CHURCHILL
MASTER AND COMMANDER

OSPREY
PUBLISHING

CHURCHILL
MASTER AND COMMANDER
WINSTON CHURCHILL AT WAR 1895–1945

ANTHONY TUCKER-JONES

OSPREY PUBLISHING
Bloomsbury Publishing Plc
Kemp House, Chawley Park, Cumnor Hill, Oxford OX2 9PH, UK
29 Earlsfort Terrace, Dublin 2, Ireland
1385 Broadway, 5th Floor, New York, NY 10018, USA
E-mail: info@ospreypublishing.com
www.ospreypublishing.com

OSPREY is a trademark of Osprey Publishing Ltd

First published in Great Britain in 2021

ISBN: HB 9781 4728 4733 1; PB: 9781 4728 4734 8; eBook 978 1 4728 4735 5;
ePDF 978 1 4728 4736 2; XML 978 1 4728 4732 4

23 24 25 26 27   10 9 8 7 6 5 4 3 2 1

Front cover image: Detail of a five cent US postage stamp of Winston Churchill. (iStock).
Author photogragh: © Mick Kavanagh.
Plate section image credits are given in full in the List of Illustrations (pages 29–30).

Foreword © Andrew Roberts

Maps by www.bounford.com

Index by Zoe Ross

Typeset by Deanta Global Publishing Services, Chennai, India
Printed and bound in Great Britain by CPI (Group) UK Ltd, Croydon CR0 4YY

Osprey Publishing supports the Woodland Trust, the UK's leading woodland conservation charity.

MIX
Paper | Supporting
responsible forestry
FSC
www.fsc.org   FSC® C171272

To find out more about our authors and books visit **www.ospreypublishing.com**. Here you will find
extracts, author interviews, details of forthcoming events and the option to sign up for our newsletter.

Contents

Foreword by Andrew Roberts   7

Introduction   9

Prologue: Death or Glory   15

List of Maps   28

List of Illustrations   29

PART ONE: BAPTISM OF FIRE   31

  1 Soldiers of the Queen   33

  2 Frontier Wars   40

  3 Great Escape   48

  4 The Sakabulas   57

PART TWO: FALL AND RISE   65

  5 A Haunting Lesson   67

  6 'Cat on Hot Bricks'   80

  7 Winston's Mercenaries   87

PART THREE: WORLD ORDER OR DISORDER   97

  8 Flying Police   99

  9 Troubled Emerald Isle   104

10 Beneath the Sphinx   114

11 Nazism or Communism   123

PART FOUR: THE WARLORD RETURNS   139

12 Master and Commander   141
13 His Finest Hour   155
14 Strategic Dilemma   168
15 Old Foes   177
16 Hitting Back   187
17 'Bands of Brothers'   196

PART FIVE: GLOBAL JUGGLING ACT   205

18 Mediterranean Showdown   207
19 An American Friend   221
20 Joan of Arc   232
21 Courting the Red Czar   242
22 Loss of Faith   250
23 India in Revolt   264

PART SIX: WAR OF WILLS   275

24 Strained Relations   277
25 Second Front Now   288
26 'Death Wish'   304
27 Miracle of Deliverance   311
28 'The Whole Scene'   318

Epilogue: Gone Painting   327
Winston Churchill's Military Career at a Glance: 1895–1945   329
Notes and References   332
Bibliography   363
Index   374

Foreword

'I felt as if I were walking with destiny,' wrote Sir Winston Churchill of the day he became Prime Minister in May 1940, 'and that all my past life had been but a preparation for this hour and for this trial.' The distinguished historian Anthony Tucker-Jones shows brilliantly just how accurate that self-observation was, by putting Churchill's achievements during his trial of World War II squarely in the context of all that he had learned about warfare since even before he attended Sandhurst half a century earlier.

Tucker-Jones is particularly strong on the ethos, assumptions, tactics and strategic overview of the British Army at the time when the young Churchill was at his most receptive, and proves that time and again personal experience was put to astoundingly good use decades later when Churchill was Minister of Defence during the greatest existential crisis in British history. Readers will be impressed by the author's extremely wide and detailed knowledge of every aspect of this extraordinary story, as well as his willingness to engage in issues forthrightly.

Churchill felt he was qualified to act as Britain's pre-eminent 'master and commander' in 1940 in part because a quarter of a century earlier he had been taught by the Dardanelles Expedition that campaigns cannot be won by committees of politicians. Tucker-Jones examines every major influence on his thinking regarding civil-military relations, what Churchill called 'the brass hats and frock-coats'.

This fine book also explores and highlights areas that are often misunderstood or elided in other works. Churchill's enthusiasm for mustard gas; his defiance of David Lloyd George over British intervention in the Russian Civil War; his implementation of Hugh

Trenchard's controversial Air Control; his access to secret intelligence regarding Nazi rearmament; how well informed he was during the Battle of Britain; what he learned from Lawrence of Arabia that helped him set up the Commandos; his appalling dilemma over saving either Cairo or Singapore in 1942; the impact of the Quit India movement on the campaign in Burma; the two occasions when he seriously considered invading neutral Ireland during World War II: all get full and fascinating treatment.

This book is certainly no hagiography; the author points out that Churchill could get important things wrong occasionally, instancing the time that he favoured the Japanese over the Chinese in the 1930s, and also showed too little interest in the Spanish Civil War. Over the issue of Churchill's involvement in the Bengal Famine of 1943, Tucker-Jones rightly concentrates on the Viceroy Lord Wavell's full awareness of the threat posed by the Japanese Navy in the Bay of Bengal.

Churchill's adherence to the Mediterranean strategy in 1943–44 ultimately brought him to loggerheads with the Americans, to the point that he threatened to resign as Prime Minister over the projected Operation *Anvil* landings on the French Riviera in August 1944, because of the way they weakened the campaign in Italy. Tucker-Jones rightly argues that Churchill's unilateral but ultimately justified intervention without President Franklin Roosevelt's approval in the Greek Civil War needs to be seen in that context of testy Anglo-American relations towards the end of the war in Europe.

This well-researched, well-written and soundly argued book is a real addition to the avalanche of books on Winston Churchill, illuminating where the military views came from that were so profoundly to affect the twentieth century and beyond.

Andrew Roberts
London
July 2021

Introduction

Winston Churchill was one of the greatest military and political chancers of all time. This is not meant as a criticism, as these were the very qualities that made him such a dynamic and energetic leader. From a young age he craved fame, or even notoriety, as long as it brought him to public attention. It was clear he had achieved this goal by 1899, when even school girls in Pretoria knew who he was. His propensity to take risks did mean that inevitably on occasions he gambled and lost spectacularly. The focus on Churchill's life tends to be his phenomenal political career and wartime premiership. Arguably his short army and long political careers ably prepared him for that pivotal moment in 1940. Despite his limited time as a soldier, his connection with the armed forces through numerous regimental and then ministerial posts was considerable. Crucially this experience with the army, Royal Navy and Royal Air Force gave him an almost unique insight into the British armed forces.

Churchill's lust for military adventure was quite remarkable. In his quest for self-promotion and glory he essentially became a war tourist. Thanks to brazen doorstepping of senior commanders and his mother's extensive network of contacts he saw action in Cuba, India, Sudan and South Africa. All of this was in a semi-official capacity and had nothing to do with his parent regiment the 4th Hussars. Churchill notably combined being a soldier, a war correspondent and an author, though this made him enemies who were annoyed by his impertinence and jealous of his rising profile. In doing so he was prepared to travel thousands of miles and at his own expense. Like many young subalterns or lieutenants, he dreamed of winning the Victoria Cross or the

Distinguished Service Order, but what set him apart from many of his contemporaries was that he actively sought to gain them by deliberately putting himself in harm's way. To get himself noticed by senior officers he regularly exposed himself to enemy fire.

On numerous occasions Churchill could have been killed, but miraculously survived his close encounters with death. These narrow escapes seem to have convinced him that he was somehow invincible. This, in consequence, persuaded him to take more risks with his safety even in later life. His dangerous behaviour on a bombed bridge over the Rhine in 1945 beggars belief, but goes a long way in illustrating what kind of man he was. Quite simply he loved to be in the thick of it. Throughout his long life he was drawn to the sound of the guns like a moth to a flame. At a young age, unable to fast-track his military career nor prepared to put the time in, he sought to emulate his father by taking up politics as soon as possible.

Churchill's monumental political achievements so eclipsed his soldiering that it is not generally appreciated that, apart from being commissioned with the 4th Hussars, he served with numerous other units. While on the North-West Frontier he was attached to the 31st Punjab and 35th Sikh Infantry and then in the Sudan to the 21st Lancers. During his time in South Africa he was first with the South African Light Horse and then the Imperial Yeomanry. Prior to World War I he was in the Queen's Own Oxfordshire Hussars. During that conflict, after resigning from the government, he was attached to the 2nd Grenadier Guards, before commanding a battalion of the Royal Scots Fusiliers on the Western Front. He liked his time in the trenches and by all accounts was respected by the men under his command. He made a point of leading by example rather than from the safety of his dugout. Once more his luck held, although he almost lost a hand to enemy shrapnel and was regularly at risk from German snipers when on patrol.

In his youth Churchill made a good impression as a leader of men, though his attitude to following the chain of command was sometimes hazy at best and on other occasions downright insubordinate. As an officer he gathered lifelong friends whilst serving in India, Sudan, South Africa and Belgium. Once in government he increasingly acted as a rule unto himself. During World War II, Churchill liked to think that his leadership style was inclusive; however, more often than not it was autocratic. Some did not altogether appreciate his long wartime working hours. There was many a night when senior politicians and the service chiefs found themselves kept up until the early hours at Chartwell having been invited for dinner and a movie. To their irritation they often found that Churchill had already made his mind up on important strategic matters. In his role as Prime Minister and the country's very first Minister of Defence he would reason that he had the full picture while they did not. Feeling exhausted after their late night, everyone then had to return to running the war the following day and carry out Churchill's bidding.

Quite surprisingly many other aspects of Churchill's military leadership are little known; particularly his continual enthusiasm for mustard gas on the grounds that it was a more humane weapon than high explosive. This, though, was completely at variance with conventional wisdom. Churchill tried, in defiance of the Prime Minister of the day, to significantly escalate Britain's involvement in the Russian Civil War in the name of crushing Bolshevism. When he failed he resorted to using mustard gas and Czech mercenaries. Fortunately, apart from the Russian Civil War, wiser counsels prevailed to curb his desire to use gas in Afghanistan, Iraq, Normandy and Germany. He was even prepared to use it in Britain and Ireland in the event of invasion by Hitler.

He supported the use of force to try and stop Irish and Indian independence, which simply led to more bloodshed. His dealings with both countries were subsequently seen as stains on his reputation. However, he never acted out of naked malice but rather from a fear of inevitable sectarian violence should British rule end. He almost invaded neutral Ireland twice during World War II and seriously contemplated violating Portugal and Spain's neutrality by seizing their Atlantic Islands. In India he was forced to contain a popular rising by the 'Quit India' movement that threatened to derail the British campaign in Burma. Equally controversially he wholeheartedly supported Truman's use of the atomic bomb against Japan. Yet during the 1930s he favoured the Japanese over the Chinese to the extent of ignoring the shocking Nanking massacre.

On a more positive note, he nurtured both Britain's key intelligence services MI5 and MI6 as well as the RAF from the start. The intelligence services repaid his support by feeding him assessments of Germany's rearmament throughout the 1930s. Yet he chose to ignore their warnings about the Japanese threat to Singapore. He also helped initiate the formation of the Commandos, which greatly supported the development of combined operations. The latter ensured the cooperation of the armed forces on land, in the air and at sea to achieve an objective. Such coordination was needed for the conduct of large-scale amphibious operations. This was particularly vital for the success of D-Day as well as the landings in the Mediterranean. In contrast, although a supporter of Bomber Command, by the end of the war Churchill had moved to distance himself from what was effectively indiscriminate carpet bombing.

One of his contemporaries described him as having an inexhaustible strategic imagination. Unlike previous Prime Ministers, Churchill saw himself as overall director of the British war effort. He reinforced this position by wearing the uniform of any of the three services as he felt appropriate. In World War II he regularly donned a uniform, most notably an RAF air commodore and while at Yalta a colonel of Hussars. One of his most familiar outfits was his 'old sea-dog outfit of an Elder Brother of Trinity House',[1] which he used for naval occasions. He never wore an admiral's uniform; such was his respect for the Royal Navy. It was Churchill's early experiences during Britain's colonial wars and World War I that firmly convinced him that he was qualified to oversee British strategy during World War II. As the conflict progressed this inevitably brought him into dispute with his own Chiefs of Staff and the Americans. In addition, as America's role expanded so Churchill's influence on military matters markedly declined, much to his enduring frustration.

Upon being appointed Prime Minister, Churchill's wartime leadership was immediately tested by the crisis in France and the need to save the British Expeditionary Force from annihilation at Dunkirk. This was followed by the touch and go Battle of Britain in the summer of 1940. Although he enjoyed further success the following year, when the British Army soundly defeated Mussolini's forces in Libya, this victory was thrown away by the disastrous campaigns in Greece and Crete. The situation continued to deteriorate in early 1942, when Britain quickly lost Burma, Malaya and Singapore to the Japanese, who then advanced into north-eastern India. By the summer of 1942 Hitler was pressing on Alexandria and threatening the Suez Canal.

Confidence in Churchill's leadership waned. For a moment it looked as if his premiership would end thanks to a disgruntled House of Commons. However, he survived public censure and that autumn the tide began to turn with the British victory at El Alamein and the Anglo-American landings in French North Africa. These pinned down the troublesome General Erwin Rommel once and for all. Then in early 1943 the Germans surrendered at Stalingrad marking the turn of the tide on the Eastern Front. Likewise, the Germans were defeated in Tunisia finally ending Hitler's campaign in North Africa. Shortly after, the Allies landed in Sicily followed by mainland Italy, knocking the Italians out of the war. For Hitler it was a gradual slide into defeat, especially after Stalin's decisive victory at Kursk. On all fronts Hitler was left on the defensive and the initiative firmly passed to 'The Big Three' – Churchill, Roosevelt and Stalin.

This book is intended to first explain what, in his formative years, shaped Winston Churchill as a military commander, and then to examine how in high office he got it both right and wrong. Churchill is widely hailed as Britain's greatest wartime leader and politician. Deep down though, he was foremost a warlord. Just like his ally Stalin, and his arch enemies Hitler and Mussolini, Churchill could not help himself and insisted on personally directing the strategic conduct of World War II. For better or worse he functioned as political master and military commander.

Again like his wartime contemporaries, he regularly had a habit of not heeding the advice of his experienced generals. He was always very impatient for immediate action. Early in the war the results of this were disasters in Scandinavia, the Mediterranean, the Balkans and the Far East. Churchill's pig-headedness over supporting the Italian campaign, in defiance of the Riviera landings, culminated in him threatening to resign and bring the British government down. Such brinkmanship was met with quite remarkable fortitude by the long-suffering Allied Supreme Commander General Eisenhower. Churchill's fruitless Dodecanese adventure in the eastern Aegean also ended in unnecessary defeat.

Yet on occasions Churchill got it just right; his refusal to surrender in 1940, the British miracle at Dunkirk and victory in the Battle of Britain, proved that he was a much-needed decisive and defiant leader. Hitler could not understand why Churchill would not see sense and sue for peace. He assumed his Blitz, without the Krieg, would be sufficient to bend Churchill to his will. He was woefully mistaken. Churchill was made of sterner stuff. Nor did Churchill shy away from painful decisions, such as the destruction of the French Fleet at anchor to prevent it falling into Hitler's hands and his subsequent war against Vichy France's colonies. Ultimately his dogged defiance in Egypt and Burma paved the way for victory against both the Germans and the Japanese. Likewise, his insistence on attacking Italy first ensured that Mussolini was knocked out of the war, thereby finally securing the Mediterranean for the Allies.

While Britain had great faith in Churchill as a warlord, it was not so keen on the idea of him in peacetime. By 1945 the nation wanted a fresh start that did not include him. Fittingly though, Churchill's association with the military came full circle. After the war he packed himself off to Italy for a well-earned rest and much to his delight was guarded by members of his old regiment the 4th Hussars. On the whole, thanks to his vast experience, Churchill felt he made a good job of being the country's political master and military commander in its dire hour of need. Despite any initial misgivings, most of his contemporaries tended to agree with him.

Prologue

Death or Glory

The breeze gently fluttered the pennants of the 21st Lancers deployed at Egeiga, just north-east of Omdurman. It was a hot day, but what could you expect at the height of the Sudanese summer. The men fidgeted in their saddles, checking their swords and carbines. They looked rather comical in their khaki pith helmets with large quilted sun shades. From a distance these made them look like Mexican bandits in sombreros. An image of Don Quixote's Sancho Panza also sprang to mind, but these men were not about to charge harmless windmills. Their armpits soaked their dust-caked uniforms as they listened to the storm of artillery and rifle fire. There was also the distinctive clatter of the Maxim machine gun going about its deadly work. The horses languidly flicked their tails and manes to keep the pesky flies at bay. The battle had been raging for several hours.

Colonel R.M. Martin, their regimental commander, and his officers had a problem that they planned to fix as soon as possible. The 21st had no battle honours and Martin was damned if he was going to miss out on the fun. It annoyed him immensely that the army had given them the unofficial motto 'Thou shalt not kill'.[1] The regiment's only real claim to fame was that it had once guarded Napoleon Bonaparte on St Helena.[2] Martin now had the means to remedy this thanks to the written orders he was holding in his hand.

At 0830 hours on 2 September 1898 Major-General Sir Herbert Kitchener, commander of the Anglo-Egyptian Army, had instructed, 'Annoy them [i.e. the enemy] as far as possible on their left flank and head them off if possible from Omdurman.'³ While this was fairly explicit, it also offered some leeway in interpretation. Furthermore, Martin was accompanied by *Times* correspondent Hubert Howard. He would ensure that the Lancers' forthcoming Omdurman exploits were recorded for prosperity. Martin also had a *Morning Post* war reporter serving with him, one Lieutenant Winston S. Churchill. The latter though, unlike Howard, was not a non-combatant. He was armed with a sword and his trusty Mauser pistol and was in command of a troop of Martin's lancers. It irked Martin that the unwanted Churchill and Howard were friends. Who knew what malicious gossip they had been spreading.

Kitchener's expedition to retake Sudan and avenge the death of General Charles Gordon some 13 years earlier was reaching its climax. Gordon had been sent to evacuate Khartoum in the face of a widespread revolt led by Mohammed Ahmed, known as the Mahdi. Instead, he stayed and the Mahdi stormed Khartoum in January 1885. The Mahdi's successor, Khalifa Abdulla, who ruled supreme, had stirred up trouble in neighbouring Abyssinia and British-controlled Egypt. Finally alarmed by the Khalifa's regime, Kitchener was ordered to retake Dongola province in Sudan. His early clashes with the Dervishes had resulted in a victory at Atbara in April 1898. He then pushed down the Nile towards the Khalifa's base at Omdurman, which lay just north-west of Khartoum. The British captured the Dervish commander, Sharif Mahmud Ahmad, at Atbara. When taken before Kitchener, he had warned ominously, 'You will pay for all this at Omdurman ... compared with the Khalifa I am but a leaf!'⁴

Churchill landed in Cairo on 2 August 1898 to discover two of the 21st Lancers' four squadrons were already on their way to join Kitchener at Atbara. Thanks to his late arrival the troop he was to have commanded was assigned to Lieutenant Robert Grenfell. Had Churchill been any later he would have had to make the long journey down the Nile to Sudan on his own. Being a supernumerary, on secondment from the 4th Hussars stationed in India and therefore an interloper, Churchill was not made to feel welcome, especially as his posting had been facilitated by the death of Lieutenant P. Chapman, one of the Lancers' own officers.

Furthermore, Churchill had made it abundantly clear he had no intentions of staying in the army as he wished to pursue a political career like his father Lord Randolph. He had gone to Egypt because he wanted to take part in the historic recapture of Khartoum. Perhaps more importantly he planned to make money from a book on the expedition and his reports for the *Morning Post*, despite initial assurances given to Kitchener that he would not write whilst on campaign. Kitchener disapproved of Churchill's appointment, not only because of his lack of commitment to his military career, but also because he had pulled political strings to get there. Kitchener fully appreciated he would be under close public scrutiny by the journalists accompanying his army. He did not need any criticism in the press from a serving officer, even if his work was published anonymously.

Churchill really wanted to be attached to the Egyptian cavalry staff, as he hoped they would have given him greater freedom. Instead, the man who got that job was one Captain Douglas Haig who later gained fame during World War I. While Kitchener had absolute say over the Egyptian Army, he had no authority over the composition of the British Expeditionary Force. The War Office arranged Churchill's secondment to the 21st Lancers on the condition that he picked up all the costs. Once kitted out and while still in Cairo, Churchill had his photograph taken. Deliberately or not, he presented the image of a rather callow and impudent-looking young man.

Churchill soon developed a dim view of the Lancers, despite six of his squadron's nine officers being acquaintances from Bangalore and Harrow. He was assigned to Major Finn's A Squadron and found himself put in charge of the pack animals carrying the officer's mess. Lionel James of the *Times* found Churchill's sense of destiny amusing. When James questioned him about his new role Churchill retorted, 'These are little people, I can afford to laugh at them. They will live to see the mistake they have made!'[5] As a Hussar officer on deployment from India Churchill should have felt an affinity to the Lancers. Not only were they formerly a hussar unit, they had originally been raised in India as a European light cavalry regiment.[6] As the 21st Hussars a detachment had first seen service in the Sudan over a decade earlier. They had only just become the 21st Lancers in 1897.

James also noted that Churchill preferred to eat with the journalists rather than his fellow officers. Nonetheless, on the journey south from Cairo, he befriended Lieutenants Grenfell and Richard Molyneux, and the three of them billeted together. If there were any historians amongst their ranks, talk would inevitably have turned to the battle of Hasheen 13 years earlier when the 5th Lancers had ridden down the Dervishes. Along with the 9th Bengal Lancers and the 20th Hussars their charge had decimated a band of enemy warriors. Notably at the time it was reported most of them had been shot by the cavalry using their carbines rather than their lances and swords. Despite clarifying the cavalry's preference for firearms, the *Illustrated London News* could not resist including a highly dramatic spread showing three 5th Lancers heroically putting the Dervishes to flight.[7] If a ten-year-old Churchill had seen this image one can only guess at the impression it made on him.

In mid-August, after leaving Atbara, Churchill got separated from his column and spent a very anxious night and day alone in the wilderness before catching up. They were some 60 miles from Omdurman by 24 August. He and his squadron then joined Kitchener's forces at Shabulka. Churchill proceeded to annoy Colonel Martin by requesting his transfer to the Egyptian cavalry. He did this on the selfish grounds he stood a better chance of gaining glory with them. Colonel R.G. Broadwood commanding the nine squadrons of Egyptian cavalry was amenable to the idea, but Martin refused to let Churchill go. It is unclear if Martin ran this request through Kitchener, but he would have certainly agreed with his decision.

To be fair Churchill had good reason for wanting this transfer. The Egyptians were tough veterans of the fighting in Sudan, whereas the 21st Lancers had only just arrived. Broadwood was said 'to have been a quick-thinking and daring leader, the ideal cavalry general'.[8] The Egyptian Cavalry Corps fought with Kitchener at Firket in 1896 and had taken part in the pursuit of the enemy after the battle. At Atbara under Broadwood it had engaged Dervish horsemen to the left of the enemy stronghold.

The 21st Lancers were Kitchener's only British cavalry unit and they spent most of their time conducting reconnaissance. They spotted large numbers of Dervishes eight miles ahead of the army on 1 September 1898. 'The 21st Lancers reported some 60,000 or more of the enemy were halted outside Omdurman, and apparently drilling,' recalled infantry officer Lieutenant Ronald Meiklejohn.[9] Churchill made a personal report to Kitchener, which went off smoothly despite their frosty relationship. That night the Lancers withdrew into the defensive positions of the Anglo-Egyptian Army. Meiklejohn chatted to some of the cavalry officers, including Churchill, about the likelihood of a battle. 'He was far less argumentative and assertive than usual,' noted Meiklejohn. 'He said the enemy had a huge force, and if they attacked during the night it would be "touch and go" about the result.'[10]

Afterwards Churchill went for a walk along the banks of the Nile with another officer. Lieutenant David Beatty, commanding the British gunboat *Fateh*, seeing them, yelled to attract their attention. He then lifted an arm and hurled a bottle of champagne towards the shore. A grateful Churchill stepped into the shallows and picked it up, little realizing that one day Beatty would become a famous admiral.

At dawn on 2 September 1898, Kitchener's Anglo-Egyptian force of about 25,000 deployed just seven miles from Omdurman in a horseshoe formation, with each flank anchored on the Nile. They were protected by a defensive barrier made from dry brushwood known as a *zareba*. This was only about waist high which meant that the front rank of the infantry, in order not to expose themselves, would have to fight kneeling.[11] Instead of deploying in the nearby hills, the Khalifa's army took the bait and advanced across a coverless plain. At about 0630 hours the Dervish forces appeared. 'The noise of something began to creep in upon us,' recalled journalist G.W. Steevens, 'it cleared and divided into the tap of drums and the far-away surf of raucous war cries … They were coming on.'[12] Kitchener coolly noted, 'I estimated their numbers at 35,000 men, though, from subsequent investigation, this figure was probably under-estimated, their actual strength being between forty and fifty thousand.'[13]

Kitchener soon discovered that his exposed mounted forces on his far-right flank were under pressure. He observed, 'By 6.30 am the Egyptian Cavalry, which had been driven in, took up a position with the Horse Artillery, Camel Corps, and four Maxims on the Kerreri ridge'.[14] Before the Anglo-Egyptian *zareba* the enemy were greeted by rifles, machine guns, artillery and howitzers. It was killing on an industrial scale and the Dervishes did not stand a chance. Kitchener's British, Egyptian and Sudanese infantry opened fire with section volleys at 2,000 yards and stopped the Dervishes at 500 yards. The fire was such that the riflemen became deafened by the din and almost blinded by the resulting smoke billowing over their ranks.

'Rifles grew red-hot; the soldiers seized them by the slings and dragged them back to the reserve to change for cool ones,' adds Steevens. 'It was not a battle, but an execution.'[15] Churchill's ears may have detected the different rates of fire by the infantry. The British were equipped with the bolt-action magazine-fed Lee-Metford rifle, while the Egyptians and Sudanese were armed with the much older single-shot breech-loading Martini-Henry rifle. The latter was a weapon he had handled as a school boy at Harrow. Lacking a magazine, the Martini had a much slower rate of fire. The Dervishes with their ancient rifles and homemade ammunition, supported by their swordsmen and spearmen, struggled to respond to the storm of searing metal. Further slaughter became a pointless task. 'Cease fire please!' Kitchener ordered one British regiment. 'Cease fire! What a dreadful waste of ammunition!'[16]

Kitchener, concerned by the prospect of the Dervishes withdrawing on Omdurman, ordered a counter-attack. His infantry brigades marched forth and prepared to advance along the Nile towards the city. Once the firing slackened off Churchill began to fret that he was going to miss out on the action. However, Kitchener had plans for his British cavalry. At 0800 hours Churchill and the four squadrons of the 21st Lancers, numbering some 310 men, left the safety of the Anglo-Egyptian camp and headed south. Fifteen minutes later they had reached the northern slopes of the Jebel Surgham. The summit was occupied by some of the Khalifa's personal guard. This rocky outcrop blocked the view to the west and the south, thereby hiding the Black Standard, the Khalifa's reserve force hiding in a dry river bed known as the Khur Abu Sunt. Patrols sent out by Martin could only see the thousands of Dervish wounded streaming back towards Omdurman. They were eventually forced to turn back by the Khalifa's riflemen hidden amongst the rocks. However, one of the patrols on the far left spotted a group of riflemen standing on the banks of the Khur. They were neither wounded nor retreating.

It was about now that Kitchener's hastily scribbled orders arrived. Colonel Martin, rather than heading for the Nile, resolved to attack this force along the Khur and cut off their retreat. 'See formed body of about 200 men six hundred yards out to our left,' noted Lieutenant Robert Smith, one of Churchill's fellow officers. 'Front troops left wheel. Immediately met by volleys fairly accurately aimed.'[17] Martin ordered the whole regiment to turn to meet the enemy.

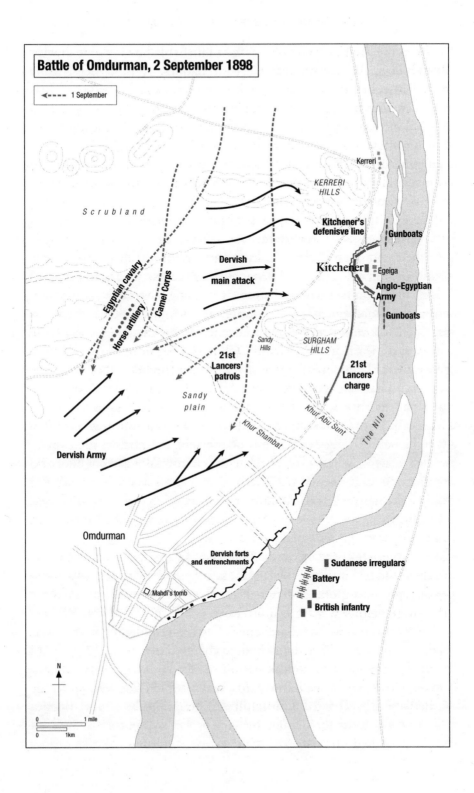

Battle of Omdurman, 2 September 1898

◄┄┄┄ 1 September

Scrubland

Kerreri

KERRERI HILLS

Kitchener's defenisve line

Gunboats

Dervish main attack

Kitchener

Egeiga

Anglo-Egyptian Army

Gunboats

Egyptian cavalry

Horse artillery

Camel Corps

Sandy Hills

SURGHAM HILLS

21st Lancers' patrols

21st Lancers' charge

Sandy plain

Khur Abu Sunt

Khur Shambat

The Nile

Dervish Army

Omdurman

Dervish forts and entrenchments

Mahdi's tomb

Sudanese irregulars

Battery

British infantry

N

0   1 mile

0   1km

Major Finn's A Squadron was on the right flank, then Major Fowle's B Squadron. To his left was Captain Eadon's D Squadron, while on the extreme left was C Squadron under Captain Doyne. Their steady trot soon turned into a gallop. The horses' hooves pounding on the dry ground, they swept forward. Churchill had injured his right shoulder in India so was unable to use his sword, but by his own account he felt no fear. He gripped the reins and knew he had to do just two things, stay alive and act heroically. Now was his chance to shine and win a medal.

Steevens reports, 'The trumpets sang out the order, the troops glided into squadrons, and, four squadrons in line, the 21st Lancers swing into their first charge. Knee to knee they swept on till they were but 200 yards from the enemy.'[18] It was at this point they realized they had ridden into a trap, because instead of fighting several hundred men, several thousand were waiting in the Khur Abu Sunt.[19] Before them was a sea of white *jibbah* decorated in multi-coloured patches – the loose cotton shirt worn by the Mahdi's followers. Many of them, though, were topless Hadendowa, reportedly one of the fiercest tribes in Sudan, whose wild hair had led to them being dubbed 'fuzzy wuzzy'. They were not afraid of cavalry and would stand their ground. Out on the Nile Lieutenant Beatty had seen the Dervishes deploying, but was unable to warn the Lancers. 'By this time we were within 200 yards of their right,' recalled Martin, 'when a large body jumped up out of a small khor and commenced a very heavy fire.'[20] Smith was aghast when he had almost reached the dry river bed, 'Looking round see Khor 12 feet wide, 6 feet deep. In front. Every side a compact mass of white-robed men.'[21] In places they were up to 20 deep.

Churchill's lack of a lance was hardly a handicap. 'The lancer's pennons attract the fire of artillery,' wrote Captain Louis Nolan, the mid-19th-century cavalry expert. 'If lances be such good weapons, surely those who wield them ought to acquire great confidence in them, whereas it is well known that, in battle, lancers generally throw them away and take to their swords.'[22] Colonel Martin charged forward without sword or pistol in his hand. At a critical moment his horse stumbled forward and he had Dervish swords swinging perilously close to his head. The startled animal recovered and he pressed on down the ravine. Behind him his men thrust their lances till they broke, swung their swords till their arms ached and emptied their revolvers. Some of the Dervishes responded by lying down so they could cut the hamstrings of the passing horses.

Unfortunately for Eadon and Fowle their squadrons hit the main body of the enemy. To make matters worse their escape route was impeded by a rough bank of boulders making it difficult for their horses to scramble up and out. Lieutenant Grenfell's troop on the far right found the enemy ranks too dense and were unable to cut their way through. Their horses were speared, stabbed and shot from all sides. The Lancers were pulled from their mounts by their feet and killed. Grenfell's horse desperately struggled to clear the river bed. The beast was cut down and he was struck by a sword. Once on the ground Grenfell was repeatedly stabbed and a spear went through his watch that stopped at 0840 hours.

In contrast Churchill galloped forward with his troop and through enemy lines that were only about four deep. Looking back, he saw one man from his troop fall and be hacked to death. Private Wade Rix with A Squadron quickly lost his lance. Just as his horse jumped into the Khor he lunged with his weapon and pierced the left eye of a Dervish. The impact was such that it shattered his lance and he quickly drew his sword. This he used to strike an enemy rifleman. 'Luck was with us,' he said. 'The horse bravely scrambled up the opposite bank of the stream bed and we were through without a scratch.'[23]

Churchill, lunging left and right, fired ten shots from his pistol, killing three men by his own reckoning and possibly three others.[24] The first swordsman who attempted to hamstring his horse was killed with two bullets. The second was so close that his weapon touched the man before he discharged it.[25] He was within 30 yards of a gathering Dervish force when he reloaded. It was then that he realized that the rest of his troop were 100 yards away, so he quickly turned and trotted after them. Churchill was extremely lucky for many of the Lancers were unhorsed, including 30 who fell on the first impact. Miraculously Colonel Martin got through without drawing any of his weapons.

Major Crole Wyndham's horse, although wounded, managed to get him beyond the river bed before dropping dead. Upon seeing this, Captain Paul Kenna galloped over, lifted the major onto his own horse and took him to safety. The unfortunate Lieutenant Molyneux found himself wounded, on foot and surrounded by angry Dervishes. He only managed to escape thanks to the actions of Private Thomas Byrne, who used his horse to block the enemy while the lieutenant made good his escape.

When Lieutenant Raymond de Montmorency dismounted to help Lieutenant Grenfell, he discovered the officer was already dead and in the chaos his horse bolted. Luckily he was rescued by Captain Kenna and Corporal Swarbrick. Kenna, using his revolver, kept the enemy at bay while Swarbrick rounded up de Montmorency's horse. 'Lieutenants T. Connally and Winston Churchill also turned about to rescue two non-commissioned officers of their respective troops,' reported war correspondent Bennet Burleigh. 'They succeeded in their laudable task.'[26] Elsewhere, some of Churchill's fellow war correspondents were not as lucky and were set upon by a lone Arab. Captain Nevill Smyth of the 2nd Dragoon Guards managed to save at least one of them, but was speared through the arm.

An exhilarated Churchill and his troop sergeant rounded up about 15 men and prepared to go again. When Churchill enquired if his sergeant had enjoyed himself, the man responded he was getting the hang of things, which caused much mirth amongst the ranks. Looking round at the battlefield Churchill witnessed, 'horses spouting blood, struggling on three legs, men staggering on foot, men bleeding from terrible wounds, fish-hook spears stuck right through them, arms and faces cut to pieces, bowels protruding'.[27]

The Khur Abu Sunt engagement had lasted barely two minutes. In that time Captain Fair broke his sword, while Lieutenant Wormwald bent his. Major Finn, like Churchill, using his revolver shot four Dervishes. Lieutenants Brinton, Nesham and Pirie were all wounded. Churchill observed, 'the blood of our leaders cooled … They remembered for the first time that we had carbines.'[28] One of Churchill's brother officers also recalled the mayhem, 'There was half a minute's hacking, cutting, spearing and shooting in all directions; then we cleared them and rallied on the far side. Halting about 300 yards off, men were dismounted and we opened a sharp fire from our carbines, driving them westward in ten minutes.'[29] Churchill noted, 'I was about the only officer whose clothes, saddlery and horse were uninjured.'[30]

Colonel Martin rallied his regiment with a view to attacking the Dervishes once more, but quickly lost enthusiasm. 'Mr Churchill wanted the men to charge the enemy again,' observed Private Rix, 'but the colonel wisely forbade it'.[31] Churchill even warned his troop that they might need to go back twice. Martin did not realize he had missed an opportunity to capture the Khalifa, who had been watching the battle seated upon a goatskin on the far side of the Khur. Instead both sides continued to shoot at each other from about 600 yards before the Dervishes finally withdrew.

At 1130 hours Kitchener observed that they had given the enemy 'a good dusting'.[32] This was a classic British understatement. The battlefield was a sea of bent and broken bodies. The Dervish Army had been completely wiped out. The Khalifa's forces suffered 9,700 dead, 11,000 wounded and 4,000 captured. Kitchener's losses amounted to 482 casualties of whom the bulk were Egyptians. By midday Kitchener's victory was complete and he marched into Omdurman followed by Khartoum. His callous treatment of the Dervish wounded and the destruction of the Mahdi's tomb was to result in a chorus of disapproval back home.

Churchill later writing his report for the *Morning Post* was evidently intoxicated by the charge. It may have been at this point that he became a fully fledged adrenalin junkie. He modestly tried to play down his experience when he wrote to a friend, claiming, 'it was not in the least exciting'.[33] Nonetheless, he also acknowledged, 'It was I suppose the most dangerous 2 minutes I shall live to see.'[34] In the *Morning Post* he floridly characterized the charge as 'two living walls crashed together with a mighty collision'.[35] In a letter to his cousin, the 9th Duke of Marlborough, he described the battle 'as a wonderful spectacle'.[36]

The 21st Lancers suffered 21 dead and 49 wounded and lost 119 horses for little tactical gain. In particular B and D Squadrons lost nine dead and 11 wounded, and seven dead and eight wounded respectively. Churchill was saddened by the loss of Grenfell and his war correspondent friend Hubert Howard. The latter had ridden with the 21st Lancers and survived, only to be killed by a friendly shell. Martin got the regimental fame and glory he wanted as Captain Kenna, Lieutenant de Montmorency and Private Byrne were all awarded the Victoria Cross for bravery as was Captain Smyth.[37] It was Churchill who identified Byrne as the gallant saviour of his friend Lieutenant Molyneux. Behind the scenes the actions of the 21st Lancers were seen as foolhardy. 'We hear the charge was a great error, and K. [Kitchener] is furious,' noted Lieutenant Meiklejohn.[38] Captain and future Field Marshal Haig viewed Martin's actions as verging on criminal recklessness. When

Churchill later asked David Beatty for his impressions of the charge, he rather bizarrely compared it to a pudding. 'It looked,' replied Beatty mischievously, 'like plum duff: brown currants scattered about in a great deal of suet.'[39]

Churchill discovered in Khartoum that Molyneux needed a graft on his wrist, so he surrendered some of his own skin from his right forearm for the operation. Whilst this was a brave and generous act, Churchill by his own admission had little choice after the doctor failed to get a graft from a nurse. It was not surprisingly a very painful procedure. 'It hurt like the devil,' admitted Churchill.[40] In later years he delighted in showing people his 'Omdurman' scar. He then travelled to Cairo to be briefed by the intelligence department in preparation for writing two books about his adventures called *The River War*. The charge of the 21st Lancers was subsequently immortalized on canvas by the artists Edward Matthew Hale and R. Caton Woodville to great effect.

It transpired it was very fortunate that Churchill did not get his way and accompany Colonel Broadwood. The Egyptian camel and cavalry forces fighting as foot soldiers on the far right were attacked by 10,000 men, backed by another 5,000. In the face of such numbers they had little choice but to mount up and quickly withdraw northwards. Although ordered back within the British defences, Broadwood continued north with the enemy host in hot pursuit. This move fortunately split the Dervish Army and weakened the pressure on Kitchener.

However, some of the Egyptian rearguard, covering Broadwood's escape from the Kerreri Hills, were overwhelmed and chopped to pieces. Notably Colonel Tudway's Camel Corps nearly did not get away as the camels struggled to cope with the broken and rocky ground. Although this action could not be seen from the British camp, artillery and nearby gunboats relentlessly shelled the Dervishes chasing Broadwood and his men. Gunboat fire alone killed about 1,000, gaining the Egyptians much-needed breathing space. In particular, the gunboat *Melik* under Major Gordon accounted for almost half this number.[41]

Later Broadwood was able to return to the battlefield to assist the British right in repelling a Dervish flank attack at 1015 hours. This culminated in a charge by the Egyptian cavalry, but by that stage the Dervishes were already retreating. While Broadwood's actions were extremely helpful to Kitchener, they offered Churchill little opportunity for glory. Knowing his taste for danger there is a good chance Churchill would have insisted on fighting with the rearguard. He certainly made a good impression with at least some of the officers and men of the 21st Lancers. 'He is a nice cheery lad and I like him a good deal,' concluded Captain Eadon, 'and I think he has inherited some of his father's abilities.'[42] Churchill would have been pleased to hear such sentiments. He had narrowly escaped death and felt that glory was calling. Equally importantly he had witnessed the full military might of the British Empire at work and this had a lasting effect on him. He learned that Britain, on occasions at least, could be truly invincible. This and his earlier escapades in India gave him an unshakable faith in the country's prowess on the battlefield.

List of Maps

Map 1: Battle of Omdurman, 2 September 1898   21

Map 2: The Boer War, 1899–1902   59

Map 3: The Dardanelles and Gallipoli, 1915   75

Map 4: Intervention in the Russian Civil War, 1919–20   92

Map 5: The Dunkirk Evacuation, 26 May–4 June 1940   150

Map 6: Britain's Air Defences in 1940   160

Map 7: The Far East in 1941   254

Map 8: Churchill and Roosevelt's competing plans for the attack on southern Germany in 1944   293

List of Illustrations

The battle of Hasheen, 1885. (*Illustrated London News*)

Main and zoomed-in views of Churchill with the Harrow School Rifle Corps. (Ocean View Group Limited. All rights.)

Churchill in his 4th Hussars uniform in 1895. (Photo © Hulton-Deutsch Collection/CORBIS/Corbis via Getty Images)

The volatile North-West Frontier in India. (Author's collection)

The battle of Omdurman, 1898. (Author's collection)

Churchill in Sudan. (Photo by Keystone/Stringer/Getty Images)

The charge of the 21st Lancers at Omdurman. (Photo by Hulton Archive/Stringer/Getty Images)

At Omdurman the 21st Lancers lost 21 killed and suffered 49 wounded. (Photo by The Print Collector via Getty Images)

Lord, later Field Marshal Kitchener. (Photo by Culture Club/Getty Images)

Churchill in the uniform of 'the Sakabulas'. (Bettmann/Getty Images)

Churchill after his capture by the Boers in South Africa. (Photo by Photo12/Universal Images Group via Getty Images)

The killing fields of Spion Kop. (Photo by Reinhold Thiele/Stringer/Getty Images)

Churchill with Archibald Sinclair. (Photo by Keystone/Stringer/Getty Images)

Churchill instigated the ill-fated attempt to force the Dardanelles with warships in 1915. (Photo by Hulton Archive/Stringer/Getty Images)

David Lloyd George was a mentor and supporter of Churchill. (Photo © Hulton-Deutsch Collection/CORBIS/Corbis via Getty Images)

Churchill played a leading role in the development of the tank. (Photo by Universal History Archive/Universal Images Group via Getty Images)

British casualties blinded by German mustard gas. (Photo by Three Lions/Stringer/Getty Images)

Hugh Trenchard, who devised Air Control as a rationale for the RAF.
(Photo by Popperfoto via Getty Images)

Churchill centre stage for the Cairo Conference. (Photo © Hulton-Deutsch
Collection/CORBIS/Corbis via Getty Images)

T.E. Lawrence. (Bettmann/Getty Images)

Mahatma Gandhi. (Photo by Central Press/Stringer/Getty Images)

On 10 May 1940 Churchill attained the highest political office in the land.
(Photo by Central Press/Stringer/Getty Images)

Churchill with Anthony Eden. (Photo by Central Press/Stringer/Getty
Images)

Churchill's first challenge as Prime Minister was Dunkirk. (Photo by
Puttnam and Malindine/Imperial War Museums via Getty Images)

The next big test of Churchill's resolve was the Battle of Britain.
(Photo © CORBIS/Corbis via Getty Images)

Air Chief Marshal Sir Hugh Dowding. (Photo by Hulton Archive/Stringer/
Getty Images)

Churchill's Chiefs of Staff, Brooke, Pound and Portal. (Photo by Keystone/
Hulton Archive/Stringer/Getty Images)

Éamon de Valera reviewing his troops. (Photo by Keystone/Stringer/Getty
Images)

Arthur Harris, Commander-in-Chief Bomber Command. (Photo by
Fox Photos/Stringer/Getty Images)

Churchill and de Gaulle in Paris. (Photo by Central Press/Stringer/Getty
Images)

Stalin, Roosevelt and Churchill at the Tehran Conference.
(Photo © CORBIS/Corbis via Getty Images)

The loss of Singapore was a terrible blow to Britain's military prestige.
(Photo by The Asahi Shimbun via Getty Images)

Tear gas being used against demonstrators in India, 1942. (Photo by
Keystone/Stringer/Getty Images)

Claude Auchinleck and Archibald Wavell. (Photo by Keystone/Stringer/
Getty Images)

Churchill with Montgomery and Brooke. (Bettmann/Getty Images)

British troops under 'The Big Three' at the end of the war. (Photo ©
Hulton-Deutsch Collection/CORBIS/Corbis via Getty Images)

Churchill, Brooke and Montgomery reviewing the 7th Armoured Division.
(Photo © Hulton-Deutsch Collection/CORBIS/Corbis via Getty
Images)

Winston and Clementine on holiday. (Photo by Daily Herald Archive/
SSPL/Getty Images)

Churchill painting in Italy. (Photo by Fox Photos/Stringer/Getty Images)

PART ONE

Baptism of Fire

Soldiers of the Queen

The infantry square looked resplendent with the front rank kneeling, bayonets fixed, poised to shoulder arms. It was like a scene from one of Victoria's military expeditions to the far-flung reaches of the empire. In fact, it looked just like a recreation of a photograph of the officers and men of the Queen's Own Cameron Highlanders forming square in Egypt in 1882. On this occasion tripod-mounted cameras had been set up on two sides of the square. Incongruously those in uniform were not soldiers, but school boys and behind them was Harrow School. The unit being photographed beneath the trees for prosperity was the Harrow School Rifle Corps. Amongst the standing second rank was Winston Churchill.

Like many young boys Churchill had grown up playing with toy soldiers. When Randolph, his father, had asked him if he would like to join the army, Winston had said yes. He assumed his father thought he had the makings of a military genius, but in reality Randolph considered his son not bright enough to go into law. Churchill wrote an essay in 1889 envisaging an imaginary British invasion of Russia, which was not such a far-fetched notion in light of the Crimean War. His 16-page manuscript included a very detailed map showing the deployment of British divisions. Notably, Churchill's English and History master, Robert Somervell, was so impressed that he kept it.

History weighed heavily on the young Churchill as he was a descendant of John Churchill, the victor of Blenheim, Ramilles, Oudenarde and Malplaquet. This had made John one of Britain's most famous commanders alongside the Duke of Wellington. One eminent military historian concluded 'England has never produced a greater soldier'.[1] John's reward was to be made the 1st Duke of Marlborough and master of Blenheim Palace. Despite his remarkable achievements and resilience, the first duke suffered from stress.[2]

As well as this family burden of overachievement Winston Churchill may have inherited what is now known as hypomanic-depressive disorder[3] from his blood line and quite possibly Asperger's Syndrome.[4] Much has been written on his 'black dog' episodes or hypomanic depression that helped fuel his drive for greatness.[5] Some clinicians though, after assessing the medical evidence, have concluded that his mood disorder is a myth.[6] In contrast his high-achieving father, Lord Randolph Churchill, would ruin a promising political career in part due to ill-health. Winston's paternal grandfather, the 7th Duke of Marlborough, served as Lord President of the Council and Viceroy of India during Mr Disraeli's administration. However, there was little chance of him inheriting the ducal seat, as his father Lord Randolph was the duke's third son. Winston's Uncle George would become the 8th Duke followed by his cousin Charles, better known as 'Sunny'. However, Blenheim was woven into his DNA, especially as he was born there prematurely on 30 November 1874 surrounded by this Gormenghastian tradition while his parents were visiting.

He grew up revering the first duke and was not the only one. Both Napoleon and Wellington were admirers of John Churchill's military skills. Crucially Marlborough appreciated from experience the value of good intelligence on the battlefield. To facilitate this, he instigated a communication system using mounted aide-de-camp and running footmen. Wellington employed similar techniques at Waterloo to keep himself informed. Marlborough's greatest claim to fame was his victory at the battle of Blenheim over a Franco-Bavarian Army on the banks of the Danube in 1704. There were many other battles, but Blenheim sealed Marlborough's reputation as a highly gifted commander.[7] What made his victory all the more remarkable was that he was outnumbered and the enemy were in a very strong defensive position. Young Winston undoubtedly learned a number of important lessons from his illustrious forebear, not least the art of deception and good intelligence in war. Over the years Churchill would be a regular guest at Blenheim. In later life when he took up painting, the interior of the house was a source of endless inspiration.[8] He was also to write a hefty biography on the first duke.[9]

Clearly Churchill felt his future lay with the military, as he had joined the Harrow Rifle Corps within a matter of weeks of arriving at the school on 18 April 1888. He delighted in getting his hands on the standard army rifle and firing live ammunition. These were no toys. The Martini-Henry rifle kicked like a mule and its soft slug easily smashed bone and cartilage creating horrific wounds. The recoil was such that after just a few rounds shoulders were bruised and it sometimes caused nosebleeds. The rifle's long sword bayonet was also a skewering accident waiting to happen. Letting schools loose with such weapons seems reprehensible, but they were the children of the Empire. The Martini-Henry was the gun that had defeated the military might of the Zulus. Every boy had heard of the heroic defence of Rorke's Drift using this weapon which had resulted in 11 Victoria Crosses being awarded for bravery. Churchill was also enthralled when he and his classmates took part in a divisional-sized exercise, that included artillery and machine guns, at Aldershot.[10] This gave him his first feel for military manoeuvres.

However, his time at Harrow was not altogether happy; he did not excel academically and his house master considered him slovenly. Churchill's main problem was that while he was undoubtedly clever, he failed to apply himself. Lady Randolph, his mother, was driven to distraction by his inability to focus and made no secret of her disappointment. In the summer of 1889 Churchill's headmaster informed Lord Randolph that his son would not get into Woolwich, which trained officers for the artillery and engineers. However, he might be better suited to the cavalry or the infantry. Churchill joined what he called the 'Army class' that prepared boys for the Royal Military College at Sandhurst, which trained future army officers.

Churchill arrived at Sandhurst in early September 1893 and he suddenly seemed to thrive amidst the heightened discipline. He graduated at the end of the following year 20th out of 130 proving he was no dunderhead. He was destined for the cavalry and it was now that his adventures really began. An ailing Lord Randolph was not entirely happy with this turn of events. He had hoped his son would join an infantry regiment to avoid the added cost of having to supply horses and uniforms for him and his groom. Churchill's hopes of bonding with his distant and disapproving father were dashed when Lord Randolph died at the end of January 1895 at the age of just 45. Churchill was commissioned as a Second Lieutenant with the

4th Queen's Own Hussars on 20 February 1895. This unit was based at Aldershot in Hampshire not far from Sandhurst.

The 4th Hussars had a very good pedigree with numerous battle honours to their name. Previously known as the 4th Light Dragoons they had formed part of the Light Brigade at the infamous battle of Balaclava. Churchill was immediately bored with peacetime soldiering and began to crave excitement, even though his regiment was due to deploy to India the following year. He was delighted to discover that officers were entitled to five months leave every year and that ten weeks of these could be taken consecutively. The failing Spanish Empire would come to his rescue in alleviating the tedium.

Casting his eye about for some action he alighted on Cuba, where there was an insurrection against Spanish rule encouraged by the arrival of exiled Cuban journalist and poet José Martí. Although Martí was killed in battle just three weeks after landing, his death inspired the revolutionaries under Máximo Gómez to carry on fighting. By June 1895 the uprising had spread to central Cuba. The only problem Churchill had was that the British press favoured the rebels and his commanding officer, Colonel John Brabazon, was keen that his trip did not look like an officially sanctioned visit. Despite being a junior lieutenant, he completely circumvented the chain of command by approaching the head of the British Army directly.

Seeking official approval Churchill tried the British Commander-in-Chief Lord Wolseley who proved to be highly receptive and sent Churchill and his travelling companion, Lieutenant Reginald 'Reggie' Barnes, to see the Director of Military Intelligence, General E.F. Chapman. He asked they collect information for him, effectively making them spies. Although Churchill's actions were wholly inappropriate, they got the desired results. He also learned a valuable lesson: to get things done you should always go to people at the top.

After writing to the British Ambassador in Madrid, an old friend of his father's, Churchill gained permission from the Spanish government to go to Cuba as an observer. In light of his request going through official diplomatic channels it was hard for the Spanish not to consider this as a British government fact-finding mission. Ever since the loss of Florida, Mexico and Texas, the Spanish were regularly seeking support for their foreign policy in the Americas. After the Mexicans firmly established their independence and the Texans joined the United States, the Americans were seen as a threat to Spain's shrinking influence in the region. By the time Churchill set sail, most of the Spanish Empire in Latin America had melted away until all that Spain controlled were the islands of Cuba and Puerto Rico. Spanish rule in its remaining colonies was dreadfully corrupt and the US was a haven for Cuban nationalists.

Thanks to the Ambassador doors would open for Churchill at the highest levels. In consequence he was to be attached to the staff of Marshal Martínez Campos, the Spanish Commander-in-Chief in Cuba. His mother arranged for him to write for the *Daily Graphic*, his first foray into journalism, so that he could earn some money. He would also be able to indulge his growing passion for smoking cigars. Churchill and Barnes sailed from Liverpool in early November 1895 travelling via New York. There they were guests of Congressman Bourke Cockran, one of his mother's former admirers, who hosted them in his well-appointed Fifth Avenue apartment. While in New York Churchill visited the cruiser of the same name and the American military academy at West Point. While he was impressed by the quality of the American sailors he was appalled by the high level of discipline at West Point. The latter probably said more about Churchill's regard for military discipline than it did of the academy.

The pair arrived in Havana on 20 November 1895 and soon discovered that the Spanish military was highly skilled in conducting counter-insurgency warfare. However, despite the commitment of a large expeditionary force, Cuba was under siege, with the Spanish authorities holding the cities, and the rebels the countryside. They were met by Marshal Campos, and then travelled to see his Chief of Staff, General Valdez, at Arroyo Blanco, who was conducting an operation in the interior. On Churchill's 21st birthday, on 30 November, they set off with a column of 2,700 Spanish troops.[11] To the south at Iguara, rebel leader Máximo Gómez had gathered around 4,000 men. Valdez's column soon came into contact with Gómez's forces, but fortunately the rebels were not very good shots. This was Churchill's baptism of fire and he was very impressed by just how cool the Spanish soldiers were when being shot at.[12] The fire fights continued for the next three days.

Churchill and Barnes had a close encounter on 1 December. They and a number of Valdez's staff officers were dressing after bathing in a river when they came under fire. Rebels appeared just 200 yards away, but luckily were driven off by about 50 soldiers who delivered a loud volley. That night Churchill and his companion's billet came under fire and an orderly was wounded. The following day they were involved in the battle of La Reforma. It was then that they discovered being with General Valdez was highly hazardous. He appeared to be fearless and in his white uniform rode to within 500 yards of the enemy attracting a great amount of fire. Valdez leading from the front bravely stayed there until his infantry had driven the rebels back. It seemed that the Spanish commander, by making himself such an obvious target, ceased to be one. His actions created a dangerous precedent for Churchill, one that he would follow time and time again for the rest of his life.

Although Churchill thought highly of the performance of the Spanish troops, he was dismayed that they then threw away the initiative and did not pursue the retreating rebels. He could not understand why, after ten days of enduring all sorts of hardship, they were content just taking a low hill. While Churchill sympathized with the Cubans' desire for independence, he considered their army little more than an undisciplined rabble. Barnes and Churchill were soon running out of leave and had to return home. Valdez, clearly impressed by the pair, recommended them for the Spanish Order of Merit. If Churchill thought the war in Cuba was a small-scale policing operation, he was very much mistaken. Spain was determined to hold onto the island and by the time he left the Spanish had flooded it with almost 100,000 troops, who were supported by tens of thousands of locally raised militiamen. The rebels, though, proved elusive and adopted increasingly brutal guerrilla tactics.

While Churchill was sailing home via America, Britain and America almost went to war. The American government had been insistent on mediating the disputed border between British Guiana and Venezuela. When Britain declined America declared that it would do it anyway and enforce the findings. For a while there was talk of open conflict, though the two countries had not fought since 1812. When Churchill got back anticipating a fight he recalled, 'vividly looking at ships off the English coast and wondering which one would be our transport to Canada'.[13] However, Britain had much more pressing concerns over growing tensions in South Africa with the Boers and agreed to arbitration. 'There followed,' said Churchill, 'a steady improvement in

Anglo-American relations.'[14] This in part he added was due to 'growing alarm at German naval expansion'.[15]

Inevitably Churchill's reports for the *Daily Graphic* and subsequent articles drew attention to his trip to Cuba. He soon found himself in trouble with the press, who were not amused that a British Army officer while on leave had gone to fight for the Spanish in the Caribbean. The *Times* declared 'spending a holiday in fighting other people's battles is a rather extraordinary proceeding even for a Churchill'.[16] He made matters worse by clarifying he had never drawn his revolver, which clearly indicated that he had been armed despite his observer status.

Churchill went on to criticize both the Spanish and rebel armies, concluding that the Spanish were the lesser of the two evils. Naturally the Spanish government expressed its displeasure to the British Ambassador in Madrid, who soon regretted sponsoring Churchill's high-profile trip. Ultimately Churchill revelled in the controversy because it brought him to the attention of the British public. Churchill in modern parlance was learning how to become a spin doctor. The Spanish should have worried more about American foreign policy than the opinions of a very young British lieutenant. The Americans intervened in Cuba in 1898 and four years later the island was granted independence. Puerto Rico became an American possession, thereby finally ending Spain's foothold in the Caribbean. Churchill had come under fire and his appetite for adventure had been whetted. Where could he go next, he pondered.

Frontier Wars

Once back in England, Churchill fretted about the 4th Hussars' deployment to India. Now under the command of Colonel William Ramsay, they were to deploy to Bangalore. This was several thousand miles from India's lawless North-West Frontier, about the only place that offered the chance of any real action. In some desperation he sought to join General Kitchener's expedition up the Nile to Sudan. His entreaties fell on fallow ground. South Africa looked far more promising. In early 1896 in the newly created state of Rhodesia there was an uprising by the Matabele. This resulted in a relief force being sent to Bulawayo and two troopers won Victoria Crosses. That summer there was also an uprising by the Mashona in Rhodesia. Local miners were trapped in the Mazoe Valley and a police captain, Randolph Nesbitt, won a Victoria Cross during a daring rescue mission.

Churchill made some enquiries and learned that the 9th Lancers were being sent to Durban and possibly on to Rhodesia. This regiment had a good lineage having fought regularly in India. When he also learned that they were short of three lieutenants, he wrote to the 9th Lancers' colonel requesting a secondment. Nothing though came of it. Lady Randolph, tired of her son's complaining and impatience, declined to intervene. The War Office was fed up with Churchill and many other young officers constantly requesting transfers in order to win medals. Indeed, Lord Lansdowne, the Secretary of State for War, warned Lady Randolph that her son's antics were making him unpopular.

Churchill and his regiment docked at Bombay in October 1896. Whilst landing on the quayside he dislocated his right shoulder, which was to give him trouble for the rest of his life. He, Reggie Barnes and Hugo Baring shared a villa complete with household staff. It is very important to remember that when Churchill arrived in India it did not exist as a political entity. It was a vast collection of diverse princely kingdoms and states that had for various reasons agreed to and cooperated with British rule. The term India was used in the same general geographic sense as that used to describe Europe.

Churchill was soon bored by peacetime soldiering and threw himself into reading, writing and playing polo with the regiment. Sergeant S. Hallaway recalled, 'Once, when I went to his bungalow, I could scarcely get in, what with books and papers and foolscap all over the place.'[1] Hallaway found Churchill's enthusiasm for his military studies annoying every time he was quizzed after an exercise. The sergeant, who was shorthanded, was responsible for getting the horses squared away. 'I was not bad tempered really,' he said, 'but I was a busy man, and had no time for tactics.'[2]

Churchill must have been inspired by tales of all the Indian colonial conflicts. The First Sikh War witnessed British and native troops win four battles in the space of just two months. At Aliwal, the penultimate engagement, the British plan had been carried out to perfection. It witnessed the 16th Lancers conduct a famous charge on the Sikh right flank. Nor could the heroic defence of the Lucknow Residency, or the charge of the 2nd Dragoon Guards at Lucknow during the Indian Mutiny, fail to stir any young lieutenant's blood. In contrast the two Afghan wars had shown that it was unwise to meddle beyond the troublesome North-West Frontier. The first had ended with the loss of an entire army, while the second resulted in a bloody nose at Maiwand. The border with Afghanistan was a constant distraction for the British administration in India. Ever since the Indian Mutiny the North-West Frontier had been the scene of continuous military expeditions to pacify the ever-restless tribes.

Churchill seemed to show none of the arrogance that many British Army officers exhibited towards the Indian Army. The latter had only come into being in 1895 with the abolition of India's regional armies. It was divided into four commands: Punjab (including the North-West Frontier and Punjab Frontier Force), Bengal, Madras (including Burma), and Bombay (including Sind, Quetta and Aden). However, some units answered directly to the Indian government and many Indian princes maintained their own private ceremonial forces. This snobbery by the British Army was not so much extended towards Indian soldiers, but British officers serving with the Indian Staff Corps. The latter was responsible for overseeing officers' postings to Indian regiments. This arrangement had come about because there were insufficient officers, so they had to be shared around as and when they were needed. There was also a distinct pecking order with how a commission was obtained.

Churchill's military ambitions and desire for adventure should be seen in the context of the times he grew up in. He was a child of the Victorian era in which the Empire barely saw a single year's peace. Queen Victoria would rule for another five years and during her 64-year reign the British Army was involved in over 60 military campaigns involving at least 400 battles across five continents. British troops conducted punitive expeditions on the Indian frontier and avenged wrongs in Abyssinia, Afghanistan and India. They fought wars of political expediency against the Egyptians, Sudanese and Zulus. Notably they fought and eventually prevailed against natural warriors such as the brave Dervishes, Maoris, Pathans, Sikhs and Zulus. Such British victories could not all be put down to superior fire power and harsh discipline. A key factor was the regimental tradition of comradeship and honour. This inspired courage, resilience and humour in the face of the most appalling conditions. Churchill was now part of that tradition; how he chose to interpret it was another matter.

He was annoyed when he learned that Captain Frederick de Moleyns, the 4th Hussars' former adjutant, had gained the Distinguished Service Order and command of the Matabeleland police. Churchill felt he had missed out in Africa. Then at the end of 1896 Kitchener agreed to put his name down for service with the Egyptian Army. Although Kitchener cautioned that he currently had no vacancies, Churchill was elated by the news. He was of the opinion that another two years' soldiering, especially in Egypt, could do no harm before he turned to politics. Churchill was due to go on three months' leave and he toyed with the idea of stopping off in Cairo to present himself to Kitchener in person.

The following year while on leave in England, Churchill heard news that the Pathan tribesmen of the Swat Valley on the North-West Frontier had rebelled under the so-called 'Mad Mullah'. His 20,000 followers soon trapped two companies of the 45th Sikh Infantry Regiment and a unit of the 11th Bengal Lancers at Fort Chakdara. The 45th Sikhs were one of the most distinguished units of the former Bengal Army. Likewise, the 22nd Punjab Infantry Regiment was caught in the fort at Malakand. Again this was a Bengal unit. Both posts held out killing 3,700 of their attackers. Although relief forces were pushed through to Malakand this did not end the uprising.

A punitive British expedition was organized by the aptly named Brigadier-General Sir Bindon Blood, who just happened to be an acquaintance of Churchill's. He immediately telegraphed Sir Bindon and set about returning to India. When he finally got to Bangalore he received a reply in late August. Sir Bindon told him that his staff was full, but he could come as a reporter. Churchill proceeded to get himself accredited to the *Daily Telegraph* and the *Indian Pioneer*. In the meantime, Sir Bindon set about pacifying the Swat Valley.

Churchill persuaded his colonel to release him to Bindon's Malakand Field Force. He then embarked on the 2,000-mile train journey to Nowshera, the assembly point for the three brigades of the Malakand expedition numbering some 12,000 men. He arrived in early September 1897. 'I sent for Churchill and suggested his joining [Brigadier-]General Jeffreys in order to see a little fighting,' noted Sir Bindon. 'He was all for it, so I sent him over at once and he saw more fighting than I expected, and very hard fighting too!'[3] Churchill was soon to form the opinion that Jeffreys, commanding Bindon's 2nd Brigade, was 'a nice man but a bad general'.[4]

While Sir Bindon's 3rd Brigade moved on Nawagai, Jeffreys advanced up the Watelai Valley where he met fierce resistance on 16 September. The Pathans waited until Jeffreys' three columns were separated and then swarmed down on the British troops. Churchill was soon in the thick of it near the village of Markhani. After 30 minutes of skirmishing he joined the 35th Sikh Infantry Regiment. Initially he fought from horseback, but the fire was such that he became concerned about the safety of his pony and dismounted.

At one point the Sikhs counter-attacked driving the tribesmen back. However, about 2,000 Pathans attacked the flank and, although cavalry helped disperse them, the Sikhs were forced to retire. During the withdrawal the Pathans pursued them very closely. In attempting to protect two wounded officers, Lieutenants Cassells and Hughes, Churchill shot a tribesman at 30 yards using his revolver. Only Cassells was saved. He and Lieutenant Bethune then carried a wounded Sikh soldier to safety. In the process Churchill's trousers became drenched in blood. Later he picked up a rifle and fired 40 rounds hitting four men.

Churchill spent the whole day under fire, during which 50 soldiers were killed and 100 wounded. In his role as an aide-de-camp he impressed not only Sir Bindon, but also the Sikh regiment he fought alongside. The colonel of the 35th Sikhs requested that Churchill be attached to them and he was to stay with the regiment for several weeks. Jeffreys came into contact with the enemy again two days later. Once more Churchill stayed mounted for as long as possible, riding up and down the skirmish line where the troops were lying down. The Sikhs suffered seven dead while Churchill went unscathed.

By the end of the month Churchill found himself attached to the 31st Punjab Infantry who were short of officers. They were in action again at Agrah on 30 September suffering 60 casualties. 'They kill and mutilate everyone they catch,' wrote Churchill of the Pathans, 'and we do not hesitate to finish off their wounded.'[5] He noted that Jeffreys' brigade suffered 270 casualties, 25 of whom were officers, in the space of two weeks. Churchill was horrified to watch the Royal West Kent Regiment abandon Lieutenant William Browne-Clayton after he went down that day. He was only a year older than Churchill. The pair had become friends and Churchill was greatly distressed when Browne-Clayton's lacerated body was retrieved. His only solace was that his friend had first been shot through the heart before the enemy had hacked him. Churchill admitted up until that point he had not been greatly moved by war; now seeing his late friend in such a state brought home the full reality of his chosen profession.

Churchill was particularly annoyed that he had to expose himself and his pony to enemy fire along the skirmish line three times before Jeffreys noticed. Nonetheless, he was happy he was mentioned in despatches by Sir Bindon. The latter wrote to Colonel Brabazon, the 4th Hussars' former commander, hinting that Churchill might be eligible for a Distinguished Service Order or the Victoria Cross, but this was not pursued. Churchill was disappointed not to be granted temporary command of the 31st Punjabis, but he was too young and too junior for such responsibility.

When Churchill returned to Bangalore in mid-October 1897, he could have taken it easy and regaled his fellow officers with tales of his daring adventures. Instead, he sat down to write a book called *The Story of the Malakand Field Force*. While on campaign he penned 15 articles for the *Telegraph*, for which he was paid £5 per column. He was unhappy that these did not have his byline; instead they were credited anonymously to 'A Young Officer'. Everyone, though, knew that it was he who had written them. It was these articles that formed the framework for his very first book. This was a doubling-up technique he was to employ for the rest of his life.

He spent two months writing five hours a day, but ideally would have liked another three or four months to polish it. Interestingly he reported the employment of dum-dum bullets by British forces against the Pathans without comment.[6] Churchill was later to use them himself in Sudan. He sent his manuscript home to his mother who got it published by Longman. The fact that the well-known and historic family name of Churchill was on it greatly helped to get it noticed. Churchill was highly delighted to have his first book, but was deeply disappointed in how his copyeditor mangled it. One reviewer noted that the book had been 'punctuated by a mad printer's reader'.[7] Churchill was later to revisit the Malakand campaign in his book *My Early Life* published in 1930. General Sir Hubert Gough, who had also been there, felt his work was full of journalist exaggeration.

Quelling the tribal unrest on the North-West Frontier continued into late October, but before that a new greater threat emerged in the Khyber Pass and the Tirah area thanks to the 50,000-strong Afridis and Orakzais tribes. They drove the garrison from the Landi Kotal fortress, which dominated the Khyber. This posed an immediate danger to the British administration in Peshawar. As far as the government was concerned the situation was as serious as the Indian Mutiny in 1857. The military authorities immediately summoned Lieutenant-General Sir William Lockhart, a North-West Frontier veteran, back from leave in England. He put together the Tirah Expeditionary Force.

The scale of this operation was much larger than Malakand and involved some 35,000 troops, plus 20,000 non-combatants and 72,000 pack animals. It was the largest army put into the field since the Indian Mutiny. Sir William warned the tribal leaders, 'The British Government has determined to despatch a force under my command to march through the country of the Orakzais and the Afridis and to announce from the heart of their country the final terms that will be imposed.'[8]

In other words the British were demanding unconditional surrender. Churchill immediately sensed the opportunity for yet more action.

On 18 October 1897 and again two days later Sir William's soldiers stormed the cliffs leading to the Dargai Heights and he eventually marched into the Tirah plain. During early December the British withdrew rather than be trapped in the Tirah over the winter. As far as Sir William was concerned the campaign was far from finished. Over Christmas he sent out two columns and by New Year the Khyber Pass had been secured as far as the Afghan border. Shortly after that, Sir Bindon led the Buner Field Force to subdue the rebellious Bunerwals north of Peshawar.

In mid-January 1898 Churchill, determined to get involved again with the operations in the North-West Frontier, travelled to Calcutta, then India's capital. As always, his name opened doors and he stayed at Government House as a guest of Lord Elgin, the Viceroy, and dined with General Sir George White, the Commander-in-Chief. By good fortune fellow 4th Hussar officer Hugo Baring was on the Viceroy's staff. Churchill made enquiries about joining the Tirah Expeditionary Force, having heard that the train keeping it supplied had a vacancy.

While at Meerut for a polo match the following month, Churchill wired his friend Colonel Ian Hamilton requesting an interview with Sir William Lockhart. By good fortune Hamilton had just taken command of the 3rd Brigade, which formed part of the Tirah force. Churchill's greatest hope was that he might eventually accompany Hamilton to Egypt, should the latter deploy with a brigade of troops. At the risk of being absent without leave Churchill took the train to Peshawar to see Sir William. He managed to persuade the general to take him onto his staff. In this he was greatly aided by the general's aide-de-camp, Captain Aylmer Haldane of the Gordon Highlanders. Churchill quickly deduced that Haldane was the power behind the throne and was grateful for his support. He wrote to his mother, 'Haldane and I get on capitally ... his influence over the general is extraordinary.'[9] He assumed that Haldane wanted to help thanks to his reputation. Nonetheless, he may have sensed that something nefarious was going on at Sir William's headquarters as he instructed Lady Randolph twice to destroy his correspondence after reading it.[10] The implication was that Haldane had some sort of hold over Sir William. Churchill characterised the former, who was by his own admission in an unhappy marriage, as 'indiscreet-overbearing ...[and] possessed by a great desire to confer favours...'[11]

By this point, though, peace had been secured and Sir William was sent to Simla to become the new Commander-in-Chief. The Pathan revolt took two years to supress and required the mobilization of 75,000 troops. Churchill could at least be grateful that he had been involved, survived and got a book out of it.

Churchill now became fixated with getting himself to Egypt to join Kitchener. He tirelessly pestered Lady Randolph to use her connections to get what he wanted. Churchill was slightly disheartened when he heard that Kitchener had defeated the Dervishes at Atbara on 8 April 1898. Nonetheless, he was confident that the battle was not the end of the campaign; Kitchener had yet to retake Khartoum. By the summer Churchill was in Sudan winning yet more battle honours at Omdurman with Kitchener and the 21st Lancers.

3

Great Escape

After his adventures in Cuba, on the North-West Frontier and in Sudan, Churchill's desire to go into politics peaked. He had finally overplayed his hand with his dual-hatted role in Sudan. Kitchener was stung by Churchill's very public criticism of his conduct of the Omdurman campaign. In response the War Office issued an edict that serving officers were not to write for the press. A stern personal rebuke from the Prince of Wales could hardly be ignored by Churchill. 'I fear that in matters of discipline in the army I may be considered old fashioned,' wrote the Prince, 'and I must say that I think an officer serving in a campaign should not write letters for the newspapers or express strong opinions of how operations are carried out.'[1] Churchill had to make a decision. On 3 May 1899, after just four years in the army, he resigned his commission.

That summer he was adopted as Oldham's Conservative candidate. When he lost the election he had to put his political ambitions on hold and find a way to make a living. War once more beckoned, but this time as a civilian. In South Africa the British were at armed loggerheads with the Boers, so Churchill arranged with the *Morning Post* to send him out as a correspondent. His fee was to be £250 a month, which at the time made him the highest paid journalist ever to go to war.

A major conflict had been brewing for almost 100 years in South Africa. Long had the Dutch farmers or Boers resented British rule of Cape Colony, which had come about as a result of the Napoleonic Wars. In the 1830s the disgruntled Boers trekked north creating the Orange Free State, Natal and the Transvaal. Britain soon saw these as a threat to its regional authority. In 1843 the British annexed Natal, but grudgingly recognized the other two states. Fearing war between Transvaal and Zululand, the British stepped in and annexed Transvaal in 1877.

This did nothing to head off conflict and two years later Britain was dragged into a war with the Zulus. The Boers watched with some amusement when the British military were humiliated at the battle of Isandhlwana.[2] Britain eventually prevailed through persistence and overwhelming firepower. Afterwards, when Paul Kruger demanded the restoration of Transvaal's independence, the British refused. This resulted in the three-month Transvaal War or First Boer War of 1880–81. British military ineptitude, particularly at the battle of Majuba Hill on the Transvaal-Natal border, ensured the Boers under Piet Joubert got their way.

It was not long before British meddling ended once again in humiliating embarrassment at the hands of the Boers. The discovery of gold in Transvaal inevitably led to the influx of Uitlanders or foreigners, many of whom were British. To the alarm of Kruger's government, by the 1890s they were beginning to outnumber the Boers and so, to stop them gaining political power, they were denied citizenship. When the Uitlanders appealed to Cecil Rhodes, the Prime Minister of Cape Colony, he offered them a column of police under Dr Leander Starr Jameson who would intervene if they rose up. On 1 January 1896, the Boers under General Piet Cronje successfully ambushed Jameson at Krugersdorp.

Over the next three years, relations between the Boer republics and Britain deteriorated. Joseph Chamberlain, the Colonial Secretary and Sir Alfred Milner, Governor of the Cape and High Commissioner for South Africa, were determined to maintain British supremacy even if it meant war. Despite numerous warnings from British intelligence the army was woefully prepared. Finally, on 11 October 1899, hostilities broke out between Britain and Transvaal and Orange Free State. The following day the Boers attacked Cape Colony and Natal. The main Transvaal force of 18,000 men moved into Natal to threaten Ladysmith, while 8,000 headed for Kimberley and Mafeking in the northern Cape. There were only 2,000 Boers available on the southern frontier of the Orange Free State for the invasion of Cape Colony. The British Army numbering almost 15,000 men was driven back and besieged at Kimberley, Ladysmith and Mafeking. Reinforcements from India began to arrive at Durban in Natal, but they were insufficient. Shortly after, Churchill sailed to Cape Town to join the mayhem. He hated the journey and was constantly seasick.

By good fortune Churchill was on the same ship as the new South Africa Commander-in-Chief, General Redvers Buller. Churchill, although now officially a civilian, proceeded to cloud his status. He did not waste any opportunity to befriend Lord William Gerard, who was an aide-de-camp on Buller's staff. Gerard was also the colonel of the Lancashire Hussars and Churchill gained the promise of a commission in his regiment. As part of his usual networking, Churchill also befriended John Atkins, a veteran war correspondent with the *Manchester Guardian*.

Churchill's attire did not help his supposed civilian occupation. He was kitted out in practical hardwearing khaki and was carrying his trusty Mauser pistol, which had proved its worth at Omdurman. He clearly looked like a fighting irregular or in modern parlance a paramilitary. His dual approach to being a war correspondent and soldier was not that uncommon. However, dressing like a combatant made him fair game and if captured he would inevitably be treated as a prisoner of war. Nonetheless, Churchill appreciated that any sort of quasi-military authority would help gain access, which was something he never struggled to get. On this occasion his actions were again to cause some embarrassment to the British government and almost get him killed.

Logically, having ingratiated himself with Buller's staff, Churchill should have stayed at their headquarters. This though was not how he liked to operate; to get good stories he needed to get to the action as quickly as possible. Likewise, if he was to get a book out of this trip he needed to have some adventures. If that meant some close shaves, as always it was a price he was prepared to pay. Once in Cape Town on 31 October 1899, Churchill and Atkins hopped on a train to East London and then a boat to Durban in advance of Buller and his staff. While in Durban, Churchill met his old friend Reggie Barnes who had been badly wounded while leading a charge at the battle of Elandslaagte north of Ladysmith. Ominously Barnes warned him that the Boers were not to be underestimated. A third of his battalion had been cut down. Churchill and Atkins then headed north to Pietermaritzburg.

On 21 October 1899 the 5th Lancers and 5th Dragoon Guards at Elandslaagte, in one of the opening battles of the war, rode down the retreating mounted Boers on the left flank. Their larger horses easily outclassed the Boers' slower ponies. The British covered a mile and a half and showed no mercy. One young Afrikaner was lanced 16 times[3] and two others on the same pony were pierced through by a single lance.[4] Lieutenant-Colonel Scott Chisholme, of the 5th Lancers, leading the Imperial Light Horse was killed on the right flank. British bravery was such that four Victoria Crosses were earned that day, two of which went to captains in the Imperial Light Horse. Afterwards the surviving Boers vowed never to give British cavalry quarter.

By now most of the British forces in Natal were trapped in Ladysmith and the railway was cut at Colenso. In the meantime, Buller joined the British Field Force of about 47,000 men, which he divided into three columns. This sizeable army had been mobilized in Britain the moment war broke out. He planned to lead the right-hand column to Fere some 25 miles south of Ladysmith. The left under Lord Methuen would advance on Kimberley, while General Gatacre in the centre moved on Stormberg. The Boers, concerned about approaching British reinforcements, sent a force of 4,000 men south under Louis Botha, while the rest continued the siege of Ladysmith. Advancing down the railway Botha overran Colenso on the banks of the Tugela beyond the hills surrounding the Ladysmith plain.

From Pietermaritzburg, Churchill and Atkins got as far as Colenso before having to turn back to Estcourt. It was held by a few thousand British and colonial troops under the command of Colonel Charles Long, a Royal Artillery officer. There Churchill came across Captain Haldane, of the Gordon Highlanders, whom he had first met on the North-West Frontier. Haldane had been slightly wounded at Elandslaagte and was separated from his battalion now trapped in Ladysmith.

Perhaps not realizing the danger, Churchill once more put his head in the proverbial lion's mouth. General Piet Joubert, the Boer Natal Commander-in-Chief, with a force of 2,000 men had got as far as Chieveley about 20 miles northwest of Estcourt. His patrols reached the outskirts of Estcourt on 14 November. The first impulse of Colonel Long was to withdraw, because the town was indefensible. He decided that they would be better near Maritzburg. Long was in the process of packing up his artillery when Churchill dissuaded him from abandoning his post. This he argued would open the road to Durban, and besides, he reasoned, Joubert would probably feel safer staying on the Tugela River. As a war correspondent Churchill had no business offering such advice.

Ironically, Churchill was the architect of his own downfall. Instead of leaving, Colonel Long now ordered Haldane to take two companies of infantry in an armoured train north towards Colenso on 15 November 1899. The train consisted of two trucks in front of the locomotive and tender with three more behind. These were protected by boiler plate with loop holes, but they had no roofs and passengers had to clamber exposed over the sides to get in and out. The first truck carried a 9-pdr muzzle-loading naval gun[5] manned by four sailors from HMS *Tartar*, the second members of the Royal Dublin Fusiliers, who were commanded by Second Lieutenant Thomas Frankland. The third and fourth trucks contained more Dublin Fusiliers and soldiers of the locally raised Durban Light Infantry. The latter were under Captain James Wylie. The fifth truck contained a breakdown gang. In total the train was carrying 150 soldiers, a telegrapher to signal back to Estcourt, six workers in case the line needed repairing, Charles Wagner the civilian locomotive driver and Alexander Stewart the stoker.

The night before, Haldane, keen to have his former comrade in arms come along, invited Churchill to join them. This was partly because Churchill had already made the same train journey on 8 November and the following day by horse, on both occasions reaching the outskirts of Colenso unharmed. Haldane recalled, 'he had been out in the train and knew something of the country through which it was wont to travel'.[6] Haldane acknowledged that Churchill was not at all keen about making the same journey a third time. Nonetheless, he agreed to go. Anyone with an ounce of sense would have sent a few cavalry; instead they sent a sitting duck.

At 0510 hours they headed north to Frere, which they reached just over an hour later and then decided to press on for another seven miles towards Chieveley. At Frere a patrol from the Natal Mounted Police informed Haldane they had been out towards Chieveley, which was encouraging. The train chugged along as if it was taking holiday-makers sightseeing. For the soldiers crammed in the trucks in full kit it was a far from comfortable journey. There were no windows and the locomotive rained soot and hot sparks down on them. To some it must have felt rather like being rats trapped in a barrel. If the Boers attacked they could only go backwards and hope for the best. The Boer patrols could hardly miss the noisy train rattling through the countryside puffing out smoke left, right and centre. It was too good a target not to attack.

Once at Chieveley at 0710 hours, Haldane's telegrapher reported all was quiet, but about 100 Boers had been sighted to the north. In response to his message Haldane was warned the Boers had briefly occupied Chieveley the night before and was ordered to return to Frere. He instructed the train to be put in reverse. Amused by the audacity of the British, the Boers waited for the train to pass some hills, having placed boulders on the line at the bottom of a steep incline. Churchill and Haldane realized they had driven into a trap when a shell struck the leading truck. The Boers continued to shell the train encouraging driver Wagner to accelerate to 40 miles an hour down the slope. The impact with the boulders was such that it derailed the breakdown truck and two armoured trucks. One was left across the rails leaving the train stranded. A Boer shell also hit the 9-pounder knocking it off its truck.

Haldane, dazed by the crash, was only too happy to have Churchill's help. He organized the defence while Churchill endeavoured to clear the track. This arrangement was quite remarkable in light of there being three commissioned officers present, consisting of two captains and a 2nd lieutenant. Churchill, though, was in his element, throwing all caution to the wind. As a civilian he had no authority to take charge, but that did not stop him from rounding up nine volunteers from the Durban Light Infantry. Captain Wylie of the Durbans was flabbergasted remarking that Churchill was 'a very brave man but a damned fool'.[7] Luckily for Churchill and his little band, despite the volume of incoming fire, the Boers were not very accurate. Their first task was to clear the rocks.

Haldane noted, 'For an hour efforts to clear the line were unsuccessful, as the trucks were heavy and jammed together ... but Mr Churchill with indomitable perseverance continued his difficult task.'[8] Churchill persuaded the panic-stricken Wagner to shunt the locomotive back and forth until the damaged trucks were barged out of the way. Despite being under continual and heavy fire, Private Walls remembered that Churchill 'walked about in it all as coolly as if nothing was going on, and called for volunteers to give him a hand to get the truck out of the road'.[9]

The locomotive and tender were eventually freed, but the coupling on the remaining truck had been broken by the shell fire and had to be left behind. Churchill 'threw off his revolver and field glasses,' observed a now wounded Wagner, 'and helped ... pick 20 wounded up and put them on the tender of the engine.'[10] Carrying 90 men, most of whom were wounded including Captain Wylie, the burning engine sped to safety. Haldane and his remaining men were left spread out along the railway line, hoping to keep up with the train in order to reach some buildings. Churchill went with the train for about a mile and a half and then hopped off and headed back to the others. He was in the railway cutting when two Boers appeared and began to shoot at him. His only escape was up the bank. At the top a Boer horseman suddenly loomed before him just 40 yards away. The man aimed his rifle and Churchill futilely reached to his waist for his pistol. For a second he waited for the Boer to shoot him, then threw his hands up in surrender. Churchill later fancifully imagined that the Boer was none other than Louis Botha. He was actually a field cornet by the name of Sarel Oosthuisen.

Four lay dead and the rest, along with Churchill, Haldane and Lieutenant Frankland, were captured. Churchill's pockets on being patted down yielded a clip of ammunition for his missing Mauser. He claimed rather disingenuously that he had picked it up as a souvenir and that he was a reporter. On being taken to the Boers' camp, Churchill immediately demanded to see General Joubert, telling his captors that he was a civilian. When he was finally taken to see Joubert, the general's entourage included Jan Christiaan Smuts, the Transvaal's attorney general. At the time Churchill had no way of knowing that Smuts, the future Prime Minister of the Republic of South Africa, would become one of his closest advisers during World War II. Smuts recalled of their first encounter, 'He was furious, venomous, just like a viper.'[11] In light of Churchill visibly commanding British troops on the railway line Joubert and Smuts were not convinced. Churchill's only consolation was that he had been involved in an action that could be career defining. He hoped that because of his conduct in rescuing the train, all those who had escaped would sing his praises.

Word that Churchill, the son of an English lord, had been taken spread far and wide, in part thanks to the reports filed by John Atkins. Even school girl Freda Schlosberg in Pretoria knew who he was. Writing in her journal on 16 November she recorded, 'An armoured train is wrecked near Estcourt and an important man by the name of Winston Churchill is taken prisoner.'[12] Three days later she added, 'Sixty prisoners taken when the armoured train was wrecked near Estcourt, including this Mr Churchill, arrived in Pretoria at noon yesterday.' Freda even knew of the details of his incarceration noting, 'Two officers and Mr Churchill were taken to the State Model School, and the rest of the prisoners to the Racecourse Prisoners Camp.'[13] The officers were Haldane and Frankland.

The Boers triumphantly photographed their prisoners and the one including Churchill has been much reproduced. Almost all those in the shot avoided making eye contact with the camera. Several looked away, while some stared resolutely at their boots. One man even stooped forward, presenting the top of his helmet. Not Churchill, he stood slightly apart from the others looking defiantly straight into the lens. He was appalled at the idea of a lengthy incarceration, so continued to make use of his rather ambiguous war correspondent status. He persisted in claiming he was a non-combatant. This included lying about whether he had been armed or not. He also offered that, if released, he would not serve against the Boers nor collect intelligence on them. The Boers who had witnessed his efforts to save the train were not convinced. 'I urge you that he must be guarded and watched as dangerous for our war,' warned General Joubert, '... he must not be released during the war.'[14] When Churchill heard talk of a prisoner exchange, he then wrote to the War Office requesting that he be considered a military officer.

Within a month Churchill, Haldane and a non-commissioned officer by the name of Brockie had concocted an escape plan. Initially Churchill suggested that they overpower the guards, make their way to the race course and release the 2,000 prisoners held there. They would then take the government hostage and await the arrival of British troops. This seemed way too risky and instead it was decided to head 280 miles to Lourenço Marques in Portuguese East Africa (modern day Mozambique). Churchill, losing patience with his dithering colleagues, went over the wall on his own on 12 December 1899. Haldane and Brockie successfully escaped three months later. The Boers immediately offered a £25 reward for Churchill. The warrant for his capture was wholly unflattering, 'medium build, stooping gait, fair complexion, reddish brown hair, almost invisible slight moustache, speaks through his nose'.[15]

Churchill jumped the freight trains and reached a colliery near Witbank, where he was helped by the English manager, John Howard, and one of his colleagues, Dan Dewsnap. By a stroke of good luck, the latter came from Oldham, where Churchill had stood as a Member of Parliament. After hiding Churchill for a time, they put him on another train and he crossed the border undetected. He then took a boat to Durban, which he reached on 23 December, where his arrival was greeted with great enthusiasm. Photographs show him being almost mobbed as he disembarked. He was treated to all the razzmatazz of a returning war hero, which included giving a speech to a large crowd outside the town hall. News of his dramatic escape flashed around the world. Churchill, not one to waste an opportunity, immediately chronicled his exploits and telegrammed them to the *Morning Post*. It shared these with numerous other international news outlets. The Churchill legend had begun to gather momentum.

4

The Sakabulas

The headlines proclaimed 'How I Escaped from Pretoria' above Winston's byline.[1] He loved all the fuss and attention, especially after a music hall song began to do the rounds: 'You've heard of Winston Churchill – This is all I have to say – He's the latest and the greatest – Correspondent of the day.'[2] If Churchill had decided it was time to return to England it would have been perfectly understandable. Instead, shortly after, he re-joined General Buller, who wrote, 'I wish he was leading irregular troops instead of writing for a rotten paper. We are very short of good men.'[3]

Meanwhile, the British military had suffered a series of utterly disastrous defeats during what was dubbed 'Black Week'. Between 10 and 17 December 1899 all three British columns were stopped at Magersfontein, Stormberg and Colenso. The War Office was furious; Buller had blown his chance not once but three times. He was diplomatically instructed to concentrate on operations in Natal and demoted. Buller received a telegram that stated, 'It has been decided … to appoint Field-Marshal Lord Roberts as Commander-in-Chief, South Africa, his Chief of Staff being Lord Kitchener.'[4] Although Buller was not asked to resign, he would now be subordinate to Roberts. For the new commander-in-chief it was a painful appointment because his only son had been mortally wounded at Colenso. Lieutenant Frederick Roberts was retrieved by the Natal Indian Ambulance Corps, formed by Mahatma Gandhi, but died at the Chieveley field hospital.[5]

Lord Roberts arrived in Cape Town on 10 January 1900. That same month Lady Randolph arrived in South Africa, with a hospital ship, along with Churchill's younger brother Jack who was seeking adventure. In the meantime, Buller, nicknamed 'Sir Reverse' and the 'Ferryman of the Tugela',[6] knew he had been given a second chance and needed a victory to avoid being sent home in disgrace. Ladysmith had to be saved at all costs, so Buller gathered 30,000 troops in northern Natal that included a fresh division under General Sir Charles Warren.

Churchill stayed in South Africa for another six months. Once more he indulged in his passion for soldiering and writing. Buller generously granted him a lieutenant's commission in the newly raised South African Light Horse. Churchill also arranged for Jack to get a commission with them. This regiment had only come into being in the Cape the previous November. Its recruits included both South Africans and loyalist Afrikaners as well as a contingent of Texans. They were known as 'the Sakabulas' because of the black Sakabula bird tail-feathers in their slouch hats.[7] When the men were dismounted this feather was a dangerous lure for snipers, as Churchill was later to discover almost to his cost. Once in his new uniform he could not resist getting his photo taken, this time presenting a rather dashing figure.

The Sakabulas' commander, Lieutenant-Colonel Julian 'Bungo' Byng would soon find, as all Churchill's previous commanders had, that he was a bit of a handful. Byng, when he was a captain in the 10th Hussars, first met Churchill back in 1894 at the request of Colonel Brabazon. Perhaps to try and keep Churchill out of trouble Byng appointed him as his personal messenger. In light of Churchill's lack of respect for the chain of command, Byng was to curse him out on a number of occasions. Churchill, though, was not the only one to lack discipline. The regiment was to became known as 'Byng's Burglars' because of their habit of pilfering whatever they wanted.[8] Rather bizarrely Byng ended up acquiring a Texan accent thanks to his American volunteers.[9]

Churchill should have stopped reporting for the *Morning Post* as this was now strictly forbidden by the War Office, but Buller obligingly turned a blind eye to his extracurricular activities. This rule had come about in part because of his actions in the Sudan. To be fair to Churchill his commission in what was a colonial unit was unpaid, so he had to find a way of earning a living. He was to see action at Spion Kop, Hussar Hill, Potgieter's Ferry and Diamond Hill. Churchill was also one of the first, or so he claimed, to get into Ladysmith and Pretoria.

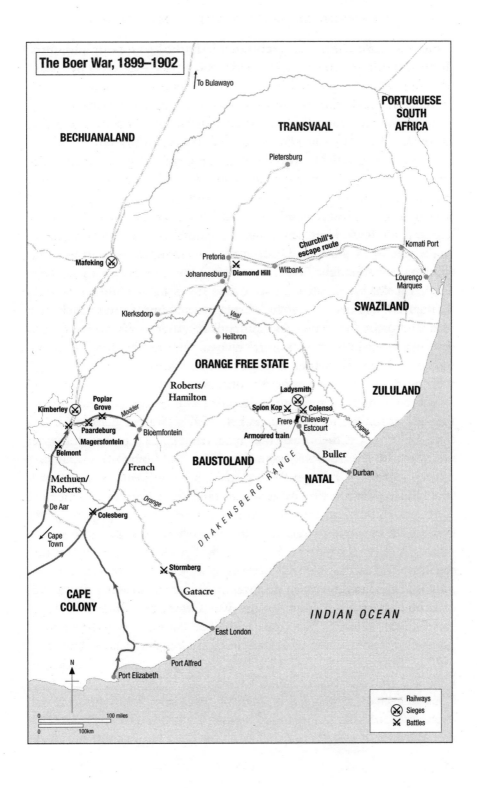

The Boer War, 1899–1902

To Bulawayo

BECHUANALAND

TRANSVAAL

PORTUGUESE SOUTH AFRICA

Pietersburg

Churchill's escape route

Komati Port

Mafeking ⊗

Pretoria

Johannesburg   Diamond Hill ✕   Witbank

Lourenço Marques

SWAZILAND

Klerksdorp

Vaal

Heilbron

ORANGE FREE STATE

Roberts/ Hamilton

ZULULAND

Ladysmith ⊗

Poplar Grove

Kimberley ⊗

Modder

Spion Kop ✕   ✕ Colenso

Paardeburg ✕
Magersfontein ✕

Bloemfontein

Frere   Chieveley
Estcourt

Belmont ✕

Armoured train

Methuen/ Roberts

French

BAUSTOLAND

DRAKENSBERG RANGE

Tugela

Buller

NATAL

Durban

De Aar

Orange

Colesberg ✕

Cape Town

Stormberg ✕

Gatacre

CAPE COLONY

INDIAN OCEAN

East London

N

Port Alfred

Port Elizabeth

0   100 miles

0   100km

Railways
⊗ Sieges
✕ Battles

General Buller's aim was to relieve Ladysmith. To do this he proposed crossing the Tugela at Trichardt's Drift and advancing across the plain north of Spion Kop. General Warren would conduct this left-flank movement round the Rangeworthy Hills (Tabanyama) and east to Dewdrop with 15,000 troops. There he would link up with General Lyttelton's brigade, some 9,000 strong, advancing north from Potgieter's Drift on the right flank. This would compromise the Boer siege lines south-east of Ladysmith. In theory it was a sound plan.

Lord Dundonald's 1,500 cavalry, which included Byng's South African Light Horse, seized Trichardt's drift. They then rode in a leftwards arc towards Acton Homes farm northwest of Spion Kop and on the road to Dewdrop and Ladysmith. Churchill, acting as an assistant adjutant with the light horse, arrived at Acton Homes on 18 January 1900. There they cut off some retreating Boers who fought to the last. Dundonald was irritated when Warren ordered him to send back 500 men to protect their camp. He was equally annoyed when his calls for reinforcements and artillery were ignored. Three days later Churchill was involved in the battle of Spion Kop, which was the bloodiest and most pointless engagement of the entire war.

Warren could not keep up, so recalled Dundonald. He stopped at Fairview at the foot of the Rangeworthy Hills. Warren under pressure from Buller decided to push the Boers off the hills to the southwest of Ladysmith by attacking Spion Kop. At 2030 hours on 23 January Major-General Sir Edward Woodgate's men, with Lieutenant-Colonel Alec Thorneycroft acting as guide, worked their way up the hill. By 0400 hours the Lancashire Fusiliers had reached the summit and launched a bayonet charge that drove off the Boers. At 0700 hours when the mist cleared the British realized they had only taken the southern end of the summit. The ground was too hard to dig and only the most rudimentary defences could be constructed consisting of shallow trenches topped with rocks. Unless the surrounding high ground was secured, Woodgate's exposed position was completely hopeless. He soon came under sustained Boer artillery and rifle fire as well as counter-attack. Just after 0830 hours Woodgate was mortally wounded and Thorneycroft took command.

Thorneycroft, reinforced by men of the Middlesex Regiment and Imperial Light Infantry, managed to hold his position for the rest of the day. However, it was not long before all the units had become mixed up hampering the chain of command. Warren had 10,000 troops available and should have immediately attacked the Rangeworthy Hills west of Spion Kop to take the pressure off Thorneycroft. Instead, they stood by all day and did nothing. Major-General Lyttelton, whose brigade had crossed the Tugela at Potgieter's Drift, vainly tried to help. He sensibly attacked up Twin Peaks to silence some of the artillery enfilading Spion Kop. Unfortunately, he was then ordered to withdraw by Buller.

The exposed defenders on Spion Kop were in a terrible state. At 1430 hours Thorneycroft sent Warren a scribbled despatch stating, 'There are many killed and wounded. If you wish to make certainty of hill for night you must send more infantry and attack enemy's guns.'[10] Churchill, with his unit standing idle, in his role as a journalist decided to reconnoitre Spion Kop. The sound of fighting inevitably drew him like a moth to a naked flame. Leaving his horse, he clambered to the spur below the summit. On the way up he passed 200 dead and numerous casualties going the other way. He was appalled by what he saw and returned to report his findings to Warren. During his trip a sniper shot the prominent Sakabula feather from his slouch hat. Later he went back up and saw Thorneycroft. Churchill thought they could hold, but the colonel responded glumly, 'Better six good battalions safely down the hill than a mop-up in the morning.'[11]

By sunset a desperate Thorneycroft decided to withdraw. Churchill, sent by Warren with instructions to hang on, met him on the way down. 'I have done all I can, and I am not going back,'[12] remarked an exhausted Thorneycroft. As he did so the Boers, who had suffered equally heavy casualties, likewise started to withdraw. However, Louis Botha quickly rallied them. By dawn a few had reached the British-held summit to find 1,200 British casualties strewn upon the ground. They photographed the dead clogging the main trench, which was barely waist deep and had afforded little protection. Afterwards distressed-looking medical orderlies searched the heaped bodies for any surviving wounded. They included Gandhi and his Indian Ambulance Corps. Vere Stent, British editor of the *Pretoria News*, visiting the battlefield had a chance encounter with him, noting, 'I came across Gandhi in the early morning sitting at the roadside eating a regulation biscuit. ... Gandhi was stoical ... cheerful and confident ... and had a kindly eye.'[13] In contrast Stent described the British troops as 'dull and depressed'.[14]

The war dragged on. At Hussar Hill, southeast of Colenso in mid-February, Churchill came across his brother Jack, who had the bad luck to be wounded in the leg in his very first action. Jack was hit while lying down, whereas Churchill as usual was striding around without a care in the world and invulnerable to the rounds whizzing about. This again convinced Churchill that he was either charmed or somehow indestructible.

In the west striking from the northern Cape, Roberts defeated the Boers on the Modder River and relieved Kimberly. Some 4,000 Boers were then trapped and forced to surrender to him at Paardeberg on 27 February 1900. This left them with just 7,000 men still in the field. The following day the Boers finally abandoned their siege of Ladysmith. Churchill was not amongst the first troops to enter the town. General Sir Hubert Gough, who also served in South Africa, was later to refute many of Churchill's romanticized descriptions of this campaign. Regarding Churchill's description of the relief of Ladysmith, Gough called it, 'A totally inaccurate account and pure fabrication'.[15] While Churchill was undoubtedly guilty of journalistic licence, Gough had taken a firm disliking to him since the days of Malakand.

After Ladysmith, Churchill's appetite for action remained unsated so he headed further north. Once more in the guise of a roving reporter he joined the Imperial Yeomanry. This was commanded by none other than his old 4th Hussars commander John Brabazon, who was now a brigadier-general. Churchill's cousin 'Sunny', the 9th Duke of Marlborough, was also serving with the Imperial Yeomanry. Originally British Yeomanry units were intended for home defence only. To get round this restriction in January 1900 new units known as Imperial Yeomanry were formed for overseas deployment. They were often enthusiastic amateurs with little or no military training.

Churchill continued to put himself in harm's way. During a patrol near Dewetsdorp south-east of Bloemfontein, he lost his horse and was separated from the others. Fortunately, his remarkable luck held out, as Trooper Clement Roberts of de Montmorency's Scouts rode forward and rescued him in the nick of time. At the end of May, he glided through Johannesburg on a bicycle disguised as a civilian in order to send some despatches by telegraph. He later took great pleasure in liberating the prison camp in Pretoria, with his cousin. Amongst those rescued was Lieutenant Frankland, who had remained incarcerated since the train incident.

Churchill's last action in South Africa was east of Pretoria at Diamond Hill with Lieutenant-General Ian Hamilton's column. Louis Botha commanding the remaining Boers was holding open the railway line east, along which the Kruger government escaped. Once more Churchill dreamed of gaining a Victoria Cross, but it was not to be. He soon gave Hamilton the slip and climbed up Diamond Hill. 'From his lofty perch Winston had the nerve to signal me,' recalled an amused Hamilton, 'if I remember right, with his handkerchief on a stick, that if I could only manage to gallop up at the head of the Mounted Infantry we ought to be able to rush the summit.'[16] For Churchill the Boer War now was over.

Once back in England, he again stood as the MP for Oldham and won, in part thanks to his well-publicized hijinks in South Africa. Churchill this time got two books out of his adventures, *London to Ladysmith via Pretoria* and *Ian Hamilton's March*. By the age of 25 he was known worldwide. Field Marshal Roberts returned home in early 1901 and was succeeded as Commander-in-Chief in South Africa by Kitchener. Notably, his column commanders, who distinguished themselves in this campaign against the Boers and became senior generals in World War I, included Colonel E.H.H. Allenby, Lieutenant-Colonel D. Haig and Lieutenant-Colonel H. Plumer.

Churchill the politician, concerned about the progress of the Boer War, wrote to Joseph Chamberlain, the Secretary of State for the Colonies, in October 1901 warning, 'Kitchener is overworked, exhausts himself on many unimportant details and is now showing signs of prolonged strain. There is no plan worth speaking of in the operations except hammer, hammer at random.'[17] Allenby also complained about Kitchener's style of leadership and what he saw as rushed police work. 'One is always at high pressure … one is probably only under the same general for about a month at a time.'[18] The Boers with their field forces knocked out of the fight resorted to guerrilla warfare and struggled on for another year and half. Eventually they grudgingly recognized British rule and in return were later granted self-government within the Empire. 'Nearly half a million British and Dominion troops had been employed, of whom one in ten became casualties,' wrote Churchill. 'The total cost in money to the United Kingdom has been reckoned at over two hundred and twenty million pounds.'[19]

Despite Churchill's criticism, Kitchener's performance in South Africa did his career no harm. In 1902 he took over as Commander-in-Chief India and, despite opposition from the Viceroy, Lord Curzon carried out many far-reaching reforms during his six years there. These included completing the unification of the Indian Army. As for Churchill, he had made himself a small fortune. Sales of *The River War*, plus his two books of war correspondence from South Africa, as well as ten months' salary from the *Morning Post* netted him over £4,000. All this writing further helped to spread the name of Churchill far and wide. It also helped him to make enemies. Some senior officers, most notably Kitchener and his circle of friends, scoffed at the notion of Churchill as some sort of self-appointed military expert. In light of his youth and having only reached the rank of lieutenant this was perhaps very understandable. Churchill, though, was old enough to know that his growing profile would inevitably attract critics jealous of his achievements.

PART TWO

Fall and Rise

5

A Haunting Lesson

It seemed at first that becoming an MP would spell the end of Churchill's military career and his involvement with the armed forces. This, however, proved to be far from the case. Determined to capitalize on his military exploits and to earn a much-needed income, he skipped the opening of Parliament. Instead, he embarked on an extensive speaking tour in Britain, Canada and America. When he eventually made his maiden speech to the House of Commons on 13 May 1901 he spoke out against military expenditure and talk of war in Europe. This did little to endear him with the armed forces who, faced with so many overseas commitments, did not welcome talk of cuts.

Churchill later caused further controversy when he 'crossed the floor' of the Commons to join David Lloyd George and the Liberals in 1904. After Russia and Japan went to war that year, Churchill's old comrade in arms, Aylmer Haldane, was sent out to be a British military observer with the Russians.[1] Likewise, Captains Thomas Jackson and William Christopher Pakenham were assigned to the Japanese fleet. Churchill would later be impressed by Admiral Pakenham during World War I.

Everyone initially assumed that Japan would be no match for the military might of the Russian Empire. Instead, at every turn the Russians were outfought and outgeneraled on land and at sea. 'Few foresaw at that time,' wrote Churchill, 'the startling defeats which Japanese arms would shortly inflict upon the Czar.'[2] The conflict also resulted in extensive trench warfare. Haldane, who inspected Russian defences north of Port Arthur, noted 'a network of barbed wire'.[3]

This heralded the shape of things to come in Europe. Notably, for the first time in modern history an Asian nation defeated a European power and the long-inward-looking Japan became ever more emboldened by this new-found success. By a quirk of fate, the official British military history of the Russo-Japanese War was written by another Boer war veteran, Captain Ernest Swinton, the man who would later come up with the idea for the tank.

The following year Churchill was appointed Parliamentary Under-Secretary of State for the Colonies under Prime Minister Sir Henry Campbell-Bannerman's new Liberal government. This post greatly helped his profile because he got to represent his department in the House of Commons, as his boss Lord Elgin, the Colonies Secretary, was a member of the House of Lords. Elgin, who had served as Viceroy of India when Churchill was there as a young lieutenant, took an instant liking to him. The job would further shape Churchill's views on the British Empire and in particular India. He would learn that the vast Empire was not strategically or politically integrated and remained wholly reliant on the Royal Navy to protect it. Traditionally Britain operated a 'two-power' navy that was capable of fighting two enemies. By the early 1900s there were simply not enough resources to go around. Britain was having to recognize American domination of the Western hemisphere and the harsh reality it could no longer defend its Far East interests without help.

During his time at the Colonial Office, Churchill had to deal with several diplomatic incidents involving America. Firstly, Sir Alexander Sweetenham, the British Governor of Jamaica, offended the Americans after he criticized their use of Jamaican labour to build the Panama Canal. Sweetenham then snubbed the US Navy by demanding a landing party from the US Marine Corps, sent to help in the aftermath of a Jamaican earthquake, leave the island immediately. This came to the notice of President Theodore Roosevelt, who complained privately to MP Arthur Lee, who in turn raised the matter with Churchill. He advised Lord Elgin that he thought Sweetenham's actions were 'indefensible and wantonly insulting'.[4] Both agreed that the governor should go and his resignation was accepted on 1 April 1907. Churchill also got to renew his acquaintance with his old South African adversary Jan Smuts, who had travelled to London with Louis Botha the previous year to present the Boers' case for self-government.

Churchill could not resist the lure of being in uniform and in 1906 and 1909 he attended German military manoeuvres as the guest of Kaiser Wilhelm II. On his first visit, rather conspicuously, he had his photograph taken alongside the Kaiser. Beforehand Campbell-Bannerman warned the outspoken Churchill not to cause a diplomatic incident by speaking too candidly to the Kaiser, which he found highly amusing. He was impressed by the German Army's discipline and organization, but doubted it fully appreciated the firepower it had at its disposal. Amusingly Churchill noted that he thought the Kaiser wanted to be just like Napoleon, but without having to fight any battles. On his second visit the Kaiser warned him of the perils of socialism. During this time Churchill joined the Cabinet as the President of the Board of Trade, a post he held for several years. He also got married to Clementine Hozier at St Margaret's Church in Westminster on 12 September 1908, which gained him yet more press coverage at home and abroad.

He gained a key high-profile Cabinet role two years later when he was appointed Home Secretary. This post was courtesy of Prime Minister Herbert Henry Asquith who succeeded an ailing Campbell-Bannerman. Once again Churchill's thirst for being in the thick of it and in the limelight was to cause him trouble. A group of Latvian anarchists on 3 January 1911 took refuge in 100 Sidney Street in the East End of London, where they were besieged by 200 police officers. The Latvians were wanted in connection with a failed jewellery shop robbery in Houndsditch the previous month that had resulted in the deaths of three policemen. Churchill was minding his own business, languishing in the bath at home in Eccleston Square, Pimlico at 1100 hours when he was informed what was happening. The War Office was enquiring if the police would like the assistance of 20 men from the Scots Guards who were better armed.

Churchill should simply have asked to be kept informed of developments, but instead he got dressed and immediately took charge. He authorized the involvement of the army and then went to the Home Office. Unable to get a clearer picture of what was happening he arrived at Sidney Street at 1150 hours. He was annoyed to discover that the soldiers had clearly arrived before the offer was made to him. He also discovered that the senior police officer, Assistant Commissioner Major Frederick Wodehouse, had gone to the War Office. This left Superintendent Mulvaney in charge, whose men were all for storming the house. Churchill urged caution, because firing was coming from the building and nobody knew just how many people were in it.

Rather than delegate, Churchill then decided to conduct his own reconnaissance of the area to make sure there were no escape routes. When he returned he was informed that the house was on fire and that the fire brigade wanted to intervene. As there was still shooting coming from the windows, Churchill told them not to risk their lives. He took cover in the entrance of a nearby yard; just in front of him were several soldiers and plain clothes officers armed with rifles sheltering in some doorways. When he glanced behind him he saw a gaggle of uniformed police officers one of whom was armed with a shot gun. In some alarm he gave orders that he was not to be shot in the backside. When the police finally entered the building they found just two bodies, both male; one had died of asphyxiation and the other had been shot by one of the soldiers. Churchill departed the scene at about 1445 hours.

The newspapers the following day were outraged at the Home Secretary's behaviour, and to make matters worse the event had been filmed by *Pathé News*. It was felt Churchill had inappropriately overridden the chain of command by taking control. It was also felt that summoning troops equipped with a Maxim machine gun and artillery was overkill. To some he was seen as little more than 'a trigger-happy boy scout'.[5] Arthur Balfour, the leader of the Conservatives, enquired pointedly, 'I understand what the photographer was doing, but what was the right honourable gentleman doing?'[6] In the inquest that followed, Churchill denied the accusations, but the damage to his reputation was done. The general perception was that the Home Secretary had been running around the streets of London taking part in street battles. In vain he attempted to explain that he had not been involved in the decision to deploy heavy weapons, which had not been used. To his critics this did not matter; it was enough the incident had happened on his watch.

Churchill suffered more criticism at the hands of the press when he was held responsible for using the Metropolitan Police and troops to quell the Tonypandy riots in south Wales during 1910–11. He was unfairly blamed for the deployment of elements of the 18th Hussars and Lancashire Fusiliers. This was not authorized by the Home Secretary or the Secretary of State for War, but the General Officer Commanding of the Southern Command pending further instructions.[7] General Nevil

Macready commanding the 2nd Infantry Brigade was sent to Cardiff to take charge should the military need to be committed. However, Churchill after discussing the situation with Captain Lionel Lindsay, the Chief Constable of Glamorgan, decided that the troops would be kept in reserve and only used as a last resort. He reassured King George V that boosting police numbers 'will obviate all risk of having to use the military'.[8]

Instead, some 1,400 police were employed to contain 12,000 striking Welsh miners who were facing financial hardship. The police responded to the protestors with their truncheons. Violence spilled out onto the streets in Tonypandy in November 1910 and one miner died after being struck on the head. Troops were sent to Llwynpia and Pontypridd to conduct patrols, but they were not involved in any trouble. By the time the strike came to an end in the summer of 1911, public perception was that Churchill had once again been heavy handed. In contrast the mine owners felt that the Home Secretary had not acted quickly enough or decisively enough. This, they argued, had allowed the riots to drag on unnecessarily.

Churchill also had to contend with a wave of dock and railway strikes that threatened food shortages in London, Liverpool and Manchester. These sparked more unrest and rioting and some local authorities feared they were facing revolution. Once more the military was called upon to support the police, with 200 members of the Yorkshire Regiment put onto the streets of Liverpool on 14 August 1911. The police and supporting troops were stoned and shots were fired. Six soldiers and two policemen were injured before peace was restored. 'Strongly deprecate half-hearted employment of troops,' George V told Churchill two days later, 'they should not be called on except as a last resource ... they should be given a free hand and the mob should be made to fear them'.[9] Asquith, although a supporter of Churchill, decided he would have to move him to distract increasing vocal condemnation of the government.

It was while he was Home Secretary that Churchill first developed what was to become a lifelong passion – an interest in intelligence. The recently established Secret Service Bureau divided into two in 1910, becoming MI5 or the Security Service responsible for counter-intelligence and MI6 or the Secret Intelligence Service responsible for intelligence gathering. Churchill had seen first-hand the failure of British intelligence during the Boer War. He was fully supportive of

MI5's work to monitor German espionage and authorized access to correspondence handled by the Post Office. Before leaving the Home Office, Churchill wrote to Sir Edward Grey, the Foreign Secretary, warning him that intelligence reports, 'show that we are the subject of a minute and scientific study by the German military and naval authorities, and that no other nation in the world pays us such attention'.[10]

Privately Churchill was in part relieved to leave the Home Office. From experience, seeing men killed on the battlefield was bad enough, but he had no stomach for judicial killings. In his role as Home Secretary he had to authorize death sentences on a regular basis, which he confided in friends, 'had become a nightmare'.[11] He found reading the appeals from prisoners with life sentences distressing. 'This was for me,' he later remarked, 'an even more harassing task.'[12]

Although Churchill lost his Home Secretary post it seemed to do his political career little harm. Before he had gone to the Home Office, Asquith had considered sending him to the Colonial Office or the Admiralty. Reginald Mckenna, First Lord of the Admiralty and the minister responsible for the Royal Navy, was under fire over the Grand Fleet's readiness to meet the growing naval threat from Germany. Asquith now needed someone to shake things up. Churchill was duly appointed First Lord of the Admiralty in October 1911. Ironically Mckenna was sent to the Home Office. Churchill arrived just in time to benefit from the reforms instigated by Admiral Sir John Fisher. The navy prospered under Churchill, with him overseeing the impressive Dreadnought battleship programme, building up the Royal Naval Air Service and introducing a naval staff for the very first time. Churchill's passion for excitement remained unabated and in 1913 he started to learn to fly. His wife, though, was naturally anxious that he would kill himself and the following year he promised to give it up.

The start of World War I in the summer of 1914 proved to be a severe embarrassment for Churchill and the Admiralty. German U-boats effectively neutralized his Grand Fleet and German cruisers reached Constantinople, inducing Turkey to side with Germany. The Turks had been incensed when Churchill impounded two dreadnoughts being built in Britain for the Turkish Navy before hostilities had even been declared against the Ottoman Empire.[13] Churchill was also soon acting as if he was once again a reckless lieutenant. One of his early escapades was to try and take charge of the defence of Antwerp.

After the German armies swept across Belgium and into France, Antwerp remained under siege. To help in the defence of the port Churchill sent a brigade of Royal Marines and two brigades of naval volunteers, forming the Royal Naval Division. Troops were also sent to Ostend and Zeebrugge with the intention of cutting their way to Antwerp. Churchill, as ever desperate to command men in the field, travelled to Antwerp on 3 October 1914 offering to resign from the government and lead the defence. Although Lord Kitchener, the Secretary of State for War, was supportive, it was not a role that Churchill was in the least qualified for, nor was he of appropriate military rank. Prime Minister Asquith was astounded and ordered him to return at once. Churchill left three days later and the city fell on 10 October.

Churchill, in a bid to help the fighting on the Western Front, proposed an assault in the Dardanelles, the narrow entrance to the Black Sea. He argued this would distract the Germans and by occupying Constantinople would open up a route to Russia. This in turn would help the Russians on the Eastern Front. Foreign Secretary Sir Edward Grey also reasoned that such an attack might trigger a coup in Constantinople, as not all Turks were happy about their country's entry into the war in support of Germany.

Before the war the Admiralty had considered amphibious operations against Germany in the Baltic. Converting such plans for operations against Turkey did not seem that great a stretch of the imagination. In the summer of 1914 Greece offered to land troops at Bulair to block off the Dardanelles, while another force landed on the outer end of the peninsula to take the Turkish forces in the rear. The Greeks, though, dropped out for fear that Bulgaria might side with Germany leaving them fighting a two-front war.

In principle Churchill's plan was sound; in its execution it was to prove a disaster. It needed to be conducted swiftly and with decisive force, but this did not happen. Churchill continued to lobby the War Office and by the end of the year Lord Kitchener had come round to the idea thanks to the lack of progress on the Western Front. Fisher, who had been recalled to serve as First Sea Lord, also backed Churchill. It seemed that the Royal Navy, by risking some of its older ships, would be able to strike a significant blow for the war effort.

The Allied Fleet in the Aegean proceeded to shell the outer forts on the Dardanelles on 3 November 1914. Vice-Admiral Sir Sackville Carden's flagship, the battle cruiser *Indefatigable*, supported by the *Indomitable*, hit the defences guarding the entrance, while two French battleships bombarded those on the Asiatic shore. This achieved little other than to alert the Germans and the Turks that the area was being targeted for some purpose. Thanks to Carden the Allies had revealed their hand thereby losing any element of surprise. Carden was considered a second-rate officer.[14] Certainly his career had been decidedly unremarkable and until recently he had been in charge of Malta's dockyard.

Churchill and the Admiralty would have done well to heed the lessons from the utterly disastrous and little-known battle of Tanga, fought on the coast of German East Africa (modern Tanzania) in the first week of November 1914. The British, using largely Indian troops, supported by an elderly cruiser, conducted a poorly organized small-scale combined operation intended to seize the territory. They were not expecting any resistance and the element of surprise was completely lost by the Royal Navy warning the Germans that hostilities were about to commence. This gave them time to summon 1,000 lightly armed men who hemmed in the 8,000-strong invasion force inflicting 800 casualties.[15] The Royal Navy commander failed to support the landings or shell the German counter-attacks. After just four days the humiliated expeditionary force, having abandoned most of its equipment, was back at sea heading for Mombasa. It was evident that cooperation between the army and navy had been non-existent. Tanga had shown how not to do things and it was vital that the same mistakes were not repeated.

By the beginning of 1915 the beleaguered Russians were calling for a diversionary attack against the Turks. Kitchener was not entirely certain what could be done in light of the British Army's losses at Ypres on the Western Front. However, he accepted that the Dardanelles seemed to offer the best option. This gave Churchill exactly the opportunity that he had been waiting for. In eager anticipation he signalled Carden on 3 January 1915 to ask, 'Do you consider the forcing of the straits by ships alone a practicable operation?'[16] Two days later Carden's response was hardly encouraging, 'I do not consider Dardanelles can be rushed. They might be forced by extended operations with large numbers of ships.'[17] Churchill hoped that the hard-pressed Russians might launch a simultaneous land and sea attack in the Bosphorous to distract Turkey. The Russians, though, were not minded to help

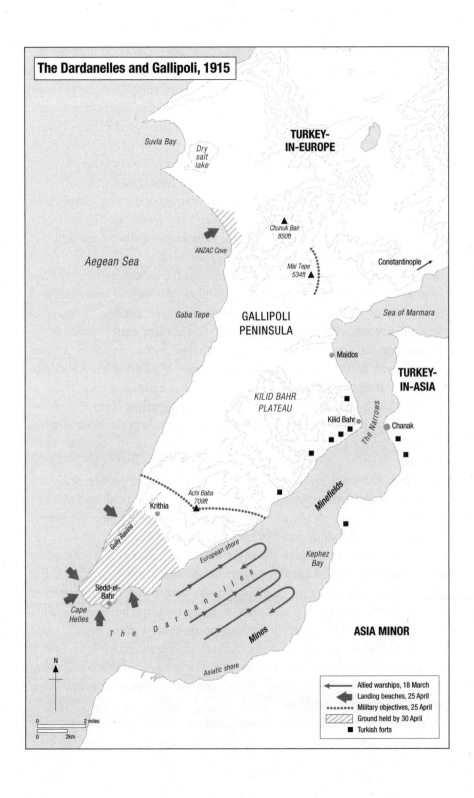

The Dardanelles and Gallipoli, 1915

Suvla Bay

Dry salt lake

TURKEY-IN-EUROPE

Chunuk Bair
850ft

ANZAC Cove

Aegean Sea

Mal Tepe
534ft

Constantinople

Gaba Tepe

GALLIPOLI PENINSULA

Sea of Marmara

Maidos

TURKEY-IN-ASIA

KILID BAHR PLATEAU

Kilid Bahr

The Narrows

Chanak

Achi Baba
709ft

Krithia

Gully Ravine

European shore

Minefields

Kephez Bay

Sedd-el-Bahr

Cape Helles

The Dardanelles

Mines

Asiatic shore

ASIA MINOR

N

Allied warships, 18 March
Landing beaches, 25 April
Military objectives, 25 April
Ground held by 30 April
Turkish forts

0   2 miles

0   2km

the Allies capture something that they had long coveted, namely the entrance to the Black Sea.

The need for 'large numbers of ships' began to ring alarm bells in the Admiralty. Fisher was concerned that a Dardanelles operation would inevitably weaken the Grand Fleet. Churchill reassured him it would remain untouched and that they could use surplus warships. Their goals he said were the same. Fisher was unconvinced and on 25 January 1915 tried to warn Asquith that the navy could not force the Dardanelles on its own and that such an operation would impact on the integrity of the Grand Fleet. Asquith chose to ignore him. Fisher understandably became increasingly frustrated that the First Lord of the Admiralty and the Prime Minister were not heeding his warnings.

A dangerous rift began to develop between Churchill and Fisher. The former was vexed by the constraints caused by the lack of resources and felt the War Council's plans were not ambitious enough. These were vague and continued to suggested that the Royal Navy could carry out the operation on its own. The directive stated they were 'to prepare for a naval expedition in February, to bombard and take the Gallipoli Peninsula, with Constantinople as its objective'.[18] Fisher remained alarmed that if the operation became too large it would divert warships from elsewhere. He was also annoyed by Churchill constantly signalling the fleet without consulting him. Things came to a head at the end of January when Churchill informed the War Council that their naval attack would be ready to commence in mid-February. When Fisher endeavoured to raise objections, Asquith silenced him. He then attempted to leave but Kitchener managed to placate the old admiral. Afterwards Churchill persuaded Fisher to once more support the operation.

The naval bombardment of the outer forts commenced on 19 February 1915, but bad weather then meant it could not be resumed until the 25th. In the meantime, the Turks had done nothing to strengthen their defences in the region. 'Up to 25 February, it would have been possible to effect a landing successfully at any point on the peninsula,' noted the Turkish General Staff, 'and the capture of the straits by land troops would have been comparatively easy.'[19] For a week Carden's landing parties were able to come ashore to destroy Turkish guns that had been abandoned in the outer forts.

Carden was essentially shooting blind as he lacked reconnaissance aircraft to spot for his guns. While waiting for aircraft to arrive he ceased the shelling and concentrated on ineffective minesweeping. He then fell sick and was replaced by his second-in-command, Admiral de Robeck. On 18 March the Allied Fleet ran into mines losing three battleships with three others damaged. Fatefully three days later de Robeck informed the Admiralty that as far as he was concerned the fleet would not get through without the help of the army. This entirely changed the complexion of the operation. While Churchill continued to support the attack, David Lloyd George serving as Chancellor of the Exchequer was alarmed by the prospect of the army having 'to pull the navy's chestnuts out of the fire.'[20]

Churchill's old comrade in arms, General Ian Hamilton, was sent out to take command of the gathering ground forces. He found the Greek island of Lemnos in the northern Aegean wholly unsuitable as a base of operations so redirected all the transport ships to Alexandria. There they had to be reloaded wasting yet more time. The Germans overseeing the Turkish defences were grateful for the delay; they needed at least eight days to prepare, but instead they got four weeks. The Turkish Army mustered six divisions in the Dardanelles, numbering 84,000 troops. Hamilton's assault force comprised five divisions totalling 75,000 men. His task was to open up the Dardanelles so the fleet could reach the Sea of Marmara. Instead of striking at Bulair he chose to land at Cape Helles and Gaba Tepe way to the south on 25 April 1915. The latter was to be assaulted by the two divisions of the Australian and New Zealand Army Corps or Anzacs.

All was not well on the Western Front either. The failure of the British Army's assault on Aubers Ridge on 9 May, costing 20,000 casualties, was blamed on a lack of high explosive shells. Kitchener, in part to distract attention from this, turned on Churchill and the navy during a meeting of the War Council on 14 May. He said the army had been let down by the navy, as it was supposed to have forced the Dardanelles. Fisher, who was in attendance with Churchill, then dropped a bombshell by announcing he had always opposed the Dardanelles operation. In response Churchill argued he would have not consented to naval operations in February and March had he known sufficient troops would not be available until May.

The following day Fisher, sick of Churchill's operational meddling, resigned. This very publicly signalled a complete loss of confidence in the First Lord of the Admiralty. It also fatally undermined Churchill's standing with the Royal Navy. The stress of working with Churchill had proved too much for Fisher who appears to have suffered a nervous breakdown.[21] This was a terrible blow to Churchill who met with Asquith to offer his own resignation. Asquith initially declined to accept it; however, it was impossible for Churchill to hang on and he was replaced on 27 May. It was a deeply upsetting time for him. When the war had broken out, he was one of the three most powerful men in the country. Just 15 months later he was a political car crash. His booby consolation prize was Chancellor of the Duchy of Lancaster. 'I thought then that I was finished,' he later remarked.[22]

Thanks to the ammunition scandal and Churchill's fall from grace Britain's last Liberal government was brought crashing down. Although Asquith remained Prime Minister, he found himself presiding over a fractious coalition government, with Lloyd George now heading the Ministry of Munitions. Churchill, in an effort to save his reputation, wrote to his successor at the Admiralty, Arthur Balfour, urging him to persevere with the Gallipoli campaign. Kitchener suggested that Churchill travel to the Dardanelles to conduct a thorough review of the situation. However, such an act would have hardly been prudent and it is doubtful Asquith and Balfour would have acquiesced to such a mission.

In the Aegean things went from bad to worse. During May and June Hamilton tried to push his troops north-east. By mid-July he had only got three miles inland from Cape Helles and was unable to reach the Anzacs. The appearance of German U-boats greatly curtailed the navy's support for the ground forces. All the major warships were withdrawn, leaving just destroyers to help out. Hamilton's subsequent landing at Suvla Bay ended in fiasco and in October he was replaced by Lieutenant-General Sir Charles Munro. Churchill, desperate to save the Gallipoli operation, shamelessly intercepted Munro on 22 October before he sailed. Churchill warned that a withdrawal would be a disaster. Nonetheless, Munro was soon calling for an evacuation and during late December the troops were withdrawn from the Anzac and Suvla bridgeheads. Those at Cape Helles remained trapped until 8 January 1916 when they were finally withdrawn.

The eight-month Gallipoli campaign was a costly political, military and human failure. It resulted in 205,000 casualties including from illness; around 43,000 were killed or died of their wounds or disease.

Unfairly Churchill was held responsible for this debacle even though he had only really exerted influence for the first month. The Australian and New Zealand governments were appalled that the sacrifice of their men had been in vain. If anyone was to blame it was Kitchener, for it was a ground forces failure as much as a naval one. Despite the bravery on the ground, which resulted in 39 Victoria Crosses being won, the campaign had been hamstrung from the start by a lack of commitment and drive. The Dardanelles were to haunt Churchill for the rest of his life. It taught him that combined operations with the army and the navy should never be run by committee. There needed to be an overall commander-in-chief with clear goals from the very start.

At this time Churchill's successor at the Home Office was facing an internal threat. MI5 sources indicated in 1915 that Indian nationalists were plotting an assassination campaign in England. This was taken very seriously because six years earlier an Indian student, Madan Lal Dhingra, had assassinated Sir William Curzon Wyllie in London. At the time Sir William was serving as the Secretary of State for India's political aide-de-camp. Churchill had been impressed by Dhingra's final words before his execution. He exclaimed, 'My only prayer to God is that I may be re-born of the same mother and I may re-die in the same sacred cause till the cause is successful.'[23] MI5 responded to this new plot by recruiting India experts and many of its staff were Indian Army, police and civil service veterans. They also succeeded in turning two of the key plotters into double agents.

During World War I MI5 on the whole did not take much notice of the pro-independence Indian National Congress Party, but that would change once it came under the influence of Gandhi. He returned to India from South Africa in 1915, where he had developed satyagraha or passive resistance. Initially the Indian Department of Criminal Intelligence did not deem him a threat. It reported Gandhi as 'neither an anarchist nor a revolutionary' rather 'a troublesome agitator'.[24] Churchill on the other hand would eventually grow to vehemently detest him. MI5 began to expand its monitoring of subversive nationalist activities beyond India to encompass the entire Empire and Commonwealth. This was intended to head off German trouble-making and required close liaison with the Colonial Office and its overseas staff. In the meantime, though, there was the question of Churchill's political future.

6

'Cat on Hot Bricks'

The urge to command continued to drive Churchill. He even asked Asquith to appoint him Governor and Commander-in-Chief in British East Africa. Churchill was hardly qualified nor of a suitable rank for such a role. Britain was engaged in a nasty guerrilla war being waged by enemy forces operating from German East Africa. Perhaps he was inspired by the hunt for the German cruiser *Königsberg* that had been cornered on the East African coast. He may have also thought he could reverse Britain's humiliating defeat at Tanga, which had all the hallmarks of a mini Gallipoli. Kitchener, though, would not have supported this. He was wholly opposed to sending inadequate reinforcements to East Africa as he felt defeating the Germans in Europe was a priority.

Instead of Churchill, Lieutenant-General Jan Smuts got the job. He was fresh from his successes with General Botha against German South West Africa (modern Namibia). It was while Churchill was Home Secretary that South Africa had been granted dominion status. This made it self-governing, effectively leaving the Boers in control, and the last British troops left Cape Town on 10 August 1914 headed for France. The Germans hoped the South African Dutch would rise up and this is what happened. Smuts had to first contend with 11,000 pro-German South Africans before he could focus on defeating the Germans in South West Africa.

Churchill, feeling humiliated and seeking to escape the political turmoil, volunteered for service on the Western Front as a major in the Queen's Own Oxfordshire Hussars. This was a Territorial Army yeomanry regiment, with which he had maintained his commission, though his membership amounted to little more than a gentleman's drinking club. It was not on active duty, which meant he would have to be assigned to another regiment and what he wanted was a combat command.

He arrived in France at the Headquarters of Field Marshal Sir John French in November 1915 and was sent to the 2nd Battalion, Grenadier Guards for training. Always the showman he stood out thanks to his habit of sporting a distinctive light blue French helmet. He was not only regularly photographed with it, but also had his portrait painted wearing it. Churchill almost suffered a terrible accident whilst visiting Vimy Ridge with Captain Edward Spears (later Major-General Sir Edward Spears) who was a liaison officer attached to the French Army. They were making their way down a trench when Churchill's automatic pistol, hanging from his neck by a lanyard, started firing rounds at his feet. 'He danced like a cat on hot bricks,' recalled Spears, 'in his attempts to get out of the unpredictable line of fire.'[1] Had Churchill been hit in the foot he would have been sent straight home, or worse had he been hit in the thigh he could have bled out.

Field Marshal French was all for giving Churchill a brigade, but the last thing Asquith wanted was to raise his profile so he vetoed the idea. When Sir Douglas Haig took over from French, Churchill, promoted to Lieutenant-Colonel, was appointed commander of the 6th Battalion, Royal Scots Fusiliers. This formed part of the 9th Scottish Division which had suffered 6,000 casualties at the battle of Loos. Churchill's second-in-command was Major Sir Archibald Sinclair, future leader of the Liberal Party and Secretary of State for Air.

Not everyone was pleased at the prospect of having a celebrity of Churchill's calibre in their midst. 'When the news spread, a mutinous spirit grew,' recalled Captain Andrew Dewar Gibb. 'Everybody liked the old C.O. and nobody could see why any prominent outsider should come in and usurp his place so easily.'[2] His arrival at Moolenacker, near Armentières, with a host of kit that included a bath, easel and paints caused further consternation in some quarters. However, Churchill worked hard to win the battalion over and he seems to have been generally well liked. His adjutant Lieutenant Jock McDavid observed that 'No detail of our daily life was too small for him to ignore. He overlooked nothing.'[3]

Churchill was amused to discover that he had met his Corps Commander, General Sir Charles Fergusson, once before at the battle of Omdurman. Fergusson had started his military career in the Grenadier Guards and then joined the Egyptian Army serving under Kitchener with the 10th Sudanese Battalion. After an inspection tour the general declared himself very pleased with Churchill's efforts. Churchill was then slightly surprised when he apologized, saying, 'I am also sorry you have been sent to this battalion which was such a very weak and shattered one.'[4]

Churchill and his soldiers were deployed to the village of Ploegsteert in Belgium at the end of January 1916. Although it was a quiet sector during his time in command 15 per cent of his men were killed or wounded by artillery fire, by snipers and in dangerous night raids on the German trenches. Some of his men were alarmed at the way he seemed to revel in danger and delight at being under fire. 'He was like a baby elephant out in no-man's-land at night,' said 19-year-old Lieutenant Edmund Hakewill Smith. 'He never fell when a shell went off; he never ducked when a bullet went past with its loud crack.'[5] Churchill's logic was that if you had heard the shot, it had already gone by. In all he led a total of 36 patrols.

Churchill had his fair share of scrapes during his time at the front. He was at his headquarters with Major Sinclair and Lieutenant McDavid on 3 February 1916 when they came under artillery fire. They were just about to head for their dugout in a nearby barn when a German shell dropped through the roof and exploded in the neighbouring room. When McDavid looked down he saw shrapnel had caught a finger; he also noted that another piece had very narrowly missed severing Churchill's right hand. Churchill had by good fortune been holding his trench lamp at the time and this shielded him from serious injury. McDavid had to be evacuated and was replaced by Captain Dewar Gibb.

Although on active service Churchill took time out to relax. Hakewill Smith was fascinated by the sight of him lugging his easel and paints around the grounds of their rather sorry-looking advanced headquarters at Laurence Farm. Each time he sat to paint he found his picture compromised by an increasing number of shell craters. Churchill's mood darkened after a week of this and Hakewill Smith bravely asked his commanding officer what was wrong. Churchill explained that he simply could not get the craters right as they ended up looking like mountains, that is until he discovered a dab of white did the job. Also, to give the painting a focal point, he got Major Sinclair to sit in the middle of the courtyard calmly reading a newspaper. On another occasion, to the alarm of his officers, Churchill insisted on painting Ploegsteert while it was under shell fire.

At the front Churchill renewed his acquaintance with Hugh Tudor who had become a friend while in Bangalore. Tudor was now a general in charge of the 9th Division's artillery. When the pair visited British positions in Ploegsteert Wood on 10 February 1916, Churchill got to experience his first sustained artillery bombardment that lasted for an hour. They went to the forward trenches to watch the fall of the rounds, which put them just 100 yards from the Germans. In response to this British shelling, the Germans lobbed shells and mortar bombs back. Churchill found the whole experience immensely exhilarating, especially when Tudor's guns accidentally dropped two rounds behind them. He marvelled at the way the earthen parapets withstood the pounding, a clear indication that relying on artillery to destroy enemy positions did not work. The ground shook violently around them and he was showered in debris but remained unscathed throughout. Churchill decided he liked the enemy mortar bombs best, because you could see them coming which gave you a chance to take evasive action. Tudor was later promoted to divisional commander.

Churchill stayed on the Western Front until May 1916 when his understrength battalion was merged with another one and he returned to London to resume his seat in Parliament. Before his departure he held a champagne lunch for his officers at Armentières. He wrote, 'I shall always regard this period ... one of the most memorable of my life.'[6] Captain Dewar Gibb observed 'he loved soldiering: it lay very near to his heart and I think he could have been a very great soldier.'[7] Back in the House of Commons, Churchill spoke out in support of the Admiralty and tried to repair his relationship with Fisher. At the end of the month the Grand Fleet finally gave battle at Jutland in the North Sea. There was no long-awaited decisive victory. It ended in an embarrassing draw, though the German fleet remained contained.

Churchill was shocked and annoyed in the summer of 1916 when the British Army's brand-new tanks were prematurely committed to the Somme offensive. He was 'shocked at the proposal to expose this tremendous secret to the enemy upon such a petty scale and as a mere make-weight to what I was sure could only be an indecisive operation'.[8] By this time only 140 British tanks had been built and only 60 of these had arrived in France, of which 49 were committed at the Somme. Haig, although a supporter of the new tank concept, abandoning any element of surprise, deployed them in penny-packets and in insufficient numbers. Fortunately for the Allies the Germans in response made little effort to develop their own tank force.

Churchill had good reason to be so vexed. While still at the Admiralty, although distracted by the Dardanelles, Churchill had found time to support the development of the tank. Lieutenant-Colonel Ernest Swinton's idea of using a caterpillar tractor on the Western Front had landed on his desk in January 1915 and he took it to Asquith, who instructed Kitchener to look into it. However, the navy, who were operating armoured cars in France, persuaded Churchill to set up the Landship Committee. This created *Little Willie*, the very first tank prototype. Asquith subsequently instructed the committee be merged with the War Office's efforts.

It is quite possible that Churchill's support for the tank was influenced by the imagination of British left-wing writer and novelist H.G. Wells, who by this stage was hugely successful. 'Wells is a seer,' remarked Churchill. 'His *Time Machine* is a wonderful book, in the same class as *Gulliver's Travels*.'[9] He had written to Wells in response to *Anticipations of the Reaction of Mechanical and Scientific Progress upon Human Life and Thought* published in 1901. Two years later Wells had a short story called 'The Land Ironclads'[10] appear in the *Strand Magazine*, which envisaged land-going warships that could traverse trenches. Before that Wells had famously conjured up 'a walking engine of glittering metal'[11] – the alien tripod war machines featured in *The War of the Worlds* first published in 1897. Although Churchill thoroughly enjoyed the general impression that he had invented the tank, it was Lloyd George as Minister of Munitions, Secretary of State for War and then Prime Minister who was instrumental in getting the army to commit to the concept. It would prove its value at the battles of Cambrai and Amiens. 'It was amateurs who were principally responsible for the tank,' acknowledged Lloyd George, 'easily the most formidable of our weapons'.[12]

Churchill had to wait a year before he was invited back into government. In the meantime, Canadian-born newspaper magnate

Max Aitken helped orchestrate the replacement of Asquith's Liberal-Conservative coalition with one led by Lloyd George on 6 December 1916. Aitken's reward was a peerage, with him becoming Lord Beaverbrook. He was also appointed Minister of Information. Six months after Lloyd George became Prime Minister, Churchill was offered the Minister of Munitions job. An enthusiastic Churchill threw himself into this role with great gusto. This was at a time when there were mounting tensions with the trade unions, but Churchill soon made his mark. He also used it as an excuse to tour the front to gather information and to network. In 1917 while on one such visit he met Major Desmond Morton, who was serving as an aide-de-camp to Field Marshal Haig. The pair struck up a friendship that later would gain Churchill access to British intelligence thanks to Morton joining MI6.

'I hold no brief for the present Minister of Munitions. I believe he has his personal and political detractors,' Labour MP William Anderson told the House of Commons, 'but in my opinion he has brought courage and a certain quality of imagination to the task.'[13] Lloyd George noted, 'between March 1st and August 1st [1918] the strength of the Tank Corps increased by 27 per cent, and that of the Machine-Gun Corps by 41 per cent, while the number of aeroplanes in France rose by 40 per cent'.[14] The troops at the front were grateful for Churchill's hard work, especially when it came to the tank. Although it was hellish fighting from inside these early armoured behemoths, the infantry was certainly thankful for their support. 'You had a certain amount of shielding because you used to follow the tanks along,' recalled John Oborne who served with the 4th Battalion, Devonshire Regiment. 'They were a great help. They'd flatten the wire. I know they were in their infancy, but Churchill did a good job with them.'[15]

Churchill also became responsible for the production of poison gas while he was Minister of Munitions.[16] The French first used gas grenades in 1914, but these were ineffective. The Germans also experimented with chemical-type projectiles that year. Then in April 1915 they unleashed chlorine gas on the British and French positions at Ypres. This was followed by the use of phosgene and mustard gas. The latter had a nasty habit of lingering on the battlefield. 'One of the shells disturbed the residue of mustard gas that had been lying there for months,' observed Cecil Withers, with the 17th Battalion, Royal Fusiliers. 'They talk about secondary smoking ... I got secondary gas.

It really hit me for six.'[17] The Allies responded in kind. German veteran Erich Maria Remarque, in his classic semi-autobiographic novel *All Quiet on the Western Front*, wrote, 'I remember the awful sights in the hospital: the gas patients who in day-long suffocation cough up their burnt lungs in clots.'[18]

Captain B.H. Liddell Hart noted in 1917, 'Moreover, by the introduction of mustard gas the Germans scored a further trick, interfering seriously with British artillery and concentration areas.'[19] In response, according to Lloyd George, the French placed 'An enormous order for poison gas and smoke shells.'[20] Churchill put into production 100 tons of mustard gas, which the British Army used at the end of September 1918.[21] Rather flippantly he had reported to his wife, 'The hamper of mustard gas is on its way.'[22] He would later be criticized for his enthusiasm for gas, but the trend had already been started before he took over the Munitions Ministry.

The British deployed 140 tons of chlorine at the battle of Loos in September 1915. Western Front veteran, poet and novelist Lieutenant Robert Graves was on the receiving end of this, recalling, 'the gas went whistling out, formed a thick cloud a few yards off … and then gradually spread back into our trenches'.[23] To make matters worse the Germans once alerted began to shell the British forward positions scoring direct hits on the gas cylinders. If Churchill was ever privy to the casualty figures this may have had some impact on his thinking; although 2,632 British troops were gassed only seven died.[24]

Whilst chemical weapons were deployed widely on both the Western and Eastern Fronts involving some 30 agents, only about 12 had any military value. Mustard gas killed up to ten per cent of its victims and for those who survived exposure caused severe blistering and blindness for weeks or months.[25] Research after World War I showed that on average only 1 in 200 mustard gas casualties were permanently affected.[26] Furthermore, of 150,000 British mustard casualties just ten soldiers suffered persistent vision damage and only a few required the removal of an eye.[27] Nonetheless, its effects could be deadly and were extremely unpleasant for those without protective clothing and gas masks. This led to it being dubbed the 'King of Gases'.[28] Churchill's view on its use was soon eclipsed by international opinion, which agreed to the Geneva Protocol banning the use of gas in warfare in 1925.

7

Winston's Mercenaries

Under Churchill's oversight Britain's weapons factories continued to feed the British armed forces. By November 1917, the army had amassed 470 tanks ready for an offensive at Cambrai. These did not prove to be as decisive as hoped and the British attack wilted in the face of a German counteroffensive. However, in part thanks to Churchill's efforts, the Allies were able to fend off Germany's last major offensive in early 1918. Then, that summer, the British launched 634 tanks against the Germans at Amiens. American and French forces also launched offensives. German morale was finally shattered. Germany, enduring starvation due to the prolonged Allied naval blockade, agreed to an armistice on 11 November 1918 bringing World War I to an end.

After Germany's defeat Churchill maintained his connection with the armed forces thanks to Lloyd George, who promoted him to joint Secretary of State for War and Air in January 1919. This made Churchill the very first Secretary of State for Air. His new concern was the outcome of the 1917 Russian Revolution and subsequent civil war, which had knocked Russia out of World War I. Churchill warned that Lenin and his Bolsheviks presented a far greater threat than the Kaiser and Germany ever did. His mantra became 'Peace with the German people, war on the Bolshevik tyranny.'[1] Much to Lloyd George's irritation Churchill became obsessed with trying to save Russia from the Bolsheviks or Reds, championing military intervention to prop up the anti-Bolshevik White Russians. Churchill seemed blind to the reality that the disunited Whites committed just as many appalling atrocities as the Bolsheviks. Furthermore, Russia was weakened by declarations of independence by the Baltic states, Finland and Poland, which had all been part of the Russian Empire.

Even though the Bolsheviks only controlled about ten per cent of Russia by mid-1918, an ill-planned intervention involving 14 countries and over 100,000[2] troops commenced before World War I even ended. Therefore, the decision had been taken way before Churchill tried to influence events. While Allied contingents were sent to protect Russia's key ports from the Germans and in some cases indulge in land grabs, few countries had any desire to become fully embroiled in the sprawling Russian Civil War. Ironically their presence, instead of bolstering the chaotic and disorganized anti-Bolshevik cause, simply roused the population to support the Red Army against the Whites and the foreign invaders. The collapse of Germany and its allies in November 1918 freed up much-needed manpower for the Bolsheviks. To complicate matters Russian allegiances amongst the many Bolshevik and anti-Bolshevik factions kept chopping and changing depending on who could offer the most security.

Lloyd George sent Churchill and General Sir Henry Wilson, Chief of the Imperial General Staff, to the Paris Peace Conference in February 1919 where the Treaty of Versailles was being negotiated. He wanted Churchill to canvass the views of the delegate nations on what if anything should be done about the chaotic situation in Russia. Churchill explained to the delegates that British troops were dying on Russian soil as they spoke and that something should be done. US President Woodrow Wilson stated that he was opposed to escalating Allied intervention and urged that their troops be withdrawn. This was not what Churchill wanted to hear. He cautioned that this would result in the destruction of the anti-Bolshevik forces enabling the Bolsheviks to take complete control of Russia. Only the French, who like the British, Americans and Japanese had soldiers in Russia, were amenable to the proposal of propping up the Whites until they could cope on their own.

Philip Kerr, Lloyd George's personal emissary at the conference, was alarmed that Churchill seemed determined to fight the Bolsheviks using international volunteers, plus the Finns and Poles who wanted to protect their new-found independence. When informed of this Lloyd George instructed Churchill not to commit Britain to a war in Russia. Churchill responded by reminding him that they were already fighting there. 'So far I am not responsible,' he said, 'for sending a single man to Russia.'[3]

Britain had deployed some 40,000[4] men to northern Russia, the Black Sea and Siberia at great cost.[5] Those in the north were under General Edmund Ironside operating from Archangel and General Charles Maynard at Murmansk. Churchill, after becoming Secretary of State for War and Air, supplied the Whites with copious quantities of munitions as Britain was awash in surplus weapons. These amounted to enough to equip an entire army.[6] 'An expensive war of aggression against Russia is a way to strengthen Bolshevism in Russia and create it at home,' warned a wise Lloyd George. 'We cannot afford the burden.'[7] He cautioned Churchill that such a war would bankrupt the country and stir up trouble with British workers. This was at a time when Europe and America were recovering from the devastating effects of World War I and socialism was spreading.

In consequence Churchill failed to persuade Lloyd George to recognize Admiral Alexander Kolchak, a senior White commander, as the official head of the Russian government. Kolchak was leader of the Siberian Provisional Government based in Omsk. This, as well as commanding anti-Bolshevik units, had nominal authority over the American, Czech, French and Japanese forces. He even had a small contingent of two British battalions that had been deployed from Hong Kong,[8] one of which was under the command of Colonel John Ward, the Labour MP for Stoke-on-Trent.[9] General Alfred Knox, the British military representative in Russia, was based in Omsk, where he oversaw the dispersal of British-supplied munitions shipped in via Vladivostok. A British mission was also sent to Ekaterinburg to form an Anglo-Russian Brigade.

Churchill was dismayed when the British government agreed to return 500,000 Russian prisoners of war, who had been captured by Germany but were now held by the Allies. He felt they should be re-equipped and sent to fight for Kolchak; instead they would now fall into the hands of the Red Army. 'This appears to me,' he wrote, 'to be one of the capital blunders in the history of the world.'[10] On 20 May 1919 he tried to muster support in the House of Commons for continued British intervention in northern Russia, claiming, 'Admiral Kolchak's advance … coupled with the growth and improvement of the Russian local troops at Archangel and Murmansk, offers us the prospect of a far better solution of our own problems than we could ever see before.'[11] His optimism was ill-founded.

Churchill had to content himself with encouraging the tough mercenary Czech Legion, who were slowly heading east to Vladivostok in order to sail for France, to fight for the Whites. He was enthralled by the romance of these 42,000[12] men, originally recruited from deserters and prisoners taken from the Austro-Hungarian Army to serve alongside the Russians on the Eastern Front. At one point their armoured locomotives controlled the entire length of the Trans-Siberian Railway, making them a force to be reckoned with. Churchill saw the Czechs rolling to and fro in their trains as landlocked buccaneers who looted and pillaged as they went. Certainly they amassed a king's ransom in Czarist treasure as well as thousands of local brides. Their haul included '29 carloads of gold, silver, platinum and gems'.[13]

American and Japanese troops had arrived at Vladivostok in the summer of 1918 to cover the Czech withdrawal. Churchill hoped that the Americans would now push inland to reinforce Kolchak and the Czechs. However, they had no desire to be drawn further into the Russian Civil War and refused. Instead, they agreed to hold the Trans-Siberian Railway between Vladivostok and Lake Baikal until the Czechs arrived. 'Surely now when Czech divisions are in possession of large sections of the Siberian Railway,' reasoned Churchill, 'and in danger of being done to death by the treacherous Bolsheviks, some effort to rescue them can be made?'[14]

'With the exception of a few battalions formed from Russian officer cadet training units, plus one division of Poles,' noted British instructor and future general Brian Horrocks at Ekaterinburg, 'these Czechs were the only reliable troops at Kolchak's disposal.'[15] The intention of the British military mission was to train and equip enough White Russian forces recruited in Siberia to eventually replace them. Horrocks was not encouraged by the quality of recruits that he and his colleagues received. His enthusiasm for the task was further dented when a British colonel told him, 'In my opinion the Reds are bound to win and our present policy will cause bitterness between us for a long time to come.'[16]

Lloyd George and his cabinet, though, did not share Churchill's unbridled enthusiasm. They had good reason, as General Knox had warned that the Czechs were untrustworthy. Nonetheless, they were well organized, disciplined and effective fighters. Their commanders, including General Radola Gajda, were prepared to side with the Whites especially after the Bolsheviks foolishly attempted to disarm them. In contrast Tomáš Masaryk, head of the Czechoslovak National Council, would have preferred the Legion to remain neutral. When the Czech Republic came into being in November 1918 under Masaryk's presidency he desperately needed the Czech Legion to help thwart German inhabitants from seceding and to halt Hungarian aspirations towards neighbouring Slovakia.

Admiral Kolchak's forces, supported by the Czechs, in the summer of 1919 hoped to march on Moscow in conjunction with the British and other White units striking from Archangel and Murmansk. Churchill backed this plan, as did his generals, and proposed pushing 17,500 British troops, which included 3,500 volunteers, to link up with Kolchak at Kotlas. The intention was that once this was achieved General Ironside could then begin withdrawing his men home. Surprisingly Lloyd George agreed, but a series of mutinies amongst the 22,000 Russian troops supporting the British thwarted their efforts. Although in a favourable military position, Kolchak hesitated. The growing Red Army counter-attacked and his forces were sent reeling. Churchill was forced to abandon the whole Kotlas pincer operation as a miserable failure.

He was exasperated that Kolchak had not pressed home his advance on the Russian capital via Kazan. 'Twenty or thirty thousand resolute, comprehending, well-armed Europeans could,' he wrote, 'without any serious difficulty or loss, have made their way very swiftly along any of the great railroads which converge on Moscow.'[17] In truth, though, Kolchaks' demoralized soldiers had run out of food, were suffering from typhus and were deserting in their thousands. His greatest handicap was that the White generals operating to the northwest and southwest of Moscow were not in a position to launch simultaneous attacks. 'The Liberating Army – or at least what is left of it,' observed Lloyd George in a conciliatory memorandum sent to Churchill, 'is now running as hard as it can back to Omsk, and is mediating a further retreat to Irkusk. The failure was certainly not due to any default on our part.'[18] General Knox ordered the instructors at Ekaterinburg not to go into action with the Anglo-Russian Brigade and called them back to Omsk. Brian Horrocks and fellow officer George Hayes were left behind to liaise with Kolchak's rearguard.

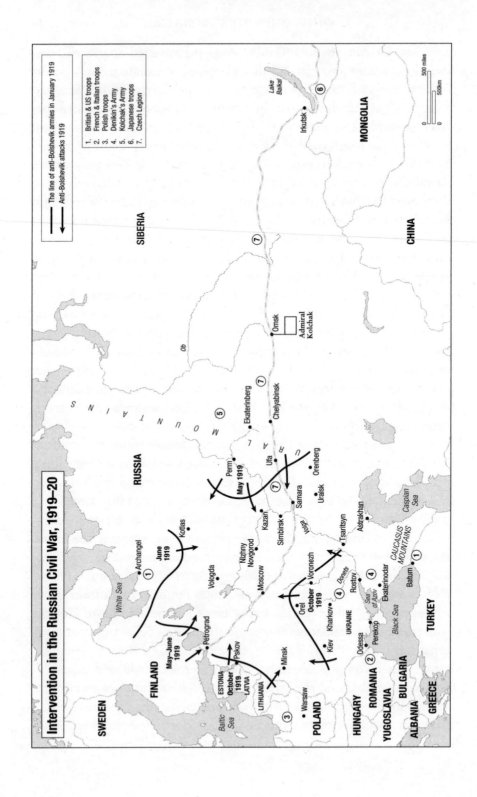

Intervention in the Russian Civil War, 1919–20

The line of anti-Bolshevik armies in January 1919

Anti-Bolshevik attacks 1919

1. British & US troops
2. French & Italian troops
3. Polish troops
4. Denikin's Army
5. Kolchak's Army
6. Japanese troops
7. Czech Legion

SWEDEN

FINLAND

White Sea

Archangel
① June 1919
Kotlas

Vologda

May–June 1919

Petrograd

Baltic Sea

Pskov
October 1919

ESTONIA
LATVIA
LITHUANIA

③

Warsaw

Minsk

POLAND

HUNGARY

ROMANIA ②

YUGOSLAVIA

BULGARIA

ALBANIA

GREECE

Moscow

Nizhny Novgorod

Kazan

Simbirsk

Volga

Perm
May 1919

Ufa

RUSSIA

URAL MOUNTAINS

Ekaterinberg
⑤

Chelyabinsk
⑦

Samara

Uralsk

Orenberg

⑦

Tsaritsyn

Astrakhan

Caspian Sea

Voronezh
October 1919

Orel

Donets

④

④

Rostov

Sea of Azov

Ekaterinodar

Kharkov

Kiev

UKRAINE

Odessa

Perekop

Black Sea

CAUCASUS MOUNTAINS

① Batum

TURKEY

Ob

Omsk
Admiral Kolchak

SIBERIA

CHINA

MONGOLIA

Irkutsk

⑥

Lake Baikal

⑦

0   500 miles
0   500km

When the Bolsheviks employed mustard gas shells captured from the Germans against the Whites, the Allies retaliated. General Sir Arthur Holland was appointed chairman of the committee charged with looking at the future of chemical warfare and continuing research at Porton Down in May 1919. The research facility had been set up during World War I and the Cabinet agreed to renewed funding. Gas warfare expert Captain Charles Nye, formerly of the Royal Engineers' Special Brigade, found himself recalled to active duty. Churchill ordered mustard gas to be sent to Russia along with Nye. When news of this became public Churchill came under attack in Parliament. 'I do not understand why, if they use poison gas,' he told the House of Commons, 'they should object to having it used against them.' When this was greeted with heckling he retorted, 'It is a very right and proper thing to employ poison gas against them.'[19] During August and early September 1919 the RAF's two-seat DH.9 bombers attacked six Russian targets using 560 gas bombs.[20] The poor results hardly justified their employment and did little to help save the Whites.

Churchill, keen to try and take the pressure off Kolchak, sought troops who could help. When he heard that there was not enough shipping to transport the Czech Legion from Vladivostok, he suggested that 30,000 of them battle their way west through Siberia to link up with Ironside in northern Russia. This he reasoned would strengthen his northern pincer. The Czechs were not receptive to this idea as it meant fighting their way through the Red Army. Instead, Ironside was authorized by the Cabinet to start withdrawing his men home. Churchill was opposed to this as he felt they were throwing Kolchak to the wolves, but there was nothing he could do.

The outbreak of war between Russia and newly independent Poland in February 1919 had been seen by Churchill as a vindication of his interventionist policy. Polish forces moved into Ukraine to support some 40,000 Ukrainian separatists. This initially helped surround the Bolsheviks and offered the prospect of destroying their regime. The writer H.G. Wells, whose work Churchill greatly admired, made his way to Prague to assess the situation for Lord Beaverbrook's newspapers. Churchill by this stage knew Wells personally, as they had met at Beaverbrook's Stornoway House.

Wells found the Czechs in Prague in a state of panic as they feared the Red Army would drive the Poles from Ukraine, take Warsaw and then attack them. They had only recently expelled the Hungarians from Slovakia, to create Czechoslovakia, and were worried their new republic would come apart. The only people Wells met who seemed confident the Red Army would be stopped were President Tomáš Masaryk and some of the hardened veterans from the Czech Legion. Masaryk reassured Wells that the Red Army would collapse and that the Bolshevik regime would not last the winter. On his return to London, Wells relayed this to Beaverbrook. This prognosis initially proved wrong when the Red Army swept to the very gates of Warsaw. There was soon talk of revolutionary governments being established in Germany and Poland. Then at the eleventh hour, in August 1920, the Poles defeated the Russians. Churchill felt that with a large chunk of the Red Army destroyed, now was the time for the Whites to renew their attack.

Wells was convinced that ruining Germany with war reparations and isolating Russia was a recipe for catastrophe. During his travels in Europe, which included Russia, he wrote a series of articles for Beaverbrook's *The Sunday Express* that were turned into a book called *Russia in the Shadows*. Beaverbrook mischievously gave it to Churchill to review, knowing full well what the reaction would be. Churchill was a fan of Wells' fiction, especially when it came to such visionary works as *The War in the Air*, and his non-fiction. However, whilst Wells' non-fiction *The Outline of History* had been a huge success, his views on Russia were completely at odds with Churchill's.

Wells' son Anthony West wrote with amusement, 'When Winston's slating and my father's counterblast appeared in *The Daily Express*, its circulation jumped just as that of *The Sunday Express* had done.'[21] Beaverbrook the consummate businessman made money out of the pair of them. Wells found this duplicity highly amusing. 'If Max ever gets to heaven,' Wells observed, 'he won't last long.'[22] Despite their ideological differences Churchill was delighted when many years later Wells dedicated a book to him.[23]

Thanks in part to international meddling, the fortunes of the Russian Civil War rapidly turned against the Whites in 1920. The Allies evacuated northern Russia and, after the British departed, the Whites in the region were soon overwhelmed. At Tsaritzyn they were defeated by a Georgian called Joseph Stalin and the city was later renamed Stalingrad in his honour. To the south French and Italian troops were withdrawn from the Black Sea and the Whites were decisively defeated in the Crimea, while in the Far East the Americans and Japanese prepared to leave. It was not long before the Bolsheviks dominated all of Russia. Churchill's undying hatred of them was not tempered until World War II, when the Soviet Union became a welcome, if strange, bedfellow.

As for Churchill's Czechs, they exchanged their loot and Kolchak with the Bolsheviks at Irkutsk for freedom and headed for their new nation of Czechoslovakia. The unfortunate Kolchak was summarily executed. Not only was the admiral betrayed by the Czechs, he was also betrayed by the Allies. The Czechs supposedly answered to General Maurice Janin, the French commander-in-chief of Allied troops in Siberia. Furthermore, there were Japanese soldiers in Irkutsk but they made no attempt to intervene. Instead, they stood by while Kolchak, his mistress and his staff officers were handed over by the Czechs to the vengeful Bolsheviks. It begs the question what happened to the Czechs' gold reserves. Furthermore, Janin later received the Czechoslovak Order of the White Lion and the French became responsible for the new Czechoslovak Army. The cynical might argue that there was some sort of stitch-up with Kolchak, but there is no evidence that Churchill was in any way complicit in this sorry affair.

The Czech Legion along with the Americans evacuated Vladivostok in April 1920; however, the Japanese were to outstay their welcome by another two years. The Czechs' long odyssey home covered over 15,000 miles and lasted two years. In awe Churchill noted, 'The pages of history recall scarcely any parallel episode at once so romantic in character and so extensive in scale.'[24] General Gajda, dubbed 'the Siberian Tiger', reached safety. Initially pensioned off he was then sent to study military theory in France. When he returned to Prague he was appointed Deputy Chief of Staff to the head of the French Military Mission. When he became Acting Chief of Staff in 1926 Masaryk forced him to retire.

It greatly rankled Churchill that his intervention strategy had failed. He felt that the Czech mercenaries could have been decisive in western Russia and unfairly held Lloyd George responsible for their failure. This stung Lloyd George who considered Churchill his protégé and his friend. 'You proposed that the Czechoslovaks should be encouraged to break through the Bolshevik armies and proceed to Archangel,' Lloyd George wrote in a frank response to such criticism. 'Everything was done to support your proposal. ... Still you vaguely suggest that something more could have been done and ought to have been done.'[25] General Wilson wrote rather uncharitably in his diary, 'So ends in practical disaster another of Winston's military attempts. Antwerp, Dardanelles ... His judgement is always at fault, and he is hopeless in power.'[26] This, though, was unfair; Churchill's attempts to help the Whites had been constantly hobbled by the Cabinet's insistence on the withdrawal of British troops.

PART THREE

World Order or Disorder

8

Flying Police

On the home front Churchill's main role as Secretary of State for War and Air was overseeing the demobilization of the army and the air force following World War I. Crucially, he safeguarded the future of the Royal Air Force as an independent organisation. It had been formed from the Royal Flying Corps and Royal Naval Air Service in April 1918. Now post-war many politicians felt it would be more cost effective to merge the fledgling RAF with the army. The appointment of Churchill to the dual-hatted role of War and Air Secretary initially indicated to some in the RAF the imminent subordination of the air service. Sir William Weir, former president of the Air Council, and Hugh Trenchard, Chief of the Air Staff and father of the RAF, were alarmed at such proposals. They were relieved when Churchill made it perfectly clear he had no such intentions and also helped set up the RAF's officer training college at Cranwell. This was to prove a vital decision come the summer of 1940 when pilot training was at a premium.

Nonetheless, Trenchard faced a terrible struggle to save the RAF from complete oblivion. The peace dividend at the end of World War I meant drastically scaling back all the armed forces. In November 1918 the RAF had 99 squadrons on the Western Front, by October 1919 only five of these still existed and by the end of that month there was just one. It was easy to see why the Admiralty and the War Office felt the RAF had become a post-war irrelevance. Churchill asked Trenchard to draw up a memorandum summarizing his proposals for building a peacetime RAF. The problem they both faced was that the Cabinet limited the RAF's funding to £15 million per annum for the next five years. Trenchard therefore had to come up with a plausible peacetime rationale for the continued existence of the RAF. It desperately needed a new role that would enable it to flourish.

Churchill was forced to consider options for cutting the escalating costs of garrisoning the sprawling and expanding British Empire. Trenchard, in late 1919, came up with a radical idea dubbed 'Air Control' that was to get Churchill into trouble. He suggested that in some instances air power could replace the army. Trenchard reasoned overseas policing operations could be conducted much more quickly and cheaply by aircraft than by slow-moving ground forces. Furthermore, local tribesmen did not normally have dedicated anti-aircraft defences. His proposal probably stemmed from operations in the North-West Frontier, where the RAF were operating in support of the army fighting rebellious tribesmen either side of the border with Afghanistan.

The Afghan Emir declared a holy war in the spring of 1919 and invaded India hoping the Muslim population would rise up against the British. Controversially, Churchill ordered the use of mustard gas against the Afghans. In response the India Office in London strongly objected pointing out it would set a very dangerous precedent in the region and the idea was quickly dropped. Churchill felt they were being very unreasonable. His enthusiasm for mustard gas seems to have been born partly out of ignorance, which is illustrated by his remarks to the India Office: 'Gas is a more merciful weapon than high explosive'.[1] Nonetheless, during World War I he had acknowledged privately that mustard gas was a 'hellish poison'.[2]

Amongst the British forces tasked with countering the Afghan Army was Squadron Leader Arthur Harris, later to gain fame as the head of Bomber Command. He was a former Royal Flying Corps pilot who had seen action during World War I and then served in India. By the summer the Afghans had been successfully driven back. Notably Harris recalled, 'on occasion we were allowed to reduce a tribe to submission by independent action', in other words by bombing and strafing them.[3] While in India he was infuriated at the way the army starved the RAF of spares to a point where their aircraft were criminally unsafe to fly. The army was responsible for funding and was therefore reluctant to prioritize Harris's aircraft, even when it came to much-needed replacement engines. He eventually deliberately caused a diplomatic stink to get the problem addressed.

Not long after, Trenchard's 'Air Control' theory was put to the test in the protectorate of British Somaliland. For two decades Muhammed Abdullah Hassan, known to the British as 'The Mad Mullah', and his followers had caused unending trouble. Numerous military expeditions had failed to defeat him, because he kept escaping into the wilderness. Through January to early February 1920 an RAF bombing campaign was waged in Somaliland to which the Mullah had no answer. This was the result of an early example of littoral warfare and combined operations, which fascinated Churchill.

A dozen of the RAF's DH.9 bombers were ferried to Somaliland by the seaplane carrier HMS *Ark Royal*, though the planes did not operate off it. This vessel was a veteran of Gallipoli and the Russian Civil War and had seen plenty of action. The Mullah's strongholds were destroyed and his forces soon dead or dispersed, along with his livestock. He fled to neighbouring Ogaden where he died at the end of the year. The army had spent almost 20 years trying to defeat him, whereas this campaign supported by the RAF flying from Berbera lasted just three weeks.[4] The success of the operation helped convince Churchill that the Royal Navy should develop its modest carrier force.

He was delighted with the outcome and reported to the House of Commons that an operation previously estimated to cost about £2.5 million using just ground forces had been carried out for £30,000.[5] This seems curiously very low, even allowing for the swiftness of the campaign, but to the government it offered endless opportunities for the deployment of the RAF overseas and for saving money. 'I propose to apply that principle to another field,' he told the Commons in February 1920. 'I have ... an alternative scheme for the control of Mesopotamia'.[6] He also wanted to create air mobile infantry which would require the construction of dedicated transport aircraft. If all this could be achieved, he proposed an RAF officer should be the next commander-in-chief in Mesopotamia. The army understandably did not like the erosion of its authority.

The Ottoman Empire had been torn apart following World War I. Under pressure from Britain and Greece, Sultan Mohammed VI was forced to sign the Treaty of Sèvres in 1920. The Allies took the Ottoman Turk's Middle Eastern territories including the Levant and Mesopotamia; Armenia was granted independence and most of Asia Minor was handed over to the Greeks. The backlash to this was the rise of Turkish nationalist General Mustafa Kemal who set up a rival government in Ankara. He drove back the Russians, reclaimed Armenia and made friends with the Bolsheviks.

In the meantime, Trenchard worked hard to make the RAF indispensable. He based seven squadrons in Egypt, eight in India and three in Mesopotamia, though these were regularly redeployed as and when they were needed. He had 33 squadrons by March 1920, although eight of them were still forming. The bulk of these forces were stationed overseas and Trenchard ensured his pilots never ceased operational flying. This was quite an achievement even though they were equipped with old aircraft and suffered from inadequate support. Without increased funding, however, there was little prospect of expanding the RAF any further. Behind the scenes Trenchard sensibly did all he could to cultivate Churchill as an ally in the Cabinet. They had a common interest, the security of the British Empire.

That same year Churchill caused yet more controversy with his handling of the uprising in Mesopotamia known as the Iraq Revolt. The Arabs and Kurds of Mesopotamia, having only just got rid of the Turks, were not happy about the presence of British soldiers. They were well armed having acquired large numbers of British and Turkish rifles as well as plentiful stocks of ammunition taken from the various battlefields and Turkish barracks. Remarkably many of these weapons were still in use in Iraq by the southern marsh Arabs well over three and a half decades later.[7] Churchill had rather optimistically told the House of Commons in March 1920, 'It is essential in dealing with Mesopotamia to get the military expenditure down'.[8] He maintained that the cheapest way to control the region would be by using the RAF who could bomb any recalcitrant tribes into submission. This idea though was not his but Trenchard's, who was constantly trying to justify the continued funding of the RAF.

By the summer of 1920 Mesopotamia was in open revolt, but Churchill, distracted by events in Russia, did not want to get involved. However, the decision was not his to make. 'Now that the Cabinet have definitely decided that we are to plough through in that dismal country,' Churchill told Lloyd George, 'every effort must be made to procure vigorous action and decisive results.'[9] That was easier said than done. 'We are at our wits end to find a single soldier,'[10] he added in despair. At great cost he somehow scraped together reinforcements from India and Iran as well as two RAF squadrons, to supplement those already there. Despite Churchill's paucity of troops, Mesopotamia was to see the deployment of 125,000 men, of whom 80,000 were Indian. The commander in Iraq was none other than General Haldane and he reassured Churchill that he would be able to crush the revolt within three months. He was true to his word. During Haldane's campaign up to 10,000 Arabs and Kurds were killed for the loss of 500 British and Indian soldiers. Rather unfairly Churchill was held responsible and the pacification of Iraq was seen as yet another example of his bloodthirsty warmongering.

Churchill gave the RAF permission to use mustard gas in Mesopotamia. Mustard gas bombs, though, were not available as the bulk of them had been sent to Russia for use against the Bolsheviks.[11] Instead, Churchill instructed the army to send 15,000 gas shells from Egypt.[12] In the event poison gas was not deployed. Churchill had once more authorized its use on the understanding that mustard gas was not considered deadly. Although potentially lethal it was designed as a long-term incapacitating agent. He rather naively scolded his hesitant colleagues, saying, 'I do not understand this squeamishness about the use of gas ... which makes the said native sneeze.'[13] Nonetheless, the RAF and the administration in Mesopotamia were against the idea from the start and did not use it.

9

Troubled Emerald Isle

During this period Churchill became embroiled in Ireland's bloody road to independence and partition. Before the outbreak of World War I Ulster's Protestants were alarmed by the prospect of Irish home rule if it meant being dominated by the country's Catholics. The issue had been defeated in the British Parliament in 1886 and again in 1893, remaining dormant for almost two decades. It was not until Asquith's Liberal minority government needed the support of the Irish Nationalist Party in 1910 that it came to prominence again. Churchill moved from opposing home rule to supporting it on the basis that Ireland remained under British authority. Randolph Churchill, Winston's son, later wrote, 'he had a waxing and reciprocal affinity with those Tories who believed that war with Germany was coming and that an Irish settlement was essential for that reason if no other'.[1]

Ireland, by March 1914, was facing potential war thanks to the impending Home Rule Act. The British government feared that Edward Carson's Ulster Volunteers militia were planning to seize the weapon depots at Armagh, Carrickfergus, Enniskillen and Omagh in order to resist rule by Dublin. There were 23,000 British troops in Ireland but only 9,000 were deployed in Ulster. This meant if trouble broke out the Ulster garrison might have to be reinforced from the main military base at Curragh near Dublin. When news of this became known it resulted in the Curragh Incident. In protest Brigadier-General Hubert Gough, commander of the 3rd Cavalry Brigade, and 57 officers resigned their commissions. There were also fears that there would be a railway strike in Ireland paralysing troop movements.

Churchill, who was First Lord of the Admiralty, warned publicly on 14 March, 'We are not going to have the realm of Great Britain sink to the condition of the Republic of Mexico.'[2] He ordered, with Cabinet approval, the 3rd Battle Squadron to Lamlash on the Isle of Arran ready to ship troops from Kingstown east of Dublin north to Dundalk and Carrickfergus. The Royal Navy was also ordered to help with the defence of the latter should the depot come under attack. Churchill signalled, 'This place is to be defended by every means … by guns and searchlights from the ships.'[3] Eight battleships were to be sent to Lamlash, with a cruiser stationed off Carrickfergus and several destroyers sent south into the Irish Sea. From a purely military point of view this was a sound tactical move; from a diplomatic one it was a complete public relations disaster. The clear implication was that the British government was prepared to shell British citizens.

When these plans became known there was outrage in the House of Commons and in the British press. Although the warships were recalled the damage was done. Churchill was accused along with the military of organizing an 'Ulster Pogrom'[4] and Lord Charles Beresford branded him a 'Lilliput Napoleon'.[5] When Churchill rose in the House of Commons on 25 March to explain why the warships had not been sent he said it was 'because the precautionary movements of the military in Ireland had been affected without opposition from an army of 100,000 which had been raised to resist the authority of Crown and Parliament'.[6] Although responsibility for the situation rested with General Sir Arthur Paget who was in command of British forces in Ireland, Churchill was still held publicly responsible by politicians in Belfast and London. International events then took over as the newly passed Home Rule Act was suspended because of the outbreak of war in Europe. Subsequently Catholic volunteers served with the 16th (Irish) Division and Protestants with the 36th (Ulster) Division on the Western Front with great distinction. This meant that large numbers of men on both sides of the sectarian divide received military training and combat experience.

The hard-line Republicans, though, could not wait for the end of the war. In 1916 Irish nationalists rose up in Dublin against British rule, but what became known as the Easter Rising was swiftly crushed by troops backed by armoured cars and artillery. Nonetheless, this came as a shock to the British government, as Dublin was considered as much a part of the United Kingdom as London, Edinburgh or Cardiff. Three years later this struggle was renewed by the Irish Republican Army (IRA) and it soon became apparent that the demoralized Royal Irish Constabulary needed help in the face of an escalating guerrilla war and terror attacks. It suffered regular casualties, and officers and their families endured intimidation resulting in mass resignations. Recruitment in Ireland stalled so the only solution was to seek volunteers in England. Lloyd George did not want to deploy the army fearing a repeat of 1916 and decided to form armed militia or paramilitaries instead.

Lloyd George was of the view that he had tried to apply self-determination to Ireland, but the Irish could not agree amongst themselves. The result was that the 1914 Home Rule Act did not come into force and a new agreement needed to be negotiated. Lloyd George was now preoccupied with trying to get a meaningful peace settlement for post-war Europe and was not greatly interested in Ireland. He should have been, as Irish security was a drain on the Treasury. Churchill, by now Secretary of State for War and Air, was well aware that the British Army had 43,000 men stationed in Ireland at a cost of almost £11 million a year. In addition, there was the cost of maintaining the 10,000-strong Royal Irish Constabulary.

It was soon apparent to both Lloyd George and Churchill that discipline was an issue. When a party of British soldiers were ambushed and one of their number killed on the way to church in Fermoy in September 1919, the following day 200 troops went on the rampage. When those soldiers responsible were posted to Cork they went on a looting spree there. Many Irishmen thought the authorities in Dublin were deliberately trying to provoke another rising to justify a military clampdown.

Lord French, the Viceroy of Ireland, Ian Macpherson, the Chief Secretary for Ireland and General Sir Nevil Macready, Commander-in-Chief in Ireland, were directly responsible for internal security, not Churchill. Macready, though, reported to Field Marshal Sir Henry Wilson, Chief of the Imperial General Staff, who answered to the Secretary of State for War. Wilson was an Irishman, but no Republican. Churchill was implacably opposed to full Irish independence and saw the problem in the same light as India: hard-line nationalists were trying to break up the British Empire, or in this case the United Kingdom.

As a result, many of Churchill's suggestions to the Cabinet were extreme. These included special tribunals to dispense summary justice and deploying the RAF to bomb and strafe the IRA. He was perhaps hoping to implement Trenchard's 'Air Control' in Ireland. However, the country was hardly the North-West Frontier or Somaliland. Both ideas were rejected. Instead, Lloyd George approached General Sir Hugh Tudor, an old friend of Churchill's since his days in India, to established what was worryingly termed 'a counter-murder association'.[7] Tudor was an artillery man so hardly seemed the best choice to command the Irish police and a new paramilitary force.

The Republicans swept the field in the district council elections in January 1920. This sparked a wave of political and sectarian violence. Thomas MacCurtain, the Lord Mayor of Cork, who also happened to be the Commandant of the Cork Brigade of the IRA, was shot by intruders on the night of 19 March. The Coroner's inquest ruled that the killers were members of the Royal Irish Constabulary taking officially sanctioned revenge for the shooting of a policeman. The inquest returned a verdict of 'wilful murder' against Lloyd George, French and Macpherson. Whether this was true or not, it was an allegation that was to persist. Macpherson, in fear for his life, resigned and was replaced by Sir Hamar Greenwood.

Churchill the historian should have known that the Republicans would not give up. They had a long history of rebellion against British rule and had never forgiven the English for the settler plantations that had permanently changed the religious hue of Northern Ireland. The Catholics had long memories and the merciless treatment of Drogheda and Wexford at the hands of Oliver Cromwell was forever burned into their collective memory. For the diehard Republicans it was all or nothing. In contrast, Ireland's Protestants always took solace from their historic victory over the Catholics at the battle of the Boyne.

Churchill largely viewed the Irish problem as economic rather than sectarian, remarking, 'If Ireland were more prosperous she would be more loyal, and if more loyal more free.'[8] When it came to the sectarian divide he felt this was an internal domestic issue. Nonetheless, he acknowledged it was very damaging internationally: 'The British Empire cannot afford to be drawn continually by these brutal Irish feuds into a position dishonouring to its general and long maintained reputation.'[9]

In his role as Secretary of State for War and Air, Churchill saw the challenge essentially as one of finding sufficient manpower to overwhelm the IRA. To assist Tudor thousands of ex-servicemen were recruited and sent to Ireland. This policy did not originate with Churchill or Lloyd George. The First Lord of the Admiralty, Walter Long, suggested it in May 1919. Joseph Byrne, the Royal Irish Constabulary's inspector general, opposed this but he was replaced. Understandably, men traumatized and desensitized to killing by their time in the trenches and in need of employment did not make the best candidates for policemen. Perhaps Churchill should have insisted on better screening and training, but this was before the concept of winning hearts and minds of the local population had ever been developed. When the initial company of volunteers arrived in Limerick in March 1920 there were insufficient green police uniforms so they ended up with green or khaki trousers and tunics, with black belts and caps. As a result, they were named the Black and Tans after a famous local pack of dogs. This was not a name to greatly encourage public confidence.

Worryingly, by 1 May 1920 the *Irish Times* claimed, 'The King's Government has virtually ceased to exist south of the Boyne and west of the Shannon.'[10] In the meantime the Black and Tans started gaining a reputation for brutality. To supplement them the Auxiliary Division was recruited from ex-officers. They were chosen, Churchill explained rather optimistically, 'for intelligence, their characters and their records in the war'.[11] Brigadier-General Frank Crozier, who arrived to command this force, found the police and their paramilitary supporters were poorly motivated and running unofficial death squads, whereas the British Army in Ireland was on the whole better disciplined. The police, enduring heavy casualties, lashed out wherever they could. This situation came about partly because General Tudor was incapable of maintaining police discipline and General Macready disliked leaving the safety of Dublin Castle.

The Auxies were to prove little better than the Black and Tans. Crozier was a former commander of the Protestant 36th (Ulster) Division, so was hardly an impartial choice when it came to sectarian politics. Like Churchill he was also a Boer War veteran and had been at Spion Kop. General Macready was not happy about his appointment, noting, 'his record in the War Office is one which is hardly a recommendation as an administrator of discipline in any capacity whatever'.[12] This was unfair on Crozier who arrived to find his new recruits already in a state of ill-disciplined disarray. He was angry that little thought had been given to supplying and quartering them. 'The original members of the division, which then had no name,' wrote Crozier, 'had to arrange their own messing and canteens ... Conditions were appalling.'[13]

The militarization of the police by General Tudor seemed to make matters worse. The Royal Irish Constabulary was not only bolstered by army veterans but was also issued with heavier weapons. Many of the senior posts were filled by British Army officers including Brigadier-General Cecil Prescott-Decie and Lieutenant-Colonel Gerald Smyth. Their preference was to fight fire with fire, which was not the best way of upholding the rule of law. They were under the impression the policy issued by Dublin Castle was one of state-sanctioned murder. This was thanks to Tudor who spoke of the 'stamping out of terrorism by secret murder'.[14] Prescott-Decie declined to carry this out only until such time as he had adequate resources. 'I have absolutely no faith,' Wilson informed Churchill, 'in the present regime as a semi-military, semi-police operation.'[15]

Churchill and Wilson were exasperated at how some senior army personnel in Ireland did not seem to take personal security seriously. Three officers, including Brigadier-General Cuthbert Lucas, commander of the 17th Infantry Brigade, were kidnapped on 26 June 1920 while on a fishing trip near Fermoy. The following evening the local troops went on the rampage trying to find them, causing £18,000 worth of damage and killing a civilian. Their brigade commander attempted to shrug their actions off as 'an over-zealous display of loyalty'.[16] Lucas and the others, though, only had themselves to blame.

Churchill was not pleased when he was informed that the Irish troubles had spread to troops stationed in India just two days after the kidnapping. Around 350 members of the Connaught Rangers Regiment, part of the British Army, mutinied in the Punjab. British soldiers occupied their barracks and, as a result, 88 mutineers were court-martialled and James Daly, one of their ringleaders, sentenced to death. This event rattled Churchill because the regiment had fought loyally for the Crown during the Boer War and World War I and had helped put down the Easter Rising. Every Irish regiment now became suspect.

Brigadier-General Lucas's actions were not unusual because government officials naively assumed the IRA would not target those engaged in sporting activities. For example, the legal adviser at Dublin Castle regularly rode with the Meath Hounds. If the authorities had been paying any attention they would have realized the IRA had ended this gentleman's agreement on 3 June 1920 when two gunmen targeted troops playing a cricket match at College Park, Trinity College, Dublin. Although no members of the military were hit a female student was killed and another woman wounded. General Macready wrote to Churchill to apologize for Lucas's 'thoughtless' behaviour.[17] However, he tried to blame the government by remarking 'it had to be remembered that under the situation as it existed no official, civil or military, was exempted from the same fate, nor would they be until such time as the Government chose to recognize that the country was in a state of war'.[18] Otherwise in Macready's view his hands were tied. As for Brigadier-General Lucas, he eventually escaped.

Although Field Marshal Wilson was responsible for British Army operations in Ireland, neither he nor Churchill had any say over the day-to-day conduct of the paramilitaries.[19] They knew what was going on though. Wilson jotted in his diary on 23 September 1920, 'Tudor made it very clear that the police and the Black and Tans … are carrying out reprisal murders. … Winston saw very little harm in this but it horrifies me.'[20] Churchill could have spoken out, but he chose not to. When an inquiry was launched it was Chief Secretary for Ireland Greenwood who sought to suppress it. On 1 December 1920 Lloyd George and the Cabinet reluctantly agreed to martial law being declared in eight counties. General Macready was not happy because he felt Prescott-Decie would act as if 'martial law means that he can kill anybody he sees walking along the road whose appearance may be distasteful to him'.[21]

The introduction of martial law put the British Army even more in the firing line. Amongst those officers who served in Ireland was a World War I veteran by the name of Bernard Montgomery; from a Protestant northern Irish family, he knew where his loyalties lay. He arrived in Cork on 5 January 1921 to take up the post of Brigade-Major with the 17th Infantry Brigade. Now commanded by Brigadier-General H.W. Higginson this was the largest brigade in Ireland, numbering some 9,000 men. 'My whole attention was given to defeating the rebels,' said Montgomery, 'and it never bothered me a bit how many houses were burned.'[22] Nonetheless, his instructions to the Brigade included 'The behaviour of the Army must be kept beyond reproach.'[23] While the military were constantly badgering Churchill and Lloyd George for more troops and weapons, Montgomery assessed that Ireland was a lost cause. Long term he felt the British Army could not win, even if it was permitted to wage all-out war. IRA Commander Tom Barry later recalled that Montgomery conducted himself in Ireland 'with great correctness'.[24]

Shortly after, Churchill, who was constantly at loggerheads with Lloyd George, was moved from the War Office to become the Colonial Secretary. While this may have taken the armed forces from him, the role still gave him a say in Irish affairs. Many in the British government did not want to lose Ireland, but ultimately the only way to address the deep-rooted divisions was partition between the predominantly Catholic south and largely Protestant north. Northern (Ulster) and Southern Ireland were created in May 1921, both with devolved governments, but remained part of the United Kingdom. This, though, did not satisfy the Republicans nor the Irish Republican Army who wanted a united independent Ireland.

Nor did it satisfy Field Marshal Wilson. 'We are having more success than usual killing rebels,' he told Lloyd George just before partition 'and now is the time to reinforce and not to parley.'[25] Churchill agreed. His suggestion was to send seven army battalions south; these he argued could be replaced by raising 30,000 volunteers in Ulster. This met favour with the Unionists in Belfast who feared the British might abandon them to the IRA. In turn Wilson suggested reforming the Ulster Division, but instead it was decided to expand the constabulary.

Despite Wilson's claims, fighting fire with fire in Ireland was simply not working. General Macready warned that by the end of October 1921 the army would be at breaking point. He reported that unless the government found a solution then it would have 'to relieve practically the whole of the troops, together with the great majority of the commanders and their staff'.[26] An exhausted Major-General Sir Peter Strickland, Montgomery's divisional commander, had already offered his resignation to Macready. In despair Strickland wrote in his diary, 'Murder and crime seem so deep-rooted that one wonders *how* it can be stamped out.'[27] The only way out of the ongoing bloodshed with the Republicans was a negotiated settlement. General Smuts was sent to persuade Éamon de Valera, the Republican leader, to accept dominion status. Smuts pointed out that the South Africa Republic had almost been destroyed in a war with Britain, but had secured its independence under such terms.

In London Churchill in his new guise found himself a member of the British negotiating delegation headed by Lloyd George on 11 October. This was to lay the ground work for the Anglo-Irish Treaty and the creation of the Irish Free State. He had, though, little influence over the proceedings and felt Britain should have been negotiating from a position of strength. Churchill agreed with Wilson and later wrote, 'I thought we ought to have conquered the Irish and then given them Home Rule.'[28] His role was to chair the defence subcommittee. The Irish understandably wanted to be responsible for their own defence and be neutral in any future wars involving Britain. Churchill was not amenable to this and demanded control of Ireland's key strategic ports. Eventually, however, he was forced to make some concessions that would have ramifications for Britain during World War II.

When the head of the Irish delegation, Michael Collins, complained to Churchill that they had put a £10,000 bounty on his head, Churchill showed Collins the framed wanted poster issued by the Boers for him dead or alive. 'They only thought me worth 25 pounds,' explained Churchill with a grin, who always felt he should have been worth double that.[29] 'You hunted me night and day! You put a price on my head,' said Collins looking at the poster.[30] 'He read the paper,' recalled Churchill, 'and as he took it in broke into a hearty laugh. All his irritation vanished.'[31] Churchill saw Collins in the same mould as Smuts and hoped he would facilitate reconciliation between the Empire and Southern Ireland. Following these talks the Irish Free State would come into being at the end of the year. Collins knew that by agreeing to partition and dominion status for the south he had signed his own death warrant. Not all members of the IRA would support a provisional government in the south still recognizing the authority of Britain or accept partition and would continue their raids in Ulster.

Churchill was given responsibility for overseeing the transfer of power to the new Irish government in Dublin in lieu of the old Chief Secretary for Ireland. He soon saw his role as the protector of the Protestants of Ulster. He bluntly told the Cabinet he would not supply the provisional government with weapons unless they used them against the IRA. He even suggested that Britain cling to Dublin. The British armed forces, though, needed to be withdrawn from the south as soon as possible otherwise they would find themselves in limbo, caught between the vengeful IRA and the provisional government's supporters.

In Northern Ireland he approved the Special Powers Act in Ulster in April 1922, which allowed for summary justice and permitted ministers to rule by decree.

The IRA's attacks in Northern Ireland were matched by Protestant pogroms against the Catholic population. Once more the British government turned to militia to keep the peace. Churchill supported the formation of the Ulster Special Constabulary, which General Macready thought was a bad idea in light of past experiences. He also wanted to hold up the southern Irish elections, but Lloyd George stepped in. When Republicans occupied the disputed border villages of Belleck and Pettigo, Churchill, without consulting Lloyd George or the Cabinet, despatched 7,000 troops to send the invaders packing. Lloyd George suspected Churchill had deliberately attempted to spark war in order to derail talks with the provisional government, take control of the south and become leader of a pro-Unionist government.

When the southern Irish elections took place on 16 June 1922 the results showed the majority were in favour of a treaty with Britain. Shortly after, Field Marshal Wilson, who was now acting as security adviser to the Ulster government, was murdered in London. Churchill and the British government demanded that the new Irish administration drive the IRA out of their Four Courts stronghold in Dublin. When Churchill ordered General Macready to do this, he refused on the grounds that British civilians in the city would be put at risk. The Irish government, knowing it had to assert its authority, attacked Four Courts on 28 June using artillery, sparking a year-long civil war. Before the summer was over Collins had been killed in a roadside ambush. Just before his death he sent a generous note saying, 'Tell Winston we could never have done anything without him.'[32]

As far as Churchill was concerned Ireland set a dangerous precedent for the rest of the Empire, in particular India. Only the previous year Éamon de Valera, speaking to Irish and Indian nationalists in New York, had declared 'Patriots of India, your cause is identical to ours.'[33] Nonetheless, the Connaught Rangers had done nothing to recruit the Punjabis. Stephen Lally, one of the mutineers, later said, 'we could have officered the Native ranks and in a very short time India would have gained her freedom'.[34] Luckily for Churchill that never happened as the Irish soldiers feared what might happen if they incited a 'native' revolt. Their fear of anarchy was greater than their nationalism.

Beneath the Sphinx

While Churchill as Secretary of State for the Colonies was grappling with Ireland, he also faced brokering the future of the Middle East. This inevitably had a military dimension to it. During the British-held Cairo Conference in March 1921 he oversaw the difficult dismemberment of the Ottoman Empire with the creation of Iraq and Transjordan. They would form a significant security buffer for British interests in the region. Churchill did not seem over burdened by this daunting task. 'I hope to paint a few pictures in the intervals …,' he wrote gleefully, 'and naturally I am taking all the right kinds of colours …'.[1] He also decided to treat it as a bit of a holiday by taking Clementine his wife with him. The conference brought together British Middle Eastern experts and amongst the military delegates were his old colleagues Haldane, Ironside and Trenchard.

When Churchill arrived in Egypt it was in a state of political turmoil. On their way to the heavily guarded Hotel Semiramis, he and Clementine had stones thrown at their car by angry Egyptian nationalists. Since the beginning of World War I the country had been a British Protectorate. Although Prime Minister Rushdi Pasha who was pro-Allies declared Egypt neutral, there were concerns many Egyptians favoured the German-Ottoman alliance. Britain, which had maintained a sizeable military presence in the country since 1882, moved to ensure the defence of the Suez Canal, the Nile Valley and the Delta.

Soon after the war ended there were demonstrations and riots throughout the country demanding full independence. The British military contained these and nationalist leader Saad Zaghloul was exiled. Conspicuously, while the Hajez, Iraq and Syria were represented at the Versailles peace negotiations, Egypt was not. The Egyptians looked to what was happening in Ireland and drew hope from this. A form of qualified independence would be granted in 1922, but even then British troops remained. Britain would maintain responsibility for the security of the country, the administration of Sudan and the Canal, which guaranteed communications with India. All this would have serious consequences for Churchill during World War II.

Notably, Churchill's two leading political advisers in Cairo were Colonel T.E. Lawrence, better known as 'Lawrence of Arabia', and Gertrude Bell the 'Queen of the Desert'. Bell had made a name for herself as an archaeologist and expert on Middle Eastern culture. Like Lawrence she had travelled extensively in the region. The three of them, mounted on camels, along with some of the other delegates, could not resist the temptation to have their photograph taken beneath the Sphinx and the Pyramids. Churchill was impressed by Lawrence's intellect, but could sense he had been scarred by the war. 'He was not in complete harmony with the normal,' observed Churchill diplomatically.[2] Western Front veteran, poet and novelist Robert Graves who met Lawrence before he sailed with Churchill recalled, 'I did not question him about the [Arab] Revolt, partly because he seemed to dislike the subject.'[3] Churchill likewise knew better than to quiz a fellow veteran. Graves noted there was 'a convention … that the war should not be mentioned'.[4]

The task of the conference was to ensure effective administration of Ottoman lands ceded to Britain by the Treaty of Sèvres signed in 1920. Territory was also ceded to France, Greece and Italy. Churchill was well aware that the Turks were not in a position to resist Allied plans, especially after Britain's military occupation of Palestine, Syria and Mesopotamia. The Ottoman Empire had dropped out of its alliance with Germany at the end of October 1918 and acquiesced to the Allied occupation of Constantinople. Ironically after the futile Gallipoli campaign, the Allied fleet simply sailed up the Dardanelles unopposed to occupy the city. By the time Churchill arrived in Egypt the Turks were embroiled in a costly border war with the Greeks.

Churchill was well aware that Britain partly wanted revenge on the Ottoman Empire, and not just for Gallipoli. British forces had been humiliated in Mesopotamia where another operation ended in defeat. A Turkish army, under the command of a German general, in

1916 had forced the surrender of the British garrison trapped at Kut numbering some 13,000 men. The bulk of these were Indian troops from the Indian Army. Four attempts to relieve Kut had resulted in further heavy losses. In addition, Lawrence had been involved in a failed attempt to bribe the Turks to let the garrison go. In response the British had mustered 166,000 troops, marched up the Tigris, retaken Kut and occupied Baghdad. The Turks also launched two determined attacks from Palestine towards the Suez Canal but both had failed. Agents in Switzerland had kept the government quite well informed of Turkish military intentions in Arabia, Palestine and Mesopotamia.[5] The end result of this was that the British took Jerusalem.

The real challenge faced by Churchill and the conference was essentially to create something from nothing. They had their work cut out not only with the competing interests of the European powers but also the Arabs themselves. Although they shared a common language and, in many instances, the same religion, the people of Arabia, the Levant and Mesopotamia were culturally and racially diverse. Prince Faisal, one of the sons of Hussein bin Ali, the Grand Sharif of Mecca, played a leading role in the Arab Revolt. In return for supporting the Allies his father declared himself King Hussein of the Hejaz. However, he only controlled part of western Arabia and was under pressure from the Sauds, the rulers of the Riyadh region. Likewise, the interests of the Palestinian Arabs and Jews had to be somehow met.

Lawrence had written, after his triumphant entry into Damascus in 1918, 'Our aim was an Arab Government, with foundations large and native enough to employ the enthusiasm and self-sacrifice of the rebellion'.[6] The underlying problem was that the Arabs did not exist as a political entity. 'A first difficulty of the Arab movement was to say who the Arabs were,' noted Lawrence.[7] He acknowledged they had been very tightly interwoven with their overlords to the extent 'nearly one third of the original Turkish Army was Arabic speaking'.[8] Bearing in mind at the start of World War I the Ottoman Empire had 800,000 men under arms this potentially meant that over a quarter of a million Arabs had received military training.

Ironically some of these troops had been sent to the Dardanelles during the war to keep them out of Arabia for fear they might join the Arab Revolt. Initially some Turkish commanders were reluctant to commit their predominantly Arab regiments due to concerns over how they would perform.[9] It may have pained Lawrence but it was beholden on him to highlight to Churchill that the bulk of Arabia had not supported the rising that commenced in Mecca. Lawrence's hope had been for a unified Arab state, though it was not to be, not with France granted the Lebanon and Syria.

Prince Faisal had attended the Versailles peace conference with Lawrence and in 1920 under the Treaty of Sèvres he became King of Syria. However, the French, having gained a Syrian mandate, conducted a brief and successful military campaign to expel him. Faisal was forced to flee to London. This left him and his younger brother Abdullah looking for Arab kingdoms to rule. The presence of the French in Lebanon and Syria, far from creating a useful security buffer with Turkey, would cause Churchill unwanted military problems during World War II.

Churchill appreciated that the treatment of the defeated Muslim Ottoman Empire would have to be handled very sensitively, not only with the Arabs, the Jews and the French. India's Muslim political leaders would inevitably watch with interest what was happening in the Middle East and the results could well fuel Indian nationalism. India had provided a million men for the Allied cause, as well as $500 million, during World War I in return for a promise of greater autonomy. Instead, alarmed at the prospect of anarchy, the British authorities tightened their grip, which was to spark off two decades of civil strife, rallies and hunger strikes.

This commenced in April 1919 with the Amritsar massacre when British-led troops opened fire on an unarmed crowd inflicting 1,516 casualties.[10] Churchill condemned the incident warning that the use of force would only serve to undermine British authority and destroy all cooperation with India. 'We have to make it absolutely clear,' he told the House of Commons, 'some way or other, that this is not the British way of doing business.'[11] He sacked the general in command, much to the fury of many Conservative right-wingers who felt the man had only been doing his job. Churchill's stance was quite enlightening, as one would have expected him to leap to the officer's defence. Nevertheless, Churchill appreciated that shooting civilians in cold blood was simply indefensible and was not the act of a disciplined soldier.

During the Cairo conference he took time out to paint the pyramids, which had witnessed the destruction of Napoleon's dream to control Egypt. Afterwards, accompanied by Lawrence, he travelled to Jerusalem and painted the city at dusk. In Palestine he was greatly impressed by the achievements of the hard-working Jewish community. Crucially he decided that Palestine would remain a British Mandate open to Jewish settlers. Under the Ottomans it was not a distinct province and its inhabitants, along with those in Lebanon, had considered themselves part of southern Syria. At this stage Arab Palestinians thought more in terms of the 'Arab nation' rather than the nation states that were to emerge from the wreckage of the Ottoman Empire. It was while he was in Jerusalem that he offered Abdullah Transjordan which formed part of the Palestine mandate.

Foremost, as Churchill saw it, his task was to protect British interests and save money at the same time. Even before World War I, Ottoman authority over Mesopotamia was waning. Soldier and explorer Wilfred Thesiger later wrote, 'From a few small towns, Turkish officials tried to assert some semblance of authority over unruly tribes in this destitute province of a tottering empire.'[12] The three Mesopotamian provinces, encompassing the Kurds of Mosul, the Sunnis of Baghdad and the Shia of Barsa, were welded together to form Iraq under King Faisal. This prevented Turkey, slowly emerging from the ashes of the Ottoman Empire, from conquering any further Kurdish territory and guaranteed British access to Mosul's oilfields. Oil had yet to be discovered in Basra to the south. Sparsely populated Transjordan, bordering Palestine and Syria, completely lacked natural resources.

All this was to store up terrible trouble for the future, but Churchill had no way of knowing that at the time. Responsibility for carving up the Middle East did not just rest with him. Both Bell and Lawrence suggested that Faisal be placed on the Iraqi throne, even though he did not come from the region and the locals owed him no allegiance. It was more a case of realpolitik; having a friendly king in Iraq looked attractive as it replicated British policy with the maharajahs in India. One of the many failings of the creation of Iraq was that although Faisal was given the kingdom the local Arab tribesmen remained armed. This posed an immediate threat to his rule. Although a small Iraqi army was established it was mainly recruited from the Kurds who lived in the north of the country and not from the majority Arab population.

Churchill was at least spared the headache of trying to sort out the various provinces in Arabia. During World War I Foreign Secretary Sir Edward Grey had envisaged Arab states being established in Mesopotamia,

Syria and Arabia. Kitchener had even wanted to see Mecca placed under British control. However, the region was dominated by shifting tribal loyalties and Britain now had no intention of getting involved in the vast interior. Although King Hussein had supported the Arab Revolt and his sons became kings of Iraq and Transjordan, his rival Abdullaziz Ibn Saud was waiting on the sidelines. He would become the founding father of Saudi Arabia and prudently avoided antagonizing the British. Nonetheless, once Ibn Saud had driven King Hussein into exile this would result in unwanted tensions with the rulers of Iraq and Transjordan.

Churchill was fascinated by Lawrence's adventures in Arabia and no doubt canvassed his views. Lawrence did not think highly of Hussein's leadership qualities describing him as 'an obstinate, narrow-minded, suspicious character'.[13] Besides, Britain already had naval access to Aden, Bahrain, Muscat and Qatar so before oil was discovered the rest of Arabia had little allure. While Churchill coped admirably with the strains of the conference, they took their toll on Lawrence. Lord Halifax noted, 'Lawrence found himself engaged in what was for him the more arduous struggle of the peace. ... The mark that these days left upon him was deep and ineffaceable.'[14]

Churchill returned to London triumphant, confident of a job well done, and to the gratitude of Lloyd George. When he addressed the House of Commons he was greeted as a great success. The Treasury was particularly happy with him as the cost of administering the region would be £30 million a year, down from £80 million in 1919–20. Money talks, and Churchill had delivered. In contrast Lawrence, who made a lasting impression on Churchill, withdrew from public life to write accounts of his exploits in the desert. Churchill thought very highly of his *The Seven Pillars of Wisdom* when it was finally published. He was later to write rather extravagantly, 'I deem him one of the greatest beings alive in our time'.[15]

Although Churchill returned to London a success, the British division of the Middle East was not completed until 1925 when the Clayton Mission officially demarked the borders between Arabia, Iraq and Transjordan. This process involved drawing a lot of conspicuously very straight lines. Nor did the issue of policing Iraq go away. In the summer of 1921 Churchill persuaded the Cabinet that it could be done on the cheap employing the RAF and limited numbers of British and Indian troops supported by local militia, which would cost about

£4 million a year. The drawback was inevitably Faisal would want to use them to extend his control over Iraq's outlying areas.

Just as Churchill had hoped, in 1922 the RAF took over Iraq with Air Marshal Sir John Salmond assuming command. His forces consisted of eight squadrons and four army infantry battalions. He had to form his own armoured car units to protect his airfields after the army refused to give him any of theirs. Squadron Leader Arthur Harris led one of the RAF's very first troop carrier squadrons. He quickly converted his aircraft into what he described as 'the first of the post-war long-range heavy bombers'.[16] Harris soon got to deploy them.

Salmond reported to Churchill that the Turks were intent on retaking Mosul and sent his squadrons to repel them. Soon after, the battered Turks gave up. 'The truculent and warlike tribes which occupied and still controlled, after the rebellion, large parts of Iraq,' noted Harris, 'also had to be quelled, and in this our heavy bombers played a major part.'[17] Onerously the RAF also found themselves enforcing Faisal's tax-raising efforts by bombing non-compliant villages. Churchill tried to put a stop to this, but there was no other way of ensuring complete compliance with Faisal's new government. In a moment of exasperation Churchill joked, 'Six months ago we were paying his hotel bill in London ... Has he not got some wives to keep him quiet?'[18]

Harris firmly agreed with Churchill and Trenchard's employment of the RAF noting, 'It was, of course, a far less costly method of controlling rebellion ... and the casualties on both sides were infinitely less'.[19] Like Churchill, Harris hated the place, 'Never shall I forget the appalling climate.'[20] The trouble with these types of missions, aside from unwanted civilian casualties, is that they sowed the germ of an idea with Harris – namely wars could be won by air power alone. Nevertheless, if the RAF had not conducted these policing operations then there would have been no rationale for its expansion and this would have greatly slowed the development of what eventually became Fighter Command.

Following the Iraq campaign Trenchard's idea of 'Air Control' was extended across the Empire, but this was nothing to do with Churchill. An India Group of half a dozen squadrons was put together to help keep order, particularly in the North-West Frontier Province. In early 1925 Wing Commander Richard Pink led a solely RAF operation against rebellious tribesmen in South Waziristan in what became known as 'Pink's War'. After 50 days of bombing the tribal leaders sued for peace.

This convinced the British authorities in India of the utility of the RAF, and it continued to conduct operations into the 1930s; nonetheless it remained the army's poorer cousin.

In the meantime, Britain almost went to war with Turkey. By 1922 after four years of conflict Mustafa Kemal had decisively defeated the Greeks, driving them from their territorial gains. This left Britain with the prospect of imposing the terms of the Treaty of Sèvres regarding the Dardanelles. Churchill was all for fighting. 'If the Turks take the Gallipoli peninsula and Constantinople we shall have lost the whole fruits of victory,' he said, 'and another Balkan war would be inevitable.'[21] The British maintained a garrison at Chanak on the eastern shores of the Dardanelles and Churchill hoped the Turks would attack it thereby sparking war. Instead, Britain backed down and a new treaty was signed in Lausanne that recognized the borders of modern Turkey. The Sultan fled and shortly after the country became a republic under Kemal.

After losing the support of the Conservatives, Lloyd George resigned as Prime Minister in 1922 and the following year Churchill lost his Liberal seat in the general election that followed. This resulted in a hung Parliament and Churchill returned as an independent in 1924. Not long after this, he crossed the floor of the House of Commons to re-join the Conservative party. He then became Chancellor of the Exchequer under Stanley Baldwin. Churchill soon found himself struggling with deflation after returning the country to the Gold standard, which fuelled unemployment. This was damaging to him personally, the Conservatives and the country. It caused economic strife and the 1926 nine-day general strike. The Conservatives lost the election three years later and a second Liberal-supported Labour government took power.

Churchill was then to endure what he called the 'wilderness years' from 1931 to 1939, during which time he remained a Member of Parliament but was granted no opposition or governmental responsibilities. Whilst he found this hard to bear, he had brought this situation upon himself largely thanks to his stance on India. Frustrated by the lack of progress over India's future, the Indian National Congress party issued a unilateral and futile declaration of independence in early 1930. Churchill pointedly resigned from the Shadow Cabinet the following year over plans to grant some level of self-government to placate the Congress. To his displeasure Ramsay MacDonald's weak Labour minority government and many Conservatives increasingly backed greater freedom for India. In particular, Clement Attlee, deputy leader of the Labour Party, fully supported granting India dominium status. This was anathema to Churchill. In contrast, Attlee from a young age was an ardent anti-Imperialist. While still at school he had taken part in a march to celebrate the series of humiliating British defeats in South Africa. For this unpatriotic act he was caned.[22]

If Churchill saw the reports of British mounted police charging the crowds in Calcutta (modern Kolkata) in January 1931 celebrating the first anniversary of the unilateral declaration of independence, it would have only convinced him even more that without British law and order India would descend into sectarian chaos. 'Not for a hundred years have the relations between Moslems and Hindus [in India] been so poisoned,' he told the House of Commons that year with foreboding, 'as they have been since England was deemed to be losing her grip, and was believed to be ready to quit the scene if told to do so.'[23] He was alarmed by the thought that 'mobs of neighbours ... will tear each other to pieces ... with their fingers'.[24] He argued in the Commons that the issue of dominium status should not be at the expense of 'peace, order and good government of the Indian Empire'.[25] However, when he tried to table an amendment to MacDonald's India policy he found few supporters. To Churchill's annoyance Gandhi, representing the Congress, came to London attending yet more futile talks. 'Gandhism and all that it stands for,' he asserted, 'must ultimately be grappled with and finally crushed.'[26] Churchill's imperial world view had been forged in Sudan, the North-West Frontier and South Africa and he would not budge from it. This was later to have ramifications for his handling of India during World War II.

Churchill was to partly occupy himself during this period by writing a four-volume biography of the illustrious 1st Duke of Marlborough. When Hitler came to power Churchill could not help but draw sinister parallels between past and present. Marlborough had saved half of Europe from a greedy continental power. Did his ancestor in part inspire him to stand up to Hitler? What was on his mind when he sat down to paint the tapestries at Blenheim Palace, which depicted the duke's great victory over France? His imagination must have been filled with the sights and sounds of battle, the crack of musket fire, the roar of cannon and neighing of terrified horses. While Britain hoped vainly for peace, Churchill immersed himself in the study of continental warfare and the perils of unchecked militarism. It was an apprenticeship that would serve him well.

Nazism or Communism

Churchill saw both Germany and the Soviet Union posing the greatest threats to European security during the 1930s. One of his first warnings came as early as 1932 when he told the House of Commons, 'Now the demand is that Germany should be allowed to rearm ... Do not let His Majesty's Government believe ... that all that Germany is asking for is equal status.'[1] Tantalizingly Churchill almost met Hitler that summer. He was in Munich with his family including his son Randolph researching his Marlborough book. Randolph, who had worked in Germany as a reporter, was acquainted with Hitler's press secretary and tried to arrange a meeting. 'I had no national prejudices against Hitler at this time,' recalled Churchill.' 'I knew little of his doctrine or record and nothing of his character.'[2] Hitler, though, did not show up.

In addition to narrowly missing a historic meeting, Churchill's tour of his ancestor's battlefields proved decidedly detrimental to his health. Once he had finished he planned to travel through Austria for a family holiday in Venice. Instead, he ended up hospitalized in Salzburg suffering from an infection caused by Salmonella after one too many picnics. After just over a week in hospital he headed home, but back at Chartwell suffered a relapse with intestinal haemorrhaging. Diagnosed with enteric fever he faced a 15 per cent chance of dying.[3] Fortunately, with rest he made a full recovery and pressed on with his book.

Churchill, like other British politicians, watched Hitler's determined rise to power with his National Socialist German Workers' Party – better known as the Nazis – with a growing sense of unease. Hitler, through guile and his skill as an impassioned orator, became Chancellor in 1933 with the Nazis dominating the German parliament. The following year Paul von Hindenburg, the German President, died and Hitler assumed the title of Führer of the German Reich in addition to that of Chancellor. Soon he was acting without parliamentary consent and banned all political parties except the Nazis. Some, though, marvelled at how Hitler pushed forward Germany's economic recovery and restored her sense of national pride, which had taken such a battering thanks to the Treaty of Versailles and the ineffectual Weimar Republic. Churchill felt that this resurgence was based on one thing and one thing alone – rearmament.

'I dread the day when the means of threatening the heart of the British Empire,' Churchill told the House of Commons on 8 March 1934, 'should pass into the hands of the present rulers of Germany.'[4] Almost a year to the day Hitler announced on 9 March 1935 the creation of the Luftwaffe or German Air Force, which in reality Germany had been building in secret for some time. The following week he stated that he was reintroducing conscription. Both acts were in contravention of the Treaty of Versailles. Churchill was especially concerned by the growth of the Luftwaffe, observing 'this very gifted people are capable of developing with great rapidity the most powerful air force for all purposes, offensive and defensive, in a very short period'.[5] In light of this development and reflecting on the state of the RAF he argued, 'We ought not to be dependent on the French air force for the safety of our island home.'[6] Likewise he was alarmed by the Germans' naval build-up, particularly their U-boat or submarine programme that could pose a threat to Britain's maritime security. 'Once Hitler's Germany had been allowed to rearm without active interference by the Allies ...' concluded Churchill, 'a second World War was almost certain.'[7]

Hitler's steady slide into totalitarianism coupled with his desire to reclaim lost German lands and his unbridled anti-Semitism did not bode well for peace in Europe. 'We cannot afford to see Nazidom ...' Churchill warned the Commons on 24 October 1935, 'with all its hatreds and all its gleaming weapons, paramount in Europe.'[8] Hitler, determined more than ever to rearm Germany, unilaterally abandoned all the military restrictions of Versailles. Churchill wrote, 'Hitler, casting aside concealment, sprang forward armed to the teeth.'[9] The German leader then set about remilitarizing the Rhineland also in violation of the Treaty of Versailles followed by claiming Austria and parts of Czechoslovakia.

Stalin in the Soviet Union had come to power a decade before Hitler when appointed General Secretary of the ruling Russian Communist Party (Bolsheviks). After the death of Lenin in 1924 he ruthlessly consolidated his hold on the country. Churchill felt that only Lenin had been capable of curbing the worst excesses of the Russian revolution. 'He alone could have found the way back to the causeway,' wrote Churchill perhaps rather generously. 'The Russian people were left floundering in the bog. Their worst misfortune was his birth, the next worst – his death.'[10] Stalin unleashed a wave of brutality. Through the late 1930s he purged his political and military rivals in what became known as the Great Terror. Parts of the Soviet Union were also blighted by terrible famine thanks to his collectivization policies. This internal upheaval ensured a distracted Stalin did nothing to hinder Japan's expansionism in China. Nonetheless, through the Communist International he fostered and sought to control foreign Communist parties bent on social revolution. This included China's Communists under Mao Zedong. 'Everyone can see how Communism rots the soul of a nation,' observed Churchill, 'how it makes it abject and hungry in peace, and proves it base and abominable in war.'[11] The Soviet Union, just like Germany, was in the throes of modernizing its armed forces. Under such circumstances it was hard to see how Europe could avoid a major war.

The Bolsheviks and Nazis clouded Churchill's global strategic judgement. He was not greatly concerned about the implications of the Chinese civil war or the Japanese seizure of Manchuria and the creation of the puppet state of Manchukuo. In the early 1930s the League of Nations refused to recognize the latter and judged Manchuria should become an autonomous part of China. The Japanese response was to withdraw from the League and refuse to relinquish their prize. In Churchill's view the failure to resolve the situation was the League's fault not Japan's. 'The moral authority of the League was shown to be devoid of any physical support,' he wrote, 'at a time when its activity and strength were most needed.'[12] The British government was loath to intervene, especially as Britain and

Japan had been in alliance for over two decades until 1923. America, which was a growing power in the Pacific, was not a member of the League of Nations and had no desire to antagonize Japan. Churchill felt that, 'There was a rueful feeling in some British circles at the loss of the Japanese Alliance and the consequential weakening of the British position with its long-established interests in the Far East.'[13] Churchill was clearly in that circle.

Churchill was pleased that Generalissimo Chiang Kai-shek's Nationalist troops had successfully driven Mao Zedong's Communists into the mountains of southeast China during the first half of the 1930s. Chiang spoke convincingly of creating 'a bulwark against bolshevism'.[14] To Churchill this evoked memories of his efforts to thwart the spread of Bolshevism in Russia. Nazi Germany, though, was the only country that was actively supporting Chiang's campaign. What Churchill did not know was that Chiang, in order to get back his son, who had been held for over a decade by Stalin, had to agree to let Mao's forces escape. This meant they would survive to fight another day. In the meantime, the Japanese conquered enormous areas of Chinese territory, eventually including the key cities of Shanghai and Nanking.

Controversially, Churchill felt that Japan provided a counterweight to the dangers posed by the spread of Communism in China and the Soviet Union. 'It is in the interests of the whole world,' he declared, 'that law and order should be established in Northern China.'[15] Japan though, would not settle for just Manchuria. It ruthlessly took Shanghai, known as the Paris of the Orient, regardless of the presence of a large international community. The British government hoped Japan would come to the negotiating table, but the Japanese took no notice of Western concerns. Churchill hoped that the Japanese would turn north and inconvenience Stalin. Instead, they marched into the heartland of China and away from the Soviet Union.

Closer to home, by the mid-1930s Churchill was regularly warning the House of Commons of the danger posed by Hitler's steady expansionism. He watched as Hitler reoccupied the demilitarized German Rhineland in March 1936. Although this violated the Treaty of Versailles and placed German troops west of the Rhine, Britain and France did nothing to oppose Hitler. In response Churchill became a prophet of doom. 'Europe is approaching a climax,' he told the House of Commons on 23 April that year. 'I believe that climax will be reached in the lifetime of the present Parliament.'[16] This glum assessment was not based just on gut instinct.

Churchill's MI6 contact, Major Morton, regularly passed him intelligence on German rearmament during the 'wilderness years'. By the early 1930s Morton had created the Industrial Intelligence Centre, which had been separated from MI6. He claimed rather fancifully that he briefed Churchill with the authorization of Prime Ministers Ramsay MacDonald, Stanley Baldwin and Neville Chamberlain. This seems highly unlikely and it is more probable that Morton was operating on his own volition because he, like Churchill, feared a resurgent Germany. In addition, he only lived about a mile away from Churchill's home at Chartwell, so had easy access.

No one, however, would listen to Churchill after he supported King Edward VIII's wish to marry his American mistress Wallis Simpson. This brought Churchill to loggerheads with Prime Minister Stanley Baldwin. The King's relationship created a constitutional crisis the like of which had never been seen before. The establishment expected him to do the right thing and end the relationship. When he refused, Baldwin forced the King to abdicate and Churchill was left isolated and looking foolish. In addition, many felt his long links with the military had made him a warmonger, hence his continual vocal opposition to Hitler. To the government, headed by Neville Chamberlain from May 1937, appeasement seemed a better option than embarking on a costly rearmament programme and another bloody war in Europe.

Hitler's land grabs continued with the annexation of Austria in March 1938. The country had been left adrift since the dismemberment of the Austro-Hungarian Empire at the end of World War I and many Austrians welcomed Hitler with open arms. This was followed by the acquisition of the German-speaking Sudetenland from Czechoslovakia. Churchill was unconvinced that Hitler would be sated by Chamberlain's Munich Agreement in September 1938. This spinelessly let Hitler take the Sudentenland and abandoned the rest of Czechoslovakia to its fate all in the name of avoiding war. 'We are in the presence of a disaster of the first magnitude,' he told the House of Commons on 5 October 1938. 'The system of alliances in central Europe upon which France has relied for her safety has been swept away.'[17]

The ensuing political meltdown in Czechoslovakia resulted in the Czechs and Slovaks splitting their country, with Hitler occupying the Czech lands in March 1939. Since the days of the Czech Legion the Czechoslovaks had steadily built up a large modern army, but this stood by without firing a shot while its homeland was dismembered. Once a valuable counterweight to Hitler's aspirations in eastern Europe, it proved to be a paper tiger. 'We certainly suffered a loss through the fall of Czechoslovakia equivalent to some thirty-five divisions,' observed Churchill.[18] Hitler's growing war machine seized all the Czechoslovaks' weapons intact. These included 469 tanks, 1,500 aircraft, over 500 anti-aircraft guns, 43,000 machine guns, over one million rifles, 1,000 million rifle rounds and three million field gun rounds. To make matters worse Czechoslovakia was a major weapons manufacturer. Churchill noted that the Skoda works, 'the second most important arsenal in central Europe ... was made to change sides adversely'.[19] Notably its military output almost matched that of Britain's. Churchill lamented, 'Czechoslovakia deserted and ruined by the Munich Pact; its fortress line in German hands; its mighty arsenal henceforward making munitions for the German armies.'[20]

Churchill also watched the developing civil war in Spain with interest. Rather unusually he had no desire to see Britain intervene. While he disliked General Franco's rebellious Nationalists, who were backed by Hitler and Mussolini, at the same time he was concerned by the revolutionary nature of the Republican government, which gained support from Stalin. 'I have found it easier to maintain this feeling of detachment from both sides,' he told the House of Commons on 14 April 1937, 'because, before we gave any help to either side we ought to know what the victory of that side would mean to those who are beaten.'[21] Essentially the highly complex conflict became seen purely in terms of a struggle between Fascism and Communism. Britain was polarized with those on the left believing the workers of the Republic should be supported, while those on the right called for the restoration of the Spanish monarchy. Churchill remarked in the case of Spain, 'It is not a question of opposing Nazism or Communism, but opposing tyranny in whatever form presents itself.'[22]

Churchill's stance was that the war in Spain should be treated with complete neutrality especially as it had no strategic relevance to Britain;

unless of course the fighting should pose a threat to British Gibraltar or other British interests in the Mediterranean. Britain, France and the rest of Europe were swift to publicly at least adopt a policy of non-intervention. Behind the scenes it was a completely different matter. Italy, Germany and the Soviet Union all pursued their own interventionist agendas regardless of international opinion. George Orwell, who volunteered to fight with the Republican International Brigades, felt, 'The outcome of the Spanish war was settled in London, Paris, Rome, Berlin – at any rate not in Spain.'[23]

In the Far East during the second half of 1937 the Japanese fought to take Shanghai. 'China, as the years pass,' lamented Churchill, 'is being eaten by Japan like an artichoke, leaf by leaf.'[24] By this stage Japan had over 700,000 troops deployed in China. Wholly unfairly Churchill blamed the Chinese for their defeats. 'If the Chinese now suffer the cruel malice and oppression of their enemies,' he wrote in early September 1937, 'it is the fault of the base and perverted conception of pacifism their rulers have ingrained for two or three thousand years in their people.'[25] Field Marshal Bernard Montgomery was later to echo this sentiment when he wrote 'their military character seems to have been subdued by the deep-rooted aversion to things military which was inherent in Chinese civilization.'[26] This was simply not true. China had been brought to its knees by the ravaging armies of the Communists, Nationalists, independent warlords and Japanese. In such a toxic war-torn environment it was hardly surprising that Japan's conquests went unchecked. 'Japan's leaders were lured on by imperial ambition,' observed Foreign Secretary Anthony Eden, 'however much they might pretext economic needs to excuse their policy.'[27]

Churchill does not seem to have appreciated the strategic implications of what was happening in China. 'For the first time in the history of warfare,' wrote British novelist J.G. Ballard who was born and raised in Shanghai, 'a coordinated air, sea and land assault was launched against Chiang Kai-shek's Chinese armies, who greatly outnumbered the Japanese, but were poorly led by corrupt cronies of Chiang and his wife.'[28] There was a certain irony that Chiang's best troops were trained by the Germans and his air force established by the Americans and the Italians. It was in part thanks to Germany that Chiang had prevailed over the Communists and China's powerful warlords. The Japanese meanwhile were teaching the West how to conduct combined operations. Their tactics also had all the hallmarks of Hitler's subsequent Blitzkrieg.

Alarmed at the prospect of the fighting in Shanghai spilling over into the British and American sectors of the neutral International Settlement, both countries' governments despatched warships. When the Chinese accidentally bombed the area it was suspected they had done it deliberately to draw in the Western powers. There were further provocations by both the Chinese and Japanese, but as in the case of Spain, Britain had no desire to get involved. The only concession to taking sides was when General Alexander Telfer-Smollett, commanding the local British forces, permitted a trapped Chinese battalion to withdraw into the settlement where they were interned. 'The Japanese surrounded the city,' observed Ballard, 'but made no attempt to confront the contingents of British, French and American soldiers, or interfere with their warships in the river.'[29]

Churchill acknowledged 'always having been a sentimental well-wisher to the Japanese and an admirer of their many gifts and qualities, I should view [war with them] with keen sorrow.'[30] This was not the view of the British government. Lord Halifax, the Lord President of the Council, told the House of Lords on 21 October 1937, 'We deplore the pursuit of policy, by Japan ... by military means and the recourse to force ... contrary to the spirit ... of the League of Nations.'[31] The situation in China would remain largely unchanged until 1941 when Japan declared war on America and Britain and swept all before them. This severed China's external supply lines.

Despite whatever Churchill thought of the situation in China, the British government were lulled into a false sense of security. Ballard noted, 'I assume that the Japanese leadership had decided that Shanghai was of more value to them as a thriving commercial and industrial centre, and were not yet prepared to risk a confrontation with the Western powers.'[32] Shanghai was a long way from British Hong Kong and the proximity of Mao's Communists in Jiangxi province to the north had always been of greater concern, until they relocated during the Long March. Yet to the north-east of Hong Kong lay the island of Taiwan, which the Japanese had controlled since 1895. This they had turned into a vast air and naval base. Strategically Hong Kong was horribly exposed as were the American-controlled Philippines. 'I had no illusions about the fate of Hong Kong,' Churchill later wrote, 'under the overwhelming impact of Japanese power.'[33] He also knew 'there is not the slightest chance of holding Hong Kong or relieving it'.[34]

The Japanese, enraged by Chinese resistance at Shanghai, massacred up to 300,000 people when they took Chiang's capital Nanking.[35] However, rather than resulting in a Chinese collapse, it hardened Chiang's resolve to fight on against the bloodthirsty invaders. He was also forced into an alliance of convenience with Mao Zedong's Communist forces in order to fight a common enemy. For Chiang this was frustrating because he had been winning the civil war. Once the news leaked out about Nanking the world was appalled. Churchill's defence of Japanese militarism then looked extremely ill-advised and he simply chose to ignore what had happened in Nanking.[36]

In the late 1930s Japan turned north and clashed with the Soviet Union in Mongolia. After being soundly rebuffed by the Red Army the Japanese were soon looking south again. Far from countering Communism, Japan became an increasing threat to the whole of South East Asia. The Japanese would soon be greedily eyeing French Indochina, which put them on a collision course with Britain and America. By that stage Britain had completely acquiesced to Japanese activities in the Far East. Historian H.H.E. Craster wrote in 1939, 'The British Government recognized that the Japanese forces in China had special requirements for the purpose of safeguarding their own security ... and stated that they had no intention of countenancing any acts or measures prejudicial to the attainment of those objectives.'[37]

When German and Italian troops began to arrive in Spain under the guise of being 'advisers' and 'volunteers', Churchill mockingly called them 'armed tourists'.[38] He hoped that the Spanish might come to their senses, remarking, 'They do not want to go on killing each other for the entertainment of foreigners.'[39] Although he leaned towards Franco, he was not in a position to influence policy. The British government remained very keen not to become dragged into the conflict. Lord Halifax, when addressing the House of Lords on the international situation on 21 October 1937, stated, 'the issue of the Spanish civil war should not be permitted materially to affect the relations of Mediterranean Powers and their position in the

Mediterranean'.[40] Interestingly he spent far greater time discussing the Far East and Japanese aggression against China than what was going on in Spain. Later Halifax, who took over from Eden as Foreign Secretary, clarified the rationale for Britain's neutrality, 'The first reason was the danger of the conflict developing into a general European war. The second was the presence of the foreign participants on both sides in the Spanish conflict.'[41]

In contrast Clement Attlee and two other Labour leaders, Philip Noel-Baker and Ellen Wilkinson, travelled to Madrid that year to visit the British volunteers fighting with the International Brigades. Attlee, pipe clenched firmly between his teeth, was photographed touring the smiling troops amongst the rubble. He also met with Republican General José Miaja who was in command of Madrid's defences. A tired Miaja could not have looked more disinterested if he had tried. Attlee was guest of honour at a dinner, during which he rather optimistically pledged to try and end the 'farce of non-intervention'.[42] At night a parade was held to mark the occasion. Afterwards the unit he had visited was renamed the 'Major Attlee Company'. Churchill did not entertain either side and branded non-intervention 'official humbug', because no one took any notice of it.[43]

The antics of Mussolini's submarines in the western Mediterranean soon brought Britain and Italy to the brink of war. Any merchant ships carrying supplies to the Republicans, including British ones, were considered fair game. Churchill was angered by this and wanted Franco warned by the British government that 'if there is any more of this, we shall arrest one of your ships on the open sea'.[44] Instead, Chamberlain sought to appease the Italian leader. Behind the scenes the Royal Navy was far from prepared to tangle with Mussolini's expanding and modern fleet. Foreign Secretary Anthony Eden, who privately supported the Republican cause, resigned in protest in February 1938 to be replaced by Lord Halifax. Churchill was disgusted by the completely one-sided Anglo-Italian Pact brokered by Chamberlain. In return for Italy maintaining the status quo in the Mediterranean, Chamberlain acquiesced to Mussolini's troops remaining in Spain until the end of the civil war. Churchill called the agreement 'a complete triumph for Mussolini, who gains our cordial acceptance for his fortification of the Mediterranean against us, for his conquest of Abyssinia, and for his violence in Spain'.[45]

The presence of the Italian Air Force and Navy in the Spanish Balearic Islands seemed to suggest Mussolini was preparing to establish a permanent foothold in the western Mediterranean that would ultimately threaten Gibraltar. A despairing Eden wrote to Churchill on 16 April 1938 and warned, 'I do not believe that Mussolini has abandoned his dream of creating a *Mare Nostrum*.' He also said that Chamberlain's weakness, 'is likely to be interpreted as giving Mussolini and Hitler a free hand to finish their campaign'.[46]

As a result of all this Churchill and other Conservative opponents of Chamberlain became increasingly pro-Republican. Interestingly even at this stage Churchill made it clear if he had to choose between Nazism or Communism, he would opt for the latter. 'It would seem today,' he declared on 30 December 1938, 'the British Empire would run far less risk from the victory of the Spanish government than from that of Franco.'[47] Churchill knew that if Fascism took hold in Spain it would inevitably pose a threat to British interests. The prospect of an alliance between Franco, Hitler and Mussolini was just too alarming to contemplate. Despite this change of heart, even if the government wanted to, it was simply too late for the Republicans who were out-gunned and driven back on every front. The fighting lasted until 1 April 1939 and ended in a victory for Franco. Luckily he was his own man and would work hard to keep his two allies at arm's length. Furthermore, Spain was exhausted by the civil war and the tiny Spanish Navy was in no position to challenge the British Mediterranean fleet.

The British government had little choice but to recognize Franco as the new leader of Spain, although this was opposed by both the Labour and Liberal parties. Beforehand the debate in the House of Commons was tempestuous. Attlee was outraged and called it 'a gross betrayal of democracy'.[48] Churchill was absent, but Eden from the back benches argued delaying recognition would accomplish nothing. Labour MP Ellen Wilkinson, who had seen the terrible destruction in Madrid, verbally turned on Sir Henry Page Croft, a Conservative supporter of Franco. Few were convinced by Franco's pledge to show the defeated Republicans mercy. Thousands of refugees were already fleeing to France and Mexico. Communist MP William Gallacher even called for Chamberlain to be impeached. George Orwell was equally dismayed that Britain threw Spain's democratically elected government to the wolves. He reasoned if

Britain and France had acted sooner, they could have helped thwart Franco's coup at the very start. 'Yet in the most mean, cowardly, hypocritical way,' wrote Orwell, 'the British ruling class did all they could to hand Spain over to Franco and the Nazis.'[49] For Churchill it confirmed his belief that the policy of appeasement towards Hitler and Mussolini simply did not work.

A harbinger of things to come in Europe was the involvement of the small 'volunteer' German Condor Legion in Spain, which consisted of ground and air force units. In theory they were part of the Nationalist army, but this arrangement fooled no one. They were there under the authorization of Hitler and led by German officers. This formation was used to test Hitler's developing weapons, most notably the Luftwaffe's bombers and the German Army's early panzers. Although Italian intervention in terms of numbers was far more decisive, the Germans gained vital tactical experience. German aircraft began bombing Madrid in late August 1936 and the city's subway stations were soon full of refugees. Most notoriously the Condor Legion carried out carpet bombing of the Basque market town of Guernica on 26 April 1937. They used explosive, shrapnel and incendiary bombs. These reduced Guernica to rubble and caused 2,500 civilian casualties sparking an international outcry. Barcelona received similar treatment at the hands of the Italian Air Force. When the Japanese bombed Chiang's new capital at Chungking in May 1939 killing 7,000 people the world was already hardened to such atrocities. The Germans also tested the Ju 87 Stuka dive bomber in Spain, which would become a key component of Hitler's Blitzkrieg.

Shamefully the British government tried to avoid criticizing Germany over Guernica. At the time Anthony Eden, still Foreign Secretary, told the House of Commons that the government did not have any 'considered reports'.[50] To deliberately confuse matters the Nationalists claimed the retreating Republicans blew up the town. Churchill was partly misled by the lessons from the air war over Spain. He concluded erroneously that bombers were not effective against warships, fortifications or weapons factories. Churchill had read with interest how Republican bombers failed to sink Nationalist and German warships moored off Ibiza. Mines and Italian submarines had proved the greatest menace. However, he did note correctly that the bombing of civilians did not break their spirit; if anything it fuelled defiance.

Although Churchill was half American and had visited Cuba and North America, he always viewed the conflicts in the Americas as of peripheral concern. On the whole American foreign policy in the region was only of interest if it affected British colonial interests in the Caribbean. Panama before World War I, backed by America, had declared independence from Colombia, thereby facilitating the construction of the Panama Canal. America also intervened in Honduras and Nicaragua. Prior to and during World War I Mexico was plagued by unrest, which sparked American military intervention in 1916. Brief American military expeditions were also conducted in the Caribbean, including Cuba.

Germany's activity in the Americas was another matter. Its influence was considerable and growing. The Germans took an active interest in South America, sending training missions to various countries. In the mid-1920s there was unrest in Brazil, and Ecuador, but by the 1930s the Americas had largely quietened down. That was until the outbreak of the Chaco War between landlocked Bolivia and Paraguay, which left both countries politically unstable. The Bolivian Army was trained and commanded for a time by a German general. Nevertheless, Bolivia lost the war at a cost of 57,000 dead; although Paraguay was victorious it suffered 36,000 dead and economic ruin. During the same period Colombia and Peru fought a brief border war.

Churchill, however, was not blind to the potential threat posed by Brazil, by far the largest country in South America. It had a very sizeable German population of almost a million and was Germany's leading trade partner. Hitler even talked of making it 'a German dominion'.[51] Brazilian President-dictator Getúlio Vargas, an admirer of Mussolini, abandoned the country's liberal constitution and established a military dictatorship. This banned all political parties including Communist and Fascist groups. Filinto Müller, the Brazilian Chief of Police who was 'notoriously pro-Axis',[52] maintained links with the Gestapo in his hunt for Communist agitators. Such a totalitarian regime did not go unnoticed.

An American reporter characterized Vargas as 'able, friendly, slippery'.[53] Churchill was moved to warn in 1938 that 'even in South America the Nazi regime … begins to undermine the fabric of Brazilian society'.[54] That year Mussolini's second son, Bruno, an Italian Air Force pilot, flew across the Atlantic to Brazil. Vargas, though, was secretly indebted to Britain. Three years earlier MI6 had tipped him off that he was facing a Communist revolution and he was able to round up the conspirators.[55] Nonetheless, in America there were concerns about a 'fifth column threat in South America'. Frank Tannenbaum reported in the *New York Times*, 'A German army of 100,000 could be raised in Brazil from among German settlers there all with military training.'[56] Vargas, however, proved to be just like Franco and would not be seduced by Hitler or Mussolini. Brazil and Mexico would eventually join the Allied cause during World War II.

Churchill should have been equally concerned about Argentina. There the military had seized power in 1930 and was greatly influenced by the Germans. Many senior officers had undergone training in Germany and this, combined with the large proportion of the population who were of Italian origin, ensured the country was very strongly pro-Axis. By the late 1930s the Argentinian fleet was the most powerful in South America, easily outnumbering the Brazilian Navy. Britain was reliant on Argentinian beef and wheat imports, but to complicate matters there was a long-standing dispute between the two countries over the British Falkland Islands.[57] In the event Argentina would remain neutral until almost the end of World War II when it belatedly sided with the Allies. Beforehand, though, Churchill would capitalize on America's concerns about the Nazi threat in South America.

In contrast, Eden's warning to Churchill about Mussolini's empire building soon proved well-founded. Mussolini noted that Britain blinked twice in the Mediterranean firstly over Abyssinia and then over Spain. He took this as a sign of weakness and promptly invaded Albania in early April 1939, as a prelude to attacking Greece the following year. Churchill and Eden appreciated that for all Mussolini's ridiculous bluff and bluster he should not be underestimated.

In Europe Churchill's worst fears about Hitler were realized on 1 September 1939 when he stormed into western Poland and subsequently divided the country with Stalin. Britain and France were pledged to defend Poland, but were simply not in a position to help. Two days later Chamberlain declared war on Germany. At the same time Churchill was finally invited back into government and appointed once again First Lord of the Admiralty. Chamberlain felt it prudent having Churchill in the fold, rather than outside causing trouble from the back benches with Eden. The significance of this was not lost on the armed forces. 'I for one was inclined to believe that Winston had been given a Department,' remarked Major-General Sir Edward Spears, 'so that he would be too busy to make a nuisance of himself.'[58] Churchill's reputation preceded him and Spears added 'had he not had his hands full he would have been running the war, and overshadowing the Prime Minister in a matter of days'.[59]

Churchill, reflecting on the situation, wrote, 'No one had ever been over the same terrible course twice with such an interval between. ... Should I have once again to endure the pangs of dismissal?'[60] On 4 September he stood on the steps outside the Admiralty and had an iconic photograph taken. Churchill was back and whether he was aware of it or not, poised to assume power. His arrival was not entirely auspicious as he had only recently criticized Admiral Sir Dudley Pound, the First Sea Lord, regarding the deployment of the Mediterranean Fleet. It was obvious Churchill was never going to mend his ways.

He had met American President Franklin Roosevelt once during World War I and was delighted to get a letter of congratulations from him. 'It is because you and I occupied similar positions in the World War,' wrote Roosevelt warmly, 'that I want you to know how glad I am that you are back again in the Admiralty.'[61] He also added that he hoped that Churchill and Chamberlain could keep him informed. 'I am glad you did the Marlborough volumes before this thing started,' concluded Roosevelt, 'and I much enjoyed reading them.'[62] Churchill recalled, 'I responded with alacrity, using the signature of "Naval Person" and thus began that long and memorable correspondence.'[63] Roosevelt's single act of kindness sowed the seeds for a future military alliance, the like of which the world had never seen before.

PART FOUR

The Warlord Returns

Master and Commander

Churchill soon had his hands full. His flat was at the top of the Admiralty building, which meant he had immediate access to the navy's operational headquarters. Although Europe quickly lapsed into an armed stand-off, the German U-boat menace rapidly made itself felt. Within weeks of hostilities commencing U-boats torpedoed the aircraft carrier *Courageous* south-west of Ireland and penetrated the Home Fleet's anchorage at Scapa Flow, in the Orkney islands, where they sank the battleship *Royal Oak*. In payback the Royal Navy damaged the German pocket battleship *Graf Spee* in the South Atlantic; trapped at Montevideo, Uruguay's capital, its crew were subsequently forced to scuttle her. On land Hitler made no move as winter approached and both sides' armies glowered at each other from behind the Maginot and Siegfried Lines. The British Expeditionary Force under the command of Lord Gort and the French Army had to endure the boredom of the so-called 'Phoney War'.

Churchill saw little point in adopting the defensive 'wait and see' policy that was prevalent in France.[1] 'The Royal Navy has immediately attacked the U-boats, and is hunting them night and day, ... with zeal and not altogether without relish,'[2] he told BBC radio on 1 October 1939. He also quickly resurrected the convoy system that had been used during World War I to protect Atlantic shipping. By the end of 1939 Lord Halifax, the Foreign Secretary, was appreciative of Churchill's efforts. 'Since this has been organized,' he said, 'something like 6,000 ships were convoyed to the end of December with a loss of only twelve ships.'[3]

Churchill also wanted to blockade Germany's ports in order to wage economic warfare against it. He cast about to find a way to take the war to the enemy. An opportunity arose when he learned that German shipping was ferrying vital Swedish iron ore to Germany from the northern Norwegian port of Narvik. The only other route for the ore was from the Swedish port of Lulea south through the Gulf of Bothnia and to the German coast on the Baltic Sea. However, for almost half of the year Lulea was ice bound, which is why a railway line had been built north to the ice-free Norwegian coast. The only problem was that the German vessels were operating within neutral Norwegian territorial waters. They were also screened by the islands running the length of the Norwegian coast known as The Leads. Only south of Stavanger did the Germans have to expose themselves in open water and by then they had reached the protection of the Luftwaffe.

Churchill suggested to Admiral Pound, First Sea Lord, that the navy lay mines in The Leads in what he quaintly dubbed Operation *Wilfred*. This would force the German merchantmen and their escorts out into international waters. The only problem with such a plan was that it would violate Norwegian neutrality. If that happened, it could invite a German attack on Norway. This meant that Britain and France faced the prospect of having to send warships and troops to defend the Norwegians. It would involve a combined operation that both countries were ill-equipped to conduct. Churchill should have known better, as Norway had all the makings of another Dardanelles, yet he and the British Chiefs of Staff thought it was a way of grabbing the initiative and somehow shortening the war. Prime Minister Chamberlain was not keen on the enterprise because he was concerned about how other neutral countries, especially America, might react. Churchill therefore approached the American ambassador Joe Kennedy to canvass President Roosevelt's attitude. The reply came back that as a US presidential election was looming America would certainly not get involved over Norway.

When Stalin attacked Finland in the winter of 1939 it was proposed that aid be sent to the Finns and that British troops deploy to Norway's key ports and the Norway-Sweden railway. In light of what had happened to Poland, both countries chose not to cooperate. Nonetheless,

Britain shipped military equipment to help the Finns in their uneven struggle against the Red Army. In Germany, Hitler was persuaded by the Commander-in-Chief of the German Navy, Grand-Admiral Erich Raeder, that Norway offered ideal bases for their submarines. This suggestion fell on fertile ground because during World War I Germany had failed to occupy Norway and paid the price. Hitler authorized an invasion.

In the House of Commons Chamberlain and his government's procrastination was winning them no friends. 'It is time we stopped saying: what is Hitler going to do?' said Churchill's old comrade in arms Sir Archibald Sinclair, leader of the Liberals. 'It is about time we asked: what is Chamberlain going to do?'[4] Likewise, Clement Attlee, the Labour leader, warned 'you cannot have a policy of wait and see'.[5] Conservative MPs were similarly concerned that not enough was being done to help the beleaguered Finns. Fortunately for Chamberlain, Finland surrendered to Stalin's demands, which meant Britain and France no longer faced the dilemma of going to war with Russia as well as Germany. His days as Prime Minister, though, were numbered as he had consistently underestimated Hitler.

Paul Reynaud became the French Premier on 21 March 1940 and he supported Churchill's plan to mine The Leads. It was agreed that although Norway and Sweden were neutral, by supplying ore to Germany they were deliberately helping Hitler's war effort. Operation *Wilfred* would be backed by Operation *R4* which would land troops in Norway in the event of the Germans intervening. Unbeknown to Churchill, Hitler's attack was scheduled for the early hours of 9 April 1940. Supported by the German fleet and the Luftwaffe his troops grabbed Norway's ports from right under the very noses of the Allies. Hitler also attacked Denmark that day and overwhelmed it within four hours. Now that the gloves were off Churchill relished the opportunity to use the power of the navy. Rather foolishly he declared 'we could liquidate their landings in a week or two'.[6]

Just like the Dardanelles, Churchill could push the naval element of the operation, but he had no bearing on what happened on the ground or in the air. Disastrously, because of military requirements in France and the need to defend British air space, the Royal Air Force was unable to spare more than a few squadrons. In contrast the Luftwaffe deployed over 400 aircraft that proved more than a match for the exposed Royal

Navy. Churchill once again despaired at military operations being run by committees, principally the War Cabinet, the ministerial military coordination committee and the Chiefs of Staff committee. The Allies proved singularly unable to dislodge the Germans from Trondheim despite their own landings just to the north and south at Namsos and Andalsnes. They decided to take Narvik, initially unaware that the Germans were already there waiting for them.

With the Germans in Denmark and Norway, Chamberlain faced a very hostile House of Commons on 7 May 1940 in what became known as 'The Norway Debate'. The rowdy MPs sensed blood in the water. Chamberlain had misjudged Hitler once too often and had again been wrong-footed. Leo Amery, an old school friend of Churchill's, invoked the words of Oliver Cromwell to the Rump Parliament crying, 'You have sat here too long for any good you have been doing. Depart, I say, and let us have done with you. God, go!'[7] This was met by cheers of approval. Churchill was in a difficult position because he had to be loyal to the Prime Minister and at the same time defend the armed services' botched handling of Norway. It was by now widely accepted that Chamberlain could not stay on, although it was unclear who could succeed him. The Foreign Secretary Lord Halifax was a possible contender, but it was felt he lacked drive. Likewise, Churchill was considered too old and too much of a wild card.

During the debate Attlee pointed out that Norway was a culmination of Chamberlain's flawed policies following Czechoslovakia and Poland. When Lloyd George rose, he put Churchill on the spot by saying the Norway campaign was 'half-baked' and had been hampered by a lack of cooperation from the navy. Churchill valiantly admitted he bore responsibility for the Royal Navy. Lloyd George, though, would accept no such deflection, replying 'the right honourable gentleman must not allow himself to be converted into an air-raid shelter to keep the splinters from hitting his colleagues'.[8] Turning to Chamberlain, Lloyd George said he should step aside, 'because there is nothing which can contribute more to victory than that he should sacrifice the seals of office'.[9]

A vote of no confidence in Chamberlain's beleaguered administration was inevitable. Forty-one Conservatives voted against their own government and another 60 MPs, mostly Conservatives, abstained. Thanks to this and the actions of the Labour and Liberal MPs the Conservative majority fell from 213 to 81. It meant a coalition government was the only way ahead. Attlee said he would support a coalition but not under Chamberlain. That night a tired Chamberlain, unaware that he had terminal cancer, summoned Churchill and informed him he doubted he could remain Prime Minister.

These must have been tantalizing days for Churchill. He had held almost every high office in the land and now the very top job was potentially within his grasp. Although Halifax was the preferred candidate by all the political parties, as a member of the House of Lords technically he could not become Prime Minister in the House of Commons. Furthermore, it appears he did not really want the job, knowing full well that the situation in Europe meant it was a poisoned chalice. On 10 May 1940 Hitler invaded the Low Countries, Luxembourg and France, and Chamberlain resigned. He had taken the country to war but could do no more. Churchill was summoned that evening by King George VI and asked to form a new government. Afterwards Churchill's bodyguard, Detective Inspector Walter Thompson, recalled, 'He looked pleased but was obviously tense and strained.'[10] The news flashed around the world, with papers in New York proclaiming 'Chamberlain Out, Churchill In.'[11]

Churchill, fed up with the muddled running of the war, created for himself the new post of Minister of Defence, thereby placing himself directly above the Chiefs of Staff. By doing this he took personal control of the war. The three service ministers were conspicuously not invited onto the War Cabinet and were unceremoniously shoved aside. His daily meetings with the Chiefs of Staff gave him immediate oversight of the progress of the war and they answered to him. He appointed his friends and allies Anthony Eden Secretary of State for War with responsibility for the War Office and Archibald Sinclair Secretary of State for Air. Sinclair had been Churchill's deputy battalion commander on the Western Front. Eden noted wryly, 'despite all my admiration for Churchill, I expected that relations with him might be choppy'.[12]

Churchill needed Chamberlain's support as he remained leader of the Conservative party, so he gave him the post of Lord President of the Council, which ensured he was in the War Cabinet. Likewise, Halifax as Foreign Secretary was also in the Cabinet. Churchill wanted to include his old Liberal mentor, Lloyd George. He had led the country during World War I so his experience could have been invaluable. Chamberlain initially was not keen on the idea, but acquiesced to Churchill's wishes. Churchill met with Lloyd George at 10 Downing Street on the evening of 16 June and offered him a role. The suggestion was that he oversee food production, distribution and rationing. Lloyd George said that he would think about it and Churchill subsequently sent Lord Beaverbrook to sound him out again.

Lloyd George gave every indication he would accept. However, at 77 years of age his stamina was waning and he had no stomach for coalition politics. 'I am not going in with this gang,' he grumbled privately. 'The country does not realize the peril it is in.'[13] Even when Chamberlain resigned from the War Cabinet at the end of September 1940 due to his failing health, Lloyd George still held back from helping Churchill. The Prime Minister made one last effort to recruit him – this time the job was ambassador to America – but once again he declined. Lloyd George did not agree with how the war was being conducted, nor did he agree with how the Cabinet was constituted. It was evident that he did not support Churchill's style of leadership. He would later write, 'We have made blunder after blunder and we are still blundering. Unless there is a thorough change of policy, we shall never win.'[14] It may have been that he vainly hoped as an elder statesman at some stage he might be called upon to replace Churchill.

Churchill appreciated that to successfully direct the war he needed to be extremely well informed. He instructed William Cavendish-Bentick, Chairman of the Joint Intelligence Committee, that his staff must be ready to produce reports 24/7 for the Prime Minister, members of the War Cabinet and the Chiefs of Staff. The Joint Intelligence Committee had only been established in 1936 to bring together the fruits of military and naval intelligence; however, its remit had expanded to encompass MI5, MI6 and the Government Code and Cypher School (which included the codebreakers at Bletchley Park). Although the Joint Intelligence Committee technically came under the Chiefs of Staff, Churchill gave it direct access to Downing Street. He understood the need for a strong centralized intelligence organization. Fortunately for him Cavendish-Bentinck rose to the challenge of dealing with all the intelligence chiefs, not all of whom were easy to work with.

At the same time Churchill acted swiftly to ensure that he had personal access to raw incoming intelligence. Desmond Morton, who was now Director of Intelligence at the Ministry of Economic Warfare, was summoned to Downing Street to join Churchill's staff. His job was to act as liaison between MI6 and the new Prime Minister. Morton would attend the Secret Service Committee whose members included all the intelligence heads. Morton was perhaps not the best man for the job as he had been highly critical of MI6's intelligence-gathering efforts.

Initially Churchill's new Cabinet had high hopes for the performance of France's powerful armed forces; after all they had withstood everything that was thrown at them in World War I. 'On land the French Army stands as ever,' remarked Halifax rather too optimistically, 'the bastion of Western civilisation.'[15] It was certainly large, though not very mobile nor very well led. Worryingly as Halifax highlighted 'our troops since the war began have been under the command of the French commander-in-chief to use and to send where he thinks fit'.[16] Crucially, less than half of France's mobilized manpower was actually deployed in the north. Although the French had greater numbers and better-quality tanks than the Germans, only a third of them were with their handful of newly formed armoured divisions. The Allied plan was that when hostilities opened the French Army would move into the Netherlands while the British Expeditionary Force (BEF) and more French troops would advance into Belgium. This strategy was totally reliant on the Germans making slow progress and the cooperation of the neutral Dutch and Belgians.

Thanks to Hitler's Blitzkrieg the challenges now facing Churchill were enormous. He was immediately confronted by a very rapidly deteriorating situation in northern Europe. Lord Gort moved the BEF forward towards the Dyle line, a few miles east of Brussels, as planned. Without knowing it he was advancing into an enormous trap devised by Hitler and his generals. Within five days the Germans overwhelmed the Dutch after the Luftwaffe flattened Rotterdam. In Belgium the Germans reached Hannut and within four days defeated two French armoured divisions. The speed of the German advance forced Gort to withdraw and the abandoned Belgians were soon to sue for peace.

To the south Hitler's panzers sliced through the wooded Ardennes over the River Meuse at Sedan and into France. The Allies threw a fleet of bombers at the Sedan bridgehead in an effort to stop them. Instead, half the aircraft were shot from the skies and Sedan fell to the Germans. Churchill received an unwelcome phone call on the morning of 15 May from his despondent French counterpart. 'We are beaten,' lamented Paul Reynaud, 'we have lost the battle.'[17] Alarmed by such defeatism after less than a week of fighting, Churchill flew to Paris the following day to try and rally his French allies. The French Army, though, was already in a state of utter disarray and its morale was plummeting. When Churchill asked about their strategic reserves he was informed there was none. Hitler's panzers sped relentlessly westward to reach the English Channel at Abbeville on 20 May. This cut off the ports of Boulogne, Calais and Dunkirk and all those Allied forces in north-eastern France and western Belgium. Desperate French and British attempts to stem the German tide were easily brushed aside.

Gort at Wahagnies, south of Lille, assessed the situation was so serious that the BEF should be evacuated and began to make plans for a withdrawal to the coast. When Churchill heard of this he was aghast; the last thing he wanted to do was abandon Reynaud. At this stage it was not clear to him and his commanders that the BEF would have to flee back across the Channel. Instead, the British and French fleets were ordered to prepare plans to resupply their isolated ground forces. British reinforcements were sent over to Boulogne and Calais. It was also hoped that counter-attacks on the northern and southern flanks of the German corridor could sever the breakthrough. In the meantime, Vice-Admiral Bertram Ramsay, at Dover, took charge of the evacuation of all British wounded and non-essential personnel from France. In the event, the highly anticipated Allied counter-attacks were poorly coordinated and too weak. Although Gort's attack at Arras failed on 21 May, it inflicted sufficient casualties on the Germans to cause Hitler to order a two-day halt while his infantry divisions caught up with the panzers.

Meanwhile, Norway had become little more than an unwanted sideshow. At Narvik the German garrison were cut off after the German fleet was severely mauled, but the Allied ground attack did not commence until mid-May. At the end of the month Narvik was taken and the Germans forced back towards Sweden and possible internment. By then facing imminent defeat in France the Allies had lost faith in Churchill's Scandinavian adventure and at the end of the first week of June they evacuated Narvik. Churchill had little choice but to abandon the Norwegians to their fate. Despite this the Royal Navy had inflicted considerable losses on the German fleet and was still able to dominate the North Sea. Both factors greatly impeded Hitler's ability to invade England that summer.

When Gort informed Anthony Eden that he was indeed withdrawing on the coast, Eden cautioned, 'It is obvious that you should not discuss the possibility of the move with the French or the Belgians.'[18] The noose began to really tighten around the BEF, the remains of the Belgian Army and the French 1st Army when the Germans took Boulogne on 25 May. The subsequent surrender of Belgium then exposed the eastern flank of the pocket, forcing Gort to redeploy two of his divisions to screen Nieuport east of Dunkirk. This meant he would be unable to conduct any further counter-attacks. Churchill was now facing a disaster of catastrophic proportions. Supported by Eden, the Secretary of State for War, and General Sir Edmund Ironside, Chief of the Imperial General Staff, he now had to make a terrible decision as it was evident that Calais would be next in line to feel the wrath of the Germans. If the garrison remained it would help distract the panzers' drive on Dunkirk. 'It was my decision,' said Churchill. 'When I made it I had a feeling I was going to be sick.'[19]

Reluctantly Eden and Ironside agreed with Churchill. 'The Calais decision was one of the most painful of the war,' recalled Eden, 'for I had served with one of the regiments and knew personally many of those whose fate I had now to decide.'[20] Churchill personally signalled Brigadier Claude Nicolson with a last stand order. 'Every hour you continue to exist is of greatest help to the BEF,' he said. 'Government has therefore decided you must continue to fight. ... Evacuation will not (repeat not) take place.'[21] The unfortunate Nicolson and his men held out until the evening of Sunday 26 May. The Germans captured 20,000 prisoners, 3,500 of whom were British, including Nicolson. 'This saved the situation,' reasoned Churchill. 'Calais made the evacuation at Dunkirk possible.'[22]

Churchill concluded that, in light of the French Army being unable to counter-attack to the south, his first priority was saving the trapped BEF. It would be a race against time as the Dunkirk pocket shrank under German pressure and the lifeline across the Channel was incessantly pounded by the Luftwaffe. Reynaud was in London on 26 May to discuss whether the Allies should continue to resist or consider negotiating

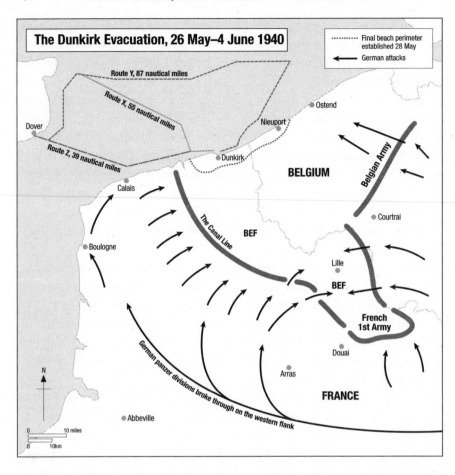

The Dunkirk Evacuation, 26 May–4 June 1940

- ·········· Final beach perimeter established 28 May
- ◄── German attacks

Route Y, 87 nautical miles

Route X, 55 nautical miles

Route Z, 39 nautical miles

Dover

Ostend

Nieuport

Dunkirk

BELGIUM

Belgian Army

Calais

Courtrai

The Canal Line

BEF

Boulogne

Lille

BEF

French 1st Army

German panzer divisions broke through on the western flank

Douai

Arras

FRANCE

Abbeville

N

0   10 miles
0   10km

with Hitler. Churchill made no mention of his plans to withdraw the BEF. The harsh reality was that he needed the French Army to carry on fighting to cover the evacuation. However, the issue of negotiating was to cause some controversy within the Cabinet, especially as Halifax felt a peaceful resolution should be pursued. Churchill was not keen on using Mussolini as an intermediary, especially as he potentially had more to gain in the Mediterranean from siding with Hitler. Likewise, any direct negotiations with Hitler would inevitably mean considerable concessions. Halifax understandably felt that Churchill was risking everything by not exploring the options, no matter how unpalatable they might be.

At this point Churchill instructed Admiral Ramsay to commence Operation *Dynamo*, the desperate bid to rescue the BEF from total destruction. Gort finally got the instructions he had been waiting for. 'The only course open to you may be to fight back to the west,' signalled Eden, 'where the beaches and port, east of Gravelines will be used for embarkation.'[23] Ramsay managed to muster an ad hoc armada of almost 900 vessels, less than a third of which were naval craft. It was felt that destroyers would be most suited for the operation, but while the Royal Navy had around 200 only 41 were available. Prompted by Churchill, Ramsay had little option but to requisition anything and everything that was available. His rescue fleet gathered at the ports of Dover, Folkestone, Margate, Portsmouth and Ramsgate included barges, ferries, paddle steamers, sailboats, trawlers and numerous small pleasure craft, many of which were not intended for ocean-going journeys.

The sight of the ancient paddle steamer *Emperor of India* heading across the Channel exemplified just how dire Britain's situation was. The irony was not lost on Churchill that, despite the wealth and might of the British Empire, the country stood impotent in the face of Nazi aggression. Gort understandably felt that it was too late and this was reflected in his response to Eden, 'I must not conceal from you that a great part of the BEF and its equipment will inevitably be lost.'[24] It was anticipated that the Germans would capture the port within two days and that at best 45,000 men might be saved. This at least was better than nothing.

Churchill ordered that Gort and his generals, Alan Brooke, Harold Alexander and Bernard Montgomery were not to fall into German hands. Understandably they wanted to stay with their men until the very end. When Churchill heard that this was Gort's intention he instructed him to hand over command and return immediately. By the end of May Churchill was informed that 150,000 British soldiers had been safely transported back to England. About 60,000 remained, which meant, allowing for the loss of the 15,000-strong rearguard, another 45,000 had to be shipped over the next few nights. By that point only 15,000 French troops, from a force of 200,000, had been evacuated. The senior naval liaison officer at Dunkirk, Captain William Tennant, reported, 'The French staff at Dunkirk feel strongly that they are defending Dunkirk for us to evacuate, which is largely true.'[25]

On 31 May Churchill endured a very frosty meeting with Reynaud in Paris, who was not happy about this situation. Churchill tried to explain how chaotic the logistical and command and control situation was inside the Dunkirk pocket. 'Moreover,' he added pointedly, 'the French have not up to the present received orders to embark.'[26] In an attempt to save the Anglo-French alliance he agreed that British and French troops would be evacuated in equal numbers from that point on and that the British would help with the rearguard. 'It will not be possible to keep Dunkirk open very much longer,' he warned Reynaud, 'forty-eight hours perhaps if we are fortunate.'[27] Churchill also stipulated that from now on only unwounded men would be evacuated as the British Army needed to rebuild its shattered divisions as quickly as possible.

Only General Alexander remained to oversee this evacuation of the Allied rearguard. After conferring with Churchill, Eden instructed him, 'You should withdraw your force as rapidly as possible on a 50-50 basis with the French Army, aiming at completion by night of 1–2 June.'[28] Although as a matter of honour Churchill was determined to rescue as many Frenchmen as possible, he was irked by their inefficiency. At 1320 hours on 3 June he signalled Reynaud. 'We are coming back for your men tonight,' he said. 'Please ensure that all facilities are used promptly. For three hours last night many ships waited idly at great risk and danger.'[29] As a result over 25,000 French troops sailed for England, most of them carried by British ships, just before Dunkirk surrendered. Remarkably between 26 May and 4 June, 338,226[30] British and Allied troops were rescued from Dunkirk, though mostly without any of their weapons or equipment. Of these over a third totalling 141,842 were allied forces, most of whom were French and the bulk of them went back to France almost immediately to face imminent defeat and capture.[31]

The cost of *Dynamo* was extremely heavy. Around 44,000 Allied troops were left behind either killed or captured. Ramsay reported he had lost six destroyers, five minesweepers, eight transport ships and over 200 other craft, plus 17 Allied vessels. When Air Chief Marshal Sir Hugh Dowding, Commander-in-Chief RAF Fighter Command, briefed Churchill it was not good news; since 10 May he had lost 432 Hurricanes and Spitfires. This represented 20 squadrons of fighters. During the nine days of *Dynamo* the RAF lost 106 aircraft. This proved that the fighters, although not entirely successful, had done their utmost to keep the Luftwaffe's dive bombers away from Dunkirk's exposed beaches.

News of the evacuation was not made official until 1800 hours on 31 May 1940 when the BBC acknowledged, 'All night and all day men of the undefeated British Expeditionary Force have been coming home'.[32] The newspapers followed suit the following day. On 4 June Churchill went before the House of Commons to announce the BEF had been saved. Looking round at the gathered MPs he warned them, 'Wars are not won by evacuations.'[33] He told them his plan was to fight on, come what may, until America entered the war. There would be no surrender even if Hitler invaded. His defiance struck a chord with the British people. 'To us, who had the honour of being members of the threatened nation, whose eyes were riveted on Winston Churchill,' wrote Major-General Sir Edward Spears, 'now recognized as the supreme leader who would give each and all of us the impulse we expected and awaited, the words conveyed a hidden meaning.'[34] Churchill's hope for rescue, though, depended on whether Franklin D. Roosevelt could win a third term in office and convince his country to intervene once again in a European conflict.

Despite the successful evacuation at Dunkirk, Churchill and Ironside still had forces in France that needed extricating. Churchill was reluctant to completely abandon Reynaud but time was fast running out. The 51st Highland Division was caught at Valéry-en-Caux to the west of Dieppe and forced to surrender on 12 June. Two days after that Paris capitulated. Churchill wanted the newly arrived 52nd Division to assist the French, but was persuaded by Lieutenant-General Alan Brooke during a 30-minute phone call to evacuate it. Brooke argued that the French were beyond help and that his first duty was to his men. Churchill hoped that Reynaud and his government would move to French North Africa to carry on the fight. Instead Reynaud resigned. The British 1st Armoured Division withdrew to Cherbourg and managed to escape by 18 June just as the panzers were arriving. Four days later France surrendered. The evacuations, however, continued until 25 June by which time another 144,171 British troops had been rescued in what amounted to a second Dunkirk.

Churchill was angered to learn that in all the chaos the French released 400 German pilots, most of whom had been shot down by the

RAF. They were supposed to have been shipped to England, but instead they were able to return to the Luftwaffe and become, as Churchill remarked, 'available for the Battle of Britain, and we had to shoot them down a second time'.[35] Thanks to the heroic efforts of Ramsey, Gort and the others, Churchill narrowly avoided what would have been the worst defeat ever in British military history. It is conceivable that, had the BEF been lost, Churchill's government would have collapsed and Britain would have sued for peace. Instead, thanks to his defiant leadership the country would continue to resist Hitler.

13

His Finest Hour

French Prime Minister Reynaud told Churchill in mid-May 1940, 'If we are to win this battle … it is necessary to send at once … ten more squadrons.'[1] Churchill could not ignore his French counterpart's plea and promised to put it to the War Cabinet. Dowding, alarmed at the attrition rate of his fighter squadrons in France, made a point of personally briefing Churchill, Sir Archibald Sinclair the new Air Minister, Sir Cyril Newall Chief of the Air Staff, and Lord Beaverbrook. This was done just before a meeting of the War Cabinet. Dowding patiently explained that although the Air Ministry assessed that 52 RAF fighter squadrons were needed to defend Britain, these had already been reduced to 36. If his Hurricanes continued to be shot down at the current rate, then they would have none left within two weeks.

Churchill may have been annoyed by this breach in the chain of command and took a dislike to Dowding. For some reason he was not receptive to this warning and Dowding was not given an opportunity to brief the Cabinet. Nor did anyone else raise the matter again. Dowding seemed to overestimate the success of his meeting with Churchill. He immediately wrote to Keith Park commanding 11 Group responsible for London, 'We had a notable victory on the "home Front" this morning. Any orders to send more Hurricanes were cancelled.'[2]

Instead, four more fighter squadrons were sent to France. To Dowding's dismay Churchill, on a visit to Paris on 16 May, promised to deploy a further six Hurricane squadrons. Although the War Cabinet wavered in Churchill's absence, they agreed to send them if they flew back to England every night. This left Dowding down to half strength. Strangely, though, Churchill refused to fully acknowledged the extent of Dowding's warning, later writing blandly 'the head of metropolitan Fighter Command, had declared to me that with twenty-five squadrons of fighters he could defend the island against the whole of the German Air Force, but with less he would be overwhelmed'.[3] It was not until 19 May that Churchill and Newall finally agreed that it would compromise Britain's air defences if any further squadrons were deployed across the Channel. By then the damage had already been done. Just 66 of the 261 Hurricanes sent to France returned.

Following Dunkirk, it was very clear that the RAF was now a priority as it was the country's first line of defence. Although Fighter Command received a battering in France, Churchill and Dowding had one particular advantage that the Luftwaffe greatly underestimated. This was an early warning radar system, called Radio Direction Finding or RDF. This could detect enemy aircraft gathering over the continent. It seemed logical that Hitler would make the destruction of Dowding's airfields and radar his first objective. Churchill would soon find that managing all the personalities with responsibility for the defence of Britain's skies would be no easy task. Dowding's Fighter Command was divided into four groups. Key amongst these were Park's 11 Group defending London and Trafford Leigh-Mallory's 12 Group protecting the Midlands. The two remaining groups, 10 and 13, were responsible for the south-west and the north, encompassing Scotland. Dowding rather unkindly was known as 'Stuffy'.[4] This was nothing to do with any outmoded views on aerial warfare, rather his austere lifestyle choices of being a teetotaller and a vegetarian.

Churchill placed the controversial newspaper tycoon Lord Beaverbrook, in charge of the newly created Ministry of Aircraft Production. This appointment quickly brought him into conflict with the Air Ministry, though fortunately he got on with Dowding. One of the first things Beaverbrook did was to shake up fighter production. He was unhappy to discover that the Nuffield organization had been given a contract to build Spitfire IIs, despite the fact that Vickers-Supermarine had designed it and were already manufacturing it. Nuffield's Castle Bromwich factory in Birmingham should have started manufacturing 1,500 Spitfires, but when Beaverbrook took over on 14 May 1940 none had been completed. In response he instructed Vickers-Supermarine to take over Castle Bromwich. Lord Nuffield was furious and tried to get

Beaverbrook sacked by complaining to Churchill. He failed. On 6 June 1940 the first Spitfire II was in the air. It was just in time. After Henry Ford refused to support the British war effort, Beaverbrook managed to persuade Packard to build Rolls Royce Merlin engines under licence in America.

On 18 June 1940 Churchill dramatically announced in the House of Lords, 'The Battle of France is over. I expect The Battle of Britain is about to begin.'[5] He then added, 'Hitler knows that he will have to break us in this island or lose the war.'[6] The figures presented to him by the time of the French surrender made for grim reading. Dowding's worst fears had come to fruition. The RAF had lost 959 aircraft in the West, plus 66 in Norway; 509 of these were fighters. The human cost had been high, as 435 pilots had been killed, captured or were missing. To defend the British Isles there were 331 Spitfires and Hurricanes supported by 150 'second-line' fighters. The prospect of a German invasion seemed imminent. Churchill, though, understood that Hitler's true goals were not in the West; 'should he be repulsed here or not try to invade,' Churchill wrote to Beaverbrook on 8 July, 'he will recoil Eastward.'[7] That very day Fighter Command shot down its first German fighter over Britain. From that point on Luftwaffe attacks in the English Channel and southern England began to escalate.

Hitler was now in possession of numerous air bases in Norway, Denmark, the Netherlands, Belgium and France from which the Luftwaffe could attack the British Isles. Those in the Pas de Calais region posed the greatest threat to London. Churchill told Beaverbrook that the country urgently needed fighters until 'we have broken the enemy's attack.' Then he added that Hitler would ultimately be defeated by 'an absolutely devastating, exterminating attack by very heavy bombers from this country upon the Nazi homeland'.[8] Churchill was very clearly flagging up the forthcoming strategic bombing campaign against Germany and the occupied territories. This also indicated that Churchill valued Dowding only for the duration of the fighter battle. Even at this early stage Churchill envisaged the defence of Britain's air space as a holding action until such time as the country was ready to strike back at its tormentors.

It was not just Dowding who was causing Churchill difficulties. He was vexed by the defeatist attitude of the US Ambassador in London. On 1 July Churchill noted, 'Saw Joe Kennedy who says everyone in

the USA thinks we shall be beaten before the end of the month.'⁹
Several weeks later he was equally annoyed when Kennedy held a press
conference to announce that Hitler would be in London by 15 August
1940. However, Kennedy wielded serious political clout and it was
an election year in America, with Roosevelt running, against Wendell
Wilkie, for an unprecedented third term in office. Roosevelt needed
Kennedy's support and in turn Churchill desperately needed Roosevelt's
help. This meant that Churchill had to avoid upsetting Kennedy at
all costs.

From 10 July until the end of the first week of August the Luftwaffe
tried to bring Dowding's pilots to battle by attacking shipping in the
English Channel. They then switched to striking his airfields and
radar stations. However, attacks on the latter did not commence
until 12 August and fortunately for Dowding the radar masts proved
to be very resilient. Few were hit and those that were were quickly
repaired. Behind the scenes, though, Churchill faced problems over
Dowding's continued command of Britain's air defences. Dowding was
very disappointed that the Air Minister and the Chief of the Air Staff
had not spoken up for him with Churchill regarding fighter losses in
France. Nor was he happy about his treatment by the Air Ministry
over his anticipated retirement. Confusingly he had received three
dates. The most recent was 14 July 1940, although the Air Ministry,
with Churchill's backing, was now asking if he could continue until the
end of October.¹⁰ He undoubtedly held Churchill, Sinclair and Newall
responsible for this uncertain state of affairs. As far as he was concerned
they were all being ungrateful at a critical time when he was struggling
to fend off the Luftwaffe.

After dining with the Prime Minister at Chequers on 13 July,
Dowding had come away under the impression that he had Churchill's
full backing and an open retirement date. He responded to the Air
Ministry saying pointedly, 'I am anxious to stay because I feel there
is no one else who will fight as I do when proposals are made which
would reduce the Defence Forces of the Country below the extreme
danger point.'¹¹ The truth was that he had stepped on so many toes
at the Air Ministry and Air Staff while creating Britain's air defences
during the late 1930s that they wanted rid of him.

On the intelligence front things were going much better for
Churchill. Even before Dunkirk, Bletchley Park had broken the

Luftwaffe's codes.[12] This meant that it was reading up to a thousand messages a day, though little of it was of much help. Then in mid-July Hitler issued instructions for the preparation of an invasion of England. A prerequisite to this was that the Luftwaffe must destroy the RAF's ability to resist a seaborne assault. Churchill was informed that an initial air offensive was anticipated to commence in early August. During that period Fighter Command's airfields and radar stations would come under growing attack. Bletchley's intelligence was so sensitive that Churchill did not include Dowding in the loop. He was only granted access in mid-October 1940 and even then Dowding was not permitted to share it with his commanders.[13] The Luftwaffe's bombers launched their first massed assault, codenamed *Eagle Day*, against the RAF on 13 August 1940, but Fighter Command managed to drive them off.

Churchill desperately wanted to be in the thick of things so he visited Dowding's Fighter Command Headquarters at Bentley Priory two days later. In the Filter Room he saw the vast table with a map of the entire country marked out in a grid, on which were tracked gathering incoming enemy aircraft. Once 'the true track' was decided the Operations Room next door was informed of the bombers' likely destination. Dowding's 'girlies', as he called his Women's Auxiliary Air Force personnel, were thrilled to have the Prime Minister watching them work.[14] 'We plotters were a bit of a sideshow,' recalled Petrea Winterbotham with evident pride.[15]

Churchill left impressed by Dowding's abilities and the professionalism of his WAAFs, many of whom were just 19 or 20 years old. They disliked being called 'girlies'. It was 'nauseating but sweetly meant' said Petrea Winterbotham.[16] They also disliked how Dowding would tease them for being hungover, whereas they were exhausted by their intense four-hour shifts. The stress was soon causing what was dubbed 'Anxiety Neurosis'. Nevertheless, no one would have ever dreamed of complaining to the Prime Minister. The raids on 15 August were heavy, although Dowding had the small consolation that they had attacked the RAF's bomber bases. If they carried on striking his fighter airfields, then it would be the death knell of Fighter Command. The Germans lost around 70 aircraft that day, the RAF about 30.

Fatefully in the small hours of 25 August a German bomber got lost and bombed London by accident. Outraged, Churchill ordered an immediate reprisal attack on Berlin and the German capital was

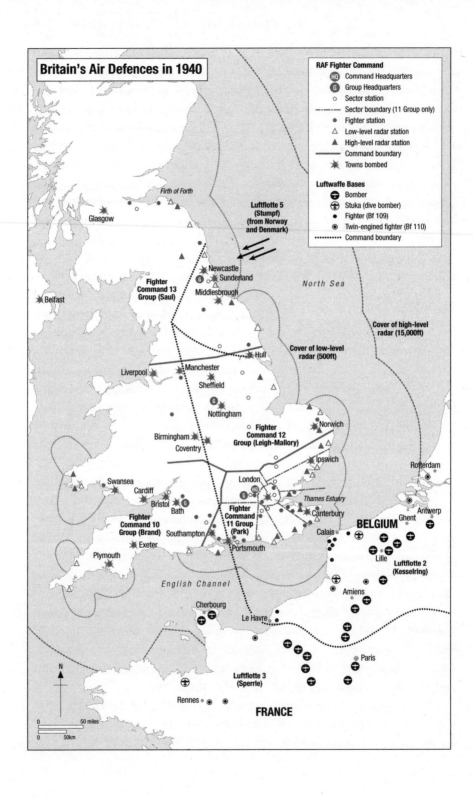

Britain's Air Defences in 1940

RAF Fighter Command
- HQ Command Headquarters
- G Group Headquarters
- ○ Sector station
- ─·─ Sector boundary (11 Group only)
- ● Fighter station
- △ Low-level radar station
- ▲ High-level radar station
- ── Command boundary
- ✳ Towns bombed

Luftwaffe Bases
- Bomber
- Stuka (dive bomber)
- ● Fighter (Bf 109)
- ◉ Twin-engined fighter (Bf 110)
- ······ Command boundary

Luftflotte 5 (Stumpf) (from Norway and Denmark)

Firth of Forth

Glasgow

Belfast

North Sea

Newcastle
Sunderland
Middlesbrough

Fighter Command 13 Group (Saul)

Cover of high-level radar (15,000ft)

Cover of low-level radar (500ft)

Hull

Liverpool
Manchester
Sheffield

Nottingham

Birmingham
Coventry

Fighter Command 12 Group (Leigh-Mallory)

Norwich

Ipswich

Rotterdam

Swansea
Cardiff
Bristol
Bath

London

Canterbury

Thames Estuary

Antwerp
Ghent

BELGIUM

Calais

Fighter Command 10 Group (Brand)

Fighter Command 11 Group (Park)

Southampton
Portsmouth

Lille

Luftflotte 2 (Kesselring)

Plymouth
Exeter

English Channel

Amiens

Cherbourg
Le Havre

Luftflotte 3 (Sperrle)

Paris

N

0   50 miles
0   50km

Rennes

FRANCE

bombed that very night. Hitler was furious and the Battle of Britain expanded to encompass England's cities, heralding the Blitz. Although this was a terrible development, Churchill's actions took the pressure off Dowding's battered airfields, especially those of Park's 11 Group.

Churchill toured Kent on 28 August visiting the fighter stations at RAF Manston, Ramsgate and Dover. Being on the front line the airfield at Manston had been almost pounded into oblivion. He was annoyed to discover that little had been done to repair the damage, noting, 'I was much concerned to find that although more than four clear days have passed since it was last raided the greater part of the craters on the landing ground remained unfilled and the aerodrome was barely serviceable.'[17]

He was also angered by the senseless destruction of local homes and shops. Churchill was caught by an air raid warning while in Ramsgate and was rushed to a public shelter. Inside he was confronted by a large 'No Smoking' sign and was obliged to stub out his newly lit cigar. It was no false alarm. Overhead two German aircraft appeared and dropped their bombs in a tip-and-run attack. When he re-emerged a little later the first thing that confronted him was a bombed-out tea shop, its smashed tables, chairs and crockery strewn across the street. Nearby stood the owner sobbing her heart out. Moved by her plight Churchill turned to those around him and said, 'Arrangements must be made for poor people like that.'[18]

At Dover, accompanied by some American military and naval observers, he watched as Hurricanes of 85 Squadron chased Messerschmitts off Folkestone. American liaison officer Colonel Raymond E. Lee witnessed a German fighter crash into the ground as its pilot descended safely by parachute. 'At the same time a German bomber came tumbling down into the sea,' noted Lee in a letter to his wife, 'where it disappeared with a good sized splash.'[19] Churchill and his entourage had no way of knowing that it was 85 Squadron's most successful action of the Battle of Britain, claiming about half a dozen enemy fighters in one go.

That evening he stopped at Church Whitfield to survey the burning wreckage of a Messerschmitt. After being reassured that it was not a British fighter he exclaimed, 'Thank God. That's another less on a long list!'[20] When he enquired after the pilot, Churchill was advised that the man had bailed out and been captured, but was in hospital very badly wounded. He then stooped and picked up a cartridge case as a souvenir, which he would add to the spears he had collected at Omdurman all those years ago.

When Churchill got back on his special train at 1945 hours he was in a foul and vindictive mood. Turning to the Americans travelling with him he announced that Berlin would be bombed that night. The Germans also conducted their first massed night-time raids hitting Liverpool docks and other targets. Throughout the Blitz Churchill resolutely toured Britain's bombed cities to show solidarity and boost morale. In stark contrast Hitler steadfastly refused to visit any of Germany's devastated cities. Wherever Churchill went he attracted great affection. 'That man was our idol,' said 18-year-old Fred Woolford with the South London Home Guard, 'and we would have died before we let him down.'[21]

By early September even Churchill's undying optimism was beginning to fail him. The widespread bombing of London on 7 September was so intense he agreed the armed forces should be put on full invasion alert that night. He had good reason to make this decision as the sustained German air raids involved almost 1,280 aircraft.[22] The RAF and Royal Navy were already largely at maximum readiness, but the codeword Cromwell was signalled to the army. Unfortunately for Churchill and his Chiefs of Staff not everyone knew what it meant and chaos ensued in some areas, particularly with the Home Guard. Originally Cromwell's key instruction was simply that 'troops were to take up their battle stations'.[23] Subsequently it was revised to 'Invasion imminent and probable within twelve hours.'[24] Others thought it signalled the invasion was actually under way and in panic the Home Guard began to ring the church bells. Joseph O'Keefe recalled being told by a frightened Home Guard despatch rider it was not an exercise and that, 'They've landed on the south-east coast!'[25] Fortunately it was a false alarm, at least for the time being.

By now the attrition rate for pilots and aircraft was such that Dowding was facing defeat. Twenty-six fighters were being lost every day and 120 pilots a week. Many of these young men were only in their late teens or early twenties and Churchill affectionately referred to them as 'Dowding's chicks'.[26] Archibald Sinclair admitted that there were just 288 fighters, or 11 days' supply, remaining in reserve. Churchill warned the nation on 11 September 1940, 'It ranks with the days when the Spanish Armada was approaching the Channel, and Drake was finishing his game of bowls; or when Nelson stood between us and Napoleon's Grand Army at Boulogne.'[27]

Inspector Walter Thompson, Churchill's close protection officer, was naturally concerned about his personal safety in London. On 12 September Thompson pointed out that as Prime Minister he should not be putting himself at risk. 'Thompson, the Prime Minister of the country lives and works in that house,' retorted Churchill pointing at 10 Downing Street, 'and until Hitler puts it on the ground, I work there.'[28] He then defiantly posed for press photographers on the front steps before setting off to review Dover's defences.

Three days later at 1030 hours on a Sunday morning he and his staff visited Park's 11 Group Operations Room at RAF Uxbridge. This was 50 feet underground and reached by 63 steps. 'I don't know whether anything will happen today, sir,' cautioned Park. 'At present all is quiet.'[29] He then apologized that Churchill could not smoke his cigar because the air conditioning would not cope. Inside the Ops Room Churchill could feel the tension as he had four weeks previously, when he had first visited shortly after *Eagle Day*. Although it was quiet, he knew very well that trouble was brewing. Bletchley Park's decoders had warned him that the Luftwaffe was going to throw everything it had at London that day prior to invasion.[30]

In light of the presence of the Prime Minister the Ops staff tried to look more vigilant than ever – if that was at all possible. Churchill surveyed the two-storey room that was 60 feet across with three levels for the men and women overseeing the air defence of southeast England. He noted Wing Commander Eric Douglas-Jones poised by six telephones linking the Ops Room with the fighter controllers. On the opposite wall were bulb-lit panels which charted every sector's squadrons.

Churchill watched impassively as the WAAF plotters at the large map table below used croupier rods to move coloured discs to show incoming enemy aircraft. This information was being relayed by the members of the Observer Corps and the RAF's vital radar stations. The plotters had initially shown 40-plus heading from Dieppe, but these soon became 60-plus then 80-plus. 'There appear to be many aircraft coming in,' observed Churchill. 'There'll be some one there to meet them,' responded Park.[31] As well as 11 Group both 10 Group and 12 Group were on heightened alert.

At 1103 hours Douglas-Jones began to instruct the fighter squadrons to take to the air. No.11 Group scrambled 11 squadrons, 10 Group one and 12 Group its 'Big Wing' of five squadrons. Very soon 21 squadrons were airborne and every squadron panel bulb glowed red next to the label 'Enemy intercepted.' 'Good lord, man,' said Churchill to Douglas-Jones, 'all your forces are in the air – what do we do now?'[32] The Wing Commander was normally unflappable, but having the Prime Minister next to him meant it was doubly important that he sounded calm. 'Well, sir,' he replied, 'we can just hope that the squadrons will refuel as quickly as possible and get up again.'[33]

No one wanted to burden Churchill with the knowledge that 501 Squadron at Kenley only had two serviceable aircraft. Even worse, 73 Squadron at Debden the day before had lost a pilot and six aircraft to trigger-happy Spitfires. It was not long before there were 148 German bombers plus their fighter escorts over the capital and the deadly aerial dogfights commenced. The bombs fell inaccurately across central and south London. It was evident that the Germans were repeating their last massed attack of 7 September. 'In a little while all our squadrons were fighting,' recalled Churchill, 'and some had already begun to return for fuel.'[34]

Wing Commander Douglas-Jones, on seeing Churchill's expression added, 'The fighter stations will report immediately when any aircraft are available.'[35] By 1230 hours the surviving Germans were heading back across the Channel ready to refuel and bomb-up. As the clock ticked Churchill and Park could only hope that their pilots could refuel and get back in the air before the Luftwaffe reappeared. Churchill understood that despite his morale-boosting speeches, fighter pilots did not think in terms of victory but simply day-to-day survival.

The Germans returned in the early afternoon and once again a titanic struggle was fought high above southern England. This second attack involved nearly 600 aircraft. When Churchill enquired what reserves Fighter Command had held back, Park responded, 'Perhaps you'd better ask the Commander-in-Chief, sir.'[36] Churchill did just that and got onto the phone to Dowding demanding to know what was left. There was a very brief pause the other end of the line. 'I have no reserves, sir' replied the harassed Dowding, 'every aeroplane is in the sky.'[37] Churchill knew all they could do was hope for the best. It was, as always, a messy battle marked out by swirling vapour trails, but the RAF seemed to have the upper hand again.

The all-clear was eventually sounded at Uxbridge at 1550 hours and Churchill departed for Chequers to get some much-needed rest.

Just before he left, Park confessed to him that for the last 20 minutes 11 Group had been swamped with information and had totally lost control of the battle. The bombers, despite the RAF's best efforts, had still got through to London. It was a frank admission but Churchill needed to know just how touch and go the situation had been. Churchill was nonetheless clearly very relieved the Luftwaffe's onslaught had been thwarted once again. On the way out he patted Douglas-Jones on the shoulder and said 'Good show, old boy.'[38]

Once back at Chequers, Churchill was informed that Mussolini's troops had invaded Egypt. News regarding the Battle of Britain was much more heartening, as the RAF had shot down an estimated 185 aircraft for the loss of under 40.[39] No one knew it at the time, but 15 September 1940 was a decisive turning point. The bombing would continue on and off until 1944, but the threat of invasion began to rapidly subside. German efforts to overwhelm the RAF had failed and it was now too late in the year for Hitler to launch his invasion. He would have to postpone this to the spring or summer of 1941. Later Churchill found Inspector Thompson flagging outside his study. Churchill put his arm around him and said, 'We're going to win, you know.'[40]

It was understandably hushed up just how close Fighter Command had come to being overwhelmed. The following day the newspapers reported triumphantly that the Luftwaffe had sent 400 aircraft against London of which almost half had been shot down.[41] Mercifully for Dowding and Parks the skies over southern England remained relatively quiet on 16 September, with individual raiders clinging to the cloud cover. An ebullient Churchill told the House of Commons, 'Sunday's action was the most brilliant and fruitful of any fought up to that date by the fighters of the Royal Air Force.'[42]

Not long after, Churchill's spirits were further lifted by an Air Ministry intelligence assessment. It stated that the results of the Luftwaffe's bombing were 'remarkably small in proportion to the considerable effort expended'. It concluded that Hitler's aerial offensive was preoccupied 'with the primary objective of lowering morale'.[43] Thanks in part to Churchill's efforts they were singularly failing to grind the British down. When Churchill travelled up the Thames on 25 September to view the bomb damage he sat with his arm around Clementine. What he saw almost reduced him to tears and she leant forward to say a few reassuring words. After seeing the pounding that London had received

Churchill was more determined than ever not to abandon the capital. Increasingly he began to worry that a frustrated Hitler might resort to chemical warfare and deploy toxic gas. The RAF informed him that they had enough gas bombs to conduct up to five days of operations against German cities. However, if they mixed them in with high explosives they could keep it up for three weeks. Desperate times called for desperate measures, but Hitler stayed his hand and so did Churchill.

During October Churchill found himself drawn into a dispute amongst Fighter Command over how best to counter the German air raids. Park was reliant on Leigh-Mallory to protect his airfields while his fighters were intercepting the Luftwaffe. When Park's airfields were regularly bombed he understandably reacted angrily, which led Leigh-Mallory to question his whole strategy. The legendary pilot 'Tin-Legs' Douglas Bader, who commanded one of Leigh-Mallory's squadrons, argued that Park was wrong in sending up just squadron-sized units. Bader reasoned that massed squadrons or Big Wings were needed to smash the German bomber formations. Whilst this had its merits there were certain practicalities, not least of which was that it took time to gather the squadrons. For 12 Group who got longer warning this was not such a problem, but 11 Group on the front line did not have such a luxury. Leigh-Mallory's Big Wings were often intercepting the Germans at the extreme limit of their fighter cover with predictable results. Also, they regularly did not arrive until the Germans were heading for home.

Bader's adjutant Flight Lieutenant Peter MacDonald, who was a Member of Parliament, contacted the Air Ministry. They were not receptive and refused to discuss matters with a serving officer. MacDonald's next step was to invoke Parliamentary privilege and meet secretly with Churchill. The Prime Minister agreed to make enquires. Leigh-Mallory also discussed Bader's theories with his friend Air Vice-Marshal Sholto Douglas, who was deputy Chief of Air Staff. Bader was subsequently summoned to brief Sholto Douglas. The upshot of Churchill and Leigh-Mallory's intervention was that both Dowding and Park were made to look bad.

Despite Dowding being under enormous stress, Churchill seemed reluctant to alleviate it. For example, it is quite remarkable that he allowed the navy to meddle with Fighter Command. The RAF would never have dreamed of questioning naval strategy. Admiral T.S.V. Phillips, Vice Chief of the Naval Staff, on the other hand wrote to Churchill with a long 12-point assessment about countering the Luftwaffe's night bombing. Churchill obligingly forwarded it to Dowding. The Air Chief Marshal was furious that he had to waste time responding to this. He concluded his reply to Churchill by saying acidly, 'You will note that Admiral Phillips suggests no method of employment of fighters, but would merely revert to a Micawber-like method of ordering them to fly about and wait for something to turn up.'[44]

Through mid to late September RAF reconnaissance flights over the Channel ports showed that the Germans had dispersed two-thirds of their invasion barges. Then on 25 October Bletchley Park reported that the Luftwaffe had disbanded one of its liaison units assigned to the invasion forces. Six days later Churchill and his Defence Committee concluded the likelihood of an invasion was relatively remote. British anti-invasion forces were stood down. Churchill could not completely relax until the following summer when Hitler attacked the Soviet Union, proving his intuition was right.

'If the Prime Minister's announcement in the House of Commons is anything to go by, it appears we have been taking part in a famous battle,' wrote Squadron Leader Sandy Johnstone on 18 November 1940. He was amused because he felt the RAF had been fighting one long exhausting defensive action, rather than a distinct battle, since October 1939. Johnstone then added rather tartly, 'He has been telling the people that they owe it to the pilots of Fighter Command for not being invaded in September. It's nice to know we have been of service.'[45]

In the meantime, Churchill and Sinclair replaced Newall with Air Marshal Sir Charles Portal. Dowding's position was also shaky despite having conducted a highly successful defence. After the disputes over daytime tactics, he now found himself at loggerheads with the Air Ministry over how best to deal with the Luftwaffe's night bombing. Churchill appointed World War I fighter ace Wing Commander Gerald Maxwell to conduct a comprehensive review of Fighter Command. At the end of November 1940 Dowding was unceremoniously sacked and Park transferred. The suspicion was that it was at the behest of Churchill, even though the Prime Minister had championed him earlier in the year. 'Stuffy' Dowding observed drolly, 'There had been hanging over my head for a long time a whole shop-full of bowler hats.'[46] Even if he felt badly treated it was now time to contemplate his belated retirement.

Strategic Dilemma

Before Mussolini showed his hand and sided with Hitler, Churchill was able to recall many of the Mediterranean Fleet's warships to help protect the British Isles, or chase German raiders in the South Atlantic and Indian Ocean. Churchill understood that safeguarding British commerce was paramount. Before the war the country had 4,000 merchant ships and on any given day over half of these were plying their trade on the high seas.[1] Such was the power of Britain's mercantile marine that it carried half of the world's trade.[2] Keeping Britain and its far flung empire supplied inevitably put British merchant seamen right in the firing line of a developing trade war with Germany. The very first casualties, lost just two days after Britain's declaration of war, as Churchill well knew, had not been members of the armed forces but passengers and crew of a torpedoed liner.

Following the fall of France Churchill faced an awful strategic dilemma. Not only would he have to contend with Mussolini threatening British interests in the Mediterranean, there was also the thorny issue of the French fleet and the fate of the French empire. Traditionally France had safeguarded the western half of the Mediterranean, while Britain protected the eastern half. This arrangement had effectively neutralized the growing Italian Navy and had worked well despite the growing tensions during the 1930s. British naval bases at Gibraltar, Malta and Alexandria ensured Britain's lines of communication across the Mediterranean to the Suez Canal. When Mussolini entered the war, Churchill anticipated he would attack Malta or Egypt, but instead he conducted feeble invasions of southern France and Greece.

Nevertheless, Britain's position was precarious, since Mussolini had a large if poorly equipped army in Libya poised to attack Egypt. However, at sea Churchill had a number of advantages, principally aircraft carriers and radar, neither of which the Italian fleet possessed. The balance of power, though, could take a shift for the worse if the French Mediterranean fleet should fall into the hands of Hitler or Mussolini. Following the surrender of France, the country had effectively been divided in half, with the north under German occupation and the south a nominally neutral zone run from the town of Vichy by Marshal Pétain. Admiral Jean François Darlan was appointed Vichy's Minister of Marine. He knew if his warships went over to the British, then Hitler would almost certainly retaliate by invading Vichy. If Hitler did that, then there was nothing to stop him taking the warships berthed at Toulon. However, the French fleet's other main sanctuary was Mers-el-Kebir on the Algerian coast well out of the reach of the Germans.

Churchill ordered Admiral Andrew Cunningham and his warships at Alexandria and Admiral James Somerville commanding those at Gibraltar to sail to Mers-el-Kebir. Once there they were to demand the French either join the war effort, be interned in British ports, sail to the West Indies or be scuttled. When the Royal Navy arrived on 3 July 1940 the French made it clear they would not comply and a shooting match commenced. Still at their moorings the French fleet struggled to escape and suffered 1,648 casualties. Just a single battleship and a few destroyers managed to flee to Toulon. Pétain vowed never to cooperate with Churchill or the Free French leader General Charles de Gaulle. Churchill had violated Vichy's neutrality and as a result was forced to fight a series of campaigns against Vichy French colonial interests around the world. The naval war against Mussolini's fleet would ebb and flow, but serious blows were inflicted on the Italians at Taranto and Cape Matapan.

After serving as head of the Admiralty twice Churchill felt qualified to direct naval operations. Whether his admirals agreed with him was an entirely different matter. Initially Admiral Sir Charles Forbes, commanding the Home Fleet, although mindful that his anchorage at Scapa Flow was not safe from German attack, vetoed Churchill's move to the Clyde. This was on the grounds it would hamper deployment into the North Atlantic. Forbes found himself in trouble while Churchill was still at the Admiralty thanks to the loss of the *Royal Oak*. The following month two German battleships slipped his grasp as they headed home following an attack on the Northern Patrol. Then he failed to intercept any of the German ships supporting the invasion of Norway until after the event. As a result, Forbes was rather unkindly dubbed 'Wrong Way Charlie'.[3]

During the summer of 1940, when the threat of German invasion was at its height, Churchill naturally took an even keener interest in the fleet's disposition. Forbes' warships were ordered by Churchill and his War Cabinet to Rosyth on the Firth of Forth so they could more readily steam south. In particular Churchill wanted the bulk of the destroyers stationed in the Humber-Portsmouth area in order to defend the English Channel. This decision was opposed by Forbes because he knew it would come at a terrible price. Disastrously the Atlantic convoys were left largely unprotected and the U-boats caused havoc during a period their captains called the 'happy time'.[4] Forbes was frustrated because he assessed that Hitler's naval forces were simply too weak to force the Channel and that Churchill's redeployment was therefore unnecessary. 'I was certain the Hun would not invade us,'[5] said Forbes. This of course was true, but at the time no one else was prepared to take the chance. Churchill would not listen and Forbes was relieved of command. Admiral Sir John Tovey was brought back from the Mediterranean to take charge. However, Forbes was of course right. If the Luftwaffe could not gain air superiority over southern England, then the Germans would be hard pressed to stop the Royal Navy getting amongst their invasion forces. Even if they got ashore determined attacks by the navy and RAF would have then cut them off. Churchill was later to tell Forbes, perhaps a little disingenuously, he 'never believed that invasion was possible.'[6]

The threat of invasion had to be taken seriously and this called for desperate measures. Churchill looked back to the dramatic defeat of the Spanish Armada. Could 'Hell-Burners' once again save England? In 1588 English fire-ships had scattered the Armada gathered off Calais prior to the battle of Gravelines. He suggested the use of fire-ships to deny British ports to the Germans, though this idea was already being explored. Also, to compensate for the loss of French sea power in the western Mediterranean a new squadron was created at Gibraltar. Churchill was adamant that, should Spain support Hitler and take Gibraltar, then the Canary Islands would have to be seized to help maintain control of the entrance to the Mediterranean.

All was not well in the Atlantic either. 'Our food, our means of making war,' wrote Churchill, 'our life, all depended upon the passage of ships across the sea.'[7] Hitler's U-boats sought to strangle that lifeline. 'The only thing that ever really frightened me during the war was the U-boat peril,' admitted Churchill. 'I was even more anxious about this battle than I had been about the glorious air fight called the Battle of Britain.'[8] During the first seven months of the war the Germans sank 29 British merchant ships. This number rapidly escalated. Despite Churchill's convoy system, between June 1940 and February 1941 the U-boats ran amok in the Atlantic. By October 1940 they had claimed 270 Allied ships. It took Britain time to develop techniques and technologies with which to counter the marauding U-boat wolf packs.

Although Hitler's invasion of the Soviet Union in the summer of 1941 created a much-need ally and finally ended the threat of invasion, it resulted in more problems for the navy. Despite their ideological differences Churchill was determined to support Stalin at all costs.[9] This meant that Tovey's warships would have to escort supply convoys through the Norwegian and Barents Seas to Murmansk and Archangel. Both were within the Arctic Circle and in the case of Archangel it was iced up from winter to spring. Churchill, supported by Roosevelt, whose country had not yet entered the war, feared if they did not save the Red Army from complete oblivion then Stalin might sue for peace with Hitler. Not everyone agreed with this approach. General Alan Brooke, now Chief of the Imperial Staff, felt that all military supplies should go the British armed forces, but he was overruled. Once Hitler realized the scale of British and American support the Arctic convoys had to run the gauntlet of Luftwaffe and U-boat attacks launched from occupied Norway.

In the meantime, the British changed tactics in the Atlantic, which included the deployment of permanent escort groups to shepherd the convoys. Churchill extended escort coverage across the entire Atlantic by asking the Canadians to protect the western convoys. In gratitude for their help, he told the Canadian Prime Minister Mackenzie King during a visit to London, 'Canada is the linchpin of the English-speaking world ... which, spanning the oceans, brings the continents into their true relation.'[10] The Americans although still neutral also extended their Pan-American Security Zone almost as far as Iceland.

The convoys did not just bring vital war materials, fuel and food. MI5 in August 1941 was presented with one of its more unusual challenges, a box of 2,400 cigars newly arrived from Cuba. These had been presented to the British Ambassador in Havana in April by the Cuban tobacco industry as a gift for Churchill. Thanks to the war it took until the summer for them to reach Britain. Upon arrival they were carted off by MI5 who conducted a series of tests to determine whether they had been poisoned. They were finally handed over to the Prime Minister in September 1941, after mice who had been injected with samples from the cigars showed no ill effects. A second batch was generously provided by the subscribers of the Cuban newspaper *Bohemia*. In America Lord Halifax also found himself the recipient of cigars from a prominent New Yorker that were intended for Churchill. The Prime Minister, an avid cigar smoker since at least 1900, could not wait to get his hands on them. MI5's advice was that he ought not to risk smoking gifted cigars until the end of the war. Churchill not only smoked them, he also handed them out to the members of the Cabinet Defence Committee. Although MI5 confirmed they were not poisonous, Churchill with a mischievous glint in his eye told the Cabinet he was conducting an experiment on whether they were toxic or not.

Even when America entered the war in December 1941 it did not immediately have a positive impact on the Battle of the Atlantic. Within the first seven months of Roosevelt joining the Allies the U-boats sank almost 400 American ships. This included 40 attacks way to the south off Florida.[11] Although most of these took place on Florida's Atlantic coast and in the Straits of Florida some occurred in the Gulf of Mexico. A number of these attacks were so audacious that crowds gathered on the shore to witness the fiery destruction.

Losses during the Battle of the Atlantic were such that Churchill became very sensitive about how they were reported by the press. For example, in early 1942 he convinced himself that cartoonist Philip Zec, who had Russian parents, was a fifth columnist. Zec, employed by the *Daily Mirror*, produced a cartoon depicting an exhausted merchant seaman desperately holding on to some wreckage from a ship. The implication was the vessel had been sunk by a U-boat. The caption read 'The price of petrol has been increased by one penny – Official.'[12] Churchill was outraged by the suggestion that oil companies were profiting from the struggle in the Atlantic. He also thought it was a deliberate attempt to undermine morale. Zec claimed he had actually meant it to be a warning about wasting precious fuel in the light of the sacrifices being made to get it to Britain. Churchill was unconvinced and ordered MI5 to look into Zec's background and his political leanings. They found nothing but the unfortunate cartoonist was publicly branded a traitor.

Tovey incurred Churchill's displeasure on 9 March 1942, when the carrier *Victorious* failed to sink or damage the German battleship *Tirpitz* operating from Trondheim. Churchill was indignant that Japanese aircraft had sunk the *Prince of Wales* and *Repulse* with such ease and yet Tovey's planes failed to even hit their target. Churchill's insistence that the Arctic convoys be maintained into the summer of 1942 during the continuous daylight hours caused Tovey to protest to Admiral Pound, Commander-in-Chief of the Royal Navy. Tovey warned that a tragedy was looming and Pound passed this on to Churchill. The Prime Minister did not heed this warning. However, in truth Churchill was forced to bow to continuous pressure from Stalin. By this point Hitler's troops had overrun huge swathes of the Soviet Union including Ukraine, the Crimea and the Caucasus. Churchill had responded to Stalin's pleas with reassurances, 'We are resolved to fight our way through to you with the maximum amount of war materials.'[13]

This was easier said than done with the German fleet loitering in the shelter of the Norwegian fjords. It was only the arrival of a US Navy task force at Scapa Flow that helped tip the balance. At the end of May 1942 Churchill pushed through the largest Arctic convoy to date, PQ16. Although the German surface ships kept out of the way, the Luftwaffe and U-boats between them sank seven ships. This was just a taste of things to come. Tovey's anticipated tragedy occurred in July 1942 involving the even-bigger convoy PQ17. Under threat of attack it was ordered to scatter and was picked off piecemeal by the merciless U-boats and Luftwaffe. Between them they accounted for 24 ships, which sank with 153 crew, 99,316 tons of supplies, plus 3,350 vehicles, 430 tanks and 210 aircraft. This caused Tovey to lament 'WC as Prime Minister is magnificent and unique, but as a strategist and tactician he is liable to be most dangerous.'[14] General Alan Brooke and Air Chief Marshal Portal were also vexed that equipment denied to them was now at the bottom of the sea. Unlike Churchill, neither fully appreciated just how essential it was to keep the Soviet Union in the war. 'We kept on supplying tanks and aeroplanes that could ill be spared,' grumbled Brooke 'and in doing so suffered the heaviest losses in shipping ... We received nothing in return except abuse.'[15]

Not surprisingly, after PQ17 Churchill found himself under pressure from his admirals to postpone any further convoys until winter darkness could provide some cover. Churchill was against this knowing full well Stalin would be furious. Instead, he suggested to Tovey that he use his heavier warships supported by aircraft carriers to fight their way through. The Royal Navy simply could not spare the resources as this was at a time when they were fighting the Battle of the Atlantic and pushing relief convoys through to a very beleaguered Malta. Likewise, the US Navy had its hands full in the Pacific. Reluctantly Churchill acquiesced and signalled Stalin, 'It is therefore with the greatest regret that we have reached the conclusion that to attempt to run the next convoy, PQ18, would bring no benefit to you.'[16] He then promptly changed his mind when he got Stalin's response, which was the usual mix of bullying and moral blackmail. After that Churchill put his foot down.

Churchill soon learned that Stalin was not grateful for the supplies nor did he care for the welfare of merchant sailors who risked their lives to deliver them. The rudimentary hospital at Murmansk was unable to cope with the influx of wounded civilians caused by the Luftwaffe's bombing and frost-bitten seamen coming off the merchant ships. Eventually the Soviet authorities reluctantly gave permission for a British naval hospital at Vaenga. Churchill was flabbergasted in September 1942 when he was informed the Soviets had instructed its staff to pack up and go home. 'I hope you will give me some solid reason,' wrote Churchill tersely to Vyacheslav Molotov, the Soviet Foreign Minister, 'which I can give should the matter be raised in Parliament, as it very likely will be.'[17] The hospital stayed open.

Although the Arctic convoys were resumed in early 1943 they were once again postponed, much to the fury of Stalin who was preparing for his summer offensive at Kursk. However, by that stage Churchill and Roosevelt had delivered over two million tons of stores and thousands of aircraft, tanks and lorries. The Soviet Union's lack of gratitude was to be brought to the fore when the American Ambassador to Moscow called Stalin's bluff. Threatened with losing American support, Stalin ensured the Soviet press was full of gushing stories about Allied help; however, he did not stop brow-beating Churchill.

Across the Atlantic shipping losses were growing thanks to the US Navy's failure to introduce a convoy system off America's east coast. Furthermore, the command and control of the US Army Air Force on the east coast was fragmented and did not come under the US Navy. The 'air gap' south of Greenland was also an area where heavy losses were occurring. At the height of the Battle of the Atlantic, Churchill was naturally dismayed by reports that 200 ships a month were being sunk.[18] Although the revised convoy system worked quite well, they still lost 654 vessels during the war. Ships sailing alone or with coastal convoys were especially vulnerable. Churchill was unhappy to learn in 1942 that 840 vessels not in convoys had been sunk. This compared to 299 with convoys that same year, many of which were stragglers who could not keep up and the convoys could not slow down.[19]

In order to improve RAF Coastal Command's capabilities Tovey wanted it strengthened and issued with better long-range aircraft. Unfortunately for Tovey, Churchill, Lord Cherwell his chief scientific officer and Air Chief Marshal Sir Arthur Harris, commanding Bomber Command, were more preoccupied by the bomber offensive against Germany. Although Churchill was anxious about the war in the Atlantic, at the same time he remained loath to divert resources from Harris. He was also critical of Coastal Command, accusing them of not looking after the aircraft they had. Admiral Pound, though, circumvented Churchill by approaching Air Chief Marshal Portal, Chief of the Air Staff, and getting his approval for the RAF shouldering more of the burden of the Atlantic air battle.

What was needed was a joint command with a supreme commander to oversee the Atlantic battle. This was indeed what Sir Stafford Cripps, now Minister of Aircraft Production, suggested to Churchill. Even though Admiral Somerville was recommended for the role, Albert Alexander, First Lord of the Admiralty was not keen on the grounds it would undercut the Royal Navy's authority. When the Americans made a similar suggestion, Pound told Churchill he was firmly against the idea. Churchill was not receptive to Cripps, because the pair had fallen out over the strategic direction of the war. Cripps had pointedly resigned from the War Cabinet in November 1942. Churchill was not only distracted by the bomber offensive, but also Stalin's constant demands for supplies to be shipped in by the Arctic convoys.

In the South Atlantic U-boat attacks ironically worked in the Allies' favour. Churchill's concerns over Brazil's allegiances were allayed in August 1942. Under President Vargas the country tried to stay neutral, but the sinking of Brazilian merchant ships by U-boats forced him to declare war on Germany and Italy, though not Japan. Vargas, under pressure from Roosevelt, had already acted against German espionage activities that included spying on Allied convoys. Vargas hoped to build up a large carrier fleet, but he simply did not have the men to crew it. The Brazilian Navy's main contribution was to escort convoys and conduct anti-submarine patrols in the South Atlantic.

For Churchill, the turning point in the Atlantic finally came in the spring of 1943, when the navy's escort carriers and Coastal Command's long-range bombers were able to offer convoys protection south of Iceland. 'In March and April 1943 twenty-seven U-boats were destroyed in the Atlantic alone, more than half by air attack,' recorded Churchill.[20] The following month he noted there was a sharp increase, 'In May alone forty U-boats perished in the Atlantic.'[21] This forced Hitler to withdraw them from the North Atlantic. Operations continued in the South Atlantic and Indian Ocean, but there were fewer ships to be hunted there. In July 1943, 37 U-boats were sunk in the South Atlantic, the majority of which were again due to air attacks. Churchill concluded with some relief 'the Atlantic supply line was safe'.[22] Nonetheless, this did not stop him from harassing Alexander and Pound every time he was presented with more shipping losses. Through 1943 and 1944 Churchill then turned his attention to the build up of forces necessary to be ready to open the Second Front. This meant that his admirals got no respite.

Old Foes

Shortly after taking up office in Downing Street, Churchill found that neutral Eire was an unwanted strategic distraction. He was particularly alarmed by the prospect of it becoming 'England's back door'. Since partition Ireland had remained a troubled island. During the early and mid-1930s there was sporadic violence in British-ruled Northern Ireland between the Catholics and Protestants. In the Irish Free State, Prime Minister Éamon de Valera and his Fianna Fáil republican government came to power in March 1932. They very slowly moved to distance themselves from Britain. De Valera avoided declaring Ireland a full republic for fear of antagonizing the British government. Four years later in the wake of the abdication of King Edward VIII he ceased acknowledging the British monarchy as full head of state. Instead, it was only recognized by external association. The Free State became known simply as Ireland or Eire, though the British still insisted on calling it Southern Ireland.

In response MI5 was tasked with monitoring Irish political machinations. A key concern was growing German contact. The Royal Ulster Constabulary was employed to cultivate intelligence contacts south of the border and ultimately MI5 oversaw these clandestine operations. Eire was now deemed a foreign country and MI6 was also tasked with intelligence collection. Churchill became obsessed with the enemy within, be they IRA terrorists, hostile foreign aliens hiding amongst the tens of thousands of refugees in Britain or his long-held bugbear – Communist agitators. Even before the outbreak of war Hitler had been cultivating links with the IRA, which had been banned in Eire in 1936. Prime Minister de Valera strenuously denied this, but intelligence showed that he was lying.

Germany had meddled in Ireland before, during World War I. For the Easter Rising it had tried to supply the Republicans with 20,000 rifles,[1] enough for two divisions of men, but the shipment had been successfully intercepted by the Royal Navy. Although at the time the IRA did not have the manpower for such a quantity of firearms, these could have fuelled a much wider rebellion. The Germans had also considered the possibility of raising an Irish Republican brigade from prisoners captured on the Western Front to join the IRA, but this never came to fruition. Roger Casement, who was supposed to have recruited this rebel unit, arrived in Ireland by U-boat only to be caught and executed for treason.

Tom Barry, the IRA's Chief of Staff, travelled to Germany in early 1937 to discuss possible cooperation should war break out. German agent Oscar Pfaus arrived in Dublin in February 1939 and met with General Eoin O'Duffy, the head of Ireland's fascist Blueshirts. He also met members of the IRA who agreed to send a representative to Germany to discuss obtaining weapons. Jim O'Donovan sailed to Hamburg, but the meeting did not go well and he returned empty handed. Nonetheless, information coming across de Valera's desk convinced him that Sean McBride, the IRA's Director of Intelligence, was more interested in assisting Hitler than furthering the cause of Irish reunification.

The fractious IRA lacked direction and was split between three main groups with different agendas. There were those who did not want to antagonize the Irish and British authorities, those who favoured a guerrilla war against Ulster and those who wanted to conduct a bombing campaign in mainland Britain. The latter faction prevailed and by mid-1939 there had been 72 IRA attacks in England. When the King and Queen visited America that June there were serious concerns that the IRA, known to be operating in Detroit and Buffalo, might try to assassinate them.[2] This was something that Roosevelt and the FBI were understandably keen to avoid. Instead, in August 1939 the IRA targeted the city of Coventry, killing five and injuring 51 when a bomb was detonated in a busy high street. These outrages did not go unpunished and in early 1940 Peter Barnes and Patrick McCormick were hanged for their involvement in the Coventry bombing. This IRA mainland campaign helped convince Churchill and his new Cabinet that the 'backdoor' threat to Britain was very real.

Despite being part of the British Commonwealth de Valera declared his country neutral at the outbreak of World War II. Churchill was infuriated by Eire's continual refusal to stand shoulder to shoulder with Britain in its hour of need. Luckily for him, Anthony Eden got on well with de Valera. 'I liked him personally and we were often of the same mind on international problems,' wrote Eden, 'always excluding, of course, the six counties of Ulster.'[3] It was Eden who secured official British diplomatic representation in Dublin with the appointment of Sir John Maffey. He was designated a 'Representative' rather than an ambassador on the grounds that Eire was still technically a Commonwealth member. De Valera also agree to Maffey being supported by a military attaché, a post initially filled by Major Pryce followed by Brigadier Edmund Wodehouse.

Churchill convinced himself that Eire was violating its dominion status. 'Legally I believe they are at war,' he remarked to Lord Halifax, 'but sulking.'[4] Regardless of the legal niceties Hitler ordered that Irish neutrality be honoured. Even so, U-boat commanders found it difficult to differentiate between ships registered in the south and the north. As a result, a number of mishaps occurred. In light of the German leader's complete disregard for the neutrality of Belgium, Denmark, the Netherlands and Norway, Churchill could not understand de Valera's stance.

Crucially de Valera's policy denied Churchill renewed use of Berehaven, Lough Swilly and Queenstown, which had remained Royal Navy bases until 1938. They had been retained as part of the Anglo-Irish Treaty of 1921. However, during the 1930s Britain and Eire were locked in a trade war and part of the settlement was relinquishing the ports to Dublin. These had helped Britain guard the approaches to St George's Channel and the North Channel leading into the Irish Sea. Furthermore, in the south Berehaven and Queenstown acted as fuelling stations for British destroyers patrolling the Atlantic. In the north, Lough Swilly screened the Clyde and Mersey. There were those, including Churchill, who felt that surrendering control of the ports at a time of growing international tension was a strategic disaster. 'I remember the looks of incredulity, the mockery, derision and laughter I had to encounter on every side,' Churchill later recalled, 'when I said,

that Mr de Valera might declare Ireland neutral.'⁵ He characterized
the decision as 'a major injury to British national life and safety', and
an 'improvident example of appeasement'.⁶ He viewed it as part of a
policy trend and he did not like it. 'A more feckless act can hardly be
imagined,'⁷ Churchill concluded.

At the time Prime Minister Chamberlain thought otherwise and the
Admiralty had not made any strong objections. Chamberlain believed
it would generate goodwill and that de Valera might agree in the event
of war in Europe to building munition factories in Eire safe from enemy
air attack. He was wrong on both counts. 'Small wonder that the seizure
of the ports by force should have been considered by the Cabinet in
October 1939,' observed Anthony Eden, 'and only abandoned with
reluctance by Mr. Churchill, as First Lord of the Admiralty.'⁸ Sir Charles
Wilson later recalled how Churchill 'had told Neville Chamberlain that
he would never ask him to use force against Southern Ireland unless
the safety of England was at stake'.⁹ In the coming months that very
much seemed to be the case. By 1940 the Admiralty was alarmed at the
prospect of U-boats being resupplied on Eire's long Atlantic coast and
the country being used as a centre for German intelligence gathering
against the Royal Navy.

Although volunteers from both north and south of the Irish border
rallied to the British armed forces, de Valera's government censored all
news regarding the war. He wanted nothing that might evoke sympathy
for Britain's plight. Censorship of news reels included a ban on images
of Churchill, Hitler and Mussolini. Likewise, any references to fifth
columnists, sabotage or refugees were removed. Although de Valera
hated the British, he was well aware that the IRA constituted a threat
to his government. When they raided the Irish Army's weapons depot
at Phoenix Park in January 1940 he instructed the police to round up
every IRA supporter they could lay their hands on and introduced
internment without trial. The following month Austrian spy Ernst
Weber-Drohl arrived in Dublin and made contact with the IRA. He
urged them to concentrate on attacking British military rather than
civilian targets. Shortly after, he was arrested and interned by the Irish
authorities.

Just five days before Churchill took up residence in Downing Street,
German agent Hermann Görtz parachuted into County Meath to
the west of Dublin. He was already well known to MI5. He had been

arrested in Britain in the 1930s for spying on the RAF and jailed for four years. During his time in Maidstone prison he became acquainted with members of the IRA. He had been deported in February 1939, but was now back with a new mission to help the IRA plan attacks in Northern Ireland. He was also to discuss Operation *Kathleen*, an IRA-supported German invasion of Ireland. Görtz's presence was compromised on 7 May 1940 when the IRA tried to capture the courier bearing correspondence to Sir John Maffey. A gun battle followed with the police and de Valera ordered another clampdown. Several weeks later Irish police raided a known safe house. They seized documents relating to *Kathleen*, £20,000, Görtz's uniform and his parachute. Görtz, though, managed to remain on the run for 18 months.

MI6 sent Charles Tegart, a veteran Anglo-Irish intelligence officer, to Dublin in May 1940 to establish if Hitler had gained a foothold. A major concern was whether the German Legation in Dublin was being used as a hub for espionage and subversion. Tegart was soon sending back highly alarming and exaggerated reports that German U-boats had delivered 2,000 agents to join the IRA, who were planning for a German invasion of western Britain.[10] The last thing Churchill wanted was a two-front war, but once Hitler was master of the Continent it was not something he could ignore.

The Joint Intelligence Committee warned Churchill that the IRA could raise 30,000 men, which posed a threat to Dublin, Belfast and London. Churchill was aware that numbers of Irish volunteers had gained valuable combat experience during the Spanish Civil War fighting on both sides. Members of the IRA served with the Republic's international brigades under Frank Ryan. Many of them preferred to fight alongside the American recruits rather than the British. On the Nationalist side the Blueshirts served with General O'Duffy. He headed the Irish Civic Guards until removed from his post by de Valera. O'Duffy's men hardly covered themselves in glory, being involved in a fatal friendly fire incident with other Nationalist troops. However, on another occasion they had supported German panzers from the Condor Legion fighting alongside the Nationalists. De Valera's Irish Army at its peak only numbered 40,000 and even with the support of the Irish police would have been hard pressed to contain a full-blown IRA insurrection. Although de Valera had no intention of siding with Churchill, if he had it would have sparked another civil war.

Churchill's solution as usual was a military one. He ordered plans be drawn up for a pre-emptive operation against Eire using recently arrived Canadian troops. This thankless task fell to Major-General Sir Hubert Huddleston who was in command in Northern Ireland. General Montgomery, who was in southern England rebuilding the 3rd Infantry Division, had been working on plans for the seizure of the Azores or the Cape Verde Islands. These were then superseded by orders to prepare for the occupation of Cork and Queenstown. 'I had already fought the southern Irish once, in 1921 and 1922,' noted Montgomery 'and it looked as if this renewed contest might be quite a party – with only one division.'[11] Churchill knew full well that to occupy Eire's ports would require resources he could not spare. Plus, such action would have pushed de Valera into Hitler's arms. General Hugo MacNeill of the Irish Army met with German officials in Dublin to request that, in the event of an invasion by Churchill, Germany provide them with weapons.

Churchill tried to sway de Valera in late June 1940 by reluctantly accepting that, if Eire declared war on Germany and Italy, the British government would recognize the principle of a united Ireland. Malcolm MacDonald, Churchill's envoy, noted, 'I repeated that the establishment of a united Ireland was an integral part of our plan, from which there would be no turning back.'[12] However, it was a hollow offer, especially as Ulster's leaders were not consulted over this proposal. After much horse trading de Valera rejected it on the grounds that the government in Northern Ireland would never sign up to it and that the British would renege on the agreement. Churchill was privately relieved, because it could have taken force to push Ulster into union with the rest of Ireland. Furthermore, de Valera said that there was no guarantee that a united Ireland would join the war. His only concession was to agree to the holding of staff talks with Britain for the mutual defence of Ireland against a German invasion. 'Eire had declared itself neutral, wished to be accepted as such,' said Eden with some irritation, 'and yet asked for a consignment of arms of various kinds at a cut rate.'[13] Churchill was of the opinion that Eire should not receive any weapons, even anti-aircraft guns, until it entered the war.

Churchill's fears of a German invasion of Eire were not unfounded. Hitler saw it as a way to either support an assault on Britain or the Soviet Union. If he held Ireland, then he could strangle Britain's transatlantic supply lines. When Hitler held talks with the German Navy in December 1940 they pointed out, unless air superiority was achieved, they did not have the strength to support an attack on Britain, let alone Ireland. Undeterred he then briefly considered invading Ireland by air.

To repel a German attack on Britain or Ireland Churchill turned to his old tried and tested weapon, poison gas. A draft directive was drawn up on 24 June 1940 for the commander of the RAF in Northern Ireland. Gas or high explosives would be flown from the mainland for use against invading German troops and any IRA irregulars supporting them. Air crews were warned to avoid incurring civilian casualties south of the border. In light of the RAF only having 12 fighters and 20 light bombers deployed in Northern Ireland they could hardly be expected to achieve much. In the event of the Germans invading Britain, General Brooke said he 'had every intention of using sprayed mustard gas on the beaches'.[14]

Churchill sent Anthony Eden to Northern Ireland in late July 1940 to review its defences and to hold talks with Major-General Huddleston, who was about to be replaced. At the same time General Brooke was despatched to Scotland to see Lieutenant-General Sir Robert Carrington. He discovered the three divisions stationed there were barely capable of defending the British Isles, never mind intervening in Ireland. After visiting the 46th Division, Brooke noted with alarm in his diary, 'Found it in a lamentably backward state of training, barely fit to do platoon training and deficient of officers.'[15] During his time there he only saw a single brigade which showed any promise. Looking across the North Sea towards German-occupied Norway the situation was far from encouraging.

Eden and Brooke's reports to Churchill did little to reassure him that the army could fend off a two- or even three-pronged attack by Hitler. He was flabbergasted when he was informed it would take almost two weeks to ship 15,000 men from the Clyde to Belfast in the event of an emergency. This was a journey that should take a matter of hours not days. In light of the huge numbers of troops shipped from Dunkirk this did not make sense. His suggestion to speed up the process was to pre-position their heavy equipment in advance, but this was not practical as it would have tied up scarce resources. He also demanded that the timetable be reviewed, instructing, 'I am not prepared to approve the transfer of the division until this enquiry has been made.'[16]

Northern Ireland and Eire were not immune to the Blitz pounding British cities. The Luftwaffe bombed Belfast on the night of 13/14 August 1940, hitting the Short's bomber factory. The city endured four more raids the following year, which caused several thousand casualties. Dublin also suffered several accidental attacks during 1940 and 1941. The Luftwaffe conducted maritime reconnaissance flights via Eire for the benefit of the U-boats. 'When the Germans held Brest and could fly over Southern Ireland to the mouths of the Mersey and the Clyde,' wrote Sir Charles Wilson, 'they could report to their submarines and then go on to Norway.'[17] Churchill was very unhappy about this and later told Wilson, 'Our food supply was balanced on a knife-edge.'[18]

During 1940 Churchill remained worried that U-boats were lurking along the Irish coast and instructed MI6 to improve its intelligence operations in Dublin. In response MI6 sent businessman Sidney Cotton to search for U-boats along the creeks and inlets of western Eire. Through the summer of 1940 and into the following year intelligence confirmed that the Germans continued to land agents in Eire, though with very mixed results. On 5 November 1940 Churchill bemoaned the Irish problem in the House of Commons, saying, 'The fact that we cannot use the south and west coasts of Ireland to refuel our flotillas and aircraft ... is a most heavy and grievous burden.'[19]

Although de Valera refused to coordinate intelligence sharing, Churchill instructed that Dublin be tipped off about Hitler's activities. By mid-February 1941 Churchill had largely abandoned the idea of sending a division to Northern Ireland. However, he still insisted that planners figure out how to get it there in less than a week. Then in April 1941 the Australian Prime Minister, Sir Robert Menzies, was sent to mediate with de Valera and the Prime Minister of Northern Ireland, John M. Andrews, in an effort to get Eire to support the Allies. A despondent Menzies reported back to Churchill that the future of Ireland remained intractable and that de Valera would not end his neutrality. Even when America entered the war, de Valera, who held American citizenship, was still not moved to join the Allied cause. On 8 December 1941, the very day after the Japanese bombed Pearl Harbor, Churchill appealed to him to declare for the Allies. The Irish leader once more refused. Churchill then sent Lord Cranborne on a secret mission to Eire to garner help, but like Malcolm MacDonald before him, de Valera rejected this approach.

Although the possibility of Germany invading Britain greatly receded after Hitler attacked the Soviet Union in June 1941, the threat remained. Despite suffering terrible casualties, the German airborne invasion of Crete that May had shown just how audacious Hitler could be. In the event of Hitler crossing the English Channel the British Chiefs of Staff discussed in mid-January 1942 occupying Eire. To prevent Hitler from launching diversionary attacks from there, plans were formulated for British troops based in Ulster, now under Major-General Vivian Majendie, to occupy Dublin and the Irish ports. Majendie, though, like Huddleston before him, had insufficient forces for such an enterprise.

While there were several divisional headquarters in Northern Ireland, there was only a single dedicated Irish combat command. The recently formed 38th (Irish) Brigade consisted of the Irish regiments from Ulster. The Royal Ulster Rifles also had several home defence battalions in Northern Ireland. These troops were hardly adequate for invading the south and would have needed considerabe reinforcing. Churchill hoped that the mere suggestion of military action would bully the recalcitrant de Valera into a change of heart. It was unclear if the Irish Army would resist, but the IRA were another matter. The occupation of Eire would most likely have sparked a renewed bombing campaign. Furthermore, containing Irish unrest would have required large numbers of troops and mass internment. Churchill fortunately wavered on the side of caution when faced with the reality of what was being proposed. He knew that Roosevelt would be incensed if Britain invaded its neutral neighbour. Nor would the President ever countenance the use of American troops, based in Northern Ireland, for such an operation.

De Valera was not blind to the threats he faced. In early February 1942 he warned his people that their country was in danger of attack by one or both belligerents. He also added rather fancifully 'we should not be satisfied until we have 250,000 men trained as soldiers'.[20] Leaders of the Irish opposition in Dublin warned him that he was risking turning their country into a 'German Gibraltar in the Atlantic'.[21] To avoid this, it was suggested he should make a deal with Churchill and Roosevelt, but he steadfastly refused to be diverted from his policy of neutrality. While remaining so, Eire suffered many of the hardships as mainland Britain thanks to the Battle of the Atlantic. 'The same British convoys brought supplies to Eire, and this not unnaturally rankled,' noted Anthony Eden, 'in particular with the Royal Navy.'[22] Eire was far from self-sufficient and its merchant marine was small. This meant the rationing of foodstuffs, fodder, petrol and other fuels. Train services were reduced and many motorists stopped using their cars.

By this stage Churchill, facing severe problems in North Africa and the Far East, considered Eire to be little more than an ongoing nuisance. When the Allies began to turn the tide during the second half of 1942 the 38th (Irish) Brigade was sent to fight in Tunisia, thereby allaying Dublin's fears of a possible British military action. Furthermore, behind the scenes developing close cooperation between MI5 and the Dublin authorities ensured that Churchill's concerns over German espionage activity were addressed. Likewise, the Irish began to unofficially cooperate with the Royal Navy, though this never really compensated for the loss of the Irish ports, especially Berehaven.

Despite winning the Battle of the Atlantic, to Churchill and the Admiralty's displeasure U-boats continued to lurk in the waters off Eire even after D-Day. Just nine days before Field Marshal Montgomery launched his daring attempt to capture Arnhem, on 8 September 1944 a U-boat sank the SS *Empire Heritage* off Malin Head. This vessel, as well as fuel oil, was carrying replacement Sherman tanks for the Allied armoured divisions fighting in Europe. Instead, they ended up scattered across the seabed. Churchill continued to put pressure on the Irish to fully cooperate throughout the war, but they never bent to his will.

Although 38,544[23] from Eire, including 5,000 from the Irish Army, volunteered to join the British armed forces Churchill still felt that Ireland betrayed Britain. Churchill the historian should have known better, but Churchill the strategist was trying to fight a global war and had desperately wanted Eire's help. Remarkably though the numbers volunteering either side of the Irish border were almost identical.[24] When going home on leave, to prevent those from the south being interned they always changed back into civilian clothing. Fortunately for Churchill, de Valera turned a blind eye to this diplomatic fudge. Despite their differences Churchill's old foes actually shed blood for him. For that he should have been grateful.

Hitting Back

Although Churchill effectively commenced the Allied strategic bomber campaign in late August 1940 when he authorized the attack on Berlin, it had actually started much earlier in the year. On 15 May 1940, just five days after he replaced Chamberlain, the RAF recorded 'the War Cabinet authorized Bomber Command to attack East of the Rhine, and that night 99 bombers were dispatched to attack oil and railway targets in the Ruhr. ... Thus began the Bomber Command strategic air offensive against Germany.'[1] The Ruhr was to become a major battle area.

Churchill also appreciated something needed to be done to counter the threat of Mussolini siding with Hitler. To that end, on 2 June 1940, he wrote to the Secretary of State for Air and the Chief of the Air Staff ordering bombers to be sent to southern France. This resulted in the RAF's Haddock Force, consisting of Wellington bombers, being deployed to Le Vallon and Salon airfields near Marseilles. Its advance guard arrived on 7 June just three days before Italy declared war on the Allies. In the event the local French authorities steadfastly refused to let the bombers take off for fear of reprisals by the Italians, even after the intervention of Churchill and Premier Reynaud. Instead, bombers flew from Britain to attack Genoa and Turin.

Just four days after the great air battle over southern England, which Churchill had witnessed from RAF Uxbridge, on 19 September Hitler instructed his invasion fleet to be dispersed. Bomber Command took the credit for this. Churchill was not entirely convinced after he saw reconnaissance imagery of the Channel ports. 'What struck me about these photographs was the apparent inability of the bombers to hit very large masses of barges,'[2] he complained to Sir Archibald Sinclair on 23 September. What of course the photos did not show was shockwave damage which had made many of the barges unseaworthy. Bomber Command had pounded them night after night, knowing full well if Fighter Command were defeated it would be up to them to prevent invasion. These attacks had started in July 1940 before the Battle of Britain gathered pace. They were conducted at night and the Channel ports were considered such easy targets that Bomber Command began to use the missions for operational training purposes.

Churchill had experienced enough wars and had a firm-enough grasp on grand strategy to know that Bomber Command were not war winners on their own. After World War I he had concluded that a strategic bombing force could not win a war by simply terrorizing an enemy population. Rather he felt that precision bombing would be far more valuable. Although the application of air power as a policing tool had been successful in Iraq, Aden and the North-West Frontier, the bombing had largely been indiscriminate. These operations were conducted by fighter-bombers rather than dedicated bombers. The Great Depression of 1929 and Churchill's term as Chancellor of the Exchequer had greatly slowed the RAF's expansion plans.

From the start Bomber Command was Fighter Command's poorer cousin in terms of resources. Although the requirement for three new heavy bomber types had arisen in the mid-1930s, none were operational until 1941. This meant Bomber Command started the war with woefully inadequate aircraft, such as the Hampden and the Whitley. In contrast Fighter Command was re-quipped with the brand-new Hurricane and Spitfire just in time, enabling it to abandon its old biplanes.

Air Chief Marshal Sir Charles Portal replaced Sir Cyril Newall as Chief of the Air Staff on 25 October 1940, and Portal's place as Air Officer Commanding-in-Chief Bomber Command was taken by Air Marshal Sir Richard Peirse. Bomber Command was based in England with Peirse's headquarters to the west of London at RAF High Wycombe. His subordinate commands consisted of 2 Group headquarters at Huntingdon, 3 Group at Exning, 4 Group at York, 5 Group at Grantham and 6 Group at Abingdon. Night bombing had become the pattern by the autumn of 1940, though daylight raids against land targets continued.

The problem that Churchill had was that in 1940 Bomber Command was the only tool available with which to hit back at Hitler. The United States Army Air Force would not arrive until 1942 so until then Bomber Command's pilots had to go it alone. Peirse was vexed that he had lost many squadrons to the Middle East and Coastal Commands and that his forces had been subordinated to the navy's campaign to hunt down Hitler's warships. The latter RAF command started in 1939 when Churchill was First Sea Lord to help protect shipping. Until Air Chief Marshal Arthur Harris's arrival in February 1942 bombing policy was overseen by Churchill. His hot and cold approach to supporting the bomber campaign against Germany would exasperate the Air Staff, who in turn tried to underpin their strategy with scientific theory.

'We have seen what inconvenience the attack on the British civilian population has caused us,' Churchill told the Air Ministry on 2 November 1940, 'and there is no reason why the enemy should be freed from all such embarrassments.'[3] The Luftwaffe's raid on Coventry on the night of 14–15 November 1940 caused uproar and Churchill and the War Cabinet found themselves under pressure to retaliate in kind. However, Portal refrained from area bombing and persisted with precision bombing on industrial targets. Between October until early March oil installations were a key priority, although attacks on the Germans' invasion barges continued into the winter. Churchill continued to push for the expansion of Bomber Command. At the end of the year he wrote to Lord Beaverbrook, 'I am deeply concerned at the stagnant condition of our bomber force.'[4]

Air Vice-Marshal Donald Stevenson's aggressive 2 Group, as well as squadrons from the other groups, conducted daylight operations throughout 1941 and 1942. They bombed from a low level and suffered a missing rate of five per cent per sortie. Accuracy by day and night remained a constant problem. Stevenson's group suffered particularly heavy losses conducting anti-shipping attacks over the Channel. When one of his men pointed out that morale was suffering as a result, Stevenson flew into a rage crying, 'Churchill wants it!'[5] Churchill continued to back Bomber Command's efforts, stating on the radio at the end of June 1941, 'we shall bomb Germany by day as well as by night in ever increasing measure ... This is not a threat only, it is a statement.'[6] His comments were clearly intended for German ears as much as British ones. Stevenson's crews did not miss their ruthless commander when he was posted to the Far East in December 1941.

Churchill was dismayed to learn from the Butt Report in August 1941 that a third of the bombers never found their primary target and only a third of those remaining got to within five miles of their target. David Bensusan-Butt, a member of the War Cabinet staff, had come to this conclusion after closely analysing over 630 photo-reconnaissance images of Bomber Command's target areas. The implications for civilian casualties were horrific. 'It is an awful thought that perhaps three quarters of our bombs go astray,' observed Churchill.[7]

The Air Staff, anxious that they should not lose Churchill's full support, presented him with a plan on 25 September 1941 for massive area attacks that would be conducted once their greatly expanded force became available. Portal argued that 4,000 bombers, targeting 43 cities with populations of over 100,000, could bring Germany to her knees within six months. It was a remarkable claim that Germany could be bombed into surrendering, based on nothing more than obscene mathematical modelling. Churchill may have ruefully recalled a speech he had given in the House of Commons on 14 March 1933 on the misuse of air power. He had said any country that 'threw its bombs upon cities so as to kill as many women and children as possible ... had committed the greatest crime'.[8]

Churchill was simply not convinced by Portal and responded two days later 'it is very disputable whether bombing by itself will be a decisive factor in the present war. ... The most we can say is that it will be a heavy and I trust seriously increasing annoyance.'[9] Portal was furious that his brave crews were seen as causing little more than an 'annoyance' to the enemy. He called Churchill's bluff and asked the Prime Minister to produce a new alternative strategy. Churchill retreated slightly replying, 'Everything is being done to create the bombing force desired on the largest possible scale, and there is no intention of changing this policy.' He concluded by adding, 'he is an unwise man who thinks there is any certain method of winning the war'.[10] Portal decided to launch an attack on Berlin that would provide the results he need to sway Churchill. In part he was urged on by Churchill's closing remark, 'The only plan is to persevere.'[11] Portal reasoned that the bombing of urban areas was easier to carry out and therefore should produce better results than the ill-fated precision bombing. When Harris arrived he adopted the same approach.

Churchill was horrified when informed that Portal's night raids conducted on 7 November 1941 against Berlin, Boulogne, Cologne, Mannheim and the Ruhr had resulted in a 15 per cent loss rate. He summoned Peirse to his country retreat at Chequers and told him that he believed the RAF could not afford such casualties, especially in light of the limited damage caused to the enemy. Churchill, though, was far more concerned about the loss rate sustained by Bomber Command during the previous three months which totalled 228 aircraft including accidents from a strength of about 800. His major worry was that this was outstripping bomber production and he urged Portal to conserve his aircraft by reducing the size of the raids. Churchill wrote to the Secretary of State for Air, CAS and the Minister of Aircraft Production on 30 December warning, 'The fighters are going ahead well, but the bomber force, particularly crews, is not making the progress hoped for.'[12] That year British factories produced 20,100 aircraft, of which just 500 were heavy bombers. It was under these circumstances that Peirse's tenure came to an end.

The 'area bombing' directive was sent to Bomber Command by the Air Ministry on 14 February 1942, eight days before Harris took charge from Peirse. This recognized that precision attacks were not working, and it had the full backing of Churchill, Portal and the Air Ministry. Instead, they would destroy Germany's larger industrial cities to break enemy morale. Harris would embrace this strategy wholeheartedly. Success would be gauged by acres flattened rather than specific targets. The tool for the job entered service on 2 March when the first two Lancaster bomber squadrons became operational. Things now began to improve for Bomber Command thanks to the introduction of the four-engine Lancaster, the Pathfinder force, improved radar aids and the development of better tactics. Also its inadequate Hampden, Manchester and Whitley bombers were withdrawn from front-line service.

While Harris was happy to attack Germany's cities, he objected to diverting his bombers against France's ports in support of the Battle of the Atlantic. Harris knew that if he was not to suffer the fate of his predecessor, he would have to demonstrate that Bomber Command was capable of delivering a deadly blow to the enemy. His solution to this was to conduct a thousand-bomber raid in a single night. Churchill was certainly receptive to Harris's idea and agreed to the very first such assault, which would be conducted against Cologne on 30 May 1942. Harris recalled during a late-night meeting with Churchill at Chequers, 'He was prepared for a loss of 100 bombers on this operation.'[13] In contrast Bomber Command's estimate was that it would cost 40 aircraft. If anything Churchill's optimism seemed to be a good influence on Harris. 'Winston's inspiring courage …' he noted, 'always sent me home whistling or singing.'[14] Harris had explained he wanted the Germans 'to look back to the days of … Cologne as men lost in a raging typhoon remember the gentle zephyrs of a past summer'.[15]

The bombers hit Cologne including the Köln-Nippes railway workshops with 1,455 tons of bombs and incendiaries. The smoke from the resulting fires was so bad that it was five days before RAF reconnaissance aircraft could take photographs of the damage. These showed 2.9 million square yards of devastation, which was ten times the damage caused by four smaller previous attacks. Nearly 60,000 people lost their homes, but 250 factories had been destroyed or seriously damaged in the process. 'The casualties among the population were certainly heavy,' reported the Air Ministry. 'All the public utility services were interrupted, for how long it is not yet possible to say.'[16] Shortly after this, Churchill was heartened by the news that Bomber Command's casualty rate was 3.3 per cent with 39 aircraft missing. Harris phoned him personally and recalled, 'I knew at once that he was satisfied then.'[17]

This devastating attack was followed by similar-sized raids on Essen and Bremen. However, the latter incurred almost a five per cent loss rate and no further thousand-bomber raids were conducted again until 1944. Churchill requested in June 1942 that Harris produce an appreciation for the War Cabinet outlining Bomber Command's strategic role and the resources it employed. In mid-August 1942 the US 8th Air Force mounted its first operation from Britain targeting the Rouen marshalling yards. This heralded the start of the Allies' Combined Bomber Offensive. The Americans were determined to conduct precision bombing of military and industrial targets and, to ensure accuracy, conducted their raids in daylight.

As a boy Churchill would have seen the very dramatic coverage of Queen Victoria's far-flung campaigns in the newspapers, such as the battle of Hasheen in Sudan in 1885. (*Illustrated London News*)

Churchill's first taste of military life was with the Harrow School Rifle Corps. He is standing ninth from the right and joined within weeks of arriving in 1888. (Ocean View Group Limited. All rights.)

Lieutenant Winston Spencer Churchill proudly
wearing his 4th Hussars uniform in 1895.
He would develop a love of military attire.
(Getty Images)

After his escapades in Cuba, Churchill saw action
on the volatile North-West Frontier in India.
There he fought with both Sikh and Punjabi
regiments. (Author's collection)

At Omdurman Churchill witnessed the full
military might of the British Empire at work
and this left a lasting impression on him.
(Author's collection)

Churchill seeking excitement with the
21st Lancers in Sudan. (Getty Images)

Looking rather like Mexican bandits the 21st Lancers charge the Dervishes at the battle of Omdurman in 1898. (Getty Images)

Churchill was lucky to survive at Omdurman, as the 21st Lancers lost 21 killed and suffered 49 wounded in the brief close-quarter combat. (Getty Images)

Lord, later Field Marshal Kitchener, the British commander in Sudan and subsequently South Africa, took an instant dislike to young Lieutenant Churchill. (Getty Images)

Churchill combined soldiering with journalism in South Africa. Here he is wearing the uniform of 'the Sakabulas' or 'Byng's Burglars'. Note the barely visible wispy moustache and prominent feather. (Getty Images)

A defiant looking Churchill (far right) after his capture by the Boers in South Africa. The other prisoners in marked contrast made a point of looking away from the camera. (Getty Images)

The killing fields of Spion Kop. Churchill was fortunate not to be amongst the corpses. (Getty Images)

Churchill with Archibald Sinclair on the Western Front in 1916. He greatly enjoyed his time as a battalion commander. (Getty Images)

As First Lord of the Admiralty Churchill instigated the ill-fated attempt to force the Dardanelles with warships in 1915. He was unfairly blamed for the failure of the subsequent landings. (Getty Images)

Liberal leader and Prime Minister David Lloyd George was a mentor and supporter of Churchill, appointing him Minister for Munitions and then Secretary of State for War and Air. (Getty Images)

Churchill played a leading role in the development of the tank during World War I, though Lloyd George was actually its greatest supporter. (Getty Images)

British casualties blinded by German mustard gas. As Minister of Munitions, Churchill was responsible for the manufacture of chemical weapons. Inexplicably he became a lifelong advocate of mustard gas. (Getty Images)

Following World War I Hugh Trenchard (centre) devised Air Control as a rationale for the RAF; the implementation of this was to get Churchill into trouble. (Getty Images)

Churchill centre stage for the Cairo Conference. T.E. Lawrence is just behind him to the right and Gertrude Bell is on the far left. The creation of Iraq and Transjordan from the ruins of the Ottoman Empire greatly stretched Britain's resources and led to the use of Air Control. (Getty Images)

The enigmatic T.E. Lawrence or 'Lawrence of Arabia' greatly impressed Churchill, who appreciated the value of irregular warfare. However, Churchill noted, 'He was not in complete harmony with the normal.' (Getty Images)

Mahatma Gandhi in London in 1931. Churchill viewed him and the Indian Congress Party as a serious threat to the British Empire. Churchill's refusal to countenance Indian independence contributed to his 'wilderness years'. (Getty Images)

On 10 May 1940 Churchill attained the highest political office in the land. Not only was he appointed Prime Minister, but he also made himself Defence Minister, becoming the country's political master and military commander. (Getty Images)

Churchill with Anthony Eden in Whitehall, London. Eden proved a valuable ally and confidant throughout World War II. (Getty Images)

Churchill's first challenge as Prime Minister was to save the British Expeditionary Force from annihilation at Dunkirk. (Getty Images)

After Dunkirk the next big test of Churchill's resolve was the Battle of Britain. (Getty Images)

Churchill was reliant on Air Chief Marshal Sir Hugh 'Stuffy' Dowding's Fighter Command to ward off Hitler's Blitz and the threat of Nazi invasion. (Getty Images)

Churchill's Army, Royal Navy and RAF Chiefs of Staff, Brooke, Pound and Portal. (Getty Images)

Irish Prime Minister Éamon de Valera reviewing his troops. Much to Churchill's displeasure he kept Ireland neutral during World War II. (Getty Images)

Arthur Harris (seated), Commander-in-Chief Bomber Command. Initially Harris's bombers were the only way to hit back at Hitler, but Churchill eventually distanced himself from the RAF's strategic bomber campaign. (Getty Images)

Churchill and de Gaulle paying their respects to the Tomb of the Unknown Soldier in Paris. Theirs was a troubled relationship. (Getty Images)

'The Big Three' smile for the camera: Stalin, Roosevelt and Churchill at the Tehran Conference. Both Western leaders mistakenly believed they could persuade Stalin of the merits of democracy once the war was over. (Getty Images)

The loss of Singapore along with thousands of Australian, British and Indian troops was a terrible blow to Britain's military prestige. Churchill knew he did not have the resources to hold both Cairo and Singapore and paid the price. He likened it to 'having to choose whether your son or daughter should be killed.' (Getty Images)

Tear gas being used against demonstrators in India protesting the arrest of Congress leaders in 1942. Containing the Quit India revolt tied down considerable numbers of British and Indian troops. (Getty Images)

Claude Auchinleck and Archibald Wavell were tasked by Churchill to maintain order in India and drive the Japanese from Burma. Wavell held Churchill responsible for the terrible Bombay famine. (Getty Images)

Churchill with Montgomery and Brooke clearly posing for the camera. Montgomery was never keen on Churchill's battlefield visits, which he found an unwelcome distraction. However, he willingly took him over the Rhine in March 1945. (Getty Images)

British troops under 'The Big Three' at the end of the war. The majority of the armed forces did not want a Conservative government. (Getty Images)

Churchill, Brooke and Montgomery reviewing the 7th Armoured Division in Berlin in July 1945. In places Churchill was dismayed by the reception he got from the troops. (Getty Images)

Winston and Clementine on holiday just before the Potsdam conference. Not surprisingly both clearly look tired and apprehensive. (Getty Images)

After losing the 1945 general election the country's former master and commander took a well-earned rest and went painting in Italy. Whilst there he happily reminisced about Omdurman, bringing his involvement with Britain's armed forces full circle. (Getty Images)

Churchill, supported by scientific adviser Lord Cherwell, Portal and Harris, became a proponent of hitting German cities. The problem was prioritizing targets: should the focus be on German oil facilities, aircraft factories, weapons factories or lines of communication? This issue was never satisfactorily resolved. Instead, Harris persisted with area bombing in order to cause as much disruption as possible, while resisting sending his bomber squadrons overseas to help the army.

By 1943 the growing preoccupation was how to support the opening of the Second Front in Europe. At the beginning of the year Harris had amassed 600 heavy bombers with more on the way. The British and American bomber commanders wanted to crush German industry and oil facilities, but the best way to support the Allied invasion of Normandy was to gain air superiority and attack German lines of communication in order to paralyse their ground forces. Ultimately though, both Churchill and Roosevelt tended to ignore considering the Combined Bomber Offensive as part of their grand strategy to bring the war to an end. Although officially integrated to support D-Day under the Pointblank Directive, Bomber Command nevertheless continued to operate largely in isolation, while pursuing its own agendas. Pointblank was clear in its goal of destroying enemy fighters in the air and on the ground. For the Allies' strategic air forces this meant destroying the factories producing the fighters and their components. This though was easier said than done.

Despite Portal being involved in drawing up Pointblank, he still gave Harris enormous leeway in how he chose to interpret the directive. In part Portal had little choice because Harris's headquarters at High Wycombe was not far from Chequers, which meant he had direct access to the Prime Minister. Although Churchill would occasionally invite Harris over for dinner, there is little evidence to show that he had any great affection for the man. Harris often found Churchill impatient and grumbled, 'I wouldn't have called Winston a good listener.'[18] However, Churchill trusted him and felt he was the right man for a difficult job.

Churchill's concerns over indiscriminate killing were realized time and time again. Notably in late July 1943 Bomber Command and USAAF visited Hamburg, Germany's second city and the second largest port in the world. Dubbed Operation *Gomorrah* it consisted of a series of four raids targeting the city's docks, factories, oil refineries and shipyards. The flames caused by the falling bombs created winds of 150 miles an hour. Those inhabitants who were not blown up or burned to death suffocated in their air raid shelters. Amongst the ruins of a once-fine city lay the bodies of over 30,000 people.[19] Germany was stunned but the war went on.

Even as the plans for opening the Second Front progressed, Harris persisted with his belief that Germany could be defeated by bombing alone. On 3 November 1943 he wrote to Churchill and claimed that his bombers had completely destroyed 19 German cities. 'We can wreck Berlin from end to end if USAAF will come in on it,' added Harris enthusiastically. 'It will cost between 400–500 aircraft. It will cost Germany the war.'[20] To Churchill there seemed no sound logic for such sacrifice, nor was it in support of the Pointblank requirements. In light of the USAAF's bloody mauling over Schweinfurt where it was attacking Germany's aircraft factories, it was hard to imagine that they would be supportive of such an undertaking. In just two raids on Schweinfurt the Americans had lost almost 140 bombers. Churchill and Portal were unconvinced and did not press the Americans to join Bomber Command's grandiose assault on Berlin.

Nonetheless, at a time when Bomber Command should have been supporting Pointblank, Churchill permitted what became known as the battle of Berlin. Between 18 November 1943 and the end of March 1944 Harris launched an incredible 9,111 sorties against Berlin, which amounted to 16 major attacks. Another 11,113 sorties were conducted against other German cities. This cost Harris 1,047 aircraft plus 1,682 damaged or written off. Although the attacks forced the Luftwaffe to focus on the defence of Berlin, it was hard for Churchill to tell just how successful this war of attrition was.

The most controversial and damning assault on Germany's cities occurred on 13 February 1945 when Bomber Command firebombed Dresden on the river Elbe. It was assessed the city was a major industrial centre and certainly hosted over 130 military factories.[21] The resulting widespread fire storm could be viewed as little more than deliberate terror bombing. The bomber crews flying over 10,000 feet could feel the 1,000-degree heat generated by the appalling blaze. The ravenous flames mercilessly consumed about 25,000 people and 13 square miles of the city. Some 48 hours later the fires were still burning. Subsequently, estimates by the German authorities put the total dead as high as 200,000, which seemed suspiciously inflated.[22] Whatever the death toll specialists had to be brought in to try and identify the charred remains. Ten days later Bomber Command firebombed Pforzheim and incinerated 17,600 inhabitants.

Quite understandably opponents of this apparently random bombing were outraged. Churchill and his government were soon under political fire. Richard Stokes, a Labour MP, stood in the House of Commons on 6 March to ask if 'terror bombing' was now official government policy and, if so, did the British people know.[23] The press immediately picked up on the reference to 'terror bombing'. Churchill realized that these types of attacks could not continue and he moved quickly to distance himself from area bombing. 'The destruction of Dresden remains a serious query against the conduct of Allied bombing,' he wrote to the Chief of Air Staff at the end of the month. 'I am of the opinion that military objectives must henceforward be more strictly studied.'[24] This could be read as nothing more than an official rebuke of the entire bomber offensive. Even worse he went on to firmly renounce area bombing, adding, 'I feel the need for more precise concentration upon military objectives ... rather than on mere acts of terror'.[25]

Portal and Harris were understandably outraged by this and Portal suggested Churchill should moderate his criticism. 'We must see to it,' Churchill wrote somewhat more diplomatically on 1 April 1945, 'that our attacks do not do more harm to ourselves in the long run than they do to the enemies' immediate war effort'.[26] Again, though, it was explicit that Churchill was warning Bomber Command that it had lost the moral high ground. Area bombing finally ceased on 16 April 1945, but it mattered little as the war was almost over and the damage had already been done both morally and politically.

Harris, infuriated that Churchill had abandoned him and his men, was to remain unrepentant about his strategy until his dying days. He reasoned 'there was nothing to be ashamed of, except in the sense that everybody might be ashamed of the sort of thing that has to be done in every war, as of war itself'.[27] Indeed at the start of the war Churchill had been fully supportive, stating 'every trace of Hitler's footsteps ... will be sponged and purged. And, if need be, blasted from the surface of the earth.'[28]

He understood that although there had been an initial imperative for bombing Germany's cities as the only way of striking back, by 1945 justification for it had long passed. After the war Harris accused Churchill of wielding 'almost absolute power', as if that should somehow excuse his own rigid strategic goals.[29]

17

'Bands of Brothers'

While Churchill was overseeing the war in the Atlantic, over Britain and in the Mediterranean he had to find ways of striking Nazi-occupied Europe. Although Bomber Command took the lead in this, Churchill looked to foster special forces that could make life unpleasant for the Germans. He understood that Britain, in order to survive, needed to evolve its outdated views about conventional and irregular warfare. He had seen the latter up close during the Boer War. The hardy self-sufficient Boer Commando military units, although fighting as infantry, always travelled by horse making their columns highly flexible. This enabled them to run circles around much superior numbers of the British troops. During World War I Churchill had tried to develop the concept of land, air and sea combined operations at Gallipoli and failed spectacularly thanks to political inertia. He had also been influenced by T.E. Lawrence's successful guerrilla tactics employed against the Turks in the Middle East. It was time to bring all these ideas together.

Immediately after Dunkirk, Churchill's impulse was to hit back at Hitler as quickly as possible and not just from the air. Just as the evacuation from France was coming to a close on 4 June 1940, he told General Sir Hastings Ismay they must 'organize self-contained, thoroughly equipped raiding units'.[1] These he explained should be up to 1,000 strong and when combined not more than 10,000. Shortly after, he added with enthusiasm, 'Enterprises must be prepared with specially trained troops of the hunter class who can develop a reign of terror down the enemy coasts.'[2] This was to prove a challenge. When World War II broke out the Royal Marines were woefully ill-prepared thanks to chronic underfunding. At this stage they were not independently mobile and traditionally were deployed for static defence on warships and to man coastal batteries. Disastrously the War Office had decided landing craft and amphibious training were unnecessary. The inter-service training and development centre in Portsmouth had just six landing craft and soldiers transported by sea had to be put ashore by boat.[3] After the British Expeditionary Force landed in France the centre was closed down.

In response to the extremely limited amphibious capabilities of the Marines, the British Army established Independent Companies, the forerunners of the Commandos, to conduct special operations overseas. These were formed in April 1940 using volunteers from the Territorial Army. Five companies were sent to Bodo, Mo and Mosjoen in Norway to support the Norwegians in early May 1940. Numbering almost 1,500 men they were collectively known as Scissorforce under the command of Lieutenant-Colonel Colin Gubbins. The idea was that the men should be able to fight as a unit or individually – in other words guerrilla warfare. Each company was lightly equipped to enable them to be as mobile as possible, which meant they could not really hold fixed defences. When the Germans outflanked them with a seaborne assault at Hemnesberget they were forced to retreat. Unable to fend off the German northward advance, Scissorforce was reinforced with elements of the Guards Brigade and fought an increasingly conventional battle.

On the evening of 4 June 1940 Lieutenant-Colonel Dudley Clarke, Military Assistant to General Sir John Dill, Chief of the Imperial General Staff, got an idea. He had served in Palestine in the mid-1930s and had witnessed first-hand how a few Arab extremists could tie down large numbers of troops. He wondered whether the British could do something similar along the newly occupied coast of western Europe. The following day he presented his suggestions in writing to Dill, who passed them on to a highly receptive Churchill. On 8 June Dill informed Clarke the Prime Minister had greenlit the project. 'The PM believes that you have something here,' he said.[4] Clarke was to set about creating 'Commando units' for cross-Channel operations. He was instructed to establish Section MO9 at the War Office to oversee this task. The problem he faced was that there were no resources to spare and service chiefs were reluctant to cooperate with this brand-new fighting force.

Just four days later Churchill appointed Royal Marine Lieutenant-General Sir Alan Bourne, temporary Head of Combined Operations, or Raiding Operations as it was then termed. A month later he was replaced by Admiral Sir Roger Keyes, but stayed on as deputy director as well as becoming Adjutant-General of the Royal Marines. When Churchill sounded out the Commander-in-Chief Home Forces about the creation of an irregular force he used the terms 'Storm Troops' and 'Leopards' to describe potential volunteers. Neither found much favour, especially the first which sounded too much like German storm troopers. Churchill agreed that 'Commando' used in Clarke's memo was just right as it drew on the Boer ethos of individualism. Churchill appreciated that the Boers, although highly independent and lacking military discipline, had fought together out of a sense of common brotherhood. These were exactly the type of men he wanted. Initially only the army was asked for volunteers. They were to be drawn from units deployed in Britain and from members of the Independent Companies, which were to be disbanded after the Norwegian campaign ended.

To Churchill's delight the first Commando raid was conducted on the night of 23/24 June 1940 in the Boulogne and Le Touquet area. Major R.J.F. 'Ronnie' Tod led 120 men, whose weapons included 20 'Tommy' guns or Thompson submachine guns, which represented half of all those in Britain.[5] Looking like some Chicago gangster Churchill was later photographed with one tucked under his right arm. This was part of a propaganda campaign to convince the Germans that the British Army had lots of these close-quarter weapons. The Commando operation did not go well; the raiders were almost attacked by the RAF and bumped into a German patrol. Lieutenant-Colonel Clarke who went along as an observer was wounded. The force landed south of Le Touquet also failed to produce any tangible results. The following month another raid was conducted, this time against the German garrison on Guernsey. Once more the results were thoroughly disappointing.

Captain Simon Fraser, 15th Lord Lovat, who was to rise through the ranks of the Commandos to command 1st Special Service Brigade, noted, 'The Prime Minister was not amused by this tomfoolery and laid it on the line in no uncertain terms.'[6] An annoyed Churchill wrote scathingly, 'It would be most unwise to disturb the coasts of these countries by the kind of silly fiascos which were perpetrated at

Boulogne and Guernsey.'⁷ Those involved were reprimanded and he ordered an immediate reorganization. 'I have asked for five thousand parachutists and we must have at least ten thousand of these "bands of brothers" capable of lightning action.'⁸

In consequence the Commando and remaining Independent Companies were amalgamated into Special Service Battalions in October 1940 and packed off to Scotland for intensive training. These battalions included around 2,000 volunteers from the Independent Companies, some of whom had been rescued from Norway. Transport was provided after a fashion by requisitioned Dutch cross-Channel steamers and trawlers. Irregular warfare schools were also created in Australia, Canada, Egypt and Singapore to spread the Commando ethos. The abbreviation of Special Service caused a number of raised eyebrows in light of Hitler's Schutzstaffel or SS rampaging through Europe, but it continued to be used until the end of 1944.

That September Colonel Clarke appointed none other than Captain David Niven as his liaison officer between MO9 and the various Commando units. Niven, a major Hollywood movie star, had returned to Britain to join the army and subsequently volunteered for the Commandos. He met Churchill several times at Ditchley Park in Oxfordshire, which was owned by mutual friends. On one occasion Niven was walking in the garden with the Prime Minister and began to explain his work with the Commandos. Churchill with a glint in his eye suddenly stopped and said, 'Your security is very lax ... you shouldn't be telling me this.'⁹ Niven was taken aback and later remarked, 'He was always a superb actor but to this day I don't know whether or not he was joking.'¹⁰

Admiral Keyes, as Head of Combined Operations, threw himself into the job with gusto. By the autumn of 1940 he was able to inform Churchill that he had gathered 5,000 men organized into ten Commandos.¹¹ In achieving this he made himself extremely unpopular with the service chiefs. However, Lord Lovat felt that Churchill had selected the right man for the job. 'The admiral believed in leading from the front,' he observed approvingly. 'I have seen him in London clothes, wet to the skin, struggle to the wrong beach in a high running sea, and then call a repeat performance.'¹²

During early April 1941 Keyes pleased Churchill with the successful destruction of the fish oil factories on the Lofoten Islands off northwest

Norway. In North Africa that year Commandos launched raids against Tobruk and attempted unsuccessfully to locate and kill General Erwin Rommel. Other operations, particularly in Crete, unfortunately went horribly wrong. Three Commando units, grouped together as Layforce numbering 2,000 and sent to defend the island, lost 600 men. That same year Churchill wanted to conduct a massive combined operation in the Atlantic. Fearing that Hitler might invade Portugal and Spain, he ambitiously authorized planning for the seizure of the Azores, Madeira, the Canaries and Cape Verdes.

Such action would prevent the islands becoming bases for Hitler's U-boats and maritime reconnaissance aircraft. It would also enable Britain to extend its anti-submarine capability towards the central Atlantic to improve convoy protection. Initially this widespread island grab was planned as a series of separate missions, but they were then combined into one. This was to involve an infantry division and the special forces, numbering in all around 24,000 men, backed by considerable resources from the Royal Navy and the RAF. Through the last six months of 1941 the units assigned to what was quaintly known as Operation *Pilgrim* were kept under orders ready to go.

The complexity of this proposed operation was slightly eased when the Portuguese government made it known that if Hitler attacked the Iberian Peninsula, they would evacuate to the Azores. Churchill and Roosevelt would then be asked to help defend the islands. *Pilgrim* was not cancelled until February 1942, when it was decided that the landing craft and warships were needed elsewhere. Behind the scenes, however, the capture of the Atlantic islands had proved well beyond the abilities of Combined Operations. 'The project terminated with a rehearsal in the Orkneys that went adrift in timing and navigation,' said Lord Lovat. 'The landing took an age, as did the arrival of the follow-up equipment, which became so muddled in the control ship that the expedition was abandoned.'[13] This did not bode well for future such operations.

Churchill's enthusiasm for what many saw as his private army caused growing resentment amongst the chiefs of the army and Royal Navy. This manifested itself as passive resistance that sought to thwart the development of the Commandos at every turn. Keyes, at constant loggerheads with the Chiefs of Staff, the Joint Planners and the Service staffs over resources, continually lobbied Churchill for support. To ease the friction Churchill tried to move Keyes sideways by appointing him

Adviser on Combined Operations and Commandant of Combined Training Centres. Keyes flatly refused. When things came to a head Churchill was obliged to replace him in October 1941 with naval Captain Lord Louis Mountbatten, King George VI's cousin. Churchill wrote Keyes an apologetic letter that concluded, 'I have no choice but to arrange for your relief.'[14]

'The old admiral – he was 68 at the time – went out in a shower of sparks,' recalled Lord Lovat.[15] Keyes, who was also an MP, angrily told the House of Commons, 'Having been frustrated at every turn in every worthwhile offensive action I have tried to undertake, I must fully endorse the Prime Minister's comments on the strength of the negative power which controls the war machine in Whitehall.'[16] He went on to say that 'procrastination' was the 'thief of time'.[17] The War Office was understandably outraged by this candid criticism and seized all his papers and pointedly sent him a copy of the Official Secrets Act. General Dill castigated Churchill by pointing out 'you can't win World War II with World War I heroes'.[18] Admiral Pound, the First Sea Lord, who was not altogether sorry to see Keyes go, remarked he 'never had much brain but whatever he has got left is quite addled'.[19]

Mountbatten, who had only just taken command of an aircraft carrier having lost his destroyer during the battle of Crete, was far from keen on his new job. He had experienced a very narrow escape when his destroyer went down. 'I felt I ought to be the last to leave the ship, and I left it a bit late,' he recalled, 'because the bridge turned over on top of me and I was trapped in the boiling, seething cauldron underneath.'[20] When summoned to London to see the Prime Minister he candidly said that he would rather be back at sea. 'Have you no sense of glory!' retorted Churchill. 'Here I give you a chance to take part in the highest direction of the war and all you want to do is go back to sea!'[21] Mountbatten shifted uneasily whilst thinking commanding a carrier was a prize job and would not involve intense inter-service rivalry.

Impishly the Prime Minister thrust out his jaw and added, 'What could you hope to achieve, except to be sunk in a bigger and more expensive ship?'[22] Mountbatten, who was not really in a position to say no, gave in. 'You will continue with the Commando raids in order to keep up the offensive spirit,' instructed Churchill. 'But, above all, I now want you to start the preparations for our great counter-invasion of Europe.'[23] Mountbatten was to oversee everything needed to ensure the opening of the Second Front was a success. Churchill also pointed out that while all the service headquarters were engaged in defensive measures, Combined Operations was only to think offensively.

Mountbatten, who joined the Combined Operations Directorate as a Commodore, was now promoted to Acting Vice-Admiral. He also became a member of the Chiefs of Staff Committee and reported directly to Churchill as Minister of Defence. The existence of his Combined Operations Headquarters effectively circumvented the established chain of command. Mountbatten upon arrival was not impressed by what Keyes had achieved and conveyed this to Churchill. He claimed he found no guidelines and had to create his own three-point philosophy from scratch, which would lay the foundations for D-Day. These consisted of: secure a beachhead, break out as quickly as possible and at the same time keep the enemy away from the landing areas.

Undeterred by the early setbacks Churchill and Mountbatten looked to the Commandos to play a leading role in Operation *Chariot*. This was an audacious attack on the dry dock at St Nazaire designed to stop the Germans using it. The plan was for the destroyer HMS *Campbeltown* packed with explosives to ram the dock gates. It took place on 27 March 1942 and was highly successful, though it was a one-way trip for most of those involved. In contrast the subsequent raid on Dieppe on 18/19 August 1942, which saw both army and Royal Marine Commandos acting on the flanks of the Canadian 2nd Infantry Division, proved poorly planned and executed. Known as Operation *Jubilee* it was supposed to test the German Atlantic Wall to see if it was feasible to capture a French port.[24] Instead, most of the attack force did not come ashore and those who did were pinned down along with the supporting tanks. Although *Jubilee* provided valuable lessons for D-Day and convinced the Allies they would need to land on open beaches it was at great cost. The Canadians suffered 3,367 dead, wounded or captured and the Commandos lost 270 men.

This was a severe blow to the developing concepts of combined operations and Churchill's expanding private army. Lord Beaverbrook, who had been campaigning in his newspapers for the opening of the Second Front as soon as possible, held Mountbatten personally responsible. He was angry that so many of his fellow Canadians had been needlessly sacrificed and the viability of the Second Front discredited deliberately or otherwise. Mountbatten could hardly disown the operation. 'Dieppe was one of the most vital operations of the Second World War,' he argued. 'It gave to the Allies the priceless secret of victory. If I had the same decision to make I would do as I did before.'[25] Churchill who was equally culpable backed Mountbatten saying, 'Dieppe occupies a place of its own in the story of war and the grim casualty figures must not class it as a failure.'[26] However you looked at it, though, Dieppe was a lamentable shambles.

During the second half of 1942 Churchill's Commandos only carried out a series of 'pinprick' raids in the Channel Islands and Normandy. From 1942 onwards, though, their role was to spearhead large-scale landings in the Mediterranean. Mountbatten was not to oversee D-Day as he would be sent to take command in South East Asia. He later recalled, 'I went to Combined Operations Headquarters and found there were just twenty-six persons … Before I left, this number had increased twenty fold … The actual sailors, soldiers and airmen in the Combined Operations Command increased to 50,000 trained experts. We really put our backs into it.'[27] By 1944 Churchill's 'bands of brothers' had expanded to four Special Service brigades encompassing both soldiers and Marines. On D-Day Lord Lovat would lead 1st Brigade ashore, which was to link up with the British 6th Airborne Division's bridgehead east of the river Orne. Churchill and Clarke's concept had come full circle.

PART FIVE

Global Juggling Act

Mediterranean Showdown

In the aftermath of France's surrender Churchill had to face down the Italians in the Mediterranean, North Africa and the Balkans. The loss of French military and naval support made this task extremely difficult. Throughout the 1930s Mussolini's interventionist foreign policy had convinced him he could challenge British dominance of the Mediterranean. The Italian leader belatedly sided with Hitler on 10 June 1940 when he declared war on both Britain and France. The following day Italian bombers in a show of strength repeatedly struck the British island of Malta, hitting Grand Harbour. This signalled the British Mediterranean Fleet would not be safe there. Churchill feared these attacks were a prelude to forces based in Italian-controlled Libya attacking Egypt, but instead Italian divisions blundered into the French Alps.

General Archibald Wavell, British Commander-in-Chief Middle East, who had been appointed before Churchill became Prime Minister, was confronted with an almost impossible task. His command based in Cairo included not only the defence of Egypt and the vital Suez Canal, but also Aden, British Somaliland, Iraq, Palestine, Transjordan and Sudan. While Mussolini had some 250,000 Italian and colonial troops stationed in Libya, Wavell could muster only 36,000 men with which to hold Egypt. To the south Mussolini had a similar number of troops in Italy's colonial possessions in the Horn of Africa, whereas the British garrisons in that part of the world were tiny.

While awaiting reinforcements Wavell moved quickly to keep Italian units along the Libyan frontier off balance. He did this by launching a series of successful border raids that caught the ill-prepared Italians by surprise. Nonetheless, it was only a matter of time before Mussolini's generals launched a full-scale offensive with overwhelming force. It rapidly transpired though that Italian forces lacked the aggressive fighting spirit of their British counterparts. On 16 June 1940 elements of the 1st Libyan Division attacked British border defences and were promptly defeated at the battle of Nezuet Ghirba. Although such skirmishes continued, much to the relief of Churchill and Wavell Mussolini did not press home his attack. The reason for this was that Italian ground forces in Libya were far from mobile and lacked logistical support, their air force although large was equipped with obsolete aircraft, and their fleet feared the Royal Navy.

Churchill taunted Italy's leader in the House of Commons on 18 June, remarking, 'we shall be delighted to offer Signor Mussolini a free and safeguarded passage through the Straits of Gibraltar in order that he may play the part to which he aspires'.[1] However, events in Europe soon favoured Mussolini. France, under attack on two fronts and with her armies in a state of chaos, signed an armistice with Hitler on 22 June and one with Mussolini two days later. Once France was out of the war Mussolini was free to redeploy his divisions in western Libya facing French Tunisia to the Egyptian border.

Despite the enormous disparity in forces Churchill knew that Mussolini needed a swift victory in North Africa because Italy was not prepared for a prolonged war. Italian industry was simply incapable of meeting the armed forces' requirements. Mussolini also appreciated that the moment he declared war, Churchill would close the Gibraltar Straits and the Suez Canal to Italian shipping thereby hemming him in. Although Mussolini had a modern fleet it had no aircraft carriers and his land-based aircraft lacked the range of the Royal Navy's carrier-borne Fleet Air Arm. Furthermore, at sea the Italians preferred to rely on speed and manoeuvrability, which meant their warships were not as well armoured as many of the Royal Navy's ships.

Through July and August 1940 Churchill and Wavell could not believe their luck as the Italians still did not invade Egypt. Mussolini, who was expecting his commander Marshal Rodolfo Graziani to attack on 4 August, became increasingly frustrated by the delays. In reaction to this he angrily threated to sack Graziani. At the same time Wavell had to contend with the large Italian army in Abyssinia, Eritrea and

Italian Somaliland which posed a threat to British-controlled Kenya, Sudan and British Somaliland. In July Italian troops had launched a very limited invasion of southern Sudan and the following month overran British Somaliland in a matter of weeks.

In the meantime, at the end of August 1940 Churchill sought to reinforce Admiral Cunningham's Mediterranean Fleet based at Alexandria. The brand-new carrier *Illustrious*, the battleship *Valiant*, the anti-aircraft cruisers *Calcutta* and *Coventry*, and other supporting vessels arrived at Gibraltar ready for action. They were escorted as far as Malta by Admiral Somerville's Force H, which also took men and supplies. Despite Malta's vulnerability to Italian aircraft flying from air bases in Italy and Sicily, Churchill was determined to hold the island. Its position in the middle of the Mediterranean made it an ideal staging point for convoys. Furthermore, its location made it an ideal base from which to attack Italy's lines of communication with Libya.

On 4 September 1940 the Mediterranean Fleet took the war to Mussolini by attacking Italian airfields on Rhodes. This helped goad the Italian generals into action in North Africa. News reached Churchill on 13 September that the long-awaited Italian assault on Egypt had commenced with the loss of Sollum. Columns of dusty Italian infantry supported by light tanks and preceded by an artillery barrage were reportedly pouring over the lightly defended border. The immediate problem for the Italians was that in negotiating the narrow border passes they were horribly exposed and RAF fighters and bombers were soon giving them a good hammering. The Italian Air Force was in the air but was in no way as aggressive as its opponents, who were determined to hamper the enemy advance at every step.

Intelligence filtering into Wavell's headquarters in Cairo indicated the Italian attack was certainly not comparable to Hitler's well-oiled and coordinated Blitzkrieg. Italian logistics and the appalling condition of the frontier roads meant that Mussolini's forces were not going anywhere in a hurry. Five days later they had got as far as Sidi Barrani some 60 miles inside Egypt, though this was only half way to the main British defences. Once again Wavell was granted valuable time when at the end of October 1940 Mussolini decided to invade Greece from Albania. Although the Greeks swiftly drove back the inept Italian Army it raised the spectre of Hitler intervening. This new campaign in the Balkans posed a dilemma for Churchill for although it slackened Italian pressure on Egypt, he felt compelled to help the Greeks.

At sea in early October, Cunningham ran a convoy from the east to Malta and escorted some empty ships back to Alexandria, during which operation the Royal Navy bumped into an Italian destroyer force. The Italians came off worst, with two ships sunk and a third damaged. The latter was taken under tow and limped away. Despite this poor showing, Cunningham was genuinely impressed by his enemy's fighting spirit, noting 'on this occasion the Italian destroyers had fought well'.[2] He signalled this sentiment to the Admiralty and Churchill reacted angrily. 'This kind of kid glove stuff,' he said, 'infuriates the people who are going through their present ordeal at home [i.e. the Blitz] and this aspect should be put to the admiral.'[3] Cunningham was unmoved by the prime minister's lack of gallantry.

Churchill and Wavell needed the Italian Navy kept at bay while British forces were reinforced in Egypt. Ever since the British attack on the French fleet at Mers-el-Kebir, Mussolini's warships largely kept out of the way at the two anchorages of Mar Grande and Mar Piccolo at Taranto. On the night of 11 November 1940 the carrier *Illustrious* approached to within striking range and her aircraft pounced on Taranto putting three Italian battleships out of action, one of which was beyond repair.[4] Mussolini was furious at the audacity of Churchill and furious at the Italian Navy and the air force for allowing themselves to be taken so completely by surprise.

Impatiently Churchill wanted the Italians driven from Egypt as soon as possible. At his behest Chief of the Imperial General Staff General Sir John Dill as early as 11 September 1940 asked Wavell when he would be able go over to the offensive. The objective would be the Libyan port of Tobruk, which if captured would severely hamper future Italian operations. Much to Wavell's displeasure, Churchill insisted on pushing the pace. He, quite rightly in his role as Commander-in-Chief Middle East, was of the view they should not act rashly until sufficient reinforcements were in place. Two days after Dill's enquiry, Mussolini had pre-empted Wavell.

It was not until 9 December 1940 that Wavell launched Operation *Compass*, employing the 7th Armoured Division and the 4th Indian Division under the command of General Richard O'Connor. They immediately liberated Sidi Barrani and on 17 December cleared

Sollum. Six days later Churchill warned the Italians that Mussolini would be their downfall. The Prime Minister stated in a radio broadcast 'that after eighteen years of unbridled power he has led your country to the horrid verge of ruin.'⁵ This was no hollow boast. During January the newly arrived 6th Australian Division stormed Bardia and Tobruk taking thousands of prisoners, reaching Benghazi in early February.

By the time *Compass* came to a halt on 7 February 1941, O'Connor had pushed right through the Libyan province of Cyrenaica, completely cutting off the Italian 10th Army at Beda Fomm on the Gulf of Sirte. He dramatically and succinctly informed Wavell, 'Fox killed in the open.'⁶ Some 25,000 trapped Italians surrendered that day handing over 100 tanks, 216 guns and 1,500 vehicles.⁷ 'I think,' reported O'Connor triumphantly, 'this may be termed a complete victory as none of the enemy escaped.'⁸ It was just the sort of good news Churchill needed. Total Italian losses over the past two months included 130,000 men captured along with 380 tanks and 845 guns.⁹ 'Very few people realize how small were the forces with which General Wavell …,' Churchill later admitted, 'took the bulk of the Italian masses in Libya prisoner.'¹⁰ He also said Wavell was a 'fine commander whom we cheered in good days and will back through bad'.¹¹

Two days later Admiral Somerville with Force H, consisting of the battleship *Malaya* and the cruisers *Renown* and *Sheffield* and the carrier *Ark Royal*, attacked Italy's western coast. His warships shelled Genoa for 30 minutes sinking four ships and damaging 18 others. At the same time aircraft from *Ark Royal* bombed Livorno and dropped mines off La Spezia naval base. Somerville then withdrew to Gibraltar successfully eluding the Italian Navy. Once more a humiliated Mussolini was enraged by Churchill's boldness in striking at the Italian mainland.

Dunkirk and the Battle of Britain in the summer of 1940 signalled that Churchill was determined to do everything in his power to save the British Isles from Nazi occupation. Beda Fomm showed that he was determined to hold Egypt and protect the Suez Canal from Italian Fascism. This victory not only safeguarded Cairo, Alexandria and Suez, it also convinced General Franco in Spain that now was not a good time to side with Germany and Italy. This decision completely thwarted Hitler's plans to take Gibraltar and seal the Mediterranean. This left the British lifeline through Malta to Alexandria intact.

Wavell had a prime opportunity to push on to Tripoli and secure all of Libya. However, Churchill had other ideas. 'Accept my heartfelt congratulations on this latest admirable victory and on the unexpected speed with which Cyrenaica has been conquered,' he signalled Wavell on 12 February 1941. 'Greece and or/Turkey must have priority ... You should therefore make yourself secure in Benghazi and concentrate all available forces in the [Nile] Delta in preparation for movement to Europe.'[12] O'Connor stopped at El Agheila to the southwest of Beda Fomm on the border of the Libyan province of Tripolitania, but wanted to press on to Sirte and Tripoli. Wavell, though, had no choice but to get ready to send troops to Greece as instructed. Less than a week after O'Connor's remarkable victory General Erwin Rommel arrived in Tripoli with instructions from Hitler to help Mussolini recover Cyrenaica.

Thanks to Churchill's commitment to Greece, Wavell lost the chance to take Tripoli before Rommel had built up his strength. Instead, Churchill sent Anthony Eden, his newly appointed Foreign Secretary, and General Dill to Cairo on 20 February to liaise with Wavell over providing military assistance to Greece. 'Do not consider yourself obligated to a Greek enterprise,' Churchill told Eden, 'if in your hearts you feel it will be only another Norwegian fiasco.'[13] This instruction seemed rather vague. It also contradicted Eden's sealed orders from the Prime Minister that instructed his 'principal object must be to send speedy help to Greece'.[14] While Churchill felt obligated to help the Greeks, he like Wavell must have grasped it was probably an operation too far. Eden, in contrast, was of the firm opinion that one too many Allies had been abandoned in recent years with the fall of Czechoslovakia, Poland and France. He was determined that Greece, once offered aid, would not suffer the same fate.

Wavell was privately irked that his successful campaign in Libya had been derailed and that politicians seemed to have no concept of what was involved in getting troops and their equipment to Greece. Nonetheless, as instructed by Churchill he had already withdrawn his better units from Cyrenaica, thereby weakening his forward defences. Although he held Churchill responsible for this state of affairs, Eden was the one there on the ground. 'As you were so long I felt I had to get started,' he grumbled at the Foreign Secretary, 'and I have begun the concentration for the move to Greece.'[15] Eden, Dill and Wavell then flew to Athens where they promised the Greek government they would send 100,000 troops, 700 guns and 142 tanks. This expeditionary force would comprise three infantry divisions, up to two armoured brigades and a Polish brigade. These forces were to include Australian, Cypriot, New Zealand and Palestinian units. The Greeks were initially reluctant to accept this offer for fear it would provoke Hitler.

Wavell commenced Operation *Lustre* in early March to ferry his forces to Greece. This requirement had become more urgent with the southward movement of German troops in February, as well as the accession to the Axis by Bulgaria on 1 March 1941. German troops entered their new ally that day and the Bulgarian Army deployed along the Greek frontier with hostile intent. In an operation that was anticipated to last two months, British convoys were run from Alexandria to the Greek port of Piraeus every three days. It was therefore vital that Cunningham, whose ships were screening the troop shipments to Crete and Greece, be kept informed of the Italian fleet's deployment.

'Admiral Cunningham left us in no doubt as to the considerable naval risks in the Mediterranean,' noted Churchill, 'which were involved in the move of the Army and Royal Air Force to Greece.'[16] There was a growing danger that Hitler might launch pre-emptive air strikes from Bulgaria against the convoys while at sea and their disembarkation ports. In addition, the Italian fleet might try to intervene. 'This could be met by our battleships based on Suda Bay in Crete,' added Churchill, 'but only at the expense of weakening the destroyer escort for the convoys and leaving the supply line to Cyrenaica practically unprotected.'[17] British plans to capture Rhodes and neutralize the Italian presence in the eastern Aegean had to be shelved for lack of resources.

At the end of March, the Royal Navy gained another victory over the Italian fleet near southern Greece. 'This timely and welcome victory off Cape Matapan,' wrote Churchill, 'disposed of all challenge to British naval mastery of the Eastern Mediterranean at this critical time.'[18] Although a stunning success the battle of Matapan was quickly forgotten, partly because of the heavy losses that were to come. Furthermore, Cunningham's triumph was not conclusive, for although the Italian Navy had been mauled again, it was not completely out of the fight. Despite Churchill's claim neither side was able to gain complete mastery of the sea. To make matters worse, Hitler's Luftwaffe was now firmly established in the Balkans poised to strike.

On land Rommel attacked the British at El Agheila on 24 March and by the end of April had rolled Wavell out of Libya. General O'Connor was captured and only Tobruk held out. Churchill was furious that everything O'Connor had achieved had been thrown away and signalled Wavell wanting an explanation. However, Wavell was distracted by the deteriorating situation in the Balkans. In support of Mussolini's bungled invasion and in response to the arrival of British forces on 6 April Hitler struck Greece and Yugoslavia. His assault was assisted by his Axis allies Bulgaria, Hungary and Italy. Wavell's expeditionary forces had only just begun to deploy and could do little to stem the tide.

'We must be careful not to urge Greece against her better judgement into a hopeless resistance alone,' Churchill advised Eden in Cairo, 'when we have only handfuls of troops which can reach a scene in time.'[19] He was particularly concerned about the impact on Britain's close allies as 80 per cent of the expeditionary force were provided by Australia and New Zealand. Their units were commanded as part of the British armed forces and little thought had been given to the long-term political implications of this. 'Grave Imperial issues are raised,' Churchill warned, 'by committing New Zealand and Australian troops to an enterprise, which as you say, has become even more hazardous.'[20] In reality he meant the situation was hopeless.

Eden, though, was adamant that they press on with their plans. 'In the existing situation we are all agreed that the best course advocated,' he responded, 'should be followed and help given to Greece. We devoutly trust therefore that no difficulties will arise with regard to the despatch of Dominion Forces as arranged.'[21] This was naïve and wishful thinking. Many members of the Australian and New Zealand governments recalled only too well the fate of the Anzacs at Gallipoli and still held Churchill responsible. Once more it seemed as if their men were being sent as sacrificial lambs as they moved forward to fight alongside the Greeks.

In the face of Hitler's Blitzkrieg, the Greek and Yugoslav armies quickly crumbled. Yugoslavia surrendered after just 11 days and Hitler's armies swept over northern Greece. This sealed the fate of the British Expeditionary Force and Churchill faced another Dunkirk. In the case of the latter the RAF had been able to help out, but the Luftwaffe with its nearby bases had complete air supremacy over Greece. Once more the exposed Royal Navy had to try and rescue the army. Over five days commencing on 24 April it retrieved 50,200 men, not all of whom were British. Just as the evacuation started Greece capitulated.

Churchill, trying to put a brave face on things, signalled Wavell saying, 'we have paid our debt of honour with far less loss than I feared'.[22] Greece cost Wavell 16,000 men, most of whom were captured, 8,000 vehicles, 1,812 machine guns, 209 aircraft, 192 field guns, 164 anti-tank guns and 104 tanks.[23] It was hard to see the operation as little more than an unmitigated disaster. Understandably Australia and New Zealand were angry that their soldiers had been needlessly thrown away on a fool's errand. Churchill sought to lay the blame for the fate of the Balkans at the feet of Mussolini. 'This whipped jackal, who to save his own skin,' said Churchill in a broadcast on 27 April, 'has made Italy a vassal State of Hitler's Empire, is frisking up by the side of the German tiger with yelps not only of appetite … but even triumph.'[24] Apart from Athens most of Greece would end up under Italian occupation. The following day Churchill wrote to Wavell trying to sound conciliatory over his expulsion from Libya, 'We seem to have had rather bad luck. I expect we shall get this back later.'[25]

The only good news for Churchill was that British operations in the Horn of Africa launched from Kenya and Sudan during the first half of the year had soundly beaten the Italians. After retreating in the face of this two-pronged attack they surrendered in Abyssinia in the second half of May, although pockets of resistance continued until late November. Churchill, in the meantime, knowing it was vital to hold the Germans and Italians at bay in North Africa sent a convoy across the Mediterranean bearing much-needed weapons for Wavell. This sailed via Malta to Alexandria and delivered 250 tanks and over 40 Hurricanes. Churchill then badgered Wavell into driving Rommel away from the Egyptian frontier and relieving Tobruk as soon as possible.

Wavell duly counter-attacked on 15 May 1941 with Operation *Brevity* but this made little headway. Rommel was a far more formidable foe than the Italians. Just five days later Hitler invaded Crete with a massive airborne assault in order to complete his domination of the Aegean. The Allied garrison consisted of 45,500 Australian, British, Greek and New Zealander troops, many of them withdrawn from Greece. When the Royal Navy tried to intervene it was quickly mauled by the Luftwaffe operating from Greek air bases.

Despite Hitler's airborne forces suffering appalling losses on Crete, by the end of the month Churchill was facing yet another humiliating evacuation. Regardless of the ever-present Luftwaffe, Cunningham's Mediterranean Fleet dutifully went to the rescue. Although they retrieved 16,500 men it was at great cost, with the loss of nine warships and a similar number needing repairs. 'The New Zealanders and other British, Imperial and Greek troops who fought in the confused, disheartening, and vain struggle for Crete,' wrote Churchill, 'may feel that they played a definite part in an event which brought us far-reaching relief at a hingeing moment.'[26] Such sentiments after Libya and Greece felt rather hollow to Wavell and his commanders.

Wavell was soon contending with yet another threat. By late May 1941, large numbers of German and Italian aircraft had landed in Syria. Alarm bells began to ring with Churchill that a German takeover was imminent, especially in the light of the daring airborne landings in Crete. Wavell responded to Churchill with gloomy news: 'This Syrian business is disquieting, since the German Air Force established itself in Syria and are closer to the Canal and Suez than they would be at Mersa Matruh. The [Vichy] French seem now wholly committed to the Germans. I am moving reinforcements to Palestine.'[27]

Churchill and Wavell were compelled to act to safeguard Egypt's vulnerable eastern flank and on 8 June 1941 Wavell successfully invaded Lebanon and Syria. In mid-June he once again attacked Rommel with Operation *Battleaxe*. Once again Rommel bested him, launching a successful counter-attack. This was Wavell's third successive defeat at the hands of Rommel in six months. 'Although this action may seem small compared with the scale of the Mediterranean in all its various campaigns,' noted Churchill unhappily, 'its failure was to me a most bitter blow. Success in the Desert would have meant the destruction of Rommel's audacious force.'[28] All the time that the Germans and Italians remained undefeated in North Africa they posed a threat to Suez and made it impossible to isolate Italy.

Churchill decided Wavell would have to be replaced. 'I have come to the conclusion that the public interest will best be served,' signalled Churchill on 21 June, 'by the appointment of General Auchinleck to relieve you in command of the armies of the Middle East.'[29] Wavell found himself swapping places with Auchinleck who was Commander-in-Chief India, so was moved sideways rather than demoted. Auchinleck, once in Cairo, just like his predecessor soon found himself under pressure from Churchill to take immediate action. 'Only by reconquering the lost airfields of Eastern Cyrenaica,' instructed Churchill, 'can Fleet and Air Force resume effective action against enemy seaborne supplies.'[30] Instead, Churchill had to wait four months before anything happened.

Facing mounting criticism in the House of Commons, Churchill addressed them in a humorous mood on 12 November 1941. 'There was a custom in ancient China that anyone who wished to criticise the Government had the right to memoralise the Emperor,' he said with a twinkle, 'and provided that he followed that up by committing suicide, very great respect was paid to his words'.[31] Six days later Auchinleck would fair slightly better than Wavell when he launched Operation *Crusader* employing the recently created 8th Army. The plan was to destroy Rommel's Afrika Korps and finally relieve the British garrison at Tobruk. Although Rommel was successfully driven back the British found themselves stalled at El Agheila once more.

The following spring Rommel defeated Auchinleck at Gazala and on 21 June 1942 took Tobruk that for so long had held out as a defiant British thorn in his rear. Churchill was in Washington at the time and he and his entourage were dumbfounded. It was a serious strategic loss and was damaging to British military prestige. To Churchill it must have felt like the loss of Singapore all over again. 'Churchill and I were standing beside the President's desk talking to him,' recalled General Alan Brooke Chief of the Imperial General Staff, 'when [General George C.] Marshal walked in with a pink piece of paper containing a message of the fall of Tobruk! … it was a staggering blow.'[32]

The news was completely unexpected and Churchill took it badly. 'I am ashamed,' he later confided in Lord Moran. 'I cannot understand why Tobruk gave in. More than 30,000 of our men put their hands up.'[33] In response Moran noted, 'The fall of Tobruk … has been a blow between the eyes.'[34] Roosevelt and General Marshal, Chief of Staff of the US Army, boosted Churchill and Brooke's spirits by promising to send 300 Sherman tanks and 100 self-propelled guns to the Middle East. It was an incredibly generous move because the equipment had already been issued to an American armoured division.

By the end of June, the British 8th Army under General Neil Ritchie was almost 400 miles from its starting point at Gazala and just 60 miles from Alexandria. Auchinleck made Ritchie a scapegoat and sacked him.

Rommel's proximity and talk of airborne attack caused considerable panic in Alexandria and Cairo. It looked as if the British were staring defeat in the face. Fearing Alexandria harbour would be bombed the Mediterranean Fleet was dispersed to Port Said and Haifa, creating yet more alarm and despondency. British families and non-essential personnel in Egypt were hurriedly sent to Palestine and elsewhere. When Churchill learned of this he instructed the British authorities in Cairo there was to be, 'No general evacuation, no playing for safety. Egypt must be held at all costs.'[35] The fear was that with Tobruk in Rommel's hands he would be able to resupply his forces and renew his advance. However, by the time Rommel reached El Alamein he was at the very end of his supply lines and time was running out for him.

To Churchill's opponents the loss of Tobruk and the threat to Cairo was the final straw. Some argued that his strategic direction of the war and his constant meddling with his generals was no recipe for victory. He had presided over a litany of defeats that showed no sign of ending. His leadership came under direct attack in the House of Commons on 2 July 1942 when he faced a vote of no confidence instigated by Conservative Sir John Wardlaw-Milne. 'The Prime Minister wins debate after debate and loses battle after battle,' observed Labour MP Nye Bevan. 'The country is beginning to say that he fights debates like a war and the war like a debate.'[36]

Churchill knew that he had to sway the Commons and win the vote with a resounding majority in order to silence his critics in the difficult months to come. 'The setting down of this vote of censure … is a considerable event,' he warned them. 'Do not, I beg you, let the House underrate the gravity of what it has done.'[37] Looking round at the gathered politicians he added 'every nation … is waiting to see what is the true resolve and conviction of the House of Commons'.[38] He had thrown down the gauntlet to back him for the good of the war effort. When the votes were counted he had won by 475 to 25. Not only had his detractors been silenced they had been shamed by their complete lack of support. Afterwards Churchill and his daughter Mary were photographed outside 10 Downing Street. Both had very broad grins upon their faces.

Although he had warded off censure, Churchill more than ever needed a victory before he faced another political challenge. The very day before the vote the fighting in North Africa had recommenced.

Throughout July in the First Battle of El Alamein, Auchinleck and Rommel fought each other to a standstill. Neither side was able to break through the other's defences. Although the American-supplied Sherman tanks arrived at Suez in early September, much to Churchill's frustration Auchinleck assessed that the 8th Army would not be able to attack again until mid-month at the soonest. Churchill flew to Cairo on 4 August with Field Marshal Smuts and Lord Moran to see Auchinleck and Brooke who was already there. Before his departure for Egypt, Churchill was overheard muttering to himself, 'There's something very wrong there, I must clear things up.'[39] He wanted to make changes and took Smuts for moral support. Churchill had decided that Auchinleck must go.

Churchill toured the Alamein and Ruweisat defences and was greeted warmly by the troops. At one location he discovered most of the men came from Oldham, which had been his very first parliamentary constituency. 'This splendid army,' he noted, 'about double as strong as the enemy, is baffled and bewildered by its defeats.'[40] His intention was to create a new Persia and Iraq command, which was offered to Auchinleck as a way of getting rid of him. Auchinleck refused, rightly seeing it as a demotion, but was still replaced in Cairo by General Harold Alexander. It fell to Brooke to break the news. 'He wanted to know what the decision had been based on,' wrote Brooke, 'and I had to explain mainly lack of confidence in him.'[41] 'There is another reason,' added Lord Moran after talking to Brooke, 'the Auk does not understand Winston.'[42]

Churchill and Brooke met with Alexander on 8 August. The Prime Minister explained that the command in Cairo was in desperate 'need of a new start and vehement action to animate the ... organization.'[43] Alexander's task was to destroy Rommel's German and Italian forces in Egypt and Libya. Churchill also told Alexander he felt really bad about removing Auchinleck. 'You know,' he said, 'it is like killing a magnificent stag.'[44] Four days later General Bernard Montgomery arrived to take command of the 8th Army, which had been under the direct control of Auchinleck since Ritchie's departure. He officially assumed his new post on 13 August which just happened to be the date of the battle of Blenheim. Churchill took this to be a good omen and in a private note to Montgomery wrote, 'May the anniversary of Blenheim which marks the opening of the new Command bring to the Commander of the Eighth Army and his troops the fame and fortune they will surely deserve.'[45]

Churchill was greatly heartened by the intelligence briefings he received in Cairo. 'Rommel is living almost entirely on transport, and food and fuel captured from us,' he wrote in a letter to his wife. 'He is living from hand to mouth; his army's life hangs on a thread.'[46] At the end of August Rommel made one final unsuccessful attempt to break through. Churchill as always was impatient for General Alexander to counter-attack. Crucially Montgomery, backed by Alexander, refused to take action until he was ready and had an overwhelming superiority in men and material. 'Prime Minister, you are telling me how to fight in battle in a way which I know is wrong,' said Montgomery firmly. 'You are not a professional soldier. I am. ... If you wish to replace me, I will go – at once.'[47] Montgomery stayed. Before he launched his attack Churchill signalled Alexander. '"Torch" [the proposed landings in North Africa] goes forward steadily and punctually,' he said. 'But all our hopes are centred on the battle you and Montgomery are going to fight. It may well be the key to the future.'[48] Churchill hoped a British victory would persuade the French in Algeria and Morocco not to resist Operation *Torch*.

Montgomery in the Second Battle of El Alamein, which commenced at the end of October, gave Churchill his long-awaited decisive victory in North Africa. Rommel was sent reeling back towards Tripoli and with the Anglo-American landings in French North Africa complete victory on the southern shores of the Mediterranean was finally assured. The fact that Montgomery let Rommel escape was quietly glossed over. In a speech at Mansion House in London on 10 November 1942 Churchill famously summed up the situation, 'Now this is not the end. It is not even the beginning of the end. But it is, perhaps, the end of the beginning.'[49] Five days later church bells throughout Britain were rung to celebrate the victory at El Alamein. Churchill's wartime leadership was now secure.

An American Friend

Churchill appreciated from the very start of World War II that Britain needed America's help. Despite the vastness of the British Empire and its dominion territories, Britain did not have the industrial capacity to fight alone. He considered Canada the 'senior dominion' but the country had neither the manpower nor financial clout of its southern neighbour.[1] He turned to Democratic President Franklin Roosevelt as a potential saviour. America had fought with the Allies during World War I and Churchill hoped it would do so again.

Churchill was no stranger to America, having visited three times since his trip to Cuba. After 1900 his second visit had been in 1929 when he undertook a lucrative lecture tour. He was accompanied by his son Randolph, brother Jack and Jack's son Johnnie and they took in the delights of Hollywood. Churchill was not entirely comfortable in the world of glittering celebrities, though he enjoyed the luxuries on offer. Their meeting with Charlie Chaplin did not initially go well. Chaplin recalled, 'Churchill's manner, though intimate, was abrupt.'[2] Churchill liked the famous actor but concluded he was 'bolshy in politics'.[3] Regarding Randolph, Chaplin observed, 'I could see that Winston was very proud of him.'[4] More importantly Churchill's schedule included a three-hour tour of the vast Bethlehem Steel works in Pennsylvania, which had built weapons for the Allies in World War I. It also produced submarines for Britain when Churchill was first at the Admiralty and he was keen to take a look around. This gave him a valuable first-hand and up-close impression of America's industrial muscle. Then while in New

York he witnessed the Wall Street Crash, which wiped out his stocks and led to the Great Depression.

Two years later he returned embarking on another lecture tour. During this he was accidentally struck by a car in New York and hospitalized for a week. The tour was also marred by large numbers of death threats by Indian Nationalists and included the stoning of his car in Detroit and an attempt on his life in Chicago. By the time he got home Churchill was increasingly critical of America's desire to build a fleet to rival the Royal Navy. 'It would have been better for us to have said to the United States:' Churchill remarked churlishly in the House of Commons on 13 May 1932, '"build whatever you will; your Navy is absolutely ruled out of our calculations, except as a potential friend."'[5] Seven years on Churchill was hoping the US Navy would come to Britain's aid.

Even if Roosevelt wanted to help his hands were tied by the US Neutrality Acts, which were enacted during the 1930s to avoid America becoming embroiled in the growing tensions in Europe. These specifically prohibited the export of weapons to war zones. Roosevelt, who had come to office in March 1933 and again in November 1936, along with his Secretary of State Cordell Hull did not like this legislation as they saw it restricting America's ability to help friendly countries around the world. This in turn greatly hampered American foreign policy. Non-interventionists or isolationists in the US Congress, though, were determined that America should not be dragged into another world war. As far as they were concerned their country must remain neutral at all costs. 'To Hell with Europe and with the rest of those nations,'[6] said Senator Thomas D. Schall, expressing popular sentiment and support for the neutrality laws. Roosevelt had no choice but to sign the legislation as he needed the continued backing of the non-interventionists with his financial New Deal, which was intended to lift America out of the Great Depression.

By the late 1930s Roosevelt wanted to help Britain and France in the event of conflict with Hitler, but needed a way round the non-interventionists. When the Neutrality Act of 1937 was passed he managed to get a 'cash and carry' provision included. This allowed for weapons sales to Europe as long as customers paid in cash and collected them. This Roosevelt reasoned would avoid America becoming embroiled in a war. However, he chose not to invoke the Act when it came to arming China to help fend off Japanese aggression. Unlike Churchill who considered the Japanese a largely stabilizing force in China, Roosevelt refused to acknowledge Japan's creation of Manchukuo.

Roosevelt suffered the same problem that Churchill did, in that whenever he spoke out against international threats he was seen as a warmonger. The crucial difference was that at the time he was in power, while Churchill was not. In response to German, Italian and Japanese policies on 5 October 1937 Roosevelt gave his 'Quarantine Speech' in Chicago. He reasoned if aggression was to be met and contained it should be on a worldwide scale. This seemed to confirm the worst suspicions of America's isolationists.

In the face of mounting tensions across Europe in early 1938 Roosevelt tried to get leaders to come to Washington to attend talks. Nobody including Chamberlain was receptive to this idea. 'Mr Roosevelt was indeed running great risks in his own domestic politics,' noted Churchill, 'by deliberately involving the United States in the darkening European scene.'[7] Roosevelt was appalled by Kristallnacht, the orchestrated attack on Germany's Jews in November 1938. In response he recalled Hugh Wilson, his new Ambassador to Berlin. The following month Anthony Eden met with Roosevelt and recalled, 'He kept insisting that we should strengthen ourselves in the air, and described his own intentions to increase the armaments of the United States.'[8] Roosevelt also endorsed Churchill's views when he highlighted 'the inferiority of the air-power of Britain and France compared with Germany's'.[9]

When Roosevelt wanted the 'cash and carry' provisions renewed in early 1939 in response to Hitler's invasion of Czechoslovakia, Congress refused. Non-interventionist Senator Burton K. Wheeler accused him of trying to trick America into a war which would 'plow under every fourth American boy'.[10] A poll that year indicated that although 80 per cent of Americans hoped the Allies would win, 90 per cent of them did not want to get involved. On the fringes of American politics there were a number of parties that did not want America getting involved either. These included the German-American Bund which was both anti-Semitic and anti-war as well as the Nazi-inspired Silver Shirt Legion and the American Communists. The latter, although anti-Nazi, changed their stance after the Nazi-Soviet Pact was signed.

Following Hitler's invasion of Poland and the seizure of the US freighter *City of Flint* by the German battleship *Deutschland* on

9 October 1939 American opinion began to turn. The freighter crew were not freed until 3 November after their captors sailed them into the neutral Norwegian port of Haugesund. The US Neutrality Act of 1939 signed the following day included the 'cash and carry' provision much to the relief of Britain and France.

One thing Churchill and the Admiralty had to do as a priority in 1939 was to protect Britain's sea lanes in the Atlantic and the Mediterranean. This meant they needed more warships in a hurry. 'Matters were made worse because the Government had not laid down any destroyers during 1938,' said Anthony Eden, 'apparently owing to Treasury pressure.'[11] While still First Lord of the Admiralty Churchill noted, 'I persevered in my correspondence with the President, but with little response. The Chancellor of the Exchequer groaned about our dwindling dollar resources.'[12]

In late May 1940 with Hitler's forces slicing through western Europe the Americans requested the use of airfields on British Bermuda, Newfoundland and Trinidad to ensure the defence of North America. Churchill, by this time Prime Minister, rejected this on the grounds that it would offer no gain to Britain. Just as the Dunkirk evacuation was coming to an end Churchill asked for American destroyers, but Roosevelt declined. Churchill then launched a charm offensive by requesting George VI write to the President. 'As you know, we are in urgent need of some of your older destroyers to tide us over the next few months,' said the King on 26 June 1940. 'I well understand your difficulties, and I am certain that you will do your best to procure them for us before it is too late.'[13] Just as the Luftwaffe was attempting to destroy RAF Fighter Command in the skies of England, on 31 July 1940 Churchill appealed to Roosevelt for 'fifty or sixty of your oldest destroyers'.[14] He also added with a clear sense of urgency, 'Mr President, with great respect I must tell you that in the long history of the world this is a thing to do now.'[15]

Roosevelt was receptive to Churchill's request, though he had to tread carefully as Congress had recently decreed that American military equipment could only be sold aboard if it was certified surplus to requirements. Furthermore, Hitler might view the transfer of warships as a clear casus belli. The only way he had to circumvent Congress was via an executive agreement with Churchill, which did not need congressional approval. Nonetheless, Roosevelt still needed a quid pro quo and in return asked that Churchill promise to safeguard the Royal Navy by dispersing it should Hitler invade Britain. Churchill did not want to give such a public undertaking for fear it might signal the government was considering abandoning the British Isles. Roosevelt then suggested the transfer of the destroyers be in return for granting basing rights on British islands in the Caribbean and the North Atlantic. Churchill was happy with this, but wanted to keep the two transactions separate. Roosevelt, though, needed to make them publicly linked to allay the suspicions of Congress and the American public that he was taking sides. He argued that such an agreement had to show a clear security benefit for America.

Secretary of State Hull authorized the transfer of 50 destroyers to the Royal Navy on 2 September 1940 in return for naval and air basing rights in the West Indies and Newfoundland. The following day Admiral Harold Stark officially certified that the vessels were no longer needed. The King wrote again to the President on 5 September saying, 'I cannot tell you how much I have appreciated your efforts to help us, and admired the skill with which you have handled a very delicate situation.'[16] Anthony Eden felt that it was a poor deal, grumbling, 'The West Indian bases alone were certainly worth more than fifty or sixty old destroyers.'[17] When Churchill complained that the vessels were in poor condition having been kept in reserve for years, Roosevelt responded by sending ten newer Coast Guard cutters as well. 'The age and condition of the fifty destroyers made unexpectedly large demands upon our dockyards,' noted Eden. 'Only nine ships were available before the end of 1940, by which time our own naval construction was catching up on our losses.'[18] The important thing for Churchill was the transaction represented a step in the right direction in terms of American cooperation.

That same month Churchill sent the Tizard Mission to Washington to discuss the exploitation of British military research. This included radar, jet engines, rockets and the possibility of an atomic bomb. Henry Tizard, leading the mission, advocated handing over Britain's latest scientific research free as a gesture of good will and to encourage greater collaboration. Initially Churchill was reluctant to do this, but as the country was in a terrible position such a policy offered a valuable bargaining chip. Nonetheless, Roosevelt remained constrained by American neutrality. In the meantime, Britain needed more weapons.

Although the British Army had been rescued from Dunkirk its losses in equipment were catastrophic. These included 600 tanks, 120,000 vehicles, 1,350 anti-tank and anti-aircraft guns, 1,000 field guns, 90,000 rifles, 8,000 light machine guns and 7,000 tons of ammunition.[19] On top of this were the losses incurred by the RAF and Royal Navy in the French and Norwegian campaigns. All this had to be replaced. The Anglo-French Purchasing Board based in New York had already placed weapons orders with America under 'cash and carry', but these now needed to be drastically increased.

In response to Churchill's appeal Roosevelt authorized the sale of $37 million worth of arms. Amongst Britain's purchases were 500,000 World War I vintage American rifles, with 250 rounds of ammunition apiece, 900 field guns with a million rounds and 80,000 machine guns.[20] Churchill also began to order much-needed fighter aircraft and bombers. British fighter requirements were to result in the famous P-51 Mustang. All deliveries had to go via Canada because it was illegal to ship military equipment direct from American ports. After France's surrender French deliveries, including 221 fighters and 452 light bombers, were diverted to Britain. Churchill and the RAF were vexed that some American-built bombers were delivered to French Morocco and subsequently fell into Vichy hands.

Towards the end of the year Roosevelt faced a presidential election and pledged to keep America out of the war. Wendell Willkie, his Republican challenger, accused him of intending to do just the opposite. Initially Roosevelt had not planned to break the presidential two-term tradition, but he was concerned about the situation in Europe. 'If our Government should pass to other hands next January – untried hands, inexperienced hands,' warned Roosevelt, 'we can merely hope and pray that they will not substitute appeasement and compromise with those who seek to destroy all democracies everywhere, including here.'[21] Much to Churchill's relief on 5 November 1940 Roosevelt was re-elected, though there remained the thorny issue of American neutrality. 'The gratitude of the British nation is due to the noble President and his great officers and high advisers,' he wrote, 'for never, even in the advent of the Third Term Presidential Election, losing their confidence in our fortunes.'[22]

At sea Churchill hoped to formulate a policy for closer Anglo-American naval cooperation. However, he was highly critical of the strategy put forward by Rear Admiral Roger Mowbray Bellairs at the

Admiralty, which he found excessively long and much too detailed. This was drafted to help those negotiating with the Americans, but Churchill had his own definite ideas. 'I think we should say,' he told Admiral Pound, 'we loyally accept the US Navy's dispositions for the Pacific. We think it unlikely that Japan will enter the war against Great Britain and the USA.'[23] This would come back to haunt him at the end of the year. 'In the meanwhile,' he added, 'apart from the admirable dispositions proposed by the US for the Atlantic ... The first thing is to get the US into the war. We can settle how to fight it afterwards.'[24] Churchill decided Bellairs' paper should not be shared with Roosevelt.

Churchill had been buying American weapons using Britain's reserves, but these were running out fast. 'By very severe measures we had been able to ... spend in America about £500,000,000 sterling,' said Churchill, 'but the end of our financial resources was in sight – nay, had actually been reached.'[25] He knew that Britain faced bankruptcy. 'Even if we divested ourselves of all our gold and foreign assets, he wrote, 'we could not pay for half we had ordered, and the extension of the war made it necessary for us to have ten times as much.'[26]

In desperation he threw himself on Roosevelt's mercy and asked for credit. He wrote the President a 15-page letter on 7 December 1940 outlining Britain's dire economic and military plight. 'The moment approaches,' he said, 'when we shall no longer be able to pay cash for shipping and other supplies.' Churchill added he was sure America would not wish to see Britain 'stripped to the bone'.[27] He argued that in the long term this would be detrimental to the American economy and security.

Roosevelt wanted to help but was still governed by the 'cash and carry' only policy. To assist Churchill, he therefore put the incredibly generous Lend-Lease bill before Congress. It was blandly titled 'An Act to further promote the defence of the United States' and the bill's number was 1776, the very year America had declared its independence. This legislation essentially permitted the President to provide weapons on any basis he saw fit, with supplies being initially leased or lent. It was passed on 9 February 1941 and was approved by the Senate the following month. Lend-Lease became law on 11 March 1941 and was subsequently extended to China and the Soviet Union. 'The Lend-Lease bill must be regarded,' said Churchill with immense gratitude and relief, 'without question as the most unsordid act in the whole of recorded history.'[28] Furthermore he acknowledged, 'The ... turning-point was when the President and Congress of the United States passed the Lend-Lease enactment, devoting nearly 2,000 millions Sterling ... to help us to defend our liberties and their own.'[29] Importantly for Churchill Lend-Lease would speed up the supply of weapons, including aircraft direct from America to British forces in the Middle East and North Africa.

In anticipation of Lend-Lease, Roosevelt established the Office of Production Management (OPM). Unfortunately, the two men he appointed to head it, Sidney Hillman, president of the Amalgamated Clothing Workers Union, and William Knudsen, the former president of General Motors, were ideologically opposed to each other. The result was that by the end of the summer the OPM was in a state of chaos and could not cope with the vast array of Lend-Lease orders. Roosevelt responded by creating another organization, the War Production Board, to work round it.

In addition to the aircraft Britain had bought and would seek under Lend-Lease, Churchill needed pilots and aircrew to man them. Despite not being at war Roosevelt permitted the RAF as part of Lend-Lease to establish seven flying schools in Arizona, California, Florida, Oklahoma and Texas.[30] There they could train in clear skies and without threat from the Luftwaffe. To avoid the involvement of the US military the RAF cadets were trained by civilian instructors. Some of the first British pilots graduated in Florida in August 1941.

Roosevelt and Churchill first met face to face in the second week of August 1941 on board the American cruiser *Augusta* in Placentia Bay, Newfoundland. Churchill then hosted the President on the brand-new battleship *Prince of Wales*. As Roosevelt had been paralysed from the waist down since 1921, by what at the time was diagnosed as polio,[31] five of the six meals the pair took together were on the *Augusta*. Churchill hoped they had come together for America to declare war on Germany and Italy, but this did not happen. Opinion polls indicated that three-quarters of Americans opposed going to war, and in addition Roosevelt faced growing tension with Japan. Instead, he pledged to aid the Soviet Union, which was now under attack by Hitler, and to provide escorts for the Allies' convoys as far as the mid-Atlantic. The latter held out the hope for Churchill that an incident between a U-boat and the US Navy might spark war.

Churchill and Roosevelt also agreed to issue what became known as the Atlantic Charter, whereby they would 'respect the right of all peoples' to form governments of their own choosing.[32] Furthermore, 'they wish to see sovereign rights restored to those who have been forcibly deprived of them'.[33] This of course raised a question mark over the future of India and indeed the rest of the British Empire. However, Churchill knew it was not the time to quibble over democratic niceties when his immediate goal was the defeat of Nazism and Fascism. While their declaration made no mention of Italy it spoke very explicitly of 'the final destruction of the Nazi tyranny'.[34] This signalled to Hitler that America was doing all it could to help Britain and Russia bar sending troops. Furthermore, Japan would see the charter as the potential foundation of an Anglo-American alliance in the Far East.

Despite this Churchill was disappointed that Roosevelt was remaining on the sidelines, as it meant Germany and Italy would take longer to defeat. He was anxious that by the time America was dragged into the war the situation for Britain would be irretrievable. At the end of the month he voiced these concerns to the Canadian Prime Minister Mackenzie King who was his guest at Chequers. 'Though we cannot now be defeated,' Churchill told him, 'the war might drag on for another four or five years, and civilization and culture would be wiped out.'[35] It would need something dramatic to speed up America's entry into the war.

Behind the scenes Churchill exploited the Nazi menace in the Americas. He was greatly aided in this by the American press that regularly reported on the Nazi threat in Brazil. For example Frank Tannenbaum warned in late May 1940 that the 'Germans have a South American Trojan horse'.[36] Churchill directed MI6 to forge a German language map showing Hitler's plans to attack South America.[37] It indicated under Nazi rule the region would be divided into five super states with the northern portion renamed New Spain. This was passed to Roosevelt as a genuine document and was used to help justify the President's support for Britain.

'Hitler has often protested that his plans for conquest do not extend across the Atlantic Ocean,' Roosevelt said in an address on 27 October 1941. 'I have in my possession a secret map … This map makes clear the Nazi design not only against South America but against the United States itself.'[38] Churchill's act of duplicity showed just how desperate he was for Roosevelt's backing. The President's remarks came shortly after a U-boat had tried to sink the US destroyer *Kearny*, which was protecting a convoy off Iceland. Although the ship survived, 11 crew were killed. Once more America refrained from declaring war.

By this stage Churchill and Roosevelt's opening courtship was coming to an end, as was America's neutrality. On 7 December 1941 Japanese aircraft attacked Pearl Harbor forcing Congress's hand. Almost at the same time the Japanese Army struck the American garrison in the Philippines and the British in Malaya. The following day Churchill and Roosevelt declared war on Japan. However, to Churchill's dismay America still did not declare war on Italy and Germany. This meant that Britain would have to continue going it alone in Europe and the Mediterranean.

Ironically Hitler, fed up with America violating its own policy of neutrality by favouring Germany's enemies with financial support, weapons and training facilities, declared war on 11 December. The Americans now had no choice but to fight Hitler and Mussolini. 'I thought of a remark which Edward Grey had made to me more than thirty years before,' observed Churchill in response to the news, 'that the United States is like a "gigantic boiler. Once the fire is lighted under it there is no limit to the power it can generate."'[39]

The following day Churchill sailed for America with the British Chiefs of Staff. Roosevelt was understandably reticent about the British prime minister's visit as he had his hands full in the days following Pearl Harbor. Nonetheless, he understood Churchill's desire for another face-to-face meeting. The British had not had a good year, having been expelled from Greece, Crete and Libya. Now they, like the Americans, would have to contend with the Japanese threat in the Far East.

One of Churchill's biggest worries was what would happen to Lend-Lease as the Americans would need all the weapons they could lay their hands on. Before he left he wrote to the King saying, 'We have also to be careful that our share of munitions and other aid which we are receiving from the United States does not suffer more than is, I fear, inevitable.'[40] During the voyage Churchill also aired such concerns with Sir Charles Wilson, his physician. 'They may concentrate upon Japan and leave us to deal with Germany,' he warned Wilson. 'They had already stopped the stream of supplies that we were getting.'[41]

Churchill arrived in Washington on 22 December and stayed for three weeks as Roosevelt's guest at the White House. Despite a night flight from Hampton Roads, a tired Churchill was launched straight into a long evening dinner for 17 people, drinks and an initial private meeting with Roosevelt. The following day the pair presented a united front for the American press. Churchill was soon wooing reporters with his wicked sense of humour. When asked how long it would take to win the war he responded, 'If we manage it well, it will only take half as long as if we manage it badly.'[42] This was met by laughter. During their time together the British and American Chiefs of Staff agreed that the war in Europe rather than the Pacific should be the priority. The defeat of Mussolini and Hitler would come first. Churchill, Roosevelt and the combined Chiefs of Staff also agreed they would fight and win a war of attrition based on overwhelming industrial muscle. Output quotas would be set and met. The fire was lit under the American boiler.

Churchill was also accorded the honour of addressing the Senate and members of Congress. He understood that it was vital to win over the assembled American politicians and worried endlessly over his speech the night before. To break the ice he said, 'I cannot help reflecting that if my father had been American and my mother British, instead of the other way round, I might have got here on my own.'[43] His joke was greeted with laughter. Churchill then told them 'twice in our lifetime has the long arm of fate reached across the ocean to bring the United States into the forefront of the battle'.[44] Steadily he gained their admiration and trust. 'There was a great scene at the end,' recalled Sir Charles Wilson. 'The Senators and Congressmen stood cheering and waving their papers till he went out.'[45] Churchill had got what he had hoped for through the dark days of 1940 and 1941, an American ally.

Unfortunately, all the excitement in Washington proved almost too much for him. After his speech he complained of chest pain and discomfort down his left arm. Sir Charles diagnosed a mild heart attack, which should have confined Churchill to bed for at least six weeks. Fearing that Churchill's work might suffer he decided not to tell him. Sir Charles reasoned 'at a moment when America has just come into the war, and there is no one but Winston to take her hand. I felt that the effect of announcing that the P.M. had had a heart attack could only be disastrous.'[46] Sir Charles simply told him that he had 'been over doing things'.[47] To which Churchill retorted that he was not going to rest. It was a calculated risk with Churchill's health, one that could have been fatal, but none the wiser he carried on regardless. After visiting Mackenzie King and addressing the Canadian Parliament he decided to head for the sunshine in Florida. He spent a week at Pompano Beach relaxing and swimming. Sir Charles observed rather unkindly that 'Winston basks half-submerged in the water like a hippopotamus in a swamp'.[48]

Joan of Arc

Churchill not only had to direct World War II, but he also had to conduct ongoing diplomacy with all the Allied leaders. None was as problematic as General Charles de Gaulle, self-appointed leader of the Free French who carried no real authority with the French military. At the time of the German invasion he was only a divisional commander, who was best known for his cutting-edge theories on the use of tanks. Then on 6 June 1940 de Gaulle was appointed Under-Secretary of State to the Minister of National Defence. He accepted on condition that France did not contemplate surrender. 'If the battle of 1940 is lost,' de Gaulle said to Premier Reynaud, 'then we must win some other battle.'[1] However, de Gaulle soon found that the French government was plagued by defeatism. In particular, he discovered that Marshal Pétain was briefing against Churchill by informing the American Ambassador in Paris he believed the British Prime Minister was planning a separate peace with Germany.

Major-General Sir Edward Spears, Churchill's personal representative with Reynaud, reported that de Gaulle 'had proved his worth as a fighting soldier'.[2] Churchill first met him just three days later at 10 Downing Street on 9 June. He was immediately impressed by de Gaulle's resolution to keep on resisting the German invasion. He was, though, brutally frank with de Gaulle, pointing out that he doubted France could hold out in light of the magnitude of her defeats and the attitude of her leaders. It was undoubtedly a difficult encounter coming just five days after the British evacuation at Dunkirk. All those remaining British forces in France were heading for the Channel ports, so it was hard to hide the reality that Britain was abandoning her ally.

De Gaulle requested, on behalf of Reynaud, ships to help the French Army withdraw to North Africa and that the BEF be re-equipped and sent back to France as soon as possible. He certainly expected a refusal of the latter, but instead Churchill pointed out that a British division was disembarking in Normandy and a Canadian division was to embark for Brittany the following day. Neither of them knew that these units would be heading home within a week minus their equipment. They became part of the smaller Dunkirk which was conducted from Brest, Cherbourg, St Malo and St Nazaire. Churchill also made it clear that he was not prepared to send any more fighter squadrons to metropolitan France.

Although de Gaulle returned to France partially satisfied, two days later the French government abandoned Paris for Tours. When de Gaulle heard that Churchill was flying to Briare on the Loire to meet the French Commander-in-Chief General Weygand he was not happy. 'It would be madness,' he told Reynaud, 'to allow the British Prime Minister to discuss the military situation with a man who is already committed to capitulation.'³ De Gaulle said Weygand should be replaced by General Huntziger, who would rally French forces in North Africa, but Reynaud wavered. To add to Reynaud's multitude of woes, Admiral François Darlan, the commander of the French Navy, refused to transport the army to North Africa. Pétain and Weygand were pressuring Reynaud to accept an armistice.

On 13 June Churchill arrived in Tours in a vain effort to bolster French morale. It was to be his last visit for almost four years. 'The cause of France will always remain dear to us,' he told his hosts, 'and we shall restore her in all her strength and dignity if we triumph.'⁴ Understandably the French were not convinced. 'History will say without a doubt that the Battle of France was lost through want of aircraft,'⁵ said Reynaud bitterly. He only had himself to blame for this, as many French aircraft had been dispersed to North Africa for safety. 'Also through want of tanks and through the numerical superiority of the enemy,' added Churchill.⁶ This again was not true as France had one of the largest and finest armies in Europe.

During this meeting Churchill quickly sensed that only de Gaulle had any stomach for carrying on the fight either from Brittany or North Africa. General Spears recalled, 'He asked me about de Gaulle, and I told him I was certain he was completely staunch'.⁷ They were both right of course, because shortly after Reynaud was overthrown by

Pétain and Weygand became Minister of Defence and Admiral Darlan Minister of the Navy. Under them France sued for peace.

On his return journey Churchill had another one of his close shaves. The weather was not good and he was informed that a fighter escort to get him back over the Channel was not available. He decided to press on regardless. Once out over water his pilot spotted German fighters below them. It was a tense few moments; all it needed was for a German pilot to glance up and they would have been done for. Luckily for Churchill and his entourage the enemy were preoccupied attacking some unfortunate trawlers. Churchill's pilot took evasive measures and was relieved beyond measure when they were finally greeted by the RAF.

Four days later in Bordeaux, de Gaulle leapt on Spears' aircraft and also flew to London. Spears took him to see Churchill in Downing Street. Although he had a lot on his mind Churchill was waiting for them in the garden. Spears noted, 'He got up to greet his guest, and his smile of welcome was very warm and friendly.'[8] Churchill agreed that as soon as Pétain asked the Germans for an armistice de Gaulle should make a broadcast to his countrymen urging them to fight on from exile. The Frenchman stated, 'I, General de Gaulle, assume the right to speak in the name of France.'[9] Few, though, chose to side with him and the country's senior leaders chose to stay in France.

'I knew he was no friend of England,' Churchill later wrote.[10] Nonetheless he decided to recognize de Gaulle as the head of the Free French Forces wherever they might be. This was a quite audacious step as de Gaulle was only a junior general and an unelected official. Pétain was the legal head of France. Churchill was fully aware that de Gaulle had no army and other than Britain no bases to operate from. All those French troops rescued from Dunkirk had elected to go home. Regardless, Churchill recalled 'I felt, there goes the Constable of France.'[11] In this instance Churchill proved to be an exceptionally good judge of character.

Churchill was evidently thinking of the military situation and gave little thought to the political fallout from backing de Gaulle from the start. This single act put de Gaulle on the road to power. Neither Halifax at the Foreign office nor Eden at the War Office liked this arrangement. They pointed out making de Gaulle head of the Free French anywhere could have political repercussion with the Americans. Eden was not happy at the thought of having to find yet more equipment for another allied unit to add to those of the Czechs, Dutch, Norwegians and Poles.

Once the armistice was signed all of France's colonies quickly paid lip service to the authority of Pétain's Vichy government.

De Gaulle rather surprisingly supported Churchill's difficult decision to attack the French Fleet at Mers-el-Kebir. Darlan's vacillation over the fate of his warships and the lack of confidence that Pétain could keep them from Hitler's grasp sealed their fate. However, de Gaulle's second-in-command, Admiral Émile Muselier, was so incensed that he threatened to resign and return to France. Many did and many on their way to join de Gaulle changed their minds. Muselier angrily wrote to Churchill suggesting that the British government should pledge to replace those warships lost at Mers-el-Kebir. He also suggested that the wounded and the families of those killed should be compensated. Churchill rightly felt that this was not the time for such a discussion, particularly as the French Fleet had resisted on the orders of Darlan. Subsequently Muselier found himself arrested by the British authorities on trumped up charges of spying for Vichy. In reality Muselier was a victim of political infighting amongst the Free French. He was eventually released and received a letter of apology from Anthony Eden. This was an embarrassing diplomatic incident and Churchill arranged for Muselier to dine with him and have an audience with the King. Churchill hoped that this had smoothed things over, but Muselier remained convinced that de Gaulle had tried to frame him.

Major Morton, Churchill's personal intelligence liaison officer, was well informed about anti-British sentiment amongst the Free French and the myriad of other French organizations in London and no doubt passed this on to Churchill. Churchill, though, did not develop a personal relationship with Sir David Petrie, the head of MI5. The result of this was that Morton was free to belittle their efforts, alleging 'MI5 tends to see dangerous men too freely'.[12] One of Petrie's many preoccupations was to make sure that the dozen Vichy consuls dotted around the United Kingdom and refugee Vichy sympathizers were not conducting espionage on British soil.

When Eden complained in August 1940 that he was getting no intelligence from the Free French or France, Sir Stewart Menzies, head of MI6, was summoned by Churchill. He was given a good dressing down and told to feed reports directly to the Prime Minister. Menzies was also instructed to keep Eden and Halifax in the loop to avoid further trouble. Although Menzies personally delivered Ultra intelligence produced by Bletchley Park's decoders to Churchill, he pointedly made sure that Morton was not on the distribution list.

While Morton saw himself as Churchill's intelligence supremo, those around him thought otherwise. The Americans were to dub him 'Desperate Desmond'.[13] Eden was to find Morton's dealings with de Gaulle and the French resistance particularly meddlesome. He was later to remark 'I wish Morton at the bottom of the Sea'.[14] Morton persuaded Churchill to hire a public relations expert to promote de Gaulle and his cause. The Frenchman was not grateful and was immediately affronted that Churchill wanted to try and turn him into some sort of film star.

Churchill was soon to find de Gaulle calling for support from scarce British military resources. In French West Africa, Cameroon, Chad and French Equatorial Africa came over to the Free French cause. However, they were neutralized by Gabon and Senegal resolutely supporting Vichy. De Gaulle reasoned that if the port of Dakar could be secured by a seaborne assault force then they would come over to the Free French. He was supported by General Spears and Major Morton. Churchill agreed because Dakar lay on the Cape supply route round to the Red Sea and Egypt. He certainly did not want it falling into German hands. Unfortunately, Vichy was well informed of de Gaulle's plans. The whole operation was compromised by leaks from the Free French and the Poles in London. The very day before de Gaulle and a British fleet arrived on 23 September 1940, Dakar received a large-scale reinforcement. The garrison resisted and damage was sustained by both sides' warships. After just two days the Allies gave up and withdrew. De Gaulle was discredited and Churchill once again looked the aggressor against his former ally. Churchill was roundly criticized in the House of Commons for acquiescing to de Gaulle's wishes, whereas the plan had really been his.

Rattled by the setback at Dakar, Churchill tried to recruit General Georges Catroux, the former governor of French Indochina, as a possible future head of the Free French. This backfired because instead Catroux pledged his loyalty to de Gaulle. Despite differences of opinion with his commanders, de Gaulle pressed on with his campaign to secure all of French Equatorial Africa. On 27 October 1940 he issued a statement from Brazzaville denouncing Pétain and declaring himself head of a newly created Empire Defence Council. Its members included Catroux and Muselier.

Although Churchill had broken off diplomatic relations with Vichy, once it was clear that the French Empire was loyal to Pétain, he had little choice but to open diplomatic channels through third parties. Churchill was influenced by Roosevelt's pragmatism. Although America was still neutral at this stage Roosevelt was committed to support Churchill. Roosevelt reasoned that the existence of Vichy and the neutral zone kept the Germans away from the Mediterranean. It also ensured, for the time being at least, the French Empire and fleet were kept out of Hitler's grasp. Likewise, after Mers-el-Kebir nothing further should be done to drive Pétain into open alliance with Germany. This meant that Churchill had little choice but to deal with both de Gaulle and Pétain at the same time, which inevitably meant he could please neither.

Pétain's unofficial emissary Professor Louis Rougier returned from London in October 1940 with what he described as a 'Gentlemen's Agreement'.[15] Churchill understood that Vichy had to maintain a policy of guarded hostility towards Britain to prevent Hitler from occupying all of France, and in this respect Mers-el-Kebir had served its purpose admirably. The so-called 'agreement' acknowledged that Britain would not attack French colonial territories and would not blockade French shipping from North Africa, as long as Vichy maintained control of the French fleet and stopped the Germans using French bases. Furthermore, the French Empire would side with the Allies once they were in a position to protect it and rearm France's colonial forces. To keep de Gaulle happy Vichy would not attempt to recapture those territories that had gone over to the Free French. De Gaulle understandably was not pleased by this, as it was little more than a diplomatic fudge. He knew Churchill had tried to supplant him with Catroux and if Churchill recognized Vichy as anything other than the enemy then it undermined the legitimacy of the Free French. Inevitably this 'Gentlemen's Agreement' did not last long.

At a time when Churchill was having to contend with fending off Rommel in the Western Desert, fighting the Italians in Abyssinia, defending Crete and suppressing a revolt in Iraq, he had to support de Gaulle's seizure of Syria. This campaign in June 1941 was driven by fears that the Germans were going to occupy Lebanon and Syria. De Gaulle and Catroux's forces were not strong enough to overwhelm the local Vichy forces and General Wavell was obliged to divert troops when he could least spare them.

Churchill then found himself embroiled in the ridiculous saga of Saint-Pierre and Miquelon, which were tiny islands owned by France south of Newfoundland. De Gaulle argued that they should be removed from the control of Vichy as there was nothing to stop them spying on Allied convoys. Churchill felt that this was a Canadian and American problem. President Roosevelt, though, was of the opinion that de Gaulle had no authority and was disinclined to help him. The Frenchman was angered to discover in November 1941 that Canada was going to take over the islands with a view to keeping them. To stop him reacting just a week after the Japanese attack on Pearl Harbor, 14 French ships were seized in American harbours. On 18 December 1941 the American government informed Eden they were opposed to the Free French securing Saint-Pierre and Miquelon. De Gaulle, though, forced the issue and on Christmas eve Admiral Muselier arrived off Saint-Pierre with three frigates and a submarine. Behind the scenes Churchill was fully aware of this operation and supported it.

At the time Churchill was in Washington visiting Roosevelt and the latter was furious with de Gaulle. However, the islanders accepted de Gaulle's authority in a referendum and there was nothing the Americans or Canadians could do. On 31 December 1940 Churchill sent de Gaulle a rather self-congratulatory telegram, 'I pleaded your case strongly to our friends in the United States. Your having broken away from the agreement about St. Pierre et Miquelon raised a storm which might have been serious had I not been on the spot to speak to the President.'[16] Churchill wanted the Free French to sign the United Nations Declaration drawn up in Washington, but Roosevelt would not hear of it. The whole incident confirmed Roosevelt's dislike of de Gaulle and left Churchill out on a limb as he continued to champion the intransigent Free French leader. In contrast Roosevelt would do his utmost to exclude de Gaulle from future Allied planning. He would also remain lukewarm to the idea of liberating other Vichy-controlled overseas possessions.

De Gaulle and Churchill would have to go it alone until it came to the invasion of French North Africa. Although Churchill and Eden tried to reassure de Gaulle that the Allies had no designs on French territory, he remained unconvinced. De Gaulle's stock rose immeasurably with Churchill in May 1942 when General Pierre Koenig's Free French troops bested three German and Italian divisions in the Libyan desert at Bir Hakeim. Nonetheless, that same month Churchill invaded the island of French Madagascar without informing de Gaulle. He hoped that by not involving the Free French the Vichy garrison would not resist. Instead, it took months to subdue the island.

Churchill knew that the Free French had a very good intelligence network and it would only be a matter of time before de Gaulle learned of Allied intentions towards French North Africa. Roosevelt wanted to persuaded French Algeria and Morocco to come over to the Allied cause without recourse to de Gaulle. He was adamant when he wrote to Churchill on the issue, 'In my view it is essential that de Gaulle be kept out of the picture and permitted to have no information whatever, regardless of how irritated and irritating he may become.'[17] Roosevelt was later amused to learn that Churchill had dubbed de Gaulle 'Joan of Arc'.[18]

The French admirals and generals in North Africa had little respect for de Gaulle, and on the surface at least were not prepared to break with Vichy. Churchill agreed with Roosevelt that, when they invaded French North Africa, if American troops conducted the landings the Vichy troops would be less likely to resist. When de Gaulle learned of the Allied landings in Algiers, Casablanca and Oran in November 1942 he was furious. He was even angrier when he discovered that Churchill and Roosevelt had agreed to Admiral Darlan serving as French High Commissioner in order to bring French North Africa over to the Allies. Churchill had to justify this odious arrangement in a secret session of the House of Commons. 'I hold no brief for Admiral Darlan,' he said. 'Like myself, he is the object of the animosities of Herr Hitler ... Otherwise I have nothing in common with him.'[19] By this stage Hitler, in retaliation to the Allied landings, had occupied Vichy and was sending troops to occupy Tunisia.

The appointment of Darlan and Hitler's invasion of southern France simply pushed the French resistance into the arms of de Gaulle. The subsequent assassination of Darlan ensured by the end of the year de Gaulle was president of the French Committee of National Liberation, which had been set up in Algiers. Rumours were soon circulating that de Gaulle's supporters were responsible for the murder and as a result his trip to Washington was cancelled by Roosevelt. It has also been suggested Churchill had a hand in Darlan's death and that he instructed Stewart Menzies, the head of MI6, to coordinate the killing with French dissidents.[20] However, the evidence to support this allegation remains circumstantial. Intriguingly, though, the assassin was reported to have had $2,000 in his possession, which had been provided by the British to de Gaulle's financial services.[21]

De Gaulle had many enemies and on 21 April 1943 they tried to kill him. He had just boarded a flight from London to Glasgow and was about to take off when the pilot aborted because the elevator controls had failed. De Gaulle and his party were given another aircraft. A subsequent investigation showed the elevator rod had been cut using acid. German saboteurs were blamed but no one was convinced. Although Churchill continued to support de Gaulle, Roosevelt was increasingly of the view that he was little more than a dictator in waiting, intent on preserving the French Empire and seizing power in metropolitan France. De Gaulle's squabbling with his colleagues, particularly General Henri Giraud appointed by the Americans to replace Darlan, did not help matters either. In a moment of exasperation Roosevelt dubbed de Gaulle and Giraud the 'Bride' and 'Groom'. 'We all thought General Giraud was the man for the job,' said Churchill, 'and that his arrival would be electric.'[22] It was not to be.

Things came to a head while Churchill was in Washington in May 1943. 'I become more and more disturbed by the continued machinations of de Gaulle,' warned Roosevelt. 'When we get into France itself, we will have to regard it as a military occupation run by British and American generals.'[23] He also suggested getting rid of de Gaulle by making him governor of Madagascar. Churchill floated this suggestion that they abandon de Gaulle with Clement Attlee and Anthony Eden. The latter noted, 'Everyone against and very brave about it in his absence.'[24] Attlee signalled back saying in taking such a course of action 'we would not only make him a national martyr but would find ourselves accused ... of interfering improperly in French internal affairs with a view to treating France as an Anglo-American protectorate.'[25] Churchill was not happy and remained concerned this refusal would harm Anglo-US relations. 'I should be very sorry to become responsible for breaking this harmony,' he said 'for the sake of a Frenchman who is a bitter foe of Britain and may well bring civil war upon France.'[26] It was clear in this respect that Churchill was echoing Roosevelt's concerns about de Gaulle's democratic credentials.

Although French troops were subsequently involved in the campaigns in Tunisia and Italy, Churchill and Roosevelt would deliberately sideline de Gaulle when it came to the opening of the Second Front. When de Gaulle arrived in London from Algiers on 4 June 1944, to be briefed

on the impeding D-Day, he found a waiting letter from Churchill
that said, 'Welcome to these shores! Great military events are about to
take place.'²⁷ In light of *Overlord* being just two days away Churchill
appreciated that de Gaulle would have to be handled carefully, but
there was no way to hide the exclusion of the Free French until the very
last minute. He invited de Gaulle to lunch before attending a meeting
with Eisenhower regarding the landings. Churchill and Eisenhower
wanted de Gaulle on board, because they needed the support of the
French resistance.

Churchill explained to de Gaulle that he could make no decision
regarding France's future government without Roosevelt's agreement.
He urged de Gaulle to take up Roosevelt's offer to visit America to
discuss matters. De Gaulle was angered saying his caretaker government
already existed and he saw no point negotiating its recognition.
Churchill retorted 'if General de Gaulle wanted us to ask the President
to give him the title deeds of France the answer was "no"'.²⁸ Much to
Churchill's consternation de Gaulle refused to cooperate with Allied
plans. De Gaulle voiced his suspicion that the Americans intended to
impose a military administration on France once they were ashore. He
then accused Britain of siding with America. 'How can you expect us,'
retorted de Gaulle angrily, 'to negotiate on bases such as these?'²⁹

Although a French army was allocated to the liberation of the
Riviera in August 1944, only a single French division came ashore
in Normandy weeks after D-Day. However, de Gaulle was to get the
last laugh by getting the credit for liberating Marseilles, Toulon and
more importantly Paris. Churchill remained unrepentant that he had
supported de Gaulle in the early days of the war, but their relationship
had been tested to the limit. Churchill later wrote, 'He had to be rude
to the British to prove to French eyes that he was not a British puppet.'³⁰
Few Frenchmen would argue with such a sentiment.

Once in Paris, whatever Churchill and Roosevelt's reservations
may have been, de Gaulle swiftly made himself master of France and
the French military. Pointedly, Britain and America did not formally
recognize his de facto government until October 1944. 'I understood
and admired, while I resented his arrogant demeanour,' Churchill
concluded of de Gaulle. 'It was said in mockery that he thought himself
the living representative of Joan of Arc ... This did not seem to me as
absurd as it looked.'³¹

Courting the Red Czar

Churchill's relationship with Stalin was problematic from the start and lacked mutual trust. Churchill made no secret of his complete disregard for Bolsheviks, whom he had castigated at every opportunity during the Russian revolution. 'Bolshevism is a great evil,' he had said. 'My hatred … arises from the bloody and devastating terrorism which they practise in every land.'[1] On Stalin's part he could never forgive Churchill's military intervention in Russia. He had fought during the civil war, starting as Director-General of Food Supplies in southern Russia, rising to Political Commissar to the South Western Front with sweeping military powers. After the war he had become the absolute ruler of the Soviet Union with an ingrained distrust of the Western powers.

To his dismay H.G. Wells discovered when he interviewed Stalin in the 1930s the Soviet state was only interested in the survival of Soviet Communism and nothing else. Stalin's international support against Fascism simply fuelled Soviet totalitarianism in the name of protecting the state. Wells was flabbergasted by this frank admission, as it was not what Communist spokesmen outside the Soviet Union were telling left and left-of-centre political parties. Wells reasoned that class war and the stifling of dissent was doing more harm than good. The Soviet leader thought otherwise. Furthermore, Stalin was not receptive to Wells' suggestion of a rapprochement with America, calling Roosevelt's New Deal a move to con the American working class. If Churchill saw Wells' resulting work published in the *New Statesman*, he would have also seen how it was rubbished by Irish playwright George Bernard Shaw.

The latter had spent that decade championing Europe's hard men, in particular Stalin. It was clear, though, that Stalin did not hold Britain or America in high regard.

By 1940, despite Stalin having gobbled up a swathe of Europe, Churchill knew that he needed the Red Czar as an ally. Germany had dissipated its strength by fighting on both the Western and Eastern Fronts during World War I. If Hitler attacked Stalin, then exactly the same thing would happen. Although the Soviet administration might be inept and murderous, it had enormous resources at its disposal. Under these circumstances Churchill had no scruples about burying, at least temporarily, his ideological differences with Communism.

He felt that Hitler's attack in the West was simply a pre-emptive strike before he turned East. It was his continued defiance after the fall of France that complicated matters for Hitler. The German leader's only real options when it came to Britain were to cross the English Channel or assist Mussolini's attack in the Mediterranean. Neither of these was appealing as they were unwanted diversions from his ultimate goal of gaining living space and raw materials in western Russia. During 1940 Churchill was alarmed by Stalin's determination not to provoke Hitler, a stance that severely compromised the defence of the Soviet Union. He was initially convinced that the Soviet Union, despite the size of the Red Army, would fall swiftly just like France.

However, through the last half of 1940 Churchill assumed that Hitler's next military adventure would be against Spain. General Franco had refused to give German troops passage to attack the British naval base at Gibraltar. Unless Hitler secured it, he was unable to close off the Mediterranean to the Royal Navy. If he did that it would greatly help Mussolini and any Axis operations in the Balkans. Therefore, up until early 1941 Churchill and the Joint Intelligence Committee assessed that Hitler was unlikely to attack the Soviet Union in the near future.

Things changed dramatically in mid-March 1941 when Bletchley Park's monitoring of German communications indicated Hitler was going to attack east. Churchill was aware that Stalin had deliberately slowed the mobilization of the Red Army to avoid confrontation with Germany. Alarmed at the prospect of being caught out, Stalin's generals, to get round this, contrived to conduct military exercises in the western Soviet Union. This, though, was an unsatisfactory compromise. Furthermore, transporting troops and their equipment from across the country took time, which left the Red Army in a highly vulnerable state.

Churchill faced a dilemma in that he wanted to warn Stalin, but could not reveal Bletchley had broken the German Enigma codes employed by their armed forces. He waited until early April 1941 before drafting a message, which was vague and not delivered to Stalin until the end of the month. The Soviet leader took no heed, suspecting it was a ruse by the beleaguered Churchill to get him to enter the war against Hitler. When Rudolf Hess, the Deputy Führer, flew to Scotland the following month this convinced Stalin even more that Churchill was up to something. Although Hess was acting on his own volition, Stalin felt that the British were secretly trying to make peace. If he went to war he would be left on his own. Besides, Hitler informed Stalin that his build-up in the east was designed to dupe Churchill before invading England. The troops in Poland were simply retraining. In addition, Churchill was well known for his hatred of Communism and had done everything in his power to prevent the birth of the Soviet Union. 'We're being threatened with the Germans and the Germans with the Soviet Union,' grumbled Stalin to his generals. 'They're playing us off each other.'[2]

While Churchill took Bletchley's intelligence about an attack on the Soviet Union at face value, the Joint Intelligence Committee took until 12 June 1941 to change their assessment. The committee revised its advice thanks to an intercepted telegram from the Japanese ambassador in Berlin. This provided clear evidence of a German attack on the Soviet Union and the committee assessed that it would take place in the second half of June. Churchill told Bill Bentick, the Joint Intelligence Committee Chairman, to warn Ivan Maisky, the Soviet Ambassador in London. Bentick told Maisky that Hitler would attack on 22 June or 29 June, but thought the 22nd was most likely. This was indeed the exact date chosen by Hitler for Operation *Barbarossa*. By this stage, though, the warning was far too late to help the assembling Red Army.

When Churchill was duly informed at eight o'clock on the morning of 22 June 1941 that Hitler's Blitzkrieg had been launched against the Soviet Union, he was relieved. However, the day before he had told everyone it would be a disaster for the Russians. 'So far as strategy, policy, foresight, competence are arbiters,' said Churchill scathingly, 'Stalin and his commissars showed themselves at this moment the most completely outwitted bunglers of the Second World War.'[3] Gathered at

Chequers were Anthony Eden, Sir Stafford Cripps, General Sir John Dill, Chief of the Imperial General Staff and John Gilbert Winant, the American ambassador. They were all of the view that the Red Army would not last much more than six weeks. Churchill, though, was suddenly brimming with optimism. 'I will bet you a Monkey to a Mousetrap [racing term for 500:1],' he said, 'that the Russians are still fighting, and fighting victoriously, two years from now.'[4] Jock Colville, the Prime Minister's private secretary, later told Churchill, 'I recorded your words … because I thought they were such a daring prophecy, and because it was such an entirely different point of view from that which everybody else expressed.'[5]

That night Churchill broadcast to the nation informing it that it had a new-found ally, though the formalities still had yet to be conducted. There was also an air of I told you so. 'At 4 o'clock this morning Hitler attacked and invaded Russia,' he said. 'All this was no surprise to me. In fact, I gave clear and precise warnings to Stalin of what was coming.'[6] This of course was not true. Churchill's efforts to help had been so imprecise, especially regarding sources, that they had had the reverse effect on Stalin. He immediately decided to supply the Red Army with military equipment as a sign of solidarity. The first convoy was codenamed Operation *Dervish* and comprised just six merchant ships; five British and one Dutch. It departed Liverpool on 12 August 1941 and sailed for Murmansk via Scapa Flow. It was well protected by the Royal Navy and arrived unmolested at Archangel 19 days later. A further 11 ships were sent from Iceland on 29 September and they too reached Archangel unharmed. The convoys throughout the autumn and winter of 1941 continued to enjoy this good luck. However, from early 1942 Churchill and Roosevelt's Arctic supply route had to run the gauntlet of continual German attacks.

Churchill, aware that Germany had stockpiles of poison gas, warned Hitler not to use them against the Soviet Union or he would have no qualms in responding in kind. He informed Stalin on 20 March 1942 that he would 'treat any use of this weapon of poison gas against Russia exactly as if it was directed against ourselves. I have been building up an immense store of gas bombs for discharge from aircraft, and we shall not hesitate to use these.'[7] At the start of the war Britain had 500 tons of mustard gas and 5 tons of tear gas and practically no means of delivery.[8] Churchill ensured by the end it had produced 40,719 tons of mustard gas and 14,042 tons of phosgene and tear gases as well as millions of shells and bombs.⁹ Churchill made sure Hitler was aware of his pledge to Stalin by making his warning public in a radio broadcast on 10 May 1942. Knowing Churchill's firmly held views on the utility of mustard gas, he was not bluffing. Fortunately, Hitler did not resort to such weapons, probably for fear of massive Allied retaliation.¹⁰

In early May 1942 Vyacheslav Molotov, the Soviet Foreign Minister, arrived in London to see Churchill and Attlee. He came demanding a Second Front and approval for Stalin's annexation of the Baltic States and eastern Poland, which were now currently under German occupation. Stalin wanted these back as a security buffer when the war was over. This was something that neither Churchill nor Roosevelt was prepared to sign up to. In particular Churchill was not prepared to abandon the Poles, as it was Poland's dismemberment that had brought Britain and France into the war in the first place. Molotov was hosted at Chequers, the Prime Minister's country retreat, and he was singularly unimpressed. 'Not a fancy old building,' he noted. 'There was a bathroom, but no shower.'¹¹ He and Stalin were used to working amongst the splendour of Russia's imperial palaces. Churchill was amused to learn that the Russian delegation slept with pistols under their pillows and had demanded the keys to their rooms.

Molotov and Ambassador Maisky then met with Eden and Winant. Churchill had briefed Eden not to make any concessions to the Russians. Winant pointed out to their guests that America was not prepared to sign a frontier treaty as this would go against the spirit of the Atlantic Charter. Instead, Eden offered an Anglo-Soviet mutual assistance alliance that made no reference to future borders. Reluctantly Molotov agreed. 'After they left Winston congratulated me most warmly ...' recalled Eden. 'He said if it came off it would be much the biggest thing I had done.'¹² Later King George VI met with Molotov and noted, 'he looks a small quiet man with a feeble voice, but is really a tyrant.'¹³ The King then added, 'We now have some sort of hold over Russia and both sides seem happy about it.'¹⁴ Churchill did not share his optimism; he knew that once the war was won Stalin would seek to get his own way.

Churchill thought he had headed off Stalin's call for the opening of the Second Front in 1942. He was wrong. Molotov flew from London to Washington. There he stressed to Roosevelt the Red Army was facing an immense superiority of German aircraft and panzers. It needed help now. He asked Roosevelt whether the Allies would land in France with sufficient troops to draw off 40 German divisions. 'If you postpone your decision,' warned Molotov sternly, 'you will have eventually to bear the brunt of the War.'[15] Roosevelt was swayed and told Molotov to inform Stalin that the Second Front would be opened that summer. Crucially he failed to consult Churchill and told his chiefs of staff to start planning for August 1942.

Churchill was now put in an extremely difficult position, knowing full well that any landing in France would have to be conducted largely by British troops. He was determined not to be rushed. Publicly though he was forced to agree with Roosevelt's communiqué otherwise it would signal to Hitler that there was discord in the Allied ranks. 'P.M. in good form,' noted General Brooke, 'and carried Cabinet with him in the proposed policy that we do not move to France in strength except to stop there, and we do not go there unless German morale is deteriorating.'[16] On the way home Molotov stopped off in London and met with Churchill on 10 June, who delivered the bad news. 'That evening the Prime Minister gave Molotov ...' Eden recalled, 'an aide-mémoire explaining that it was not possible to say whether the plan for a landing on the Continent was feasible that year. We could therefore give no promise.'[17] Molotov did not seem greatly upset by this; indeed he seems to have got on well with Churchill. 'So I came to be friends with the bourgeoisie,' he later ruminated. 'My journey and its results were a great victory for us.'[18]

In sharp contrast when Stalin heard about the delay with the Second Front he was outraged because Roosevelt had promised him. This spelled an end to any special relationship Churchill may have believed he was forging with Stalin. 'Later in the summer,' observed Eden, 'when the Americans admitted that the operation could not take place, Russian reproaches, particularly against Britain, became violent.'[19] Churchill felt compelled to conduct the disastrous and pointless Dieppe raid in August 1942 using Canadian troops. It was a gesture largely designed to please Stalin and distract the German military. The operation achieved neither, though it did force the Germans to accelerate fortifying the Channel ports, thereby further hampering plans for D-Day.

Churchill faced a difficult challenge selling Stalin to the British public. Many people knew that he was a dictator who had wrought terrible suffering on his own people throughout the 1930s. Only the far Left could argue that Stalin's actions had been for the greater good.

However, the appalling famine in Ukraine, the constant purges and the existence of the Gulag hardly painted a picture of an enlightened leader. By mid-1942 the military might of Britain, America and the Soviet Union was immense. According to Churchill, combined they could muster almost 20 million men, three-quarters of the world's air forces and a large proportion of its naval power. Against this there could be only one outcome for the Axis powers. In September 1942 Churchill indulged in some spin in the House of Commons by extravagantly singing the praises of the Soviet leader. 'This great rugged war chief ...' he told the assembled MPs. 'He is a man of massive outstanding personality, suited to the sombre and stormy times in which he has been cast; a man of inexhaustible courage and will-power.'[20] All this was true but Churchill naturally chose to ignore his murderous dark side.

Churchill was, though, greatly heartened by the Red Army's decisive victory at Stalingrad in the winter of 1942–43. 'The Russians, both on land and in the air, had now the upper hand,' he wrote, 'and the Germans can have had few hopes of ultimate victory.'[21] His prognosis was backed by the Joint Intelligence Committee, which seriously doubted Hitler could achieve victory on the Eastern Front. He was also reassured by the committee's assessment that Hitler would not get a separate peace settlement with Stalin.

Churchill then incurred the wrath of Stalin when in March 1943 he postponed the Arctic convoys until the return of the darkness in the autumn. Stalin, who was planning his counteroffensive that summer at Kursk, was livid because Churchill's decision delayed the delivery of 660 fighter aircraft. He also knew that the southern and Pacific supply routes could simply not make up for the shortfall. In turn Churchill was not happy about the inadequate air defences at Murmansk, which was the only accessible port once Archangel iced up. Churchill and his admirals understandably felt that it was a bit much for merchant ships to bravely reach sanctuary only to be sunk whilst in port. Stalin, who was fighting to drive the Germans from huge areas of the Soviet Union, was not prepared to boost fighter cover using the Red Air Force. Nor did he care that Churchill and Roosevelt were fighting the desperate Battle of the Atlantic. Stalin's petulance over supplies is hard to fathom, especially as relatively few Allied-built tanks and aircraft were deployed at Kursk. However, Allied trucks were of far greater use as Soviet factories were concentrating on tank production.

Nonetheless, Churchill still did everything he could to warn Stalin about Hitler's own impending offensive at Kursk scheduled for the spring or summer of 1943. By this stage Bletchley had not only cracked Enigma, but also the Lorenz system used by the German High Command. Stalin was informed on 30 April 1943 that Hitler was planning an ambitious pincer attack at Kursk, as well as what army groups and what panzer units were to be involved. To mask the activities of Bletchley the Soviet leader was told the information had come from spies and other sources. Once again Stalin was not grateful and suspected Churchill's motives. In addition, Stalin had a lifelong dislike for spies, whom he considered the lowest of the low.

Ironically Churchill's attempts at source protection were a waste of time as Stalin had British spies leaking Bletchley intelligence directly to him. Captain John Cairncross smuggled out secret documents, and Leo Long, an intelligence officer at the War Office, also leaked Bletchley intelligence via Anthony Blunt who worked for MI5. The ease with which Cairncross carried out his activities has led to speculation that Churchill was aware there was a traitor at Bletchley, but turned a blind eye.[22] Ultimately, though, Stalin did not greatly need Churchill, Cairncross or Blunt's help as Hitler's military build-up around the Soviet's Kursk salient was impossible to conceal.

Stalin felt he did not need Allied intelligence to win the war and was angry that they kept postponing the Second Front. What he wanted was a major Allied diversion. Churchill had a completely different strategic agenda from the Soviet leader, who did not appreciate Britain and America's preoccupation with the Mediterranean. Ironically the Allies' decision to invade Sicily in July 1943 could not have come at a better time. It forced Hitler to break off his attack at Kursk. He was also obliged to send reinforcements to Italy just at the very moment Stalin opened his decisive counteroffensive at Kursk.

Despite Stalin's ingratitude, Captain Jerry Roberts, one of Bletchley's codebreakers, was convinced that Churchill's actions helped ensure the Red Army's victory at Kursk. He noted the Prime Minister 'gave the Russians full details of the plans three months before the battle took place and allowed them to deploy the maximum number of tanks and win the Battle of Kursk'.[23] It was this that helped eventually put the Red Army on the road to the Vistula and then the Oder. In the meantime Stalin would have to wait until the summer of 1944 for the Second Front to be opened.

Loss of Faith

While war raged in Europe and North Africa, Churchill faced an impossible strategic task trying to protect British interests in South East Asia. China was prostrate and fractured by civil war. The Japanese had capitalized on this throughout the early 1930s carving out for themselves a vast land empire that encompassed Manchuria and parts of Inner Mongolia and stretched north and west of Japanese-occupied Korea. It was a mistake to underestimate the ambitions of the Japanese military, for it was well-equipped and wholly ruthless, having won countless battles against the Chinese. The warning signs of potential Japanese aggression towards Western interests were plain to see.

The Japanese had the options of striking north into the Soviet-backed Republic of Mongolia or south from their territories in China into French Indochina and the Pacific. Traditionally the Japanese Army preferred the northern approach, while remaining on the defensive in the south. The expanding Japanese Navy favoured a strike south. When the Japanese Army attacked into Mongolia in 1939, it was soundly thrashed by the Red Army under rising star General Georgi Zhukov. The balance of probability was that rather than pick another fight with the Soviet Union the Japanese would now push southwards. This was especially the case after the British were driven from Europe and facing eviction from North Africa. The Japanese knew that British resources were stretched to breaking point. Furthermore, it was hard to imagine the Japanese would ignore the strategically important Burma Road for long. Running from Rangoon to Lashio this was used to ship vital American military supplies to Chiang Kai-shek's Nationalist Chinese armies struggling to keep the Japanese at bay. A push into Indochina would enable the Japanese to cut this route and threaten India.

India's north-eastern frontier was screened by British-controlled Burma and the British naval base at Singapore was likewise shielded by British-controlled Malaya. These defences, though, were compromised by supposedly neutral French Indochina, now controlled by Vichy France and neutral Siam or Thailand. The latter's long Kra Isthmus formed an unwelcome wedge between Burma and Malaya. In the South China Sea America's defences in the Philippines were poor. Likewise, the Dutch military in the Dutch East Indies was weak and could expect no help from their Nazi-occupied homeland.

The whole British mindset in India had always been focused on the North-West Frontier. During the late 1930s Churchill's old adversaries, the Pathans, had once again been in revolt. The Waziristan campaign required the deployment of some 40,000 troops, who suffered almost a thousand casualties.[1] There remained a constant danger that trouble might flare up again, especially if Afghanistan got involved. The Afghans had avoided direct confrontation with India since 1919 and the Third Afghan War. To deter them and the Pathans the Indian Army had established divisional headquarters at Rawalpindi and Quetta ready to deal with any emergencies.

In contrast, Burma had never really been a significant security concern because to the east the Chinese Nationalists held the neighbouring Yunnan province. As a result, although it offered a buffer for India it was now an unwanted burden that soaked up funding. The country had been administered as a province of India until 1937 and Burmese military units served as part of the Indian Army until that date. Now it was the responsibility of the Governor, Vice-Admiral the Hon. Sir Archibald Cochrane. Defence of the country fell to Major-General D.K. McLeod, General Officer Commanding Burma, who was trying to build a new force independent of the Indian Army. Worryingly McLeod, who was starved of resources, did not consider the Thai border to the south a security risk.

While all this was going on Churchill had to contend with the ongoing thorny issue of Indian nationalism. Although there were provincial governments, no progress had been made over the issue of a federal government and therefore any meaningful steps towards independence. The Viceroy of India, Lord Linlithgow, had alienated the Hindu-dominated Indian Congress Party[2] by taking the country into war in 1939 without consulting it.[3] Nonetheless, he had to contend with Mahatma Gandhi, the charismatic leader of the opposition to British rule. Gandhi gave a vague pledge that he would 'not embarrass the British government'.[4] He said the Congress would only support the war in return for independence. However, it did not speak on behalf of Muhammed Ali Jinnah's Muslim League, which supported the war in return for greater protection for Muslims. Churchill, an ardent advocate of British rule, did not want to make any concessions to either side. Despite vocal objections from the Congress, Indian divisions were rapidly sent to Egypt and Malaya.

Churchill and the India Office were able to closely monitor the activities of Indian nationalists thanks to Indian Political Intelligence, which had been set up before World War I, and the Delhi Intelligence Bureau. The latter's job was to monitor subversive activities in India. Nationalist sympathizers in Britain were kept under surveillance by Special Branch, the security wing of the police. Neither of the intelligence organizations in India were certain that Gandhi and Jinnah would be able to work together. There would certainly be a struggle for political ascendancy, which conceivably could result in open violence between the Congress and the League. It was hard to see how the political division would not be on sectarian lines. A lot depended on who the British-run provinces and the princely states sided with.

For Churchill the Japanese threat in the Far East was always an unwanted distraction. He appreciated the risks, but simply did not have the resources with which to beef up British defences in the region. Throughout 1940 his priority was defending the British Isles against the ravages of the Luftwaffe, facing off the threat of invasion and protecting Egypt from Italian aggression. Once Rommel was on the loose in North Africa, Churchill knew if he had to decide between Egypt or Malaya, the latter was a sacrifice he was prepared to make. Suez was key to British interests in the Mediterranean and the Indian Ocean. Nor could Churchill conceive of a real threat to Singapore.

Ironically the British military had already accurately predicted how the Japanese might take Singapore. Lieutenant-General Sir William Dobbie and his Chief of Staff, Brigadier Arthur Percival, in 1937 carried out a threat assessment for the island. They concluded the Japanese would grab the airfields of southern Thailand, then conduct amphibious landings in southern Thailand and northern Malaya. These attacks would be followed by a push down the Malayan peninsula to Singapore. They refuted the long-held view that the Malayan jungle would impede any Japanese attack. Therefore, they concluded Singapore was vulnerable to land attack from the north. They recommended strengthening the RAF in northern Malaya and deploying tanks with the army. The War Office was not receptive to these findings, pointing out there was no money for rearmament and that tanks were unsuitable for jungle warfare.

The inertia in London was compounded by inter-service rivalries. By the late 1930s it was clear that air power as much as naval power posed a potential threat to British interests in the Far East. Japanese bombers ranged far and wide over China with impunity, devastating Chinese cities. Although the Royal Navy was responsible for the naval base at Singapore, it fell to the army and RAF to create a credible forward defence. To facilitate this, the RAF sensibly set about building air bases in northern Malaya. The army, though, was annoyed because this meant it would have to forward deploy to defend the RAF's ground facilities. This obliged the army to hold most of Malaya and stretched its meagre resources to breaking point.

The British chiefs of staff in 1940 argued that a regional defence in South East Asia was required, because it would be impossible to hold Singapore on its own. Churchill was not convinced. 'As Singapore is as far away from Japan as Southampton is from New York,' he reasoned, 'the operation of moving a Japanese Army with all its troopships and maintaining it during a siege would be forlorn.'[5] Churchill also assessed that it would take 50,000 Japanese troops five months to take Singapore. He clung to the notion that the Royal Navy would act as an effective deterrent to any attack on Singapore. If such an attack did take place, then the navy would steam to the rescue. This ignored the inconvenient fact that the Royal Navy had its hands full in the Atlantic and the Mediterranean. Nor did it have any aircraft carriers to spare to provide maritime air cover in the South China Sea. This represented a fatal capability gap.

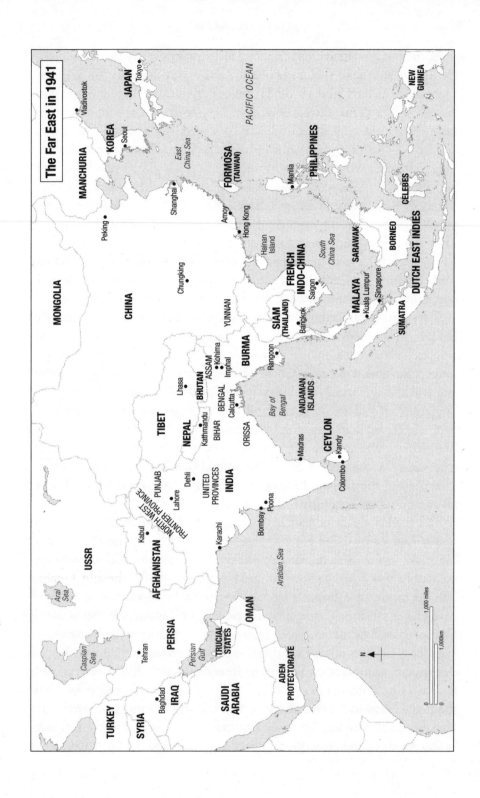

The Far East in 1941

In reality air defence was the key to protecting Malaya and Singapore. When in late 1940 the chiefs of staff recommended defending Malaya with 336 aircraft and the RAF revised this to 556, Churchill flatly refused. 'The political situation in the Far East does not seem to require, and the strength of our Air Force by no means warrants,' he said in January 1941, 'the maintenance of such large forces in the Far East at this time.'[6] When the war in Europe spread the Far East fell even further down Churchill's list of priorities. Once Hitler attacked the Soviet Union in June 1941, Churchill resolved to do all he could to help his new ally. This included shipping hundreds of fighter aircraft and tanks to Murmansk to equip the Red Army. The consequence of this decision was that Malaya ended up with just 158 second-rate aircraft that were easily outclassed by Japanese fighters and no tanks. In contrast the Japanese massed 700 aircraft and several hundred tanks in Indochina. As far as they were concerned trees were not an impediment to the deployment of their tank regiments.

The 62-year-old Air Chief Marshal Sir Robert Brooke-Popham was appointed Commander-in-Chief Far East in April 1941. Called out of retirement, he had an unfortunate habit of nodding off during meetings. His area of responsibility was vast, covering Hong Kong, British Borneo, Singapore, Malaya and Burma. He commanded all air and land forces, while naval operations came under Vice-Admiral Sir Geoffrey Layton, Commander-in-Chief China Station based in Singapore. Confusingly although Burma was operationally under Brooke-Popham's headquarters in Singapore, at the same time India was responsible for its overall defence policy. This in effect hamstrung the Commander-in-Chief Far East's autonomy when it came to defending Burma. When General Sir Archibald Wavell became Commander-in-Chief India in July 1941, he wanted Burma returned to the fold. General Dill, Chief of the Imperial General Staff, in response to this said that because of Britain's ongoing relationship with Chiang Kai-shek it would be better subordinated to Singapore. Meanwhile Brooke-Popham was highly concerned about the resources available to defend Malaya and Singapore, but his requests for reinforcements fell on deaf ears. In May 1941 Major-General Percival, Dobbie's former Chief of Staff, was sent to take charge of Malaya's defences under Brooke-Popham.

Churchill reassured General Dill in May 1941 that should the Japanese enter the war then America would side with Britain. This seemed to presuppose the Americans would be able to spare any resources from the Philippines. Besides, the American fleet was thousands of miles away at Pearl Harbor. Churchill then added 'in any case Japan would not be likely to besiege Singapore at the outset'.[7] During the discussion he got the distinct impression that Dill favoured Singapore over Cairo. It was a terrible dilemma and Churchill likened it to 'having to choose whether your son or daughter should be killed'.[8] Time was running out, because by the end of July the Japanese had secured southern Indochina having pressured the French to cooperate.

This firmly focused both Churchill and Roosevelt's attention. Now that the Japanese were in Indochina they were well placed to attack Burma, Malaya, the East Indies, Thailand or even the Philippines. For the Americans this was the final straw. Roosevelt called on the Japanese on 24 July 1941 to withdraw and for good measure froze all Japanese assets in America. The British and Dutch followed suit; in particular the Dutch stance severed Japan's oil supplies. The following month Roosevelt was even firmer. He warned that if Japan attacked any of its neighbours, including the oil-rich Dutch East Indies, America would not sit idly by. The Japanese were faced with the choice of complying or going to war.

In the meantime, Brooke-Popham conceived Operation *Matador*, a bold pre-emptive strike into southern Thailand to safeguard Malaya. He argued British forces should grab Singora and Patani on the eastern coast of the Thai Kra Isthmus. This would thwart any Japanese amphibious operations conducted across the Gulf of Thailand from Indochina. Such an operation, though, required the political will to violate Thai neutrality and needed to be implemented as soon as possible, but nothing happened. Burma also remained out on a limb.

In Rangoon in October 1941, Wavell met with McLeod and the new Governor, Sir Reginald Dorman-Smith. He was not encouraged by what he found. The Governor was of the view that war was unlikely. Wavell then flew on to Penang and toured the newly built and unimpressive defences in north-west Malaya. In Singapore he discovered that the defence of the 'Gibraltar of the Far East' rested solely on the Sembawang naval base on the northern side of the island facing the Johore Straits. This was protected by batteries intended to ward off naval attack. Wavell recalled from his days at the War Office in the 1920s, 'There was a hot controversy between the RAF, which claimed to be able to defend

Singapore with torpedo-bombers alone, and the Navy and the Army, who challenged them to prove their case.'[9] It seemed the navy had won the argument, as the mindset was Singapore would face attack by the Japanese Navy rather than the Japanese Army.

Singapore, through which almost 25 per cent of the Empire's and 60 per cent of Australia's trade passed, was dubbed a fortress. This was a fallacy. For a start the naval base was far from complete. The powerful 15-inch naval guns, designed to protect the island, could rotate inland, but only had armour piercing shells, which were no help against enemy infantry and artillery.[10] Furthermore, visibility to the north was not good. This left the nagging concern of what would happen if the Japanese attacked through the Malayan jungle and across the Johore Straits.

Churchill made it clear at a War Cabinet meeting on 12 November 1941 that the Middle East would have first call on resources and that large-scale reinforcements were not available for Malaya. He persisted in his vain hope that a simple show of force by the Royal Navy would deter the Japanese. On 4 December the brand-new battleship *Prince of Wales* and elderly battlecruiser *Repulse* along with their destroyer escort sailed into Singapore. Their presence immediately boosted the morale of the civilian population and the garrison. However, there was no hiding the lack of an aircraft carrier to protect them. The one earmarked to support the operation had been damaged and none of the others were free thanks to the Battle of the Atlantic. Churchill foolishly overruled repeated Admiralty objections about sending the warships without air cover. Worryingly the RAF was not in a position to effectively protect them either.

Churchill fully appreciated that it was only a matter of time before there was war in the Far East. During one of his visits to Ditchley Park when actor turned Commando Captain Niven asked him if he thought America would enter the war, Churchill was emphatic: 'Mark my words – something cataclysmic will occur!'[11] Four weeks after their meeting on 7 December 1941 the Japanese attacked the American Pacific fleet at anchor in Pearl Harbor. Privately Churchill was relieved. Although he called their actions irrational, it ended his concerns that the Japanese might only strike European colonial territories, thereby leaving America on the sidelines. The following day the Japanese assaulted Hong Kong, while a task force, as predicted, landed troops at Singora and Patani as well as at Kota Bharu in north-eastern Malaya. Shortly after, Roosevelt cabled Churchill to say, 'Today all of us are in the same boat with you and the people of the Empire and it is a ship which will not and cannot be sunk.'[12] Sometime later Churchill bumped into Niven again at Ditchley, who wanted to know how he had made his prophecy. 'Because, young man,' replied Churchill, 'I study history.'[13]

This was a pithy sound bite, but in truth Churchill was also studying the regular intelligence reports, which indicated that attack was imminent. MI6 gained information in early November 1941 that Japanese troops were gathering at Hainan Island ready to be deployed to Indochina. In mid-November another report stated that the Japanese were poised to attack both Burma and Thailand. In the space of just a week, between 30 November and 7 December 1941, MI6 issued no less than 21 reports warning of Japanese 'preparations for Southward Move'.[14] On 5 December they noted the Japanese were landing in Cam Ranh Bay in Indochina and that 48,000 troops had come ashore supported by 250 aircraft.[15] These reports were issued to the War Office and were no doubt shared with Churchill. By the outbreak of war MI5 had expanded overseas with six defence security officers permanently stationed abroad; locations included Hong Kong and Singapore.[16] Their task was to help monitor internal unrest and foreign subversion. Furthermore, the Government Code and Cypher School had an interception station at Kranji, on the north coast of Singapore, which was monitoring Japanese communications.[17]

The British situation in the Far East deteriorated rapidly. Churchill was informed on 10 December that the *Prince of Wales* and *Repulse* had been caught by Japanese bombers and sunk in the South China Sea. As part of Force Z these warships had deployed from Singapore to intercept Japanese transport ships at Kota Bharu. Lacking air cover they had been sitting ducks. It was hard to see them as little more than sacrificial lambs and their loss was a crushing blow to national morale. Churchill only had himself to blame. The Japanese invaded the Philippines the day after and Borneo a week later. 'It means,' wrote General Brooke, Chief of the Imperial General Staff, 'that from Africa eastwards to America through the Indian Ocean and Pacific, we have lost command of the sea.'[18]

'You must now look east. Burma is placed under your command,' signalled Churchill to Wavell belatedly on 12 December. 'You must resist the Japanese advance towards Burma and India and try to cut their communications down the Malay peninsula.'[19] Churchill also promised him reinforcements, but it was too little too late. Six days later the Japanese occupied the city of Penang on the west coast of Malaya.

Churchill and Roosevelt met in Washington on 22 December and proceeded to draft a joint declaration to fight the common enemy, pledging not to make a separate peace. They also opted for a 'Europe First' policy in terms of prosecuting the war. Understandably Churchill and Roosevelt were worried that this might send the wrong signal to Chiang. If his forces were to collapse that would free up Japanese divisions that could overwhelm Australia, New Zealand and indeed the rest of the Pacific. It was therefore agreed to create a China Theatre of War with Chiang as Supreme Commander. His Chief of Staff would be an American, Major-General Joseph W. Stilwell. This declaration was made public on New Year's Day.

Churchill and Roosevelt also agreed that the Pacific, including Australia, should come under the American Joint Chiefs of Staff. It would then be divided between General Douglas MacArthur's Southwest Pacific Command, encompassing Australia, New Guinea, the Philippines and most of the Dutch East Indies and Admiral Chester Nimitz's Pacific Command. This clumsy arrangement resulted from American inter-service rivalry and gave rise to two divergent strategies for driving the Japanese from the Pacific. The US Navy felt it could defeat the Japanese at sea, but MacArthur was determined to liberate the Pacific island by island, from where his bombers could then attack the Japanese mainland.

The Japanese commenced air raids on Rangoon on 23 December 1941. Shortly after, Churchill was informed of the British surrender at Hong Kong. By that point Brooke-Popham had left Singapore and Wavell assumed his responsibilities. Under mounting Japanese pressure, General Percival made the decision to abandon central Malaya on 5 January 1942. All that lay between Singapore and the Japanese was Johore. Nine days later Wavell informed Churchill that there was no fortress; the island's fixed defences were all but non-existent. He also told him that the island's batteries could only fire seaward. This was not true and Wavell should have known from his inspection of Singapore's defences that the guns could face landward. However, Major-General Sir John Kennedy, the Director of Military Operations, observed,

'The [Johore] channel was narrow, mangrove swamps impeded the fire of the defences; and the aerodromes, water supply and other vital installations were within artillery range from the mainland.'[20]

A dismayed Churchill told the Chiefs of Staff the situation was 'one of the greatest possible scandals that could possibly be exposed'.[21] Rather disingenuously he claimed 'The possibility of Singapore having no landward defences no more entered into my mind than that of a battleship being launched without a bottom.'[22] This seems rather hard to credit from a man who was a master of detail. He certainly knew that Wavell's comment regarding the guns only firing seawards was inaccurate. Churchill seemed to be in denial over the situation. 'Why didn't they tell me about this?' he raged. 'Oh, no; it is my own fault. I ought to have known.'[23] He cast about, uncertain who to blame, 'I could have asked. I cannot understand it. Did no one realize the position?'[24]

There was yet more bad news for Churchill. Japanese ground forces crossed the Thai-Burmese border on 20 January 1942 and pushed north intent on cutting the railway line to China. Meanwhile the Japanese advance down the Malaya peninsula remained unchecked. On 28 January General Percival signalled Wavell to inform him that within two days he would be forced to withdraw onto Singapore island. Percival faced an impossible task with the Japanese controlling both the air and the sea. The time was ripe to save the garrison and conduct a seaborne evacuation to echo Narvik, Dunkirk and Crete. The tragedy was that there was no real way to retrieve them. Churchill hoped that Singapore would be the rock upon which the Japanese tide broke. Wavell anticipated that the garrison could at least pin down the Japanese for a time. They launched their assault on Singapore on 8 February.

Two days later Churchill seemed to lose the plot, worrying more about the reputation of the British Empire than the fate of those trapped at Singapore. He signalled Wavell and said the garrison must fight to the bitter end and that commanders and senior officers should die alongside their men. In what could be seen as emotional blackmail he invoked the performance of the Red Army on the Eastern Front and the Americans in the Philippines. This rather missed the point that the Russians were fighting for their motherland, as were the Americans' largely Filipino troops. The British and Commonwealth forces in Singapore were thousands of miles from home.

Wavell should have known better, but he passed on Churchill's sentiments in his Order of the Day. He warned 'the Chinese, with almost a complete lack of modern equipment, have held back the Japanese for 4 and a half years. It will be disgraceful if we yield our boasted Fortress of Singapore to inferior enemy forces.'[25] Percival also indulged in this pointless shaming exercise on 11 February by complaining, 'In some units the troops have not shown the fighting spirit which is to be expected of men of the British Empire. It will be a lasting disgrace if we are defeated by an army of clever gangsters, many times inferior in numbers to our own.'[26] These were hollow platitudes.

Four days later Churchill was informed that Percival had capitulated along with 80,000 Australian, British and Indian troops. They joined the 50,000 taken during the conquest of Malaya. Some of the dazed prisoners blamed their commanding officers, but many others believed the blame rested higher up. 'Years later I read Churchill's memo to General Wavell, ...' recalled Reg Twigg captured with the Leicestershire Regiment. 'Yet Percival had surrendered.'[27] Alistair Urquhart, who was captured with the Gordon Highlanders, felt 'The government was more culpable and Churchill even more so. It was a view that I never missed an opportunity to express.'[28] Not long after, the Japanese annihilated a hastily gathered fleet of American, Australian, British and Dutch warships in the battle of the Java Sea.

Percival's surrender was humiliating for Churchill, his government and the country. The 'Gibraltar of the Far East' was no more. The Japanese had anticipated it would take 100 days to secure Singapore, but they had done it in 70. The campaign to defend Malaya and Singapore was characterized by poor planning, extreme ineptitude, inflexibility and plain bad luck. Churchill had gambled with the security of the region, preferring to help Stalin, and lost in spectacular fashion. Understandably the Australian and Indian governments were furious that their divisions had been thrown away in such a cavalier manner.

Churchill saw no point in trying to hide or delay the news. He immediately informed the nation the day of the surrender via the BBC, urging everyone to 'draw from the heart of misfortune the vital impulses of victory'.[29] Few were convinced on this occasion. Telling the House of Commons was perhaps a much harder job, but he still tried to put a brave face on things. 'We are hard pressed,' he admitted. 'But I am sure even in this dark hour that "criminal madness" will be the verdict which history will pronounce upon the authors of Japanese aggression.'[30] When a despondent Churchill met Foreign Secretary Anthony Eden on 16 February he told him, 'I am in a truculent mood.'[31] Eden recalled, 'I told him I had gathered this from his broadcast. Nonetheless he gradually softened to the extent at least of admitting that changes would have to be made.'[32] King George VI was dismayed at the furious backlash against Churchill and remarked, 'I do wish people would get on with the job and not criticise all the time'.[33] Churchill also confirmed to the King that there would have to be a reshuffle.

In that moment it may have been that Churchill considered stepping down or at least relinquishing some of his duties. Two days later the head of Churchill's map room, Captain Richard Pim, recalled the Prime Minister 'hinted that he was very seriously thinking of handing over his responsibilities to other shoulders'.[34] Instead he rallied. Churchill made Clement Attlee Deputy Prime Minister, but he refused to step down as Minister of Defence. A week later he told the House of Commons, 'However tempting it might be ... to step aside ... and put someone else up to take the blows ... I do not intend to adopt that cowardly course.'[35] During a secret session in April 1942 Churchill promised the Commons a public enquiry into the fall of Singapore as soon as the time was right.[36] In the meantime there were much more pressing matters to attend to. He later confessed 'I cannot get over Singapore' and the loss of the *Prince of Wales* and the *Repulse* gave him nightmares.[37]

If the House of Commons and general public had been fully aware of the ample intelligence warnings about the Japanese threat, it is hard to see how Churchill could have survived the political fallout. Both he and Brooke-Popham steadfastly refused to heed what they were being told. Remarkably, despite inter-service friction and inadequate funding, intelligence was good largely thanks to MI6 and the team at Kranji. The Far East Combined Bureau responsible for co-ordinating intelligence was controlled by the navy, which led to service and departmental conflict. The local MI5 and Special Branch offices did not get on either. Kranji was not only eavesdropping on the Japanese Navy, it was also monitoring diplomatic traffic to the Japanese consul-general in Singapore. This meant that in the spring of 1941 Churchill was well aware the Japanese were escalating their subversive activities on the island. By the summer it was apparent they were planning to occupy Indochina. Alarm bells should have rung when the Japanese fleet was recalled from manoeuvres and changed its codes.

It was evident trouble was brewing when intercepts showed the Japanese consul-general had been ordered to quit Singapore by mid-November 1941. At the same time the British Consul in Saigon warned that the Japanese build-up in southern Indochina was a definite threat to Thailand. It was at this point that the Far East Combined Bureau warned that war was imminent. However, Churchill, Brooke-Popham and Percival refused to believe this. Even if they had there was little they could do by that stage. The only tiny consolation with this sorry debacle was that the staff at Kranji were evacuated, so the Japanese did not learn their communications had been compromised.

India in Revolt

Just three days after the fall of Singapore, Gandhi was causing mischief for Churchill. 'The West,' he told Chiang Kai-shek, who was visiting India, 'will never voluntarily treat us orientals as equals. Why, they do not even admit your country to their Combined Chiefs-of-Staff conferences.'[1] Chiang took this to heart and continued to berate Churchill for withholding self-rule from India. Churchill's stance would soon have serious ramifications. In the meantime, he had to contend with the Japanese threat to Burma and the Indian Ocean.

Churchill hoped to reinforce Burma with the Australian 7th Division, which was on its way home from North Africa. He approached John Curtin, the Australian Prime Minister, and requested that it be sent to Rangoon. Curtin and his government, though, were thoroughly dismayed by the bungled defence of Singapore and the loss of the Australian 8th Division. They were also rattled by the Japanese bombing of Darwin. Curtin flatly refused Churchill's plea, on the grounds that home defence was now a greater priority in the face of a potential Japanese invasion. Ironically Dill had lobbied Churchill, without success, in September 1941 to ask the Australians to send their 7th Division to Malaya rather than the Middle East.

There was yet more bad news for Churchill when the British were forced to abandon Rangoon on 7 March 1942. Although Chiang committed troops under Stilwell in southern Burma, these were largely deployed to stop the Japanese advancing eastward into China. They fought well at Toungoo and Yenangyaung and helped to save the trapped 1st Burma Division. Nonetheless, by June 1942 the Japanese were in control of all of Burma. The defence of north-eastern India now rested on holding the strategic high ground at Imphal and Kohima.

Churchill had little respect for Chiang's corrupt government or its military capabilities. Once Burma had been lost he had no strategic interests other than liberating Burma, Malaya and Singapore. Therefore, Churchill had little sympathy with America's determination to break the Japanese blockade of China and ultimately use it as a base of operations against Japan. Churchill's aims in the China-Burma-India theatre of operations were to remain much more modest compared to those of the Americans. The latter were focused on creating an air supply route from north-east India into China. In contrast Churchill wanted to counter-attack into Burma as soon as possible.

Churchill knew that he could not ignore the political situation in India and the Indian Congress's demands for independence. 'With the Japanese at the gates of India,' noted Sir Charles Wilson, Churchill's doctor, 'he dreaded the effect on the Indian Army of opening up an issue which must divide Muslim from Hindu.'[2] In late March 1942, under pressure from members of his own government including Attlee, Roosevelt and Chiang Kai-shek, Churchill sent a special mission headed by Sir Stafford Cripps. 'He carries with him the full confidence of the Government,' said Churchill, 'and he has in their name to procure the necessary measure of ascent, not only from the Hindu majority but also from those great minorities'.[3]

In light of the momentum the independence movement had gathered, Churchill should have gone in person. Indeed, he wanted to, but there was a war on and he was preoccupied by the Atlantic and the Mediterranean. In some quarters it was unkindly felt that Churchill was not up to the journey because of his health. When diplomat Lord Harvey heard that Churchill hoped to fly to India he uncharitably said 'how gallant of the old boy … But his age and more especially his way of life must begin to tell on him.'[4] Harvey was referring to Churchill's fondness for alcohol, but his remark was scurrilous as Churchill conducted considerable international travel.

Some Indians who did not support the nationalist cause felt that Churchill was very unwise to bow to American pressure. 'The Americans in general, and more especially President Roosevelt, with their utter ignorance of the Oriental mind,' wrote Nirad Chaudhuri, working for All India Radio in Delhi, 'thought that Indian nationalist co-operation was essential for winning the war against Japan. Therefore they insisted an offer should be made ... Even Churchill had to yield ... and a mission was sent.'[5]

Cripps was armed with a promise that India would be granted self-governing dominion status at the end of the war. A new constitution would be drawn up and any state or province could opt out of the proposed union. This was complete anathema to those nationalists who wanted a united states of India. Congress leaders were particularly unhappy as this provision clearly offered the prospect of Jinnah's Muslim League creating a separate 'Pakistan' homeland for India's Muslims. Ironically Congress wanted to preserve the very thing the British had created, a subcontinent-wide administration. This incorporated 11 British provinces and over 560 princely states. Gandhi had characterized the latter 'as being nothing more than British nominees'.[6]

In the face of the Congress and Muslim League's intransigence, Cripps' mission was doomed to failure and simply frustrated India's nationalists even further. Gandhi likened his offer to a 'post-dated cheque'.[7] Chaudhuri noted with resignation that there was 'another round of the old futile game of words.'[8] Cripps had no magic wand with which to heal the rifts in Indian domestic politics nor could he speed up the process of granting greater autonomy. This impotence fuelled resentment towards British rule. At the beginning of April, he warned Churchill that anti-British feeling was running high and that British prestige was the lowest it had ever been. He also advised that unrest was growing. Chiang, alarmed at the prospect of Churchill losing control in India, cautioned Roosevelt, 'Should however the situation be allowed to drift ... any attempt on the part of the British to cope ... by resorting to military force ... will only help spread disturbances and turmoil.'[9]

In the short term, Roosevelt and Chiang were not so much concerned about Indian independence, rather the prospect of Britain dropping out of the war in the Far East in the event of serious unrest in India. Roosevelt suggested that interim self-government for the duration of the war might ensure Indian loyalty to the British Empire. However, he did not want to become a go-between and cabled Churchill saying 'for the love of Heaven do not bring me into this, though I do want to help'.[10] Privately Churchill was infuriated by what he saw as Roosevelt's unwanted meddling in Britain's domestic affairs. He would have never dreamed of giving the American president advice on the future of the Philippines.

At sea the Japanese pressed home their attacks. Churchill instructed that a new Eastern Fleet be put together under Admiral Somerville, hero of the Mediterranean. To keep it out of harm's way it was stationed on the far side of the Indian Ocean at Trincomalee, on the north-east coast of Ceylon, what is now Sri Lanka. However, in early April 1942 marauding Japanese aircraft from a carrier group bombed the ports in Ceylon as well as those on the coast of Madras. Japanese warships also set about British convoys off Orissa, claiming to have sunk 20 merchant ships and damaged 23 others. The Royal Navy did not escape unscathed either. Japanese aircraft pounced first on two British cruisers and then an aircraft carrier, sinking all three. The cruisers *Cornwall* and *Dorsetshire* were lost near the Maldives Islands, while the carrier *Hermes* went down off Ceylon. The latter was lost because its air wing had been deployed elsewhere and it was unable to defend itself.

Churchill broke the bad news to the House of Commons on 13 April. He was quick to point the finger, stating, 'I cannot make any statement about the strength of the forces at Admiral Somerville's disposal, or the reasons which led him to make the dispositions of his fleet for which he is responsible.'[11] Churchill also had to acknowledge that retaliatory air attacks on the enemy carrier group failed. He continued to blame Somerville and he wrote pointedly to the Admiralty complaining, 'No satisfactory explanation has been given by the officer concerned of the imprudent dispersion of his forces.'[12]

Admiral Layton, who was now in command in Ceylon, alarmed Churchill and Wavell when he reported, 'The Japanese Fleet has retired to Singapore, to refuel and rearm, and organize an invasion force, which we think is coming back to attack us.'[13] In response Churchill authorized the deployment of three British Army divisions to Ceylon, to defend the island and guard against civil unrest being stirred up by the Japanese. The following month Japanese bombers struck Chittagong rather than Trincomalee. Fortunately for Churchill, the Japanese refrained from launching a sustained air offensive against Assam and north-east India, though at the end of the year they hit Calcutta causing panic. Instead, the Japanese fleet sought to defeat the US Navy in the Pacific and suffered a decisive defeat at the battle of Midway. However, it was not until 1943, when the Japanese naval threat in the Bay of Bengal had receded, that it became possible to bring in supplies through Calcutta.

Coastal and river navigation in the region was also greatly restricted thanks to the Japanese threat. Wavell, fearing invasion and spying activities, instructed that all privately owned boats in southern Bengal be either impounded or destroyed. Such a move was not well thought through. 'To deprive the people in East Bengal of their boats,' warned Gandhi, 'is like cutting off a vital limb.'[14] The Governor of Bengal reluctantly first enacted this measure in March 1942 and by the end of the year over 20,000 vessels had been taken out of service. Local commerce simply ground to a halt and fishermen lost their way of making a living.

After the shocking loss of Singapore, the retreat from Burma and the losses in the Indian Ocean, Indian confidence in the British administration was at its lowest ebb. Some felt if the British left India then the Japanese threat would melt away. Churchill knew that with the British and Indians squabbling amongst themselves this would signal disunity in the face of the Japanese advance on Assam. He cabled Roosevelt in late July trying to reassure his American allies, 'the Congress party in no way represents India ... and can neither defend India nor raise a revolt'.[15] When the Congress Party adopted Gandhi's resolution for the British to Quit India on 9 August 1942 it was clear trouble was brewing. Gandhi called for countrywide passive resistance to British rule until they agreed to leave India.

Lord Linlithgow the Viceroy, with the support of the Muslim League, the Indian police and the Indian Army authorized a clampdown on the Congress, which he declared illegal. When the authorities raided Congress headquarters they seized documents showing Gandhi was prepared to negotiate with the Japanese once the British were gone. Congress leaders along with Gandhi were immediately arrested, sparking the very revolt that Churchill had reassured Roosevelt would not take place.[16] There were demonstrations, sit-ins, riots, murders and acts of sabotage across India. Police stations were burned to the ground, railway tracks torn up and telegraph wires cut. Some of the attacks seemed to be coordinated rather than just spontaneous outbursts of violence. This though was a largely Hindu revolt. Jinnah's Muslim League refused to support the Quit India resolution on the grounds that Congress was trying to 'establish a Hindu raj under the aegis of the British bayonet'.[17]

Whilst buildings were set on fire in Delhi, including the railway offices, order was quickly restored and a curfew imposed. Surprisingly, although the North-West Frontier was predominantly Muslim, it was a Congress stronghold. This was thanks to Pathan nationalist Abdul Gaffar Khan who was a Gandhi supporter. He felt Congress was mounting a better challenge to the British than the Muslim League. His pacifist approach, which was unusual for the region, resulted in him being dubbed 'the Frontier Gandhi'.[18] While there were some disturbances in the North-West Frontier, they were nothing compared to what was happening in the north-east.

In Calcutta rioters set fire to the trams, attacked government vehicles and tried to decapitate motorcyclists by tying wire across the roads. A great pall of black smoke ominously spread over the city. The Indian Communist party, alarmed by the situation, took provocative photographs of police vehicles ablaze on the streets. These were published in its newspaper appropriately titled the *People's War*. Gandhi did not like Bolsheviks and made no common ground with them. 'India does not want Communism,' he declared. 'I do know that in so far as it is based on violence and denial of God, it repels me.'[19] India's Communists although opposed to British rule did not support mass disorder for fear it would weaken the war effort against Hitler and therefore increase pressure on Stalin. Churchill, seeing them as a wartime ally, had only just lifted a ban on them. In contrast the Congress Socialist party planned to occupy Delhi, until, that is, their leader Jai Prakash Narayan was arrested. He even called on American troops based in India to support Indian nationalism.

The Congress party tried to deny that its followers were rebelling. However, even pacifist Gandhi was unambiguous about what was happening. 'This is open rebellion,' he acknowledged.[20] Alarmingly at one point all the bridges connecting Bengal and those forces fighting the Japanese were cut. The shipment of supplies to the front was severed for days at a time, creating a threat to the main railheads at Chittagong, Dimapur and Jorhat. For a while the cities of Calcutta, Patna, the capital of Bihar and Gaya were cut off. The British 26th Division had to be deployed in Bengal and the 70th in Bihar to help quell the spreading unrest.

Bengal, full of desperate refugees from Burma and Assam, was already facing famine. The RAF operating from Assam did what they could to help those still trapped in northern Burma by conducting food drops to isolated camps and villages. However, they were hampered by the heavy rains of the monsoon season. Whilst tens of thousands of people made the arduous trek northwards to India on foot, British, American and Chinese pilots managed to fly almost 13,000 from Burma to safety. Thousands more sailed to Calcutta and Chittagong.

Getting food to Bengal was already greatly hampered by India's inadequate transportation system. This was not capable of moving large quantities of supplies from western India. Even if sufficient trucks had been available, the country's road network was woefully underdeveloped. This meant that the burden fell on India's railways, which were subject to numerous delays and breakdowns. The unwelcome civil unrest further exacerbated these problems. For the British armed forces, the developing trans-India air cargo ferry service somewhat alleviated the situation, but it did not help the civilian population. Military necessity required improvements to the Assam-Bengal railway up the Brahmaputra Valley, but this was intended to help fend off the Japanese, not feed people. Nor did Churchill want to expose additional Allied shipping in the Bay of Bengal to the risk of attack by the Japanese operating from the Andaman Islands.

On India's western coast in the summer of 1942 elements of the newly arrived British 2nd Division were put onto the streets of Bombay to face down demonstrators. The Congress tricolour had been raised above the city and the police were forced to fire on crowds of stone-throwers in half a dozen locations. The police also used teargas to disperse protestors. When the division moved inland to its new base at Ahmednagar it had to conduct internal security duties there as well. In a state of panic Lord Linlithgow warned Churchill, 'I am engaged here in meeting by far the most serious rebellion since that of 1857, the gravity and extent of which we have so far concealed from the world for reasons of military security.'[21] Churchill, though, could not conceive the Indian Army might mutiny. After his experiences on the North-West Frontier and their loyal service during World War I he took it for granted Indian troops would continue to serve their British officers without question.

However, families were split. Krishen Tewari, a young cadet in Bangalore, was well aware of the Quit India movement and recalled his family arguing, 'Why should you join the British Army to fight on the British side? We want independence!'[22] The slow 'Indianisation' of the armed forces caused resentment, especially as Indian officers were paid less and were not permitted to command British troops. Likewise, the Auxiliary Force designed for internal security was only open to Europeans and Anglo-Indians. Its Indian counterpart had European officers. Worryingly intelligence indicated that 60 per cent of Indian officers were nationalists and that the rest were far from content with current conditions.[23] It seemed India might be on the cusp of a countrywide rebellion, which, if supported by the Indian Army, could only have one outcome.

It may have felt to Churchill as if Linlithgow was being unduly alarmist, but if the Indian Army's divisions turned on the British there would have been wholesale slaughter on both sides. Linlithgow had every right to be anxious at the prospect of the Indians pointing their guns at their political masters. Wavell had an armoured unit on hand to intervene in Calcutta and Bengal if necessary. The 50th Indian Tank Brigade was made up of three British tank battalions and initially deployed to Ahmednagar before it moved to Ranchi west of Calcutta in July 1942.[24] However, the last thing Linlithgow and Wavell wanted was another Amritsar-style massacre on their hands. Furthermore, the sight of British tanks on the streets would have inflamed the situation.

Miraculously the Indian Army and police remained steadfastly loyal. The former was in the middle of raising three new infantry divisions, while training three others.[25] 'We get all the recruits we want,' reported Wavell. 'There is no sign of any disloyalty in the Army.'[26] This was not entirely correct as members of a single Indian artillery battery tried to desert, but they were arrested and court-martialled.[27] Likewise General William Slim observed, 'The astonishing thing is, not that there were some mutinies and troubles in the police, but that so many remained true to their salt.'[28] The Indian police were around a quarter of a million strong. This helped foster Churchill's view that the Congress's supporters were no better than a bunch of traitors. He hoped that Linlithgow would uncover proof that the Indian nationalists were in league with Germany or Japan. The intelligence from northern India proved otherwise. Churchill's hoped-for fifth columnists turned out to be largely politically motivated students, school children and desperate refugees from Burma.

Churchill was reassured by news that the violence in Calcutta had been swiftly and firmly contained. This helped to safeguard the vulnerable lines of communication to Assam. 'With practically no casualties among the troops,' reported Slim, 'and very few among the rioters, the disturbances in Calcutta petered out.'[29] Pacifying the rural areas proved much more problematic. Linlithgow reported to Churchill, 'Mob violence remains rampant over large tracts of the countryside.'[30] The Indian police resorted to firing on troublemakers, baton charges, floggings and burning villages. Linlithgow even considered setting the RAF on the saboteurs, and bombers were put in the air just in case. Leo Amery, the Secretary of State for India, told the House of Commons that some strafing attacks had taken place. By the end of August 1942 about 2,500 people had been killed and 66,000 thrown in prison, around half of whom were Congress supporters.[31]

The Indian police bore the brunt of the trouble, with at least 28 deaths reported and 65 police stations attacked, two-thirds of which were destroyed. British fatalities included seven servicemen murdered in Bihar in two separate incidents. The number of fatalities clearly indicated that this was no 1857-scale revolt. Crushing that had cost the lives of 2,000 soldiers killed in action, while another 9,000 had perished from disease and heatstroke while on campaign. In addition, hundreds of thousands of civilians and mutineers were killed. The volume of arrests certainly severely hampered Quit India supporters in trying to coordinate their efforts. By mid-September the trouble had died down and rail communications were restored.

Nonetheless, internal security operations were a massive drain on Churchill and Wavell's military resources. These tied up 57 battalions, or the equivalent of roughly 30 regiments, of British and Indian troops. One of these battalions was deployed from Lahore to Lucknow in case the latter become the focus of a new Indian mutiny. Troops were called to 60 different locations to assist the civil authorities. Around 100,00 men, including the RAF, were required to put down the insurrection.[32] In manpower terms this equated to almost seven divisions. Wavell established the Indian Army's 33rd Corps, which included the British 2nd Division, with responsibility for the defence of southern India. Although considered a reserve formation, it no doubt had a crowd control function should things get out of hand again. Likewise, 15th Corps at Ranchi, responsible for 50th Tank Brigade and 70th Division, had a secondary internal security role. All this greatly hampered Wavell's preparations for operations in Burma. Nonetheless, Churchill showed Roosevelt and

Chiang that the British could and would preserve order in India whatever the cost.

Churchill likewise acted to reassure Parliament that all was under control. He told the House of Commons on 10 September 1942 that in the past two months alone the Indian Army had attracted 140,000 recruits, which had surpassed all records.[33] He would later emphasize that, 'No one has been conscripted or compelled.'[34] This was quite remarkable when every other army was using conscription. Churchill's faith in the Indian military proved well-founded. 'There was a conflict, there's no doubt in my mind,' recalled Krishen Tewari, by now a junior officer in the Indian Army. 'It was not so much anti-British as hesitation whether we should join the Army to be on the British side or not. But I think better sense prevailed.'[35] Churchill chose to minimize the seriousness of the situation, informing the Commons that fewer than 500 people had died in the unrest and that only a few British brigades had been needed to help out. This was far from the truth as the revolt had required the commitment of up to 350,000 members of the police and armed forces to ensure public order.

To be fair to Churchill, India is so vast that many Indians were unaware of the scale of the problem or simply did not believe it. Nirad Chaudhuri in Delhi wrote, 'I certainly thought Churchill was right when he told the House of Commons that order had been restored ... with remarkable ease and quickness and with very little loss of life.'[36] Beforehand, Chaudhuri's English manager had informed him that communications in eastern Uttar Pradesh and western Bihar to Assam and Bengal had been severely disrupted. 'I heard afterwards that artillery had been brought into action against some villages there. Even that I did not take very seriously,' he concluded dismissively.[37]

Churchill also ignored the reality that some 40,000 Indian troops captured in Malaya and Singapore had volunteered to serve in the Japanese-sponsored Indian National Army. Likewise, some 10,000 Burmese also sided with the Japanese to fight for the Burma Independence Army.[38] 'This was significant, as it indicated an intention to advance into India,' reasoned General Slim, 'where the renegades would be used to rouse the population to rebellion.'[39] Slim, like Churchill, was impressed by the loyalty and fighting qualities of his Indian troops. 'My Indian divisions after 1943 were among the best in the world,' he wrote proudly. 'They would go anywhere, do anything, go on doing it, and do it on very little.'[40] Deserters from the Indian Army who sided with the Japanese would later be considered 'Patriots not Traitors' by nationalist sympathizers.[41]

After those tense weeks in the summer of 1942, Churchill knew deep down that Indian independence could not be ignored forever. Nor could the cooperation of the greatly expanded Indian Army be guaranteed for much longer. Once the Japanese had been defeated, it would be a formidable battle-hardened force confident of its own abilities. Slim accelerated the 'Indianisation' process because he found segregated units fought better and it made administration and logistics far easier.[42] This also gave them greater autonomy. After victory was secured India's war heroes might make good political figureheads, or worse orchestrate a coup. Britain would have a duty to oversee a peaceful transition of power that satisfied all the major players. As Churchill appreciated, it would be a difficult task.

PART SIX

War of Wills

Strained Relations

Roosevelt, despite his very close relationship with Churchill, grew ever more unsympathetic towards British imperial policy. The American Chiefs of Staff began to take the view that Britain was mainly concerned with retaining power in India, rather than actively fighting the Japanese. Churchill rather reinforced this perception when he declared famously, 'I have not become the King's First Minister in order to preside over the liquidation of the British Empire.'[1] Furthermore, it was clear that Churchill did not altogether trust even the most loyal of Indians. His Highness the Maharajah Jam Sahib of Nawanagar and Sir Ramaswami Mudaliar had seats on the Imperial War Cabinet, helping to coordinate the British Empire's War effort. They had equal status to Britain's dominion representatives. However, Churchill instructed that any papers passed to them be edited of anything sensitive regarding India.

While Churchill worked very hard to foster the alliance with Roosevelt, behind the scenes it was far from cordial. Churchill and Menzies appointed Sir William Stephenson to represent MI6 in New York. This was far from just an intelligence liaison post. Stephenson headed British Security Coordination, which was an umbrella organization for MI5, MI6 and the Special Operations Executive with almost a thousand staff.[2] It conducted black ops or propaganda operations and espionage on American soil, including spying on Indian nationalists in the United States. Such activities convinced the Americans and the Chinese that Churchill's first priority was maintaining control of the British Empire.

Chiang wanted the Burma Road reopened to allow Roosevelt to supply his armies. For this he needed Churchill's cooperation. Chiang, still smarting after the loss of his best forces in southern Burma, in October 1942 put forward an ambitious plan to drive the Japanese from the country. He suggested that British, Chinese and Indian troops strike south from Assam in India, while other Chinese units created a pincer movement by attacking westward from Yunnan. Also, a supporting seaborne attack would be made against Rangoon. When Wavell pointed out that all this was beyond current British capabilities, Chiang in a huff withdrew his support for the idea. Wavell also highlighted that the jungle and the monsoon season would impede any attack.

Churchill then promoted Wavell to Field Marshal. However, he was far from grateful, feeling that he should have been rewarded earlier for his exploits in North Africa. 'After all I feel it was in 1941 that I earned it not in 1942,' grumbled Wavell, 'and that it will look rather like an old age pension in the New Year List.'[3] Just as Churchill had pressured Wavell in North Africa to get quick results, he did the same with Burma. Although Wavell had 15 divisions available in India, most of these were newly formed and lacked equipment, training and experienced officers. For example, the British 2nd Division required two whole years of training in India.[4] Only three divisions were actually ready to be committed to combat against the Japanese. Part of the problem was that Slim's 4th Corps overseeing training in Bengal had been very distracted by the widespread civil unrest.

Nonetheless, Wavell was obliged to move forward and he attacked the Japanese in the Arakan in north-western Burma. Through late 1942 to early 1943 British operations in the region did not go smoothly. Initially in September 1942 they started quite well when Major-General Wilfred Lloyd's 14th Indian Division advanced to Donbaik. Unfortunately, it then paused, due to supply problems and bad weather, giving the Japanese time to reinforce their defences. All subsequent British attacks were beaten off, with the final one launched on 18 March 1943 resulting in the loss of three entire brigades. Churchill observed, 'This campaign goes from bad to worse, and we are being completely outfought and out-manoeuvred by the Japanese.'[5] Always the spin doctor, he feared a public relations disaster, adding, 'Luckily the small scale of the operations and the attraction of other events has prevented public opinion being directed upon this lamentable scene.'[6]

Churchill was not only annoyed by Roosevelt's stance over India, he was also annoyed when William Phillips, head of the American Office of Strategic Services (OSS; the forerunner of the Central Intelligence Agency) in London, was made Roosevelt's personal representative in India in 1943. This gave the clear impression that the OSS was not only supporting anti-Japanese nationalist movements in South East Asia, but also in India. Churchill's fears were confirmed when it became apparent that Phillips was very pro-Indian independence and did not support the British administration. Phillips further incurred Churchill's displeasure when he suggested a meeting of imprisoned Indian leaders adjudicated by an American. To keep Roosevelt happy Churchill had agreed to the establishment of a 'special OSS mission' in New Delhi, but he was not pleased about it.[7] He responded by permitting the interception of mail to the American consulates in India and the tapping of their telephones. This included bugging General Albert Wedemeyer, the most senior American officer in India.[8] Indian Political Intelligence also kept a close eye on Phillips' efforts to encourage mediation, even after he had returned to America.

Churchill further retaliated against the presence of Phillips by appointing an MI6 officer, Gerald Wilkinson, as his secret liaison with General Douglas MacArthur the US commander in the south-west Pacific. MacArthur disliked Roosevelt immensely and saw himself as a future presidential candidate. Wilkinson, although he reported to Menzies, briefed Churchill personally. He was later sent to Washington to monitor both American and Chinese economic threats to British commercial interests in the Far East.

During the Trident Conference in Washington in May 1943 Churchill made it clear he saw the liberation of Singapore as a priority, not Rangoon. This was the third strategic conference between the British and American leaders. Amongst the topics for discussion were the Second Front, the forthcoming Italian campaign and how to help China. Churchill knew that the Burma campaign in the long run only helped the Chinese with the opening of the Burma Road, whereas liberating Singapore and its naval base would restore British prestige in the region. Roosevelt and his commanders, looking at the bigger picture, wanted China as a base of operations against Japan to help terminate the Pacific war, so were not supportive.

The only good news for Churchill from Burma was that Major-General Orde Wingate's Chindits, named after the griffin-like creatures that guard Burmese temples, had crossed the Chindwin River and successfully penetrated enemy lines. Although the Chindits' results were modest and their losses heavy, they stung the Japanese into action. To improve their hold on Burma and prevent further incursions, they decided to launch a large-scale invasion of India via the rugged Assam-Burma frontier. This would eventually put them on a decisive collision course with Slim's newly formed 14th Army.

An enthused Churchill summoned Wingate to London. He was impressed and took him to the Quebec Conference to brief Roosevelt, the British Chiefs of Staff and Joint Chiefs of Staff. They were so enamoured of Wingate's tales from the jungle that they agreed to let him expand his brigade into a full division with independent air supply. This idea was not universally popular. General Claude Auchinleck opposed it on the grounds that it would be too unwieldy for operations behind enemy lines and soak up valuable supplies. Brigadier Joe Lentaigne and Major John Masters of the 111th Brigade were unhappy at being taken over by Wingate as part of his empire building. Masters recalled, 'We were appalled because we believed that the new force was much too big.'[9]

The general consensus, though, was that two brigades rotating behind enemy lines were sufficient to tie down the Japanese while the main British force capitalized on this diversion. Instead, thanks to Churchill's direct meddling, Wingate ended up with 24 battalions. An aghast Masters noted this 'was the infantry strength of two and a half divisions, but we were not even as powerful as one standard division, where the infantry were supported by guns, tanks, and engineers. The number of aircraft that would be needed to supply and support us was enormous.'[10]

Churchill wanted to go even further. 'I consider Wingate should command the army against Burma,' he wrote on 24 July 1943 to the Chiefs of Staff before sailing to Canada. 'He is a man of genius and audacity and has rightly been discerned by all eyes as a figure quite above the ordinary level.'[11] Few shared his enthusiasm for a man who was politely described as eccentric. On board ship Churchill chose to ignore the scar across Wingate's throat, where he had once tried to kill himself. During the voyage Lord Moran,[12] Churchill's personal physician, noted 'he seemed to be rather unbalanced, and talked like a man full of undigested ideas'.[13]

Thanks to Churchill's patronage Wingate got his division, but he did not get an army. He proved that he was completely unsuited to command the latter when he suggested that it should be broken up into long-range penetration groups on the same line as the Chindits. He seemed to give little thought for who would defend the depots and air bases supplying these groups. It soon became apparent to Churchill that Wingate was no Lawrence of Arabia and he lost interest in him for the rest of the journey to Quebec. 'He seemed to me hardly sane,' adds Lord Moran, 'in medical jargon a borderline case.'[14] Moran does not record whether he warned Churchill of his concerns. 'The appointment of Wingate to command the 14th Army,' observed Masters, 'would have led to a major disaster on the field.'[15]

Churchill was undoubtedly concerned about the impact of Indian nationalism on other parts of the Empire. This was especially the case when two West African divisions arrived in India in 1943 ready for deployment to Burma. When Aziz Brimah, a chieftain's son, landed with the Gold Coast Regiment in Madras (modern Chennai) he was invited to a speech given by Gandhi. Brimah recalled he said 'that when we get back we must spearhead our own drive for independence'.[16] Slim, who was very impressed by the West Africans, could not help but note their number of white officers far outweighed those with Indian units. This seemed to indicate there was a problem with discipline or trust. Luckily for Churchill the tough West African forces proved to be just as loyal as the Indian Army to the British crown.

Churchill had lost confidence in Wavell after the failure of the Arakan campaign. He was replaced as Commander-in-Chief, India by Auchinleck and by way of compensation appointed Viceroy. As both generals had been sacked as Commander-in-Chief Middle East, there was a sense in some quarters that India had to make do with second best. Notably, Auchinleck's responsibilities would not include operations against the Japanese in South East Asia. Although Wavell was honoured to be made Viceroy, it made him the senior political figure in-country and as such he wanted a game plan. His military mind abhorred the idea of a vacuum. During his meetings in London, he was frustrated by Churchill and Amery who were not prepared to offer any meaningful concessions on the future of India. There was to be no talk of a transfer of power and Churchill did not want any dialogue with Gandhi. Wavell, after meeting with Churchill, came away with the impression that the Prime Minister 'has always really disliked me and mistrusted me, and probably now regrets having appointed me'.[17] Wavell wanted to get together the leading Indian politicians including those Congress members who were in prison. This proposal was rejected.

Wavell was also aware of the worsening situation in Bengal after the failure of the 1942 winter rice crop, but found the Cabinet was only concerned with Europe. 'Apparently it is more important to save the Greeks and liberated countries from starvation than the Indians,' he wrote indignantly in his journal, 'and there is reluctance either to provide shipping or to reduce stocks in this country.'[18] Wavell soon set about touring India and tried to alleviate the famine in Bengal. This had been exacerbated by a cyclone, the inefficiency of the local government, panic buying and profiteering. Rivalries between the Congress Party and Muslim League did not help matters. Furthermore, with the Japanese occupying all of South East Asia, rice supplies from this region were no longer available. The rising death toll was far worse than that caused by the revolt. Between mid-August and mid-October 1943 some 8,000 people died of starvation in Calcutta alone.[19] Wavell threatened to resign if nothing was done. He called in the army to assist on 28 October 1943 just eight days after taking office. It was instructed to set up relief camps with free kitchens and get food moving from military depots and other stores to the most affected areas.

Auchinleck was quick to comply. He appointed Lieutenant-General Mosley Mayne, commanding India's Eastern Command, as the senior military liaison officer with the Bengal government. Likewise, Major-General Arthur Wakely was put in charge of getting food supplies into Bengal using military transport and implementing rationing. The security of these supplies and the lines of communication from Calcutta was the responsibility of Major-General Douglas Stuart. Auchinleck described Stuart as, 'A most enthusiastic and zealous officer.'[20] Barley was shipped in from Australia, Canada and Iraq, but it was not enough. Besides, what was really needed was rice. Churchill's decision to restrict the release of shipping supporting the war effort to carry grain imports to India was harsh but understandable. When he turned to Roosevelt to request American ships carry Australian wheat to India, the American military likewise refused to be distracted from the war.[21]

This situation provided ammunition for the Congress who claimed the diversion of food to British forces had caused the crisis. Making Churchill shoulder all the blame when he was thousands of miles away is extremely unfair. The famine had occurred on Linlithgow and the Acting Governor of Bengal Sir Thomas Rutherford's watch. Furthermore, they did not answer to Churchill or to Anthony Eden, but the Secretary of State for India, Leo Amery. However, Churchill insisted on seeing all telegrams between Amery and Linlithgow, so was fully aware of the situation.[22] Slim firmly blamed the locals, writing 'The Non-Congress Government of Bengal, a coalition of Indian politicians … showed the feebleness of its moral and administrative standards in the terrible famine'.[23] The official inquiry that followed came to a similar conclusion.

To try and inject some strategic dynamism into the region Admiral Mountbatten was appointed to head the new post of South East Asia Command. His headquarters was designed to oversee the conduct of the war on land, air and sea. Stilwell, while remaining assigned to Chiang, became the theatre deputy supreme commander. In light of Mountbatten being a sailor and not a soldier there was some question over his suitability. Mountbatten, though, was highly experienced and had just come from commanding Combined Operations. If outflanking amphibious operations were conducted along the Burmese coast, then his maritime expertise would be ideal. His Chief of Staff, Lieutenant-General Sir Henry Pownall, was also highly experienced. The Americans had suggested that Wingate get the job, but the British Chiefs of Staff rejected him. Mountbatten's American Deputy Chief of Staff was General Wedemeyer, the very man who had been bugged by Churchill. Wedemeyer would later replace Stilwell as Chiang's senior military adviser. He came to view the China front as more important than Burma and was receptive to Chiang's views on British imperialism, namely that they should leave the region.

Churchill certainly felt that Mountbatten was suited to the job and was won over by his enthusiasm for Wingate's Chindits. Auchinleck and Slim in contrast continued to consider them a waste of resources. Wingate's close relationship with Churchill was to cause Slim trouble: 'Such had been his romantic success with the Prime Minister that he claimed the right to send him messages direct, with his views and recommendations, irrespective of whether Admiral Mountbatten or any other superior commander agreed with them or not.'[24] Slim refused to be browbeaten by such tactics and Wingate backed down.

To keep out of Auchinleck's way, Mountbatten transferred his headquarters from New Delhi to Kandy in Ceylon. His main tasks were mandated by the Combined British and American Chiefs of Staff, who wanted him to divert the Japanese from the Pacific, where the Americans were conducting their island-hopping campaign. This was to be achieved by conducting an operation that would spark a major response by the Japanese. He was also to expand air and road routes through northern Burma into China.

Inevitably the Prime Minister had his own ideas about how to divert the enemy. 'Mr. Churchill had for this purpose strongly urged an amphibious operation against Sumatra,' noted Slim.[25] The logic of this was that it would have turned the Japanese flank in Malaya, cut the Malacca Straits and placed British bombers close to Singapore. Churchill had got it into his head that bombing Singapore would be a good idea. Such an operation could have also cut Japanese sea communications between Rangoon and Singapore. When Churchill consulted Brooke he was not at all supportive. 'It was not a suitable base for further operations against Malaya,' grumbled Brooke, 'but I could not get any definite reply from him as to what he hoped to accomplish from there.'[26] Churchill got angry over this and shaking his fist yelled, 'I do not want any of your long term projects, they cripple initiative!'[27] Their argument was pointless because this operation was far too ambitious for the resources available.[28]

All ambitions for an amphibious attack on Burma were completely derailed by the Tehran Conference at the end of 1943. This involved 'The Big Three', Churchill, Roosevelt and Stalin. The main purpose of their meeting was to discuss the opening of the Second Front, but Japan was also on the agenda. Stalin agreed to join the war against the Japanese only once Germany was defeated. Churchill and Roosevelt accepted this condition and as a result over half the amphibious equipment in South East Asia was recalled to Europe in order to launch the Second Front. It greatly annoyed Churchill that while the Americans went island hopping towards Japan, the resources could not be found to support British amphibious operations against Japanese-occupied territories in the Far East.

Churchill's itinerary had been punishing. Before flying to Tehran, he had sailed to Algiers to meet with Allied commanders. He then sailed to Malta to dine with the governor. By this stage Churchill was feeling unwell. Upon arrival in Alexandria he flew to Cairo to hold a conference with Roosevelt and Chiang to discuss the war against Japan.

This they agreed would continue until the unconditional surrender of the Japanese. Japan would then be stripped of all territories it had seized. When an exhausted Churchill returned to North Africa from Tehran he was diagnosed with pneumonia. He was extremely frustrated that what he dubbed his 'Bay of Bengal Strategy' was derailed.[29] Churchill saw this as vital to his ultimate goal of liberating Singapore. The problem he had, aside from the issue of resources, was that his Chiefs of Staff tended to agree with their American colleagues' desire to advance on Japan from the south-west Pacific and not via the Indian Ocean.

While Churchill was recuperating in Morocco, he felt that his Chiefs of Staff had gone behind his back in postponing the proposed operation against the Andaman Islands south-west of Burma. Crucially if they had been taken the airfield at Port Blair, on South Andaman, it would have enabled the Allies to strangle the Japanese maritime lines of communication between Burma and Malaya. This could have been decisive because the railways and roads were completely incapable of sustaining the Japanese Army in Burma. Furthermore, any assault on Sumatra was reliant on taking the Andamans, which would then have facilitated securing the Malacca Straits and a push on Bangkok and Singapore. Churchill issued a directive insisting that the Bay of Bengal remain the centre of British strategy until mid-1945. Brooke took it as a warning that if the Prime Minister did not get his own way, he would face the consequences. The harsh reality, though, was that this was simply wishful thinking on the part of Churchill, because there were insufficient resources.

Although Somerville's Eastern Fleet returned to Ceylon in September 1943, it was too weak to conduct offensive operations. To make matters worse, both Japanese submarines and German U-boats were operating in the Indian Ocean from the Malayan island of Penang. Between September and December 1943 some 27 Allied ships were lost in the Indian Ocean, most of which were claimed by these submarines. Field Marshal Smuts,[30] the South African Prime Minister, was concerned when U-boats attacked shipping in the Mozambique Channel, the waterway between the island of Madagascar and Mozambique. He approached Churchill with the proposal that they should occupy the latter which was a Portuguese colony. Churchill opposed this because of the impact it could have on Portugal and Allied operations in the Atlantic and Mediterranean. At the end of the year the Allies would be granted access to the Azores and Churchill did not want to do anything that would jeopardize that.

When the Japanese fleet moved its main base to Singapore in February 1944, Churchill became impatient for Somerville to take action. The admiral conducted his first major offensive operation in April 1944 by attacking northern Sumatra. These operations continued into September and were followed by raids on the Nicobar Islands. Determined to play a role in the defeat of the Japanese homeland, Churchill chose to divide the Eastern Fleet to create a Pacific Fleet to fight alongside the Americans.

The constant shelving of Churchill and Mountbatten's proposed combined operations meant they had no option but to fight it out with the Japanese in the jungles of Burma. This of course suited the Americans, as their only real interest in the region was in opening an overland supply route to China. Long term, Churchill's hope for China was that at the end of the war with US backing Chiang would defeat Mao's Communists once and for all. In Chungking, General Wedemeyer found himself not only working alongside Churchill's envoy General Carton de Wiart but also MI6. Although Mao was treated as an equal by the Allies, Carton de Wiart reported to Churchill that Mao's forces were little more than a nuisance to the Japanese. The implication was that they were either not very good fighters or were deliberately holding back their strength. Stilwell similarly accused Chiang of holding back his better divisions ready for the resumption of the Chinese civil war. Oddly Wedemeyer ordered American and British intelligence not to concern themselves with Chinese internal affairs. In other words, they were not to conduct surveillance against Mao's Communists.[31] This seemed to take a dangerously narrow view of post-war China. Churchill's capabilities there were extremely limited; MI6 only had 41 staff in-country, so there was little he could do to influence the situation.[32]

Meanwhile in Bengal, despite the intervention of the military, the dire effects of the famine rumbled on. In mid-August 1944 Brooke met with Amery who was worried about grain supplies in India. 'He is calling for our assistance,' wrote Brooke in his diary, 'and is very nervous lest Archie Wavell should resign the Viceroyship owing to the lack of support he is obtaining from the Government.'[33] The implication was that Wavell still blamed Churchill for the situation almost a year after being appointed. If Amery and Wavell's intention was to put themselves on the right side of history, then they succeeded admirably. Churchill would be held responsible, not them.

Even if more supplies had been shipped into India the ports were struggling to clear them. In early December 1943 the Japanese bombed Calcutta and the dock workers fled leaving a massive backlog of cargo. Roosevelt was so annoyed by this that he told Churchill he wanted the lines of communication from the port to Assam put under military control. He also sent two American battalions to help out, but it still took until the end of the year to clear the port. Then in April 1944 a ship carrying ammunition and explosives caught fire and blew up in Bombay's docks. Seventeen ships were destroyed and 900 people killed. In the blaze that followed 36,000 tons of foodstuffs were lost. The port was not fully functional until October. The British administration was held to blame for this sorry state of affairs by both the Indians and the Americans.

Second Front Now

After America entered the war Churchill stepped up his shuttle diplomacy. He knew that he needed Roosevelt's help to defend and ultimately safeguard British interests. Stalin's Red Army could tie down the bulk of Hitler's forces, but beyond that there was nothing further the Russians could do to help. If western Europe was to be liberated, then that would require American armed forces. Even before the Japanese attacked, American assistance was already quite significant. They had taken over the defence of the western Atlantic in April 1941 and in October 1941 Britain and America had combined their efforts to build an atom bomb.

Churchill flew to Washington to meet Roosevelt shortly after Pearl Harbor and they agreed that Germany should be defeated first. Roosevelt was also keen to help Stalin by opening a Second Front in Europe as soon as possible. In order to defend Suez, Churchill was already committed to North Africa fending off the Axis forces. He persuaded Roosevelt that they should adopt an 'Africa First' strategy. Since the bulk of the Allied forces in the Mediterranean were British, Roosevelt agreed to a campaign to clear the Axis from North Africa. This put Churchill in a difficult position with the Russians, as Molotov, their Foreign Minister, was initially given the impression that the Second Front would be opened in 1942. This left Churchill with the disagreeable task of visiting Moscow to tell Stalin that this would not happen until 1943 at the earliest. Understandably this looked like Britain and America were putting their strategic interests first, leaving the Russians to do the lion's share of the fighting.

The Allies landed in Algeria and Morocco in November 1942, but it took them until May 1943 to defeat the Axis armies trapped in Tunisia. At that point Churchill, Brooke and Eden flew to Tunis to congratulate everyone and to bask in the glory of another Allied victory. America had won at Midway, Britain at Alamein and Russia at Stalingrad. Tunis represented the first decisive Anglo-American triumph. Although the Mediterranean was secured, giving passage for shipping to the Far East, Churchill and Roosevelt faced their next problem. In January 1943 they had got together at Casablanca to discuss the way ahead. The Americans wanted to land in western Europe, but Churchill was all for taking the war to Hitler from the Mediterranean through Italy. Although he prevailed with his Mediterranean-first strategy there were two unwelcome provisos. The Pacific front, where the Americans were struggling to contain the Japanese, would get priority with landing craft production and the Second Front would now open in 1944. The latter understandably did not please Stalin and his beleaguered Red Army.

These conditions were to cause constant problems throughout 1943–44 over resource allocation for the campaign in Italy, the opening of the Second Front (which would encompass separate landings in both northern and southern France) and the war in the Far East and Pacific. The result was constant operational delays, especially in the case of the Far East, and the Russians were left feeling that they were doing all the hard work. Although the war began to turn in the Allies' favour their insistence of an 'unconditional surrender' of the Axis powers did not help shorten the war either. This demand convinced the Germans and Japanese to fight on, and in the case of Italy after the fall of Mussolini left the country in a terrible state of limbo.

Sicily was taken by the end of August 1943, and in the meantime Mussolini fell from power and Hitler occupied half of Italy to block the Allies' advance north following the Italian armistice with the Allies. Churchill saw Italy as the Second Front, which he wanted extended into central Europe with Vienna and Prague as the goal. Such a move he felt would forestall Stalin's occupation of eastern Europe. Roosevelt, though, would not be swayed from his commitment to opening the Second Front in France. When Churchill and Roosevelt were hosted by Canadian Prime Minister Mackenzie King in Quebec in August 1943, the American president insisted on a greater build-up for Operation *Overlord* and diverting landing craft to the Pacific. This inevitably weakened the attack on mainland Italy and when this took place in September 1943 the Germans fought a dogged defence.

Despite this, following the Italian armistice Churchill once more overreached himself by trying to gain a foothold in the Aegean. Liberating Crete was ruled out because Hitler refused to withdraw his large German garrison and it quickly disarmed the Italians. Instead, Churchill ambitiously wanted to occupy Rhodes, but General Maitland Wilson, the Allied commander-in-chief in the Mediterranean, simply did not have the resources in light of the landings in Italy. Churchill was personally familiar with the island having visited it while on holiday in the autumn of 1934. Instead, some 8,000 German troops swiftly disarmed the 35,000-strong Italian garrison leaving Hitler in control of Rhodes and its vital airfields. Churchill was insistent that Wilson counter the Germans, so weak forces were sent to Kos, Leros and Samos to rally the Italians to the Allied cause.

Unable to establish forward airfields in time, British units were left without fighter protection when the Germans moved to occupy the three islands involving airborne operations. In a replay of Greece and Crete the Royal Navy tried to help the army but was left exposed to the Luftwaffe. Not only were the British garrisons captured with the loss of 5,000 men, but naval losses included five destroyers sunk and six other vessels damaged. The campaign was a complete disaster and Churchill should have known better than to make Wilson overextend himself.[1] As in the case of northern Italy, Churchill underestimated the speed with which the Germans would react. In a case of understatement he later called the Aegean campaign, 'Most unfortunate'.[2]

Churchill's shuttle diplomacy continued with a series of conferences with the Allied leaders. Between November and December 1943, he attended Cairo I with Roosevelt and Chiang Kai-shek, Tehran with Roosevelt and Stalin, and Cairo II with Roosevelt. Crucially Churchill and Roosevelt, thanks to their determination to defeat the Axis powers, made their decisions largely on military rather than political grounds. Stalin in contrast took a much longer-term view of the war. He was determined to safeguard Soviet soil by protecting it from any future surprise attack by Germany. He wanted to ensure the great sacrifices made by the Red Army and the Soviet people were suitably rewarded, which meant gaining territory in eastern Europe to create a security buffer.

At the same time Churchill and Roosevelt had very different agendas once the war was ended. Foremost in Churchill's mind was his determination to preserve the British Empire at all costs. He knew that the war would inevitably weaken Britain's hold on its territories and damage British military prestige, particularly in the Far East. He also wanted to stop Eastern Europe from becoming a Soviet sphere of influence. Roosevelt, in contrast, had no intention of propping up the British Empire, or restoring the French Empire for that matter. His main concern was the Far East and the Pacific; both he and Chiang Kai-shek needed Stalin's help to defeat Japan. Securing this help would inevitably mean making considerable concessions. The East Europeans were Hitler's allies, so Roosevelt could understand Stalin's desire to punish them. Furthermore, Roosevelt saw Chiang as a long-term ally who should be supported against Mao's Communists once Japan was defeated.

Stalin cunningly moved to co-opt Roosevelt during the Tehran conference. He conveniently discovered a plot to kill the President, who was invited to the Soviet Embassy. Roosevelt met with Stalin privately three times and unfortunately for Churchill was completely won over by the Soviet leader. During these meetings Stalin explained all he wanted was to ensure the safety of his own country and that he would work towards democracy and peace. To that end the Red Army should liberate the Balkans. Stalin was not pleased when he discovered his allies had not nominated a commander for the opening of the Second Front. Churchill did not help matters when he reasoned that taking Rome and Rhodes should be a greater priority. Stalin then put Churchill on the spot by asking him if he actually supported *Overlord*. Under pressure, Churchill and Roosevelt pledged themselves to launch D-Day in May 1944.

Stalin advocated a British and American attack on northern France and once Rome had been taken all available forces in Italy should be diverted to southern France (initially these operations were codenamed *Sledgehammer* and *Anvil*, but became *Overlord* and *Dragoon*). As far as Stalin was concerned any operations in the Mediterranean should only be of a diversionary nature. This meant that three Allied Fronts, two in France and one in Italy, would be vying for the same resources. Stalin having got his own way agreed to attack Japan once Germany was defeated. He had set his heart on Manchuria and Korea.

When Churchill and Roosevelt returned to Cairo, the latter made it clear that British dominance of the Alliance was now at an end. General Dwight Eisenhower would be Allied supreme commander for *Overlord* as America was now supplying the majority of the resources. Churchill had hoped that an attack in the Balkans would unhinge the German defence and help forestall Stalin. Roosevelt, convinced of Stalin's sincerity, sought to prevent this by backing the Allied operation in southern France, which is just what Stalin wanted. Churchill and his generals saw the south of France landings as an unwelcome distraction. General Harold Alexander in Italy wanted to force his way northward, while General Maitland Wilson, the Allied commander in the Mediterranean, wanted to conduct a seaborne assault at the head of the Adriatic followed by a thrust east to Zagreb then an advance towards Austria and the Danube. The Americans though were not receptive.

Churchill's attitude to the opening of the Second Front was shaped not only by the failure of the Gallipoli landings, but also the failure of the Dieppe raid. He became acutely aware that a seaborne assault of the magnitude of *Overlord* had to be planned down to the finest detail. It also convinced him that trying to capture a French port straight off was impossible so some form of artificial harbour would be needed. In fact, Churchill had suggested the idea of floating piers to Mountbatten before the Dieppe raid took place. This led to the development of the top secret Mulberry Harbours used to support D-Day.

Churchill was lucky in that Lieutenant-General Sir Frederick Morgan, who was appointed Chief of Staff to the Supreme Allied Commander in April 1943, proved to be a highly capable planner. He had General Brooke to thank for finding Morgan. Much of the ground work had already been done when Eisenhower arrived at the end of the year. Normandy was selected as the best location to attack Hitler's Atlantic Wall. However, Churchill could not stop himself from being indiscreet and showing Montgomery the initial plans for D-Day before Eisenhower had even taken up his new post. Montgomery's response was the landings were on too narrow a front and should be expanded. This actually coincided with Eisenhower's views and pleased Churchill because he hoped an expansion of *Overlord* would lessen the need for Operation *Dragoon* and therefore lessen the impact on Italy.

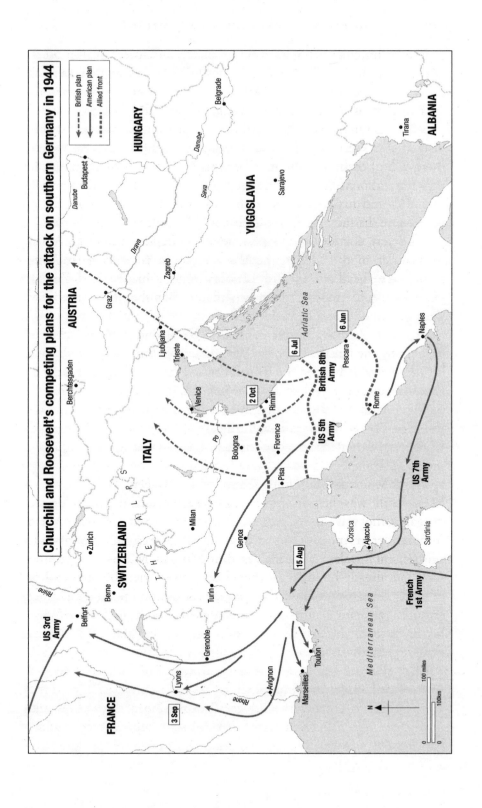

Churchill and Roosevelt's competing plans for the attack on southern Germany in 1944

By January 1944 Churchill was completely and utterly set against the landings in southern France and he began to argue that they were too far away to be of any help to *Overlord*. Preparations for both operations soaked up a lot of resources and the plans for *Overlord* kept changing, which meant the operation slipped to late May. Roosevelt was also distracted by ongoing American operations in the Pacific. As a result, there were simply not enough landing craft to spare, which meant that the south of France landings could not be conducted in parallel with those in the north. Montgomery supported Churchill's opposition on the grounds that more resources could be committed to *Overlord*.

Churchill, still haunted by past failures and concerned at how easily the Germans had bottled up the Allies in Italy, began to fear that D-Day would be a bloodbath. He drove Brooke and Eisenhower to distraction with his ideas. Amongst them was that within a week of *Overlord* a second assault should be conducted on the French Atlantic coast from Bordeaux to St Nazaire. He gave little thought to how it would be organized or where the troops would come from. He also persisted with his desire for Italy to be the focus of Allied effort; in light of it taking the Allies almost a year to reach Rome this gained no traction in the American camp. Furthermore, Brooke advised that campaigning in the Alps during the winter would be an impossible task. Nor would Eisenhower countenance abandoning all the hard work that had gone into developing *Overlord*.

Eisenhower was to find Churchill's involvement in *Overlord* meddlesome in other areas. Notably Churchill and Air Chief Marshal Portal did not want to put all of Harris's Bomber Command at Eisenhower's disposal. Nor did General Carl Spaatz, commander of the United States Strategic Air Force in Europe, want to play ball with *Overlord*. They had convinced themselves the strategic bomber campaign was finally producing dividends. At one point Eisenhower got so exasperated that he warned Air Chief Marshal Sir Arthur Tedder, his British deputy, that if the bomber barons did not get in line he would tender his resignation.

After all the horse trading over the location and size of Operation *Overlord*, Churchill was determined to be directly involved. On 30 May 1944 he got together with George VI at the Palace for their weekly luncheon. The pair, acting like irresponsible school boys, quickly hatched a plan to watch the D-Day landings from one of the supporting warships. When Sir Alan Lascelles, the King's private secretary, heard of this he was aghast. He reasoned that it would be a disaster should both the Sovereign and Prime Minister be killed at the same time. The following morning Lascelles persuaded the King to see sense. The King wrote to Churchill with an air of regret, 'I have been thinking a great deal of our conversation yesterday and I have come to the conclusion that it would not be right for either you or me to be where we planned on D-Day.'[3]

The following day Churchill met with the King and Admiral Sir Bertram Ramsay at Downing Street. The Admiral knew of the Prime Minister's plans, but was unaware that the King wanted to tag along as well. Ramsay explained that Churchill being on Admiral Sir Frederick Dalrymple-Hamilton's flagship was really not a good idea. When Churchill informed him that the King intended to come as well Ramsay became angry. Churchill quickly backtracked and said he would have to get the Cabinet's approval for the King's participation, but would recommend that it was not given. He then made it clear he was still going. When the King and Lascelles tried to deter Churchill he refused to change his mind. Even when it was pointed out that he needed the Sovereign's permission to leave the country, Churchill argued he would be on a British warship and therefore British territory. Ramsay and General Ismay, Churchill's Chief of Staff, were left in a state of panic. If the Prime Minister was killed it would be a major propaganda coup for Hitler.

Only one person had the power to stop Churchill. On 2 June the King noted in his diary, 'Ismay sent me a message early to say that the P.M. was wavering & hoped that I would send him another message imploring him not to go.'[4] He wrote again to Churchill saying, 'There is nothing I would like better than to go to sea but I have agreed to stop at home; is it fair that you should then do exactly what I should have liked to do myself?'[5] Churchill, who had gone to see Eisenhower in Portsmouth, did not reply. It was only when Lascelles telephoned the Prime Minister's train that Churchill agreed to respect the King's wishes.

When Churchill wrote back he was at pains to point out that the King's request should set no precedent in restricting a prime minister's movements. He then added, 'Since Your Majesty does me the honour to be so much concerned about my personal safety on this occasion, I must defer to Your Majesty's wishes & indeed commands.'[6] The King noted in his diary with an air of resignation, 'He has decided not to go on the expedition, but only because I have asked him not to go.'[7] More poignantly he added, 'I asked him as a friend not to endanger his life & so put me & everybody else in a difficult position.'[8] Churchill was bitterly disappointed but if there was one person he was prepared to listen to it was King George VI. Operation *Overlord* commenced on 6 June 1944 without either of them in attendance. Dalrymple-Hamilton was able to heave a sigh of relief.

That day Churchill informed the House of Commons that the long-awaited Second Front had commenced with the D-Day landings. 'This vast operation is undoubtedly,' he told them without exaggeration, 'the most complicated and difficult that has ever taken place.'[9] This was the kind of fully fledged all-arms amphibious assault that he had for so long envisaged. 'It involves ...' Churchill added, 'the combined employment of land, air and sea forces in the highest degree of intimacy.'[10]

Churchill having missed D-Day was determined to get across the English Channel as quickly as possible. He began to badger Eisenhower as early as 9 June for authorization. When he heard that the American Joint Chiefs of Staff were planning such a trip, he saw his chance and took it. Along with Brooke and Smuts, he visited Montgomery just six days after *Overlord*. They sailed from Portsmouth on the destroyer HMS *Kelvin*, but did not take the King. Montgomery, who had more than enough to deal with, was understandably not overjoyed by the prospect of this VIP visit to the Second Front. He was busy planning a breakout to the west of Caen at a place called Villers-Bocage involving the 7th Armoured Division. However, he knew he would be unable to deflect Churchill. Monty appreciated only too well that Winston saw himself as a warlord and he did not want the Prime Minister meddling at this crucial opening phase of the battle.

Montgomery wisely decided to set some ground rules and signalled Brooke beforehand, 'Roads not – repeat not – 100% safe owing to enemy snipers, including women. Much enemy bombing between dusk and dawn. Essential P.M. should go only where I take him, and you must get away from here in early evening.'[11] Brooke must have smiled at this, knowing it was easier said than done where Churchill was concerned. Nonetheless, Montgomery was aware that just two days after the landings, the Luftwaffe had retaliated with four air attacks involving up to 60 fighter-bombers. Although the Germans were struggling in the face of the massive Allied aerial superiority, there was still a danger and the last thing he wanted was Churchill killed in a surprise air raid.

Montgomery met his visitors on the beach with a fleet of jeeps and drove them to his headquarters. 'The P.M. was in first class form,' observed Monty. 'For once he was prepared to admit that I was in charge in the battle area and he must do what he was told!'[12] It rapidly became evident that Churchill was in very real danger. Upon arrival Smuts sniffed the air suspiciously and announced, 'I smell Boche.'[13] At that point a terrified teenage German deserter was brought in having been found hiding not 50 yards from Churchill and Smuts in some nearby woods. Immediately the patrols were stepped up and Monty's guard platoon was beefed up by some commandos backed by tanks just to be on the safe side. If the lad had been a more ardent member of the Hitler Youth armed with a rifle who knows what might have happened. Once again Churchill's remarkable luck held.

After lunch, during a tour of the area Churchill was amazed at how the French seemed to have thrived under German occupation. 'We are surrounded by fat cattle,' he said to Brooke, 'lying in luscious pastures with their paws crossed!'[14] Even Monty who noted the abundance of food was moved to write, 'The French civilians in Normandy do not look in the least depressed.'[15] Churchill and the others also got to meet some of Montgomery's senior commanders including Lieutenant-General Sir Miles Dempsey, commanding the British 2nd Army, and Lieutenant-General Sir Richard O'Connor, commanding the British 8th Corps. Before leaving Monty, the Prime Minister rather cheekily wrote in his visitors' book, 'As it was in the beginning so may it continue to the end.'[16] This could be open to interpretation, but presumably was recognition that the fighting in Normandy was in good hands.

Churchill, thirsting for excitement, watched as the Luftwaffe conducted an ineffectual attack on the harbour at Courseulles. When they re-embarked later that day he saw a vessel bombarding a target inland. Despite his time at the Admiralty Churchill had never been on a ship engaging the enemy and now desperately wanted to do so. 'Luckily we could not climb up owing to seaweed on the bulges,' noted Brooke with some relief, 'as it would have been a very noisy entertainment had we succeeded.'[17] Instead, they sailed up the beach to witness several other ships providing fire support. Churchill, in search of further thrills, hoped that the Germans might retaliate. They did not oblige and the *Kelvin* returned unscathed to Portsmouth with its VIPs intact.

Churchill, perhaps feeling a little guilty, met with the King on 13 June and said he would get the Cabinet's approval for him to visit Normandy. It was agreed that the King would make the crossing three days later on board the cruiser *Arethusa*. Montgomery was not pleased about this latest imposition and made his position perfectly clear to Sir James Grigg, Secretary of State for War. 'It is not a good time for important people to go sight-seeing and visiting forward areas,' he explained. 'I have made this clear to the P.M. My Corps and Divisional generals are fighting hard and I do not want their eyes taken off the ball.'[18] Montgomery also voiced his displeasure to Eisenhower. 'Whatever date is settled, keep anyone else away that day,' he instructed his chief of staff, 'i.e., warn Eisenhower off if he proposes to come the same day. I cannot deal with more than one VIP – and told the P.M. today he must not come again just yet.'[19] The King, though, was grateful for Churchill's intervention on his behalf.

'It was most encouraging to know that it was possible,' noted the King, 'for me to land on the beaches only 10 days after D-Day.'[20] He was hosted by a reluctant Montgomery and came away very impressed by what had been achieved. His sense of optimism was quickly dampened when he returned to London to find that Hitler was now attacking the capital with V-1 flying bombs. It was imperative that the Allies overran the launch sites in France as soon as possible. Churchill, by early July 1944, was frustrated by the slow progress being made in Normandy and raised the issue of using mustard gas with the Chiefs of Staff in order to break the deadlock. 'We will want to gain more ground in Normandy,' he reasoned, 'so as not to be cooped up in a small area.' He also suggested, 'We could drench the cities of the Ruhr' as a way of curbing Hitler's flying bomb attacks. Once more he argued that while gas attack was 'unpleasant ... nearly everyone recovers'.[21] He gave an undertaking to clear such a course of action with Roosevelt and Stalin and told the planners to get to work. Fortunately, nothing came of it.

Following D-Day Churchill renewed his campaign to stop Operation *Dragoon* disrupting the push in Italy. He cabled Roosevelt saying, 'Let's not wreck one great campaign for the sake of another. Both can be won.'[22] Roosevelt, though, was not for turning and pointed out that he could not change their plans without Stalin's approval. Churchill tried unsuccessfully to resurrect an operation in the Adriatic. He then turned his guns on Eisenhower. 'This argument, beginning almost coincidently with a break-through [in Normandy] in late July,' wrote Eisenhower, 'lasted throughout the first ten days of August.'[23]

The pair dined together at Eisenhower's headquarters near Portsmouth on 5 August. Churchill pointed out that, with the way things were going in Normandy, the Breton ports were within their grasp, which meant they did not need to take Marseilles. Two days later Churchill arrived at Eisenhower's Normandy headquarters asking him to shift *Dragoon* to Brittany or the Channel ports. Neither suggestion was practical as the Breton ports were too far away and German garrisons were resolutely clinging onto them and those on the Channel. Eisenhower said no and continued to do so for the next six hours. To his horror, when he met Churchill at Downing Street on 10 August the Prime Minister threated to resign if he did not change his mind about *Dragoon*. Eisenhower bravely stood his ground and told him the invasion was set for 15 August 1944 and that was that.

Brooke, who had supported Churchill, knew that any further resistance was futile. He appreciated that the row over diverting resources from Italy was counter-productive and understood that the campaign in Italy was a means to an end and not the end in itself. Eisenhower, who was fully occupied with the protracted battle for Normandy, which was reaching its climax, acted impeccably throughout his run-ins with the Prime Minister. Despite Churchill's behaviour Eisenhower affectionately called him 'a cantankerous yet adorable father'.[24] Churchill knew that this war of wills was a high-water mark. Whereas previously the British and American Chiefs of Staff had largely agreed on everything, from now on they would rarely see eye to eye.

On 12 August Churchill arrived in Italy to see Wilson and Alexander. He was taken to a beach to bathe and on the way saw two convoys heading for the French coast. The troops standing on the decks spotted him and cheered. Churchill later observed, 'They did not know that if I had had my way they would have been sailing in a different direction.'[25] Three days later Churchill was aboard the destroyer *Kimberley* to watch the landings he had so vigorously tried to prevent. These went without a hitch and Churchill found it a little boring. He later told the King rather pointedly, 'Your majesty knows my opinion of the strategy, but the perfect execution of the plan was deeply interesting.'[26] Brooke was beginning to despair of Churchill's antics. 'Personally I have found him almost impossible to work with of late,' he confided in his diary just as *Dragoon* was taking place, 'and I am filled with apprehension as to where he may lead us.'[27]

By now the Red Army had torn the beating heart from the German Army and had reached Warsaw and the Vistula. Churchill was increasingly concerned about Stalin's plans for the future of Poland and indeed the rest of Eastern Europe. 'Poland must be mistress in her own house,' he said, 'and captain of her own soul.'[28] The Allies needed to capitalize on their victory in Normandy and strike another decisive blow. At the second Quebec conference in September 1944 Roosevelt made it clear that he supported Eisenhower's broad front advance into Germany. Churchill, backing Montgomery, wanted to concentrate their efforts in northern Europe. This was in part to overrun the German V-1 and V-2 launch sites, which were bombarding England, but also to thrust towards Berlin while Stalin was preoccupied overrunning the Balkans. This strategy though was completely discredited by the failure of Montgomery's attempt to cross the Rhine at Arnhem that same month with the loss of most of the 1st Airborne Division.

Roosevelt, with elections looming in America, knew that with the bulk of the British and Canadian forces fighting in northern Europe he could hardly let his smaller allies take all the glory. Roosevelt and Eisenhower, quite rightly, felt that the US Army should at least share in the glory of forcing the Rhine. They got their own way and the focus of the Allied advance shifted south. When the American and French armies fanned out this caused enormous logistical problems and resulted in the generals squabbling over priority for resources. This meant that the Allied advance had lost momentum by the winter. It was this situation that encouraged Hitler to counter-attack the Americans in the Ardennes. Nonetheless, by the New Year Hitler's troops had been driven back to where they had started.

The grand strategist in Churchill would not let the future of the Balkans rest. He knew that once the Red Army was in Yugoslavia, Tito's Communist partisans would easily take power.[29] Albania and Bulgaria would also eventually end up with Communist governments. This left the fate of Greece hanging in the balance despite Stalin's promise not to get involved there. When Hitler's occupation forces began to withdraw, Greek Communists quickly moved to fill the vacuum. If they succeeded it would stop King George II of Greece and Georgios Papandreou's government-in-exile from returning. To fuel Greek infighting and cover their retreat the Germans left behind considerable stocks of weaponry.

Churchill acted by despatching 5,000 troops under Lieutenant-General Ronald Scobie along with Anthony Eden to Athens in October 1944 to ensure democratic elections. The irony was that these units had to be drawn from Italy. This intervention was not popular with some members of the House of Commons nor the British and American press, who saw it as unwarranted meddling in the internal affairs of a sovereign nation in defiance of the Atlantic Charter. However, Churchill called the Commons' bluff and easily won a vote of confidence. Roosevelt did not approve either, as he felt Churchill was attempting to prop up a monarchy against the people's wishes.

In the meantime, the well-armed Greek Communists took control of the port of Piraeus and most of Athens. Scobie was left holding just Kalamaki airport and the centre of the capital where the British Embassy was largely under a state of siege. Alexander, who had taken over from Wilson as commander in the Mediterranean, was instructed by Churchill, 'Deal with the situation as you think fit, but keep me closely informed.'[30] By the beginning of December 1944 fighting had broken out on the streets of Athens between Communist and pro-monarchist supporters, catching Scobie and his men in the crossfire. Feeling gung-ho, Churchill instructed him to take over the city, which was an impossible task. Nonetheless, Scobie set about attacking Communist strongpoints using machine guns and tanks. Alexander, after a fact-finding tour, ordered the deployment of a division from Italy to secure Piraeus and the airport and link up with Scobie. Alexander claimed rather optimistically, 'Once these arrangements had been effected, the military situation rapidly improved.'[31]

Churchill's military intervention was actually looking increasingly precarious. On 19 December the RAF headquarters at Kifissia, outside Athens, was attacked. The Communists gained the upper hand and 57 British airmen were killed or wounded. When it became apparent that help could not reach them, the defenders had no choice but to surrender and 563 members of the RAF were captured. Churchill now decided to personally intervene. Along with Eden and Alexander he arrived in Athens at the end of the month to try and broker peace between the waring Greek factions. By this stage the British had suffered over 1,500 casualties. Those involved knew that this was one quagmire too many, but Churchill was insistent on continued involvement. Perhaps he was acting out of guilt over not being able to save the Greeks at the start of the war, and more recently the Poles. Once again he put himself at great risk.

When he landed at Kalamaki on 25 December he first held a conference with senior British officials on board his aircraft, where everybody soon froze without the engines running. Churchill was dictating a press release when he heard something above the howling wind that was violently buffeting the fuselage. 'That was cannon fire,' he explained to the others.[32] Later, whilst lunching on the cruiser *Ajax*, moored in Piraeus harbour, he came under mortar fire and had to travel into the city in an armoured car. There a ton of explosives with a German detonator was discovered underneath a hotel next door to Scobie's headquarters. Ever unflappable Churchill reassured Clementine that he did not think the bomb was intended for him. Tense talks took place with gun fire and RAF rocket attacks clearly audible in the background. Despite the pleasantries there seemed to be little stomach for a negotiated settlement.

While staying on *Ajax*, Churchill informed Alexander and Scobie that he wanted to visit some British forward positions to get a feel for the situation. Both were horrified as it was simply too dangerous, especially as snipers were on the prowl. 'I hope he won't go ashore,' said Scobie to Lord Moran, 'it isn't safe. I simply can't compete if the P.M. will keep going ashore.'[33] Churchill later suggested using 60 tanks to clear the Communists from Athens; in response Alexander diplomatically pointed out that street fighting was a slow business and that it was very difficult to tell friend from foe. Eden found Churchill's refusal to delegate increasingly annoying and grumbled to Moran, 'I do wish he'd let me do my job.'[34] Although the city was eventually secured for the provisional government, despite Churchill's best intentions the rest of the country plunged into civil war that lasted until 1949.

'The Big Three,' Churchill, Roosevelt and Stalin, met for their last important conference before the defeat of Germany at Yalta in the Crimea in February 1945. Roosevelt, still determined to secure the Red Army's help in the Far East, made a series of decisions that did not bode well for the future of Europe or indeed the Pacific. Churchill had by now fully resurrected his fear of the Red menace and was convinced that Stalin was indeed a threat. Through the early years of the war he had steadfastly supported Stalin, but it was clear that the Soviet leader was going to reap all the benefits regardless of what the Western leaders might want.

Now that Churchill was the junior partner there was little he could do to influence Allied strategy in Western Europe. Eisenhower wanted to link up all the Allied armies stretched across France and in Italy. This would take precious time. Although Eisenhower believed that Hitler's last stand would be from a redoubt in southern Germany, he accepted that the Red Army should be the first into Prague and Vienna. Likewise, he felt that it was a pointless exercise to try and reach Berlin when the Red Army was that much closer. American troops would halt on the Elbe. This meant future access to Berlin would be reliant on Stalin's goodwill or a show of military strength by Western leaders.

26

'Death Wish'

Operation *Plunder*, the crossing of the Rhine, was to be the Allies' last great set-piece battle on the Western Front. The reckless young lieutenant still trapped inside Churchill was not prepared to miss out playing a part in this. He had been prevented from being there on D-Day and in consequence had to make do with the poor compensation of observing the pointless Allied landings on the Riviera. He arrived in the Netherlands on 2 March 1945 during the fighting between the Meuse and the Rhine. Along with General Ismay, his Chief of Staff and Brooke, Chief of the Imperial General Staff, he was a guest on Eisenhower's train located in a siding near Eindhoven. There they discussed plans for the forthcoming Rhine assault.

Whilst at the front visiting General William Simpson, the commander of the US Ninth Army, Churchill insisted on making a 30-minute journey so that he could symbolically take a pee on the German Siegfried Line defences. Before embarking on this trip he inadvertently left his dentures behind and they had to be sent for. Suddenly a jeep with outriders roared up to Churchill's convoy and someone handed him a sealed package. 'The onlookers thought that here was a signal of great importance ...' recalled Monty's Chief of Staff Major-General Francis de Guingand. 'Churchill, however, took the packet and slipped it into his pocket – unread. A ghost of a smile crossed his face. Here were, of course, the missing dentures!'[1]

When the convoy reached its destination, Churchill and the others made their way on foot to some concrete anti-tank bollards known as Dragon's Teeth. On the way Churchill was amused to see an American tank which the crew had dubbed 'Alcoholic Bitch'.[2] Simpson must have rolled his eyes and made a mental note to chew someone out over that. 'This is one of those operations connected with this great war,' Churchill said impishly to the accompanying photographers, 'which must not be reproduced graphically.'[3] He then proceeded to unbutton his trousers. 'I shall never forget the childish grin of intense satisfaction,' wrote Brooke, 'that spread all over his face as he looked down at the critical moment.'[4]

Churchill knew full well that Field Marshal Montgomery would not be receptive to his presence during the attack over the Rhine, so began to lay the ground work beforehand. At dinner, hosted by Eisenhower, after Montgomery had retired for the night, Churchill approached de Guingand to discuss his intentions. De Guingand was stunned to hear that the Prime Minister wanted to ride in a tank with the second assault wave. The hapless Chief of Staff proceeded to make excuses as to why this was not a good idea. 'De Guingand, not knowing the PM,' observed Brooke, 'unfortunately adopted quite the wrong attitude with him and I at one time was afraid that we might have trouble.'[5] Brooke appreciated that the more opposition Churchill encountered the more determined he would be to join the attack.

Churchill was very persistent and de Guingand promised to raise it with Montgomery. Churchill almost gave the impression that he had a death wish. 'I even began to wonder whether this great man had decided that he would like to end his days in battle,' remarked de Guingand, 'at a time when he knew victory was upon us!'[6] When Montgomery heard of the Prime Minister's request his response was predictable. 'It was just not on,' he said firmly, adding that he did not want Churchill 'wandering about in the middle of the battle disturbing the commanders who were running it.'[7]

Once back in London on 6 March the impish Churchill did not let the matter rest and Brooke was obliged to write to Montgomery. 'If the Prime Minister is not allowed to come, you have the seeds of serious trouble,' he warned. 'When the PM gets such ideas in his head nothing can stop him.'[8] Brooke then added Churchill 'would get into another of his rages if he felt that Monty was again trying to dictate to him, and stop him coming out'.[9] Privately, though, Brooke agreed with Montgomery and he knew Churchill would inevitably get in the way and be a general nuisance.

While de Guingand was attending a meeting in London he was summoned to see Churchill. The Prime Minister quizzed him on arrangements for his participation in the Rhine crossing and de Guingand promised he would get a tank but not in the opening waves. 'After discussing dates and timings,' recalled de Guingand, 'I left him clutching a big cigar, and grinning gently from his arm chair.'[10] On 10 March Churchill received a formal invitation from Montgomery. Brooke was tipped off by Montgomery, who wrote, 'I have written him a letter; Simpson will show it to you; it should please the old boy!'[11] The Field Marshal, though, was far from happy about this and also wrote grumbling to Sir James Grigg, Secretary of State for War, 'I didn't want him but he was determined to come; so I have invited him in order to keep the peace.'[12]

The Chief of the Imperial General Staff, the most senior officer in the entire British Army, was similarly displeased about Churchill's latest adventure. 'Tomorrow I start off with P.M. on his visit to see the Rhine Crossing,' Brooke recorded in his diary. 'I am not happy about this trip; he will be difficult to manage and has *no* business to be going.'[13] Churchill set out for Montgomery's tactical headquarters at Straelen just inside Germany on 23 March. He took with him Brooke, his private secretary Jock Colville and his naval aide Commander Charles Ralfe 'Tommy' Thompson. Churchill decided that the occasion required him to wear the uniform of his old regiment the 4th Hussars, which he had joined all those years ago as a subaltern. From RAF Northolt they took off for the two-hour flight.

Upon arrival Monty briefed Churchill and Brooke about his plans for the coming battle before going to bed early as was his habit. Afterwards Churchill was restless so he and Brooke went for a walk in the moonlight. He took this opportunity to thank Brooke for the first time for all his hard work and for standing up to him. 'He was in one of his nicest moods,' recalled a somewhat surprised Brooke, 'and showed appreciation for what I had done for him in a way in which he had never done before.'[14]

Montgomery was not taking any chances with Operation *Plunder*. He massed over a quarter of a million men to take the 1,500-feet-wide Rhine held by just 85,000 German troops. The exhausted and largely demoralized German armed forces in the Rhineland were in tatters as were their defences. According to Montgomery's figures, since

8 February 1945 they had suffered 250,000 casualties in the battles for the Rhineland. Upriver from Wesel, Montgomery's 30th Corps assaulting Rees was faced by the remains of three German parachute divisions, which were supported by just two armoured units with hardly any tanks. To the south 12th Corps' assault at Wesel was only faced by a single German division as was the US 16th Corps' attack at Walsum. German defences were to be deluged with almost 50,000 tons of bombs and shelled by over 3,000 guns. This did not mean the crossings would be a pushover – the Germans still had some 500 guns facing the British sector alone – but the outcome would be inevitable.

On the morning of 24 March 1945 Churchill stood on a hilltop at Xanten, overlooking the west bank of the Rhine, with all the other commanders, to watch the opening bombardment and the vast Allied airborne armada fly overhead. The excitement was too much for him. 'They're coming,' he shouted like an excited child. 'They're coming!'[15] Eisenhower turned up to meet with Churchill, Brooke, Montgomery and Simpson. He found Churchill brimming with unbridled enthusiasm, 'My dear General, the German is whipped. We've got him.'[16] Frustratingly though, the weather was hazy and smoke had been laid down, which made it difficult to see the river assault. Churchill and Brooke later relocated to some high ground south of Calcar. The ever-suffering Brooke had to rein in his boss who 'wanted to go messing about on the Rhine crossings'.[17]

The following day Eisenhower left to see General Bradley. The moment he was gone Churchill turned to Montgomery and said mischievously, 'Now I'm in command. Let's go over.'[18] Montgomery, who was equally as keen as the Prime Minister, agreed. 'However, had I been present,' Eisenhower later wrote, 'he would never have been permitted to cross the Rhine that day.'[19] To Simpson's horror Churchill clambered into an American landing craft followed by the others. Once they reached the other side Churchill, with a cigar clamped between his lips and his mackintosh pulled tightly round him, strode purposely ashore with Brooke, Montgomery and Simpson in tow. Orbiting them were photographers, intent on capturing this historic moment.

'This is no place for the PM,' grumbled Simpson to Montgomery. 'I'd hate to have anything happen to him in my area!'[20] While Montgomery was sympathetic to his plight there was nothing he could do and he just shrugged. Simpson caught up with Churchill and said half-jokingly,

'If we keep going, we'll soon be in the front line.'[21] Begrudgingly Churchill turned back to the river. Montgomery, sensing the Prime Minister's disappointment, asked the landing craft captain if they could head down stream towards Wesel. He was informed that this was not possible because a barrier had been placed across the river to stop the Germans using mines to attack the Allied pontoon bridges. Instead, Montgomery suggested when back across they drive to the damaged Wesel railway bridge.

Once there, before anyone could stop him, Churchill, cigar in mouth and walking stick in hand, picked his way up the steep rubble obstructing the approaches to the bridge. The ground was strewn in loose debris including half a dozen railway sleepers and smashed pieces of concrete. He then hoisted himself onto one of the bridge's steel girders and began to move out over the water. Brooke and the others watched in horror as Churchill was fearlessly 'scrambling along it for about forty yards'.[22] German artillery began to bracket the bridge dropping shells into the river either side. It was almost as if they knew he was there. The German spotters had been alerted by the construction of an Allied pontoon bridge just downstream. The crack of rifle fire also showed that snipers were in the vicinity. It was when the Germans began to shell the road behind them that Simpson realized it was definitely time to leave, even if it meant physically prising Churchill off the bridge. Desperately he pleaded with the Prime Minister 'to come away'.[23] Instead of immediately returning, Churchill suddenly grasped one of the damaged girders with both arms and looked back at the waiting officers with a sulky expression. 'It was a sad wrench for him; he was enjoying himself immensely!'[24] said Brooke. 'However, he came away more obediently than I expected.'[25]

De Guingand was good to his word and Churchill did get to ride in a 'tank', albeit not quite in the manner he had hoped. Along with Brooke, Montgomery, Dempsey and Thompson he was driven across the Rhine using a newly installed pontoon bridge to Bislich on 26 March.[26] There a special treat had been laid on. They all piled into the back of a tracked amphibious Buffalo and motored along the river. It was an ungainly smoke-belching monster that rode alarmingly low in the water. The engine was so noisy that it was almost impossible to communicate without a throat mike and radio headphones. Nonetheless, a gleeful-looking Churchill could not resist the temptation to pose with the vehicle's heavy machine gun as it lurched back up the bank. Monty tactfully rode in the back keeping well out of the way of the warrior Prime Minister. Any hopes Churchill may have had of heading off inland were thwarted by the Buffalo's tracks, which were not designed to stray far from water.

'A beaten army, not long ago Master of Europe, retreats before its pursuers,' Churchill wrote in Montgomery's visitors' book. 'The goal is not to be denied to those who have come so far and fought so well under proved and faithful leadership.' Then with a flourish he added, 'Forward all on wings of flame to final victory.'[27] Churchill returned to London that day, but before he left he took another symbolic pee, this time in the Rhine. Brooke, like de Guingand, was convinced that Churchill had hoped to die at the front. Certainly his extreme risk-taking seemed to indicate a total disregard for his own safety. Brooke was alarmed at just how excited Churchill had appeared while on the Wesel bridge. On the other hand, Brooke noted, 'Winston, I think, enjoyed his trip thoroughly and received a wonderful reception wherever he went.'[28]

Shortly afterwards American armies encircled the Ruhr and by mid-April it had been overrun. The Allies then raced to the Elbe to meet the advancing Red Army. On 12 April 1945 Churchill received the sad news that his close wartime ally President Roosevelt had died. For many years Roosevelt's health had been declining and the stresses and strains of the war had taken their toll. Five days later Churchill told the House of Commons, 'I conceived an admiration for him as a statesman, a man of affairs, and a war leader.'[29] Less than a month after Roosevelt's death Germany surrendered. Churchill later remarked, 'He was the greatest American friend that Britain ever found.'[30]

Although 8 May 1945 is considered Victory in Europe Day, the German surrender was actually a staggered affair that lasted a week either side of this date. German troops in Italy capitulated on 29 April and laid down their arms on 2 May. Although Hitler committed suicide on 30 April, the Berlin garrison fought on until 2 May before surrendering. Two days later, on 4 May, a German delegation surrendered to Montgomery on Luneberg Heath. 'At last the goal is reached,' wrote Churchill triumphantly.[31] Another delegation yielded to the Americans in Reims on 7 May; they then formally surrendered to the Russians in Berlin on 8 May. Churchill stayed up until 3.45am writing his victory speech. However, German forces in Czechoslovakia continued fighting until 11 May, with sporadic resistance lasting until 19 May.

On VE Day Churchill announced Germany's unconditional surrender to the nation over the radio from Downing Street. Although he said it was a time for rejoicing, he cautioned that Japan remained unvanquished. 'Japan, with all her treachery and greed, remains unsubdued,' he warned. 'The injury she has inflicted ... and her detestable cruelties, call for justice and retribution.'[32] He was mobbed by ecstatic crowds that day wherever he went. 'Outside, through the Horse Guards Parade, along Birdcage Walk and Great George Street, through Parliament Square,' recalled Elizabeth Layton, one of Churchill's secretaries, 'the whole place was cram-jammed with people waiting to welcome him.'[33]

Churchill stood on the balcony at Buckingham Palace with George VI and the rest of the royal family and was cheered by 20,000 people. As he made his way from the House of Commons to St Margaret's Church for a service of thanksgiving, mounted police had to keep the revellers at bay. He also appeared on a balcony in Whitehall that evening with his cabinet and received a rapturous ovation. 'Flags and bunting had been put up,' observed Layton, 'and floodlights were directed upon the balcony.'[34] He told the crowd, 'In all our long history we have never seen a greater day than this ... God bless you all.'[35] They then sang 'Land of Hope and Glory'. The nation was extremely grateful for all his incredible hard work and self-sacrifice, or so he thought.

Brooke's comments about Churchill's leadership in his diary on 8 May seem to reflect a certain bitterness harboured by him, Cunningham and Portal. 'Without him England was lost for a certainty,' he wrote, 'with him England has been on the verge of disaster again and again. And with it all no recognition hardly at all for those who help him except the occasional crumb intended to prevent the dog straying too far from the table.'[36] When the Chiefs of Staff had got together with Churchill the previous day at Downing Street to toast the German surrender, Ismay noted, 'I hoped that they would raise their glasses to the chief who had been the master planner; but perhaps they were too moved to trust their own voices.'[37] In pursuing his war aims the publicity hogging Churchill had bruised one too many egos. 'On the whole,' grumbled Brooke, 'the PM ... has never once in all his speeches referred to the Chiefs of Staff.'[38]

Miracle of Deliverance

Some of Churchill's colleagues were dismayed if not appalled at his continuing intransigence over the future of India. In his opinion it should remain part of the British Empire. They also found his ingratitude galling. A vexed Leo Amery, the India Secretary, noted in the summer of 1944 a 'long tirade on the worthlessness of the Indian Army was too much for me and I went for him ... pointing out what India had done ever since it saved the Middle East'.[1] Besides the Middle East and Italy, Indian troops served in North Africa. Indian divisions were likewise instrumental in the ongoing fighting to drive the Japanese from Burma.[2] At the end of 1944 they were even sent to Greece. Amery likened Churchill's behaviour on the issue of India to 'a rather amusing but quite gaga old gentleman'.[3] Even Wavell was moved to castigate the Prime Minister, when he wrote 'I feel that the vital problems of India are being treated by HMG [His Majesty's Government] with neglect, even sometimes with hostility and contempt.'[4] Dogged old imperialist that he was, Churchill knew that without India, Britain's status as a world power would inevitably be greatly diminished. Wavell, though, warned that it was better to keep India as a friend than an enemy.

In the meantime, thanks to competing interests, Churchill's Bay of Bengal strategy was thwarted until the very end of the war. His key opponent to this turned out to be Chiang Kai-shek, not Roosevelt. Auchinleck had hoped to conduct a three-pronged assault into Burma unimaginatively called Operation *Tarzan*. This envisaged, in March 1944, Chinese forces in Yunnan taking Lashio and Bhamo, with Stilwell's northern forces advancing from Ledo on Myitkyina and on to

Bhamo. British airborne forces would take and hold Indaw. To divert the Japanese, the 4th and 15th Indian Corps would advance the month before.

Chiang was unhappy with the plan as he felt it put too much burden on his forces. Instead, he unreasonably called for the complete liberation of Burma, which was beyond the Allies' capabilities and forced Mountbatten to cancel the operation. Similarly, Chiang refused to support less-ambitious plans for landings in the Arakan until amphibious operations had retaken the Andaman Islands, Moulmein or Rangoon. Likewise, he wanted the British to first retake Lashio or Mandalay. To Churchill this was clearly a case of the British having to take the pressure off the Chinese and not the other way round as he intended.

Despite the enormous demands for resources elsewhere, prior to the Japanese attacks on Imphal and Kohima, Churchill signalled Mountbatten, 'Let nothing go from the battle that you need for victory … I will back you to the full.'[5] Foremost they remained reliant on the loyalty of their Indian soldiers. Most of the British 14th Army's 4th Corps defending Imphal was made up of Indian Army infantry divisions, comprising Indian, Gurkha and British troops. The Japanese, in March 1944, attacked Tamu on the main road to Imphal. The following month they attacked Kohima with the objective of the Kohima Ridge, which dominated the road along which supplies were ferried to 4th Corps. To Churchill's delight through the spring and summer of 1944 the advancing Japanese were held. By the time their attacks came to a halt they had suffered 55,000 casualties. This victory safeguarded the strategic Bengal and Assam railway and the airfields that were being used to fly military supplies to Chiang and Stilwell.

Churchill's blind faith in the Indian Army was not misplaced.[6] Far from siding with the rebel nationalists, it mauled the 6,000-strong 1st Indian National Army (INA) Division at Imphal. The renegades thought that they could persuade the Indian soldiers to join them simply by yelling the rallying cry 'Jai Hind!' (Victory to India).[7] Instead, they were greeted as traitors. Around 400 were killed in action, 800 surrendered and 1,500 were lost to disease and starvation. Most of the survivors who withdrew were hospitalized. 'Our Indian and Gurkha troops were at times not too ready to let them surrender,' observed Slim, 'and orders had to be issued to give them a kinder welcome.'[8] He prudently decided to treat them as prisoners of war rather than deserters and sent them back to India to be dealt with. Nirad Chaudhuri, with All India Radio, wrote, 'It should be kept in mind that no one stirred in India when the INA was supposed to be fighting at Kohima and Imphal. Not a hand was raised.'[9]

Churchill's desire to retain India was understandable, as its independence would inevitably unravel the British Empire, but it was not a sustainable position. By 1945 India had 2.5 million men under arms and their aspirations for independence could not be kept in check forever. Those divisions deployed overseas would eventually come home. Wavell noted Churchill became concerned about officer training in India, as it was creating more and more potential future nationalist leaders. There were at least 8,000 Indian officers who could form the professional cadre for a post-independence Indian armed forces.[10] They could also lead a rebellion if there was no peaceful transition of power. No one in the British government had the stomach to fight another Quit India revolt.

In Burma the Japanese were then driven back beyond the Irrawaddy River and in early 1945 defeated at the battles of Mandalay and Meiktila. After this they withdrew towards Thailand. Once Germany was out of the war, Churchill stated, 'The new phase of the war against Japan will command all our resources ... We owe it to Australia and New Zealand to help them remove for ever the Japanese menace to their homeland as they have helped us on every front in the fight against Germany.'[11] He firmly believed the only way to restore British prestige in the Far East was the liberation of Singapore. Churchill seemed to ignore the fact that more Japanese had been killed in Burma than in any other campaign. Unfortunately, this achievement was overshadowed by events in Europe and the speed of American island hopping.

Churchill resurrected his long-favoured plan to assault northern Sumatra. Mountbatten, though, with the prospect of finally getting adequate troops and equipment, did not want to be distracted from landing on the Malaya peninsula and then on to Singapore. He also decided to carry out a combined operation to take Rangoon. It was known rather ominously as Operation *Dracula*. The airborne element commenced on 1 May 1945, but the Japanese withdrew from the Burmese capital before the seaborne force could engage them. Churchill also pledged forces to assist the planned American assault on Tokyo and the island of Honshu. This was scheduled for early 1946 and was to follow on from the planned seaborne attack on Kyushu.

For Churchill time was running out for his wartime premiership and the coalition government. Following Victory in Europe national unity collapsed. He wanted to continue in office until Japan was defeated but Clement Attlee and the Labour party demanded a general election. This was called just two months after Germany surrendered. 'I remember feeling horrified by the certainty with which Winston asserted that the coming election would go in his favour,' recalled Air Marshal Harris. 'I was equally certain that this showed a complete blindness to political realities …'.[12] Churchill and the Conservative party assumed they would gain a parliamentary majority and remain in power. It was not unreasonable for Churchill to believe that his wartime leadership had won him great favour with the British public. Although the election took place on 5 July, rounding up all the votes from the troops overseas would take until the end of the month.

Deep down Churchill knew, after five gruelling years, he ought to step down, but he was reluctant to relinquish the reins of power. He had risen to the task of warlord and revelled in it. Churchill decided he wanted to lead the country in peacetime, to oversee its recovery. The armed forces were not so keen. 'In one of my son Simon's last letters from Burma,' wrote Anthony Eden, 'he had hinted that many of the fighting forces were not likely to vote for us and, from my contacts I had in the army, I shared his opinion.'[13] Eden refrained from sharing this feedback with Churchill as he knew it would 'not be welcome'.[14] Captain David Niven noted that most servicemen he came into contact with 'held the Conservative party entirely responsible for the disruption to their lives and in no circumstances would they vote for it next time there was an election – Churchill or no Churchill.'[15]

While awaiting the results Churchill and Attlee travelled to Potsdam in Germany to meet Roosevelt's successor Harry Truman and Stalin to discuss the future of Europe and Asia. They issued the Potsdam Declaration which renewed the demand for Japan's unconditional surrender, the Allied occupation of Japan and an end to its empire. Truman without going into details hinted that he had an 'ultimate weapon' ready for use that would force the Japanese to lay down their arms. He later recounted that when he 'casually mentioned to Stalin that we had a new weapon of unusual destructive force', the Soviet leader somewhat worryingly 'showed no special interest'.[16]

Mountbatten, who was heading for London seeking reinforcements for the Far East, was diverted to Potsdam to see Churchill. There the pair dined together. 'You are going to have to revise your plans,' explained Churchill apologetically. 'The war with Japan will be over in less than a month. We are going to use a new bomb, an atomic bomb, against the cities of Japan, and the Emperor will be forced to capitulate.'[17] Mountbatten was also told that Japan would probably surrender around mid-August and that all his operations should be put on hold until then. This was a blow to Mountbatten and Slim.

In Germany the signs of Churchill enjoying electoral success were not encouraging. Lord Moran, who accompanied him, was amused to discover that the men of the 11th Hussars had voted Socialist. However, their voting papers had gone missing, and having seen the disgusting mess Russian soldiers left in the German barracks they were now occupying, they wanted to vote Conservative. Another regiment was also dismayed by the behaviour of the Russians and chose not to vote at all. When Churchill attended the British Victory Parade in Berlin his reception was not as warm as he might have expected. 'Winston Churchill, the great war leader,' noted John Peck, Churchill's Private Secretary, '... got a markedly less vociferous cheer than Mr Attlee, who ... had not hitherto made any marked personal impact upon the fighting forces.'[18] The assembled media preferred to focus on the impressive spectacle of the march past by the men and tanks of the British 7th Armoured Division – Monty's famous 'Desert Rats'.

Something far worse happened in Berlin that stunned Churchill and signalled his political position was indeed far from secure. Members of the British Army deliberately shunned him. 'When we were on parade in the Wilhelmstrasse,' recalled Londoner Private Sam Meltzer, 'Clement Attlee came down in a car with Winston Churchill. ... the British soldiers turned their backs. It was something they'd learned from Gandhi during the civil disobedience in India.' Churchill could not have missed this act and it must have greatly saddened him. 'They turned their backs on that car,' adds Meltzer, a Dunkirk veteran. 'Churchill wasn't popular ... It was the mood of that time.'[19]

The political blow fell on Churchill on 26 July 1945 with Attlee gaining an absolute landslide victory. Eden felt terribly sorry for

him: 'this was a devastating, and especially a personal, defeat'.[20] Lord
Moran valiantly tried to comfort him saying, 'there was great unrest
in the country; that demobilization, housing and unemployment
would add to it; and that it was inevitable that the Government in
power would get the blame'.[21] Hiding his pain, Churchill tried to be
stoical and responded, 'The public will be staggered when they hear
tonight at nine o'clock that I've resigned. ... This is not necessarily
the end.'[22] Certainly not everyone had anticipated this turn of events.
'The decisive defeat of the Churchill government came as a great
surprise to all,' remarked Field Marshal Montgomery.[23] His brother in
arms, Field Marshal Alexander, wrote 'our great war leader was turned
out of office by the people's vote'.[24] Many of their officers were of a
similar view. 'Look what they've done to Churchill, for God's sake!'
lamented actor turned soldier Captain Dirk Bogarde. 'Surely the most
dishonourable, ungrateful, behaviour ever given to a Leader.'[25]

The armed forces were blamed for this state of affairs, but this was
not the complete picture. The euphoria of VE Day quickly evaporated
and Japan had yet to be defeated. 'Looking at the English people around
me, it was impossible to believe that they had won the war,' wrote James
Ballard who arrived in Britain after being interned by the Japanese in
China. 'They were clearly exhausted ... Everything was rationed ...'.[26]
Although Churchill was immensely popular, the country looking to
the future wanted a fresh start. It was a parliamentary election, not a
presidential one and the country preferred what Labour had to offer.
The dogged Churchill would become Prime Minister one last time in
the 1951 general election, though his second premiership was marred
by increasing ill-health.

Churchill supported President Truman's difficult decision to use the
atomic bomb if it hastened the end of the war in the Far East. He viewed
it as 'a miracle of deliverance'.[27] Churchill and the late Roosevelt had
agreed in principle as early as September 1944 that once the atomic bomb
was operational they should consider using it against Japan. Truman was
desperate for the Japanese to end the needless slaughter in the Pacific. He
was also concerned that if Stalin declared war before they surrendered, the
Soviet Union could gain a significant foothold in East Asia. It was doubtful
that the poorly equipped and supplied Japanese forces and their allies in
Manchuria would be able to stand up to the overwhelming firepower of
the Red Army.

It was the long and drawn-out conquest of Japanese-held Iwo Jima and Okinawa during the first half of 1945 that convinced the Allies that invading the Japanese home islands would be a bloodbath.[28] On 6 August 1945, the first atomic bomb to be used in modern warfare fell on the city of Hiroshima. Three days later a second one was dropped on Nagasaki. They killed about 200,000 people, many of whom died of horrific burns and radiation sickness.[29] That very day, on 9 August, Stalin invaded Manchuria and crushed the Japanese puppet state within less than two weeks. At this point continued Japanese resistance became completely pointless. Japan finally accepted unconditional surrender on 15 August 1945. 'We were glad that VJ came so soon after the election results,' said Elizabeth Layton, 'since now it could never be said that Victory in the Far East was not every bit as much *his* victory as Victory in Europe had been.'[30]

Churchill's belated grand imperial gesture to reclaim Singapore involving 200,000 men ended in farce. Mountbatten's forces, spearheaded by his battle-hardened Indian divisions, came ashore in south-west Malaya on 9 September 1945 under Operation *Zipper*. It was fortunate the Japanese did not resist, as the landings could have ended in disaster. When the assault craft disgorged their vehicles, many of them sank in the mud and it took 12 hours to get the armour ashore. As the war had already ended it was easier to forget Mountbatten's shambolic version of D-Day. Poor intelligence and constant delays imposed by Churchill stole Mountbatten's long-awaited moment of glory.

That same month Indian divisions were deployed to help the Dutch and French reassert control of the East Indies and Indochina. Responsibility for these military misadventures, like Malaya, fell to Attlee not Churchill. Truman understandably struggled to comprehend why Attlee's Labour government was propping up its colonial neighbours. However, Attlee feared if he did not help there would be a wholesale massacre of Europeans, which had already commenced in the East Indies. Indian troops were also sent to help with the occupation of Japan. In the Middle East, Indian divisions remained stationed in Egypt, Iran, Iraq and Palestine until Indian independence in 1947.

28

'The Whole Scene'

'We all think back to Sir Winston Churchill as a man who bespoke confidence,' said General Eisenhower.[1] That confidence was the result of a life well lived. Churchill viewed his military and political career as one long apprenticeship for the day he became Prime Minister. Regarding his appointment he memorably wrote, 'I felt as if I were walking with destiny, and that all my past life had been but a preparation for this hour and for this trial.'[2] On the basis of what he experienced and achieved it would be churlish to argue with such a notion. No one was as well qualified as he was. 'Never has any land found any leader,' remarked Field Marshal Montgomery, 'who so matched the hour as did Sir Winston Churchill.'[3]

Notably though Churchill's school days never suggested that he was destined for high office. He struggled terribly to apply himself. His school report in 1884 lamented, 'He is not to be trusted to do any one thing.'[4] Four years later the prognosis had not got any better when his house master at Harrow reported, 'As far as ability goes he ought to be at the top of his form, whereas he is at the bottom.'[5] Churchill's father even went so far as to threaten to disown him: 'if your conduct ... at Sandhurst [Royal Military College] is similar to what it has been in the other establishments ... my responsibility for you is over.'[6] Thankfully for Winston and indeed the nation, Sandhurst was the making of him. He made a very good impression on his first regimental commander, Colonel Brabazon, who wrote, 'I personally knew the boy, liked him and was anxious to have him.'[7]

From Churchill's earliest brushes with death on the dusty battlefield of Omdurman, in the mountains of the North-West Frontier and on the

South African veldt he developed an unshakeable sense of invincibility and destiny. In his youth he was clearly an adrenalin junkie, publicity seeker, spin doctor and flouter of rules; these were key elements of his character that helped shape his unshakeable political ambition. Churchill forged himself a formidable reputation and became a deep thinker with a strategic grasp on domestic and international affairs. He also sought and achieved political office, serving in all the top jobs.

His world view was anchored on him being an ardent imperialist and monarchist for which he made no apology. He saw the British Empire as sacrosanct and it should be remembered he was far from alone in this. He viewed British rule in India and Ireland as a stabilizing force which in both countries kept at bay historical sectarian tensions. To this end he considered nationalists to be a threat not only to the British Empire but also to law and order. In both instances he was paddling against the tide of history and in both instances he hoped a military solution would keep them wed to Britain. Instead, partition proved to be the only solution. Likewise, he saw Britain's involvement in the Middle East in terms of a security problem as much as a diplomatic one. The use of air power to keep order in the empire helped safeguard the RAF's future and was done in the name of economy. Nonetheless, the policy of 'Air Control' was Hugh Trenchard's, not Churchill's.

In World War I Churchill did all he could as the First Lord of Admiralty, a battalion commander and then Minister of Munitions to support the British war effort. In his role as Secretary of State for War and Air his ambitions in the post-war years were very much restricted by the austerity measures imposed on Britain's defence spending. His attempts to shape Russia's future were founded on his fear of Bolshevism and the impact it could have on the world order. Unfortunately, by championing international intervention, he helped ensure that the Soviet Union became an enemy of the West until 1941. Once World War II was over that historic mistrust quickly returned leading to the Cold War.

Although a devout supporter of parliamentary democracy, Churchill learned during World War I and in its aftermath that running military campaigns by committee stifled initiative. He was blamed for the failure at Gallipoli but it was really the result of poor coordination and timeliness by the services. By holding both the premiership and defence minister post during World War II he was truly the country's political master and military commander. 'At last,' said Churchill, 'I had the authority to give directions over the whole scene.'[8] Churchill wanted to lead and lead he did. 'He certainly dominated the events and persons surrounding him in the war years,' observed Montgomery, 'as should all good leaders.'[9] Eisenhower came to appreciate that Churchill embodied 'the age-old truth that politics and military activities are never completely separable.'[10]

After the dark days of appeasement, the Phoney War and the opening of Hitler's Blitzkrieg in the West, Churchill's arrival gave the British government a much-needed sense of direction and backbone. General Spears who attended Churchill's first speech as Prime Minister recalled 'suddenly he was transformed into an inspired leader, the High Priest of a great religion dedicating a nation to measureless sacrifice'.[11] His words of defiance galvanized the wavering House of Commons and the country. 'He was always at his best when things were worst,' observed Air Marshal Harris, 'which, of course, is the mark of real leadership, especially in wartime.'[12] Despite paying brief lip service to opening negotiations with Hitler via Mussolini, it seems very doubtful that Churchill ever intended to sue for peace. He described the Nazis on 19 May 1940 as 'the foulest and most soul-destroying tyranny'.[13] He had watched their rise and knew what they represented. The Nazis, said Churchill, had left in their wake 'shattered States and bludgeoned races'.[14] He appreciated that a power based purely on military resurgence did not make for a good neighbour.

When it came to continuing the war Churchill observed, 'I thought I knew a good deal about it all, and I was sure I should not fail.'[15] Anthony Eden who was a member of his War Cabinet wrote, 'It was the combined creation of the Prime Minister's leadership and the men he chose.'[16] Although it was beset by differences of opinion it functioned thanks to the presence of Churchill. 'The machinery for the military and political conduct of the war had been discerningly built and it worked,' said Eden. 'Churchill knew how to get the best out of it.'[17] Field Marshal Alexander agreed with Eden. 'This balance, as between chiefs of staff and political chiefs, is not easily achieved,' he wrote. 'During the ... war it worked out pretty satisfactorily in the end, but not without blood, sweat and tears.'[18] Churchill wrote to Montgomery in 1945 saying, 'Certainly the relations which I had with you, with Alexander and with the High Command of the three Services generally, were of a most intimate character in spite of the great stresses ... . How different from the rows ... which characterized the last war.'[19]

Churchill's Chiefs of Staff and other senior commanders were not so keen on his regular late-night working practices especially at Chequers on weekends. 'If it was a mixed party [i.e. with wives] – which was not very often,' said Harris, 'I knew that we might get home somewhere between midnight and one ... but when I was asked alone, it would be anywhere between three and four.'[20] Churchill liked to host dinner followed by a film and then after midnight get down to business. On one occasion Field Marshal Brooke was kept up until 2.50am after Churchill insisted on calling for sandwiches and playing the gramophone. Beforehand they had watched German and Russian newsreels before discussing the war. 'I hoped that this might at last mean bed!' Brooke wrote in his diary. 'But no!!'[21] Eisenhower recalled how his weekly meetings at Chequers 'often continued into the morning'.[22] 'These,' he added, 'sometimes lasted until three.'[23] Only Churchill's South African confidante, Field Marshal Smuts, politely refused to put up with this punishing routine. 'Well, Winston, I suppose you are going on with the argument all night,' he once said after dinner. 'I am going to bed, good night.'[24]

Churchill convinced himself that he was a good commander. 'Winston never had the slightest doubt that he had inherited all the military genius of his great ancestor, Marlborough,' observed Brooke. 'His military plans and ideas varied from the most brilliant conceptions at one end to the wildest and most dangerous ideas at the other.'[25] Brooke admitted that he always struggled to steer Churchill away from his wilder ideas and when he succeeded Churchill had a vexing habit of returning to them. 'Churchill, who can jump from one subject to another with the agility of a grasshopper,' wrote Spears, 'has nevertheless the same power of concentration that was so characteristic of Napoleon.'[26] 'During the war Mr Churchill maintained such close contact with all operations as to make him a virtual member of the British Chiefs of Staff,' wrote Eisenhower, 'I cannot remember any major discussion with them in which he did not participate.'[27]

'People say my speeches after Dunkirk were the thing. That was only a part ...' explained Churchill. 'They forget I made all the main military decisions.'[28] His initial instincts to defy Hitler, rescue the British Expeditionary Force from Dunkirk and fight the Battle of Britain saved the country from ignominious defeat. His decision to hold Malta, despite the heavy cost, was also the right one. Although it had to endure constant air attack, thanks to the losses incurred by Hitler taking Crete, it was never subjected to an airborne invasion. British forces operating from Malta were then able to strangle Rommel's supply lines, which greatly aided victory at El Alamein.

His subsequent strategic judgement in the Mediterranean left much to be desired. He had no option other than face down Mussolini, but the wisdom of his decision to attack the French fleet at Mers-el-Kebir has been hotly debated ever since. What it did do was signal very firmly to Vichy that Britain would not tolerate France or indeed its colonies siding with Germany. When Vichy did not heed this warning he had no compunction about occupying France's overseas territories.

The resounding victory over Mussolini at Beda Fomm in February 1941 was rapidly thrown away by Churchill's well-intended but foolhardy decision to help Greece. Eden should share responsibility for this as he was fully committed to the enterprise on purely political grounds. Wavell and Eden should have opposed Churchill rather than let him weaken British forces in North Africa. 'I have ... always considered from the very start that our participation in the operations in Greece was a definite strategic blunder,' remarked Brooke. 'Our hands were more than full at that time in the Middle East, and Greece could only result in the most dangerous dispersal of force.'[29] In consequence Rommel was able to gain a firm foothold in Tripoli and British forces were ejected from Libya, Greece and Crete. The climax of this was that Rommel menaced Cairo.

Churchill's ceaseless impatience drove his commanders to distraction. 'There were times when it would appear,' noted Air Chief Marshal Tedder, 'that he would almost prefer action at any cost providing it was immediate.'[30] In North Africa Churchill's impulsiveness made life very difficult for Wavell and Auchinleck, who understandably were more concerned with lasting military results than political ones. Churchill's constant insistence on attacking meant that Wavell launched a series of operations that lacked sufficient power to deliver the desired outcome. In the case of Operation Crusader, it threw away precious equipment that the Royal Navy had shed blood to shepherd across the Mediterranean.

Churchill's meddling in the Far East needlessly sent the Repulse and the Prince of Wales to their fates. After the fall of Singapore, he largely left the conduct of the war against the Japanese to his admirals and generals. Although the Viceroy panicked in the face of the Quit India revolt in August 1942, Churchill's faith in the loyalty of the Indian Army remained unshakeable and well-founded. Notably, regarding the Quit India movement, reporter Nirad Chaudhuri assessed, 'I think its seriousness and magnitude has been grossly exaggerated after independence in the interest of the Indian nationalist myth.'[31] Certainly its timing was premature and the only tangible results were to delay operations in Burma and further sour British relations with the Indian nationalists.

After the Battle of Britain there can be little doubt that El Alamein was Churchill's most important victory as it heralded the turn of the tide in North Africa and in the Mediterranean. Only this made possible the opening of the Second Front. Churchill acknowledged, 'Up to Alamein we survived; after Alamein we conquered.'[32] It made Montgomery the man of the moment and ensured his place in history as one of Britain's most famous generals. 'We did not always see eye to eye,' said Montgomery, 'I doubt if any soldier ever has done with his political chief, and certainly not with that one.'[33] On the eve of the battle the supremely confident Montgomery was forced to scold Churchill for meddling, remarking, 'You do not know how to fight this battle, or when. I do know.'[34] Nonetheless, Montgomery admired Churchill as a leader and came to regard him as a valued friend. Furthermore, Montgomery's desert triumph finally silenced critics of Churchill's conduct of the war. Churchill reciprocated Montgomery's friendship, saying, 'It has been my fortune and great pleasure often to be with him at important moments in the long march from Mersa Matruh to the Rhine.'[35]

Although King George VI initially hoped Lord Halifax would succeed Chamberlain he wrote in his diary in February 1941, 'I could not have a better Prime Minister.'[36] Churchill worked hard to form a bond with the monarch, whom he greatly respected. 'I valued as a signal honour the gracious intimacy with which I,' he noted, 'as first Minister, was treated, for which I suppose there has been no precedent since the days of Queen Anne and Marlborough during his years in power.'[37] Churchill also cherished the friendship and counsel of his former enemy Field Marshal Smuts. 'We could work together with utmost ease,'[38] wrote Churchill gratefully of his 'old friend and comrade.'[39] Lord Moran observed, 'He is the only man who had any influence with the P.M.'[40]

'The friendship of Churchill and Smuts always fascinated me,' noted Eden. 'They were such contrasting personalities; the one with his neat philosophic mind, the other a man "so rammed with life".'[41] Smuts regularly worried about Churchill's health, because as Moran recorded he felt 'Winston is irreplaceable.'[42] This closeness inevitably rankled with some of the other dominion leaders, who felt they were perhaps not consulted as much as they should have been. Although they were fighting shoulder to shoulder Churchill did not seem to have much time for John Curtin and Mackenzie King, the respective prime ministers of Australia and Canada. Churchill's long relationship with Smuts had been forged during the Boer War and World War I so the two men had more in common with each other than the others.

Despite frequently making life difficult for his commanders Churchill was certainly no warlord tyrant. 'I think the first thing that impresses one about Winston,' noted Harris, 'is the extraordinary mixture in him of real human kindness and of sometimes impish mischief.'[43] Montgomery was the victim of the latter on a number of occasions. When he captured General Wilhelm von Thoma at El Alamein he drew criticism for inviting his captive to eat with him. 'I sympathize with General von Thoma,' said Churchill when he heard. 'Defeated, humiliated, in captivity and dinner with Montgomery.'[44] Churchill could also be very cruel to old friends. Lloyd George launched a withering criticism of how the war was being run in the House of Commons on 7 May 1941. In response Churchill remarked, 'It was the sort of speech with which, I imagine, the illustrious and venerable Marshal Pétain might well have enlivened the closing days of M. Reynaud's Cabinet.'[45] Lloyd George never forgot this accusation of cowardice and refused to cooperate with Churchill's wartime government.

Brooke, as Chief of the Imperial General Staff, endured the most of Churchill's wrath during their often-stormy relationship. He was amazed that Churchill never sacked him. A regular angry refrain from the Prime Minister in 1942 had been, 'Have you not got a single general in that army who can win battles?'[46] Brooke was angered that Churchill insisted on making such ungrateful remarks to the War Cabinet, thereby undermining confidence in the army. 'For all that I thank God that I was given an opportunity of working alongside such a man,' concluded Brooke, 'and of having my eyes opened to the fact that occasionally such supermen exist on this earth.'[47]

Whereas Churchill met very regularly with his Chiefs of Staff, other senior commanders and Allied leaders, General Slim and his 14th Army were completely neglected. Slim was abroad for over seven years and in all that time he noted, 'I had never met the Prime Minister.'[48] Even when he launched his successful offensive around Imphal and Kohima, Churchill and Brooke showed little interest in the campaign. It was not until after Germany surrendered that Slim returned home on leave and met the pair.[49] Churchill wrote of 'the welter of inefficiency and lassitude which has characterized our operations on the India front' and this criticism was not forgotten.[50] This lack of recognition and gratitude came at a political cost. Slim's soldiers considered themselves 'The Forgotten Army'[51] and most of his British units voted against Churchill in 1945.[52]

One of Churchill's greatest achievement was the bond he forged with America. He did this by sheer force of character alone, winning over Roosevelt's support and admiration even before America had entered the war. This was no mean feat when the country was so predominantly isolationist. Churchill recognized that America was a global power in waiting and that it had the means with which to defeat Nazism and Fascism. In Britain's darkest hour Churchill was not too proud to plead for help. He regularly impressed upon Roosevelt the gravity of the situation and in the process gained a like-minded ally. By the time of Pearl Harbor the ground work for their wartime relationship had already been laid. Subsequently, during the preparations for the invasion of French North Africa and then the liberation of Europe, it was Eisenhower's turn to experience just how 'restlessly impatient' Churchill could be.[53] Eisenhower recalled, 'Often, unheralded, he descended on me to present a new idea, to argue once again a rejected proposal, to get the latest word on battle – or just to chat.'[54]

Churchill's dealings with Stalin were much more problematic because of their ideological differences. Nevertheless, Churchill did all he could to support the Soviet Union. Prior to, and indeed after, the opening of the Second Front the Red Army did the lion's share of the fighting. Britain and America's Arctic convoys were therefore a costly but necessary show of solidarity. This undoubtedly weakened Britain's war effort at a critical time in North Africa. Soviet leader Nikita Khrushchev wrote, 'I think Stalin was more sympathetic to Roosevelt than Churchill because Roosevelt seemed to have considerable understanding for our problems.'[55] Furthermore, Khrushchev claimed, 'Roosevelt and Stalin had a common antipathy for monarchy.'[56] He could have added to this British imperialism.

Once the Axis surrendered in Tunisia, Churchill increasingly struggled to dominate the strategic conduct of the war. For Roosevelt and Stalin, the Second Front was the priority as this would trap Hitler and take some pressure off the Red Army. After the Allies secured Sicily, mainland Italy did not prove to be the soft underbelly of Europe as Churchill had hoped. His attempts to forestall the German takeover in the Aegean after Italy surrendered were ill-considered and under-resourced. The subsequent stalemate on the Italian Front dashed his aim of keeping Stalin out of the Balkans and meant he failed to discourage the invasion of southern France. After D-Day, Eisenhower, quite rightly, was firmly in control of the Western Front. He found Churchill's interference increasingly tiresome, but he never yielded. By the time of the Rhine crossing Churchill was little more than an excited bystander.

Nevertheless, there is no denying Churchill's quite extraordinary personal achievements especially during World War II. Whilst his mistakes were legion and in some cases quite unforgiveable, he restored the country's faith in itself in its direst hour and provided firm leadership when it was needed the most. His drive and energy representing the interests of the nation proved to be quite phenomenal despite bouts of ill-health. At the end he was feted as a hero on both sides of the Atlantic and as an inspirational leader. It would be fair to conclude that he achieved his ultimate goal of being both master and commander.

Churchill was no superman nor an egotist. He chose a role in life and played it well. A decade after World War II ended, Nirad Chaudhuri witnessed one of Churchill's final appearances in the House of Commons. 'It was surprising how successfully he had divested himself of all atmosphere,' wrote Chaudhuri, 'of all suggestion of being not only a writer, historian, and political thinker, but also a statesman and war leader.'[57] This seemed a rather harsh observation, until Chaudhuri explained, 'I meant these words to be complimentary, and not censorious, as if he was an English incarnation of one of the early heroes of Rome.'[58] Churchill would have been highly pleased by such an epitaph.

Epilogue

Gone Painting

Remarkably Churchill did not take a single holiday during the war. After VE Day, rather than wait for the declaration of the polls, it was decided he and Clementine would go on a well-earned break to southern France. They left London on 7 July 1945 for a chateau south of Bordeaux overlooking the Bay of Biscay. Churchill hoped to relax by painting, but he was exhausted and very restless. He had only painted a single picture during the entire war and that had been a view of Marrakech in January 1943.[1]

Churchill and Clementine were photographed on the beach together and both looked tired and pensive. It was not surprising that he was unable to settle; not only was there the question of the election results, but the war against Japan still loomed large. President Truman was about to test the atomic bomb in the Nevada desert and Churchill was anxious to hear of the outcome. During a visit to St Jean-de-Luz he did manage to start painting again, though the weather proved temperamental. He also bathed at Hendaye, ironically the town where Hitler had met Franco in a futile bid to get Spain to enter the war against Britain. After just over a week he flew to Berlin for the Potsdam conference and subsequent electoral defeat.

At the end of the war Churchill was physically and mentally exhausted by his crushing schedule of continual conferences, meetings and travel.[2] To sustain six years of constant life-or-death decision-making would have taken a terrible toll on any lesser mortal. Perhaps it was just as well that he lost the election otherwise he would have got no rest at all. There was military intervention in Greece and Java in the immediate post-war years. Indian independence and partition loomed large as did the Berlin Blockade, heralding the start of the Cold War, followed by the Korean War. Eire severed all ties with Britain and declared itself an independent republic. All this would have rested on his shoulders had he won the premiership in 1945.

Instead, he took a much-needed holiday on the shores of Lake Como in northern Italy in September 1945 to do some more painting and take stock. He stayed in the villa La Rosa which was arranged by Field Marshal Alexander. For several days Churchill and Alexander sat side by side painting the same scene. Alexander was just being companionable, because as Churchill put it the Field Marshal had not 'handled a brush for six years'.[3] During their conversation Churchill remarked, 'The war is over, it is won and they have lifted the hideous aftermath from my shoulders.'[4] Alexander, grateful 'for the trust, friendship, and support' Churchill had shown him during the war, offered his commiserations over losing the election.[5] 'You know, when I was turned out of office,' replied Churchill, 'I felt it to be a very hard thing after all I had done.' Pointing to the Italian landscape he added with a smile, 'But life has its compensations.'[6]

Although he had taken a battering his optimism showed through in his brush strokes. One of his pictures captured golden sunlight reflected in the sky-blue waters of the lake, which were framed by a natural canopy of green foliage.[7] Churchill was clearly invigorated by his trip to Italy because in 25 days he produced 15 paintings.[8] 'With my painting I have recovered my balance,' he told Lord Moran. 'I'm damned glad now to be out of it.'[9] War, though, was never far from his mind. Over lunch he reminisced about the Boer War with Alexander who had showed an interest in the exploits of General Buller. His daughter Sarah delighted in recalling, 'Night after night Charles [Lord Moran] and I would sit back while the boys fought the battles from Omdurman to Alamein.'[10] Churchill as ever was in his element.[11]

Winston Churchill's Military Career
at a Glance

1895–1945

1895

Commissioned as a 2nd Lieutenant with the 4th Queen's Own Hussars
Observer and war correspondent with the Spanish Army, Cuba

1896

Lieutenant with the 4th Hussars, India

1897

Aide-de-camp and war correspondent with the Malakand Field Force, India
Lieutenant with the 35th Sikh Infantry Regiment, MFF, India
Lieutenant with the 31st Punjab Infantry Regiment, MFF, India

1898

Lieutenant and war correspondent with the 21st Lancers, Sudan

1899

Resigned commission
Civilian war correspondent with the Royal Dublin Fusiliers and Durban
   Light Infantry, South Africa

1900

Commissioned as a Lieutenant with the South African Light Horse, South
   Africa
War correspondent with the Imperial Yeomanry (Lancashire Hussars/
   Queen's Own Oxfordshire Hussars), South Africa
War correspondent with Montmorency's Scouts, South Africa

1902

Captain with the Queen's Own Oxfordshire Hussars, Territorial Army

1905

Major with the Queen's Own Oxfordshire Hussars

1906

Attended German military manoeuvres

1909

Attended German military manoeuvres

1910

Attended British Army manoeuvres at Aldershot

1911

First Lord of the Admiralty (political head of the Royal Navy)

1914

Took charge of the defence of Antwerp at the outbreak of World War I

1915

Forced to resign from the Admiralty due to the Gallipoli Campaign

1915–16

Major with the 2nd Battalion, Grenadier Guards, Western Front
Lieutenant-Colonel (temporary) commanding 6th Battalion, Royal Scots
    Fusiliers, Western Front

1917

Minister of Munitions

1919–21

Secretary of State for War and Air

1939

First Lord of the Admiralty
Honorary Air Commodore No.615 (County of Surrey) Squadron, RAF
Honorary Colonel Queen's Own Oxfordshire Hussars
Honorary Colonel Royal Artillery

1940

Honorary Colonel 6th Battalion, Royal Scots Fusiliers

1940–45

Prime Minister and Defence Minister

1941

Honorary Colonel 4th Hussars
Honorary Colonel 4th/5th (Cinque Ports) Battalion, The Royal Sussex
    Regiment

1942

Honorary Colonel 489th (Cinque Ports) Heavy Anti-Aircraft Regiment,
    Royal Artillery

1945

Honorary Colonel 4th Battalion, The Essex Regiment

CHURCHILL'S MILITARY DECORATIONS, MEDALS AND ORDERS 1895–1945

Although Churchill never won the coveted Victoria Cross[1] or Distinguished
Service Order, he gained an array of other awards, including:

Cross of the Order of Military Merit (Spain, 1895)
India Medal with clasp (Punjab Frontier, 1898)
Cuban Campaign Medal (Spain, 1899)
Queen's Sudan Medal (1899)
Khedive's Sudan Medal with clasp (Khartoum, Egypt, 1899)
Queen's South Africa Medal, with six clasps (Diamond Hill, Johannesburg, Relief
    of Ladysmith, Orange Free State, Tugela Heights, and Cape Colony, 1901)
1914–18 British War Medal (1919)
1914–15 Star (1919)
Distinguished Service Medal (Army) (US) (1919)
1914–19 Victory Medal (UK) (1920)
Order of the Companions of Honour (1922)
Territorial Decoration (1924)
Defence Medal (1945)
Africa Star (1945)
France and Germany Star (1945)
Italy Star (1945)
1939–1945 Star (1945)
1939–45 War Medal (1945)
Order of Leopold with Palm (Grand Cordon) (Belgium, 1945)
War Cross with Palm (Belgium, 1945)
Military Medal (Luxembourg, 1945)

Notes and References

INTRODUCTION

1 Roy Jenkins, *Churchill: A Biography*, New York: Farrar, Straus and Giroux, 2001, p.52

PROLOGUE

1 Robert Wilkinson-Latham, *The Sudan Campaigns 1881–1898*, London: Osprey, 1976, p.35
2 This rankled for good reason as the British Army's lancer regiments, which had first been formed in 1816, gained numerous battle honours. The 5th Lancers fought at Hasheen or Hashin in the Sudan on 20 March 1885, suffering five dead and two severely wounded. The 9th Lancers were involved in defeating the Indian Mutiny and along with the 16th Lancers served in the First Sikh War. The 12th and 17th Lancers made a name for themselves during the Crimean War. In particular, the 12th took part in the infamous charge of the Light Brigade at Balaclava. The 17th also fought in the Zulu War.
3 Wilkinson-Latham, *The Sudan Campaigns*, p.33
4 Donald Featherstone, *Omdurman 1898: Kitchener's Victory in the Sudan*, Oxford: Osprey, 1994, p.53
5 Michael Paterson, *Winston Churchill: His Military Life, 1895–1945*, Newton Abbot: David and Charles, 2005, p.119
6 This was the 3rd Bengal European Cavalry Regiment. In late 1857 the Bengal government, short of cavalry as a result of the mutiny, raised four new regiments that were recruited in England. It became the 21st Regiment of Hussars in 1862.
7 'The War in the Soudan', *The Illustrated London News*, Saturday, 11 April 1885, pp.368 & 382–3.
8 Featherstone, *Omdurman 1898*, p.10
9 Paterson, *Winston Churchill*, p.120
10 Ibid., p.121
11 John Fabb, *The Victorian and Edwardian Army from Old Photographs*, London: B.T. Batsford, 1975, pp.143–7

12 Wilkinson-Latham, *The Sudan Campaigns*, p.34

13 Featherstone, *Omdurman 1898*, p.53

14 Ibid, p.61

15 Wilkinson-Latham, *The Sudan Campaigns*, p.34

16 Donald Featherstone, *Weapons & Equipment of the Victorian Soldier*, Poole: Blandford Press, 1978, p.33

17 'Ismat Hasan Zulfo, *Karari: The Sudanese Account of the Battle of Omdurman*, London: Frederick Warne, 1980, p.203

18 Wilkinson-Latham, *The Sudan Campaigns*, p.33

19 Accounts vary, with sources stating the force ranged from 1,500 to 4,000 men. Not long after the battle William H.G. Kingston's *Our Soldiers: Gallant deeds of the British Army during the reign of Queen Victoria*, London: Griffith Farran Browne, 1899, recorded they numbered over 2,000, p.350. Interestingly the account of Omdurman made no mention of Churchill's exploits.

20 Zulfo, *Karari*, p.203

21 Ibid.

22 Featherstone, *Weapons and Equipment of the Victorian Soldier*, p.53. General Stewart decided the British Army needed lancers in the Sudan after the battle of El Teb in 1884, where the Dervishes waited for the cavalry to pass before leaping up to hamstring the animals.

23 Paterson, *Winston Churchill*, p.127

24 Churchill's recollection of these fatalities varied. He wrote to his mother on 4 September 1898 saying he had shot five and possibly two others. When he wrote to Colonel Ian Hamilton 12 days later he clarified he had killed three for certain, plus possibly three others. See Randolph S. Churchill, *Winston S. Churchill*, Volume 1, Youth 1874–1900, London: Heinemann, 1966, p.414 & p.418. Andrew Roberts in *Churchill: Walking with Destiny*, London: Penguin, 2019, p.58 records that he killed four, citing Peter Midgley (ed.), *The Heroic Memory: Memorial Addresses to the Rt. Hon. Sir Winston Spencer Churchill Society, Edmonton, Alberta, 1965–1989*, Edmonton, 2004, p.13. When Churchill later wrote to his cousin, the Duke of Marlborough, he only mentioned he thought he had killed three, adding 'It's difficult to miss at under a foot's range.' Nigel Blundell, *Winston Churchill: The Pictorial History of a British Legend*, Barnsley: Pen & Sword, 2011, p.17. Andrew Roberts astutely noted 'Can't be easy to be certain in such a fast-moving situation … The surprising thing is that he revised downwards!'

25 Author Clive Ponting was highly critical of Churchill's actions at Omdurman and basically accused him of murder: 'Churchill's contribution was, after the charge, to shoot down five men in cold blood with his Mauser pistol loaded with dum-dum bullets.' Ponting, *Churchill*, London: Sinclair-Stevenson, 1994, p.30

26 Paterson, *Winston Churchill*, p.131

27 Colin R. Coote, *A Churchill Reader: The Wit and Wisdom of Sir Winston Churchill*, Boston: Houghton Mifflin, 1954, p.255

28 Ibid.

29 Michael Glover, *Warfare from Waterloo to Mons*, London: Cassell, 1980, p.206

30 Max Arthur, *Churchill: The Life: An Authorised Pictorial Biography*, London: Cassell, 2017, p.45

31 Paterson, *Winston Churchill*, p.132

32 Featherstone, *Weapons and Equipment of the Victorian Soldier*, p.31

33 Randolph Churchill, *Winston S. Churchill*, Vol. I, p.418 – WSC to Ian Hamilton, 16 September 1898

34 Ibid.

35 *The Morning Post*, 29 September 1898

36 WSC to the Duke of Marlborough, 29 September 1898, Marlborough Papers Manuscript Division, Library of Congress

37 Max Arthur, *Symbol of Courage: The Men behind the Medal*, London: Pan, 2005, pp.150–2

38 Paterson, *Winston Churchill*, p.133

39 Winston Churchill, 'The Cavalry Charge at Omdurman,' in Ernest Hemingway (ed & intro.), *Men at War*, London: Fontana, 1972, p.45

40 Lord Moran, *Winston Churchill: The Struggle for Survival 1940–1965*, London: Constable, 1966, p.522

41 War artist Frederick Villiers filmed the battle from the *Melik*, but unfortunately his camera was knocked over and the footage ruined.

42 Martin Gilbert, *Churchill: A Life*, London: Pimlico, 2000, p.100

CHAPTER I: SOLDIERS OF THE QUEEN

1 David Chandler, *Marlborough as Military Commander*, London: Batsford, 1979, p.331

2 John Churchill regularly experienced severe migraines, dizziness and silent rages. Ibid., p.316

3 Dr Andrew Norman, *Winston Churchill: Portrait of an Unquiet Mind*, Barnsley: Pen & Sword, 2012, pp.199–200

4 Richard Holmes, *In the Footsteps of Churchill*, London: BBC Books, 2005, p.23

5 It has been speculated that this first manifested itself during Churchill's teenage years. See Norman, *Winston Churchill*, p.200

6 See Allister Vale and John Scadding, *Winston Churchill's Illnesses 1886–1965*, Barnsley: Frontline Books, 2020. Both medical consultants, they state, 'Our view, then is that the available evidence suggests that Churchill suffered no major psychiatric disorder', p.397. They also conclude that 'he was not an alcoholic', p.409

7 The French and Bavarians had some 56,000 troops facing 52,000 Allies, of which no more than 9,000 were British. The Franco-Bavarian force also had two-thirds more artillery. See David Green, *Blenheim*, London: Purnell, 1974, p.69 and Chandler, *Marlborough as Military Commander*, p.144

8 Amongst his works was *Tapestries at Blenheim Palace* which he painted in the 1930s. See Mary Soames, *Winston Churchill: His Life as a Painter*, London: Collins, 1990, pp.110–1

9 Winston S. Churchill, *Marlborough: His Life and Times*, 4 vols, George G. Harrap & Co. Ltd, 1933–8.

10 This exercise in March 1889 involved 11,000 regulars and over 1,300 public school boys. Brian Lavery, *Churchill Warrior: How a Military Life Guided Winston's Finest Hours*, Oxford: Casemate, 2017, p.4

11 Sources vary enormously on how strong this Spanish force was.

12 Andrew Roberts says that Churchill's claims to have heard shots on his birthday are untrue, but he did come under fire on 1 December: see *Churchill: Walking with Destiny*, p.37, citing Hal Klepak, *Churchill Comes of Age: Cuba 1895*, Stroud: The History Press, 2015, p.129

13 Winston S. Churchill, *A History of the English-Speaking Peoples*, Volume IV, The Great Democracies, London: The Folio Society, 2003, p.275

14 Ibid.

15 Ibid.

16 Holmes, *In the Footsteps of Churchill*, p.45

CHAPTER 2: FRONTIER WARS

1 Paterson, *Winston Churchill*, p.104

2 Randolph Churchill, *Winston S. Churchill*, Vol. I, p.325, citing David Scott Daniell, *The History of the Fourth Hussars*, Aldershot: Gale & Polden, 1959

3 Paterson, *Winston Churchill*, p.110

4 Randolph Churchill, *Winston S. Churchill*, Vol. I, p.363, WSC to Lady Randolph, 22 December 1897

5 Ibid., p.360, WSC to Lady Randolph, 2 October 1897

6 These were first produced by the Dum Dum Arsenal, near Calcutta.

7 Jenkins, *Churchill: A Biography*, p.32

8 Jules Stewart, *The Savage Border: The Story of the North-West Frontier*, Stroud: Sutton, 2007, p.127

9 Randolph Churchill, *Winston S. Churchill*, Vol. I, pp.374–5, WC to Lady Randolph, 31 & 7 March 1898

10 Ibid, 7 March 1898

11 Ibid, 31 March 1898

CHAPTER 3: GREAT ESCAPE

1 George and Anne Forty, *They Also Served*, Speldhurst: Midas, 1979, p.133, citing Frederick Woods (ed.), *Young Winston's Wars*, London: Leo Cooper, 1972

2 There are numerous fine books on the Zulu War, but one of the most outstanding is Ian Knight's *Zulu Rising: The Epic Story of Isandlwana and Rorke's Drift*, London: Macmillan, 2010

3 Rayne Kruger, *Good-bye Dolly Gray: The Story of the Boer War*, London: Pan, 1974, p.85 and Featherstone, *Weapons & Equipment of the Victorian Soldier*, p.55

4 Denis Judd, *The Boer War*, London: Granada, 1977, p.43

5 Some accounts say this was a 7-pounder gun.

6 Gilbert, *Churchill: A Life*, p.110

7 Carlo D'Este, *Warlord: A Life of Churchill at War, 1874–1945*, London: Allen Lane, 2009, p.139

8 Arthur, *Churchill: The Life*, p.47

9 Gilbert, *Churchill: A Life*, p.110

10 Ibid., p.110

11 D'Este, *Warlord*, pp.140–41
12 Judd, *The Boer War*, p.53
13 Ibid.
14 Jenkins, *Churchill: A Biography*, p.54
15 Arthur, *Churchill: The Life*, p.48

Chapter 4: The Sakabulas

1 Winston Churchill, 'How I Escaped from Pretoria', *Pearson's Illustrated War News*, and 'How I Escaped – Six Days of Adventure and Misery', *London Morning Post*, 30 December 1899

2 Forty and Forty, *They Also Served*, p.133, citing Woods (ed.), *Young Winston's Wars*

3 Arthur, *Churchill: The Life*, p.51

4 Robert Wilkinson-Latham, *The Boer War*, London: Osprey, 1977, p.21

5 Gandhi's ambulance corps consisted of 300 Indian volunteers and 800 indentured Indian labourers on furlough. Louis Fischer, *The Life of Mahatma Gandhi*, London: HarperCollins, 1997, p.75

6 Judd, *The Boer War*, p.75

7 Also known as the long-tailed widow bird and found throughout southern Africa.

8 Philip J. Haythornthwaite, *The Colonial Wars Source Book*, London: Caxton, 2000, p.204

9 Ibid., p.209, citing J. Williams, *Byng of Vimy, General and Governor-General*, London: Leo Cooper, 1983, p.47

10 Kruger, *Good-bye Dolly Gray*, p.194

11 Holmes, *In the Footsteps of Churchill*, p.67

12 Eversley Belfield, *The Boer War*, London: Leo Cooper, 1975, p.74

13 Fischer, *The Life of Mahatma Gandhi*, p.76

14 Ibid.

15 Paterson, *Winston Churchill*, p.168

16 Ibid., p.172

17 Belfield, *The Boer War*, p.140

18 Ibid.

19 Churchill, *History of the English-Speaking Peoples*, Vol. IV, pp.319–20

CHAPTER 5: A HAUNTING LESSON

1 Denis and Peggy Warner, *The Tide at Sunrise: A History of the Russo-Japanese War 1904–1905*, London: Angus & Robertson, 1975, p.288, citing A.L. Haldane, *Reports from British Officers Attached to the Japanese and Russian Forces in the Field*, London, 1908

2 Churchill, *History of the English-Speaking Peoples*, Volume IV, p.309

3 Warner, *The Tide at Sunrise*, p.288, citing A.L. Haldane, *Reports from British Officers Attached to the Japanese and Russian Forces in the Field*.

4 Randolph S. Churchill, *Winston S. Churchill*, Volume II, Young Statesman 1901–1914, London: Heinemann, 1967, p.203

5 Jenkins, *Churchill: A Biography*, p.195

6   Stephen Wynn, *Churchill's Flawed Decisions: Errors in Office of the Greatest Briton*, Barnsley: Pen & Sword, 2020, p.125

7   Randolph Churchill, *Winston S. Churchill*, Vol. II, p.374

8   Ibid., p.375

9   Ibid., p.383

10 Christopher Andrew, *The Defence of the Realm: The Authorised History of MI5*, London: Allen Lane, 2009, p.37

11 Vale and Scadding, *Winston Churchill's Illnesses*, p.377

12 Ibid.

13 These were the *Sultan Osman* and the *Reshadiye*; both were completed and paid for. Klaus Wolf, *Victory at Gallipolli 1915: The German-Ottoman Alliance in the First World War*, Barnsley: Pen & Sword, 2020, pp.30–31

14 Stephen Roskill, *Churchill and the Admirals*, Barnsley: Pen & Sword, 2013, p.42

15 Major J.R. Sibley, *Tanganyikan Guerrilla: East African Campaign 1914–18*, London: Pan/Ballatine, 1973, p.34

16 Barry Gough, *Churchill and Fisher: Titans at the Admiralty*, Barnsley: Seaforth, 2017, p.335

17 Ibid., p.338

18 B.H. Liddell Hart, *History of the First World War*, London: Cassell, 1971, p.218

19 Ibid., p.215

20 Ibid., p.224

21 Roskill, *Churchill and the Admirals*, p.50

22 Moran, *Winston Churchill*, 489

23 Dr Shreerang Godbole, 'Madan Lal Dhingra: A Lion Hearted National Hero', *Hindu Janajagruti Samiti*, 14 August 2010

24 Andrew, *The Defence of the Realm*, p.93

CHAPTER 6: 'CAT ON HOT BRICKS'

1   Major-General Sir Edward Spears, *Assignment to Catastrophe*, London: The Reprint Society, 1956, p.467

2   Major Andrew Dewar Gibb, *With Winston Churchill at the Front: Winston in the Trenches 1916*, Barnsley: Frontline, 2016, p.61

3   Ibid., p.177

4   Richard Hough, *Winston and Clementine: The Triumphs and Tragedies of the Churchills*, London: Bantam, 1991, p.378

5   Ibid., p381

6   Dewar Gibb, *With Winston Churchill at the Front*, p.178

7   Ibid., p.176

8   Anthony Tucker-Jones, *Armoured Warfare in the First World War 1916–1918*, Barnsley: Pen & Sword, 2016, p.45

9   Moran, *Winston Churchill*, p.328

10 D'Este, *Warlord*, p.248 and Lavery, *Churchill Warrior*, p.166

11 H.G. Wells, *The War of the Worlds*, Harmondsworth: Penguin, 1971, p.50

12 David Lloyd George, *War Memoirs of David Lloyd George*, Volume II, London: Odhams, 1937, p.2039

13 Ibid., p.1160

14 Ibid., p.1877. By this stage the Allies had 21,843 pieces of artillery, 5,646 aircraft and 1,572 tanks. The Germans had 18,100, 4,000 and almost none respectively. Manpower was 4 million against 3.5 million.

15 Max Arthur, *Last Post: The Final Word from our First World War Soldiers*, London: Weidenfeld & Nicolson, 2005, p.205

16 Roberts, *Churchill: Walking with Destiny*, p.254

17 Arthur, *Last Post*, p.83

18 Erich Maria Remarque, *All Quiet on the Western Front*, London: Mayflower, 1972, p.50

19 Liddell Hart, *History of the First World War*, p.428

20 Lloyd George, *War Memoirs*, Vol. II, p.1264

21 Roberts, *Churchill: Walking with Destiny*, p.262

22 Mary Soames (ed.), *Speaking for Themselves: The Personal Letters of Winston and Clementine Churchill*, London: Black Swan, 1999, p.215

23 Robert Graves, *Goodbye to All That*, Harmondsworth: Penguin, 1977, p.128

24 Richard Holmes, *The Western Front*, London: BBC Worldwide, 1999, p.71

25 Philip Stevens puts fatalities as low as one per cent in *The Great War Explained*, Barnsley: Pen & Sword, 2014, p.184.

26 G.B. Carter, *Porton Down: 75 Years of Chemical and Biological Research*, London: HMSO, 1992, p.26

27 Ibid., p.7

28 Ibid.

CHAPTER 7: WINSTON'S MERCENARIES

1 Coote, *A Churchill Reader*, 1954, p.89

2 Sources vary enormously over how many foreign soldiers were sent; some put it as high as 180,000, for example D'Este, *Warlord*, p.346.

3 Gilbert, *Churchill: A Life*, p.411

4 Nicholas V. Riasanovsky, *A History of Russia*, New York: Oxford University Press, 1993, p.483

5 Only 13,000 British troops were in northern Russia and 1,000 in Siberia. For a detailed account of British intervention see Clifford Kinvig's *Churchill's Crusade: The British Invasion of Russia 1918–1920*, New York: Hambledon Continuum, 2006.

6 These included 200,000 rifles, 6,000 machine guns, 500 million rounds of ammunition, 800 pieces of artillery, 1.7 million rounds of ammunition and 500,000 uniforms. See Ponting, *Churchill*, p.235

7 Paterson, *Winston Churchill*, p.239

8 Jenkins, *Churchill: A Biography*, p.351

9 Ibid.

10 Gilbert, *Churchill: A Life*, p.412

11 Frank Owen, *Tempestuous Journey: Lloyd George His Life and Times*. London: Hutchinson, 1954, p.515

12 Robert T. Elson, *Prelude to War*, New York: Time-Life Books, 1976, p.42. Sources vary enormously on the strength of the Czech Legion; some report it was as strong

as 70,000: see Jenkins, *Churchill: A Biography*, p.351; 55,000: Edgar O'Ballance, *The Red Army*, London: Faber and Faber, 1964, p.47; and 50,000: Norman Stone, *Europe Transformed 1878–1919*, Glasgow: Fontana, 1983, p.378. Other sources have even claimed it was 100,000. Whatever its size it must have been quite considerable to hold the Trans-Siberian Railway. Churchill was not the only one who was keen to employ the services of these mercenaries. Sir Mansfield Cumming, the head of MI6, had already authorized a secret mission to enlist Czech and Slovak émigrés in Russia to support the Allied cause. British novelist and playwright Somerset Maugham, an MI6 agent, arrived in Petrograd in September 1917 with a Czech émigré leader, Emanuel Voska, and made contact with Masaryk. Maugham took with him $21,000 (now worth $350,000), which was hardly just travelling money. To get to western Russia Maugham sailed from America to Vladivostok and during his train journey to Petrograd is likely to have met many of the Czech Legion's officers. A month later the Bolsheviks seized power in Petrograd and Maugham returned to London apparently empty handed.

13 Elson, *Prelude to War*, p.42
14 Lavery, *Churchill Warrior*, p.281
15 Lieutenant-General Sir Brian Horrocks, *A Full Life*, London: Collins, 1960, p.38
16 Ibid., p.39
17 Brian Moynaham, *The Claws of the Bear: A History of the Soviet Armed Forces from 1917 to the Present*, London: Hutchinson, 1989, p.40
18 Owen, *Tempestuous Journey*, p.518
19 Ponting, *Churchill*, p.237
20 Ibid.
21 Anthony West, *H.G. Wells: Aspects of a Life*, London: Hutchinson, 1984, p.82
22 David J. Bercuson and Hologer H. Herwig, *One Christmas in Washington: Churchill and Roosevelt Forge the Grand Alliance*, London: Phoenix, 2006, p.104
23 This was *Star-Begotten*, see Clarke, *Mr Churchill's Profession*, p.135
24 Elson, *Prelude to War*, p.42
25 Owen, *Tempestuous Journey*, p.520
26 Gilbert, *Churchill: A Life*, p.421

CHAPTER 8: FLYING POLICE

1 Ponting, *Churchill*, p.258
2 Soames, *Speaking for Themselves*, p.215
3 Marshal of the RAF Sir Arthur Harris, *Bomber Offensive*, London: Collins, 1947, p.21
4 See Roy Irons, *Churchill and the Mad Mullah of Somaliland: Betrayal and Redemption 1899–1921*, Barnsley: Pen & Sword, 2013, pp.198–210
5 Lavery, *Churchill Warrior*, p.305
6 Ibid., p.306
7 Wilfred Thesiger, *The Marsh Arabs*, Harmondsworth: Penguin, 1967, p.37
8 Wynn, *Churchill's Flawed Decisions*, p.40
9 Gilbert, *Churchill: A Life*, p.424
10 Ibid., p.425

11 Ponting, *Churchill*, p.258
12 Ibid.
13 Ibid.

CHAPTER 9: TROUBLED EMERALD ISLE

1 Randolph Churchill, *Winston S. Churchill*, Vol. II, p.509
2 Ibid., p.489
3 Ibid., p.498
4 Ibid., p.501
5 Ibid.
6 Ibid., p.499
7 Gilbert, *Churchill: A Life*, pp.422–3
8 Sean Lamb (ed.), *The Wisdom of Winston Churchill: Words of War and Peace*, London: Arcturus, 2019, p.211
9 Ibid., p.212
10 Owen, *Tempestuous Journey*, p.565
11 Ibid., p.566
12 Charles Messenger, *Broken Sword: The Tumultuous Life of General Frank Crozier 1879–1937*, Barnsley: Praetorian Press, 2013, p.145
13 Ibid., p.131
14 John Gibney (ed.), *The Irish War of Independence and Civil War*, Barnsley: Pen & Sword, 2020, p.34
15 Chris Ryder, *The Fateful Split: Catholics and the Royal Ulster Constabulary*, London: Methuen, 2004, p.9
16 Richard Bennett, *The Black and Tans*, Barnsley: Pen & Sword, 2020, p.58
17 Ibid., p.59
18 Ibid.
19 Churchill has since been held responsible for the actions of the Black and Tans, but even former policeman Stephen Wynn failed to produce any credible evidence of him being directly complicit in their conduct; see *Churchill's Flawed Decisions*, pp.41–56
20 Ponting, *Churchill*, p.247
21 John Borgonovo and Gabriel Doherty, 'Smoking gun? British government policy and RIC reprisals, summer 1920', in Gibney, *The Irish War of Independence and Civil War*, p.34
22 Nigel Hamilton, *Monty: The Making of a General 1887–1942*, London: Hamish Hamilton, 1981, p.158
23 Ibid., p.157
24 Ibid., p.161
25 Bennett, *The Black and Tans*, p.197
26 Owen, *Tempestuous Journey*, p.573
27 Hamilton, *Monty: The Making of a General*, p.156
28 Coote, *A Churchill Reader*, p.34
29 Owen, *Tempestuous Journey*, p.582

30 Coote, *A Churchill Reader*, p.111
31 Ibid.
32 Arthur, *Churchill: The Life*, p.130
33 Michael Silvestri, 'Nationalism, empire and memory: the Connaught Rangers mutiny, June 1920', in Gibney, *The Irish War of Independence and Civil War*, p.63
34 Ibid., p.64

CHAPTER 10: BENEATH THE SPHINX

1 Hough, *Winston and Clementine*, p.426
2 Dominique Enright, *The Wicked Wit of Winston Churchill*, London: Michael O'Mara, 2001, p.69
3 Graves, *Goodbye to All That*, p.243
4 Ibid., p.244
5 Keith Jeffrey, *MI6: The History of the Secret Intelligence Service, 1909–1949*, London: Bloomsbury, 2011, p.129
6 T.E. Lawrence, *Revolt in the Desert*, London: Jonathan Cape, 1927, p.431
7 T.E. Lawrence, *Seven Pillars of Wisdom*, Vol 1, London: Reprint Society, 1939, p.31
8 Ibid., p.46
9 Wolf, *Victory at Gallipoli 1915*, p.122
10 It is remarkable that India did not go up in flames after this, especially when the Hunter Report revealed that the troops had fired 1,650 rounds killing 379 people and wounding 1,137. The officer in charge, Brigadier General Reginald Dyer, admitted he would have used the machine guns on his armoured cars had he been able to deploy them; see Fischer, *The Life of Mahatma Gandhi*, p.232.
11 Coote, *A Churchill Reader*, p.322
12 Thesiger, *The Marsh Arabs*, p.96
13 Lawrence, *Revolt in the Desert*, p171
14 H.H.E Craster (ed.), *Speeches on Foreign Policy by Viscount Halifax*, London: Oxford University Press, 1940, p.29
15 Nicholas Rankin, *Churchill's Wizards: The British Genius for Deception 1914–1945*, London: Faber and Faber, 2009, p.176
16 Harris, *Bomber Offensive*, p.22
17 Ibid.
18 Ponting, *Churchill*, p.253
19 Harris, *Bomber Offensive*, p.23
20 Ibid.
21 Ponting, *Churchill*, p.271
22 Trevor Burridge, *Clement Attlee*, London: Jonathan Cape, 1985, pp.14 & 16
23 Winston S. Churchill, *The Second World War, Volume I, The Gathering Storm*, London: Cassell, 1948, p.53
24 Ibid.
25 Ibid.
26 Fischer, *The Life of Mahatma Gandhi*, p.452

CHAPTER 11: NAZISM OR COMMUNISM

1 Dwight D. Eisenhower, 'Introduction', in *Churchill The Life Triumphant: The Historical Record of Ninety Years*, New York: American Heritage Publishing, 1965, p.72
2 Churchill, *The Second World War, Volume I, The Gathering Storm*, p.65
3 Vale and Scadding, *Winston Churchill's Illnesses*, p.55
4 Coote, *A Churchill Reader*, p.295
5 Konrad Heiden, *Der Fuehrer: Hitler's Rise to Power*, London: Victor Gollancz, 1944, p.556
6 Ibid.
7 Churchill, *The Second World War, Volume I, The Gathering Storm*, p.148
8 Lamb, *The Wisdom of Winston Churchill*, p.262
9 Eisenhower, *Churchill The Life Triumphant*, p.72
10 Coote, *A Churchill Reader*, p.73
11 Lamb, *The Wisdom of Winston Churchill*, p.83
12 Churchill, *The Second World War, Volume I, The Gathering Storm*, p.69
13 Ibid., p.68
14 Richard Overy and Andrew Wheatcroft, *The Road to War*, London: Macmillan, 1989, p.246
15 Ponting, *Churchill*, p.360
16 Coote, *A Churchill Reader*, p.200
17 Lamb, *The Wisdom of Winston Churchill*, p.253
18 Churchill, *The Second World War, Volume I, The Gathering Storm*, p.263
19 Ibid.
20 Ibid., p.271
21 Lamb, *The Wisdom of Winston Churchill*, pp.77–8
22 Ibid., p.77
23 George Orwell, *Homage to Catalonia and Looking Back at the Spanish Civil War*, Harmondsworth: Penguin, 1984, p.240
24 Coote, *A Churchill Reader*, p.349
25 Ibid., p,355
26 Field Marshal Viscount Montgomery of Alamein, *A Concise History of Warfare*, London: Collins, 1972, p.124
27 The Rt. Hon. The Earl of Avon, *The Eden Memoirs: The Reckoning*, London: Cassell, 1965, p.305
28 J.G. Ballard, *Miracles of Life: Shanghai to Shepperton: An Autobiography*, London: Harper Perennial, 2008, p.25
29 Ibid., p.27
30 Coote, *A Churchill Reader*, p.345
31 Craster, *Speeches on Foreign Policy by Viscount Halifax*, p.105
32 Ibid., p.28
33 Winston S. Churchill, *The Second World War, Volume III, The Grand Alliance*, London: Cassell, 1950, p.562
34 Ibid., p.157
35 Iris Chang, *The Rape of Nanking: The Forgotten Holocaust of World War II*, London: Penguin, 1998, pp.99–104 and Dick Wilson, *When Tigers Fight: The Story of the Sino-Japanese War 1937–1945*, London: Hutchinson, 1982, p.81

36 Chang takes Churchill to task for making absolutely no mention of the Nanking massacre in his history of World War II, *The Rape of Nanking*, p.7

37 Craster, *Speeches on Foreign Policy by Viscount Halifax*, p.298

38 Hugh Thomas, *The Spanish Civil War*, London: Eyre & Spottiswoode, 1961, p.337

39 Lamb, *The Wisdom of Winston Churchill*, p.323

40 Craster, *Speeches on Foreign Policy by Viscount Halifax*, p.106

41 Ibid., p.149

42 Thomas, *The Spanish Civil War*, p.505

43 Antony Beevor, *The Spanish Civil War*, London: Orbis, 1982, p.231

44 David Mitchell, *The Spanish Civil War*, St Albans: Granada, 1982, p.164

45 Thomas, *The Spanish Civil War*, p.531

46 Avon, *The Eden Memoirs: The Reckoning*, p.14

47 Ponting, *Churchill*, p.391

48 Thomas, *The Spanish Civil War*, p.531

49 Orwell, *Homage to Catalonia*, p.240

50 Piers Brendon, *The Dark Valley: A Panorama of the 1930s*, London: Jonathan Cape, 2000, p.338

51 Overy and Wheatcroft, *The Road to War*, p.282

52 Stanley E. Hilton, *Hitler's Secret War in South America 1939–1945*, Baton Rouge: Louisiana State University Press, 1981, p.23

53 George Pendle, *A History of Latin America*, London: Penguin, 1990, p.201

54 Hilton, *Hitler's Secret War in South America*, p.3

55 Jeffrey, *MI6*, p.270

56 Hilton, *Hitler's Secret War in South America*, p.315

57 In 1940 Churchill did consider ensuring continued Argentinian cooperation by offering sovereignty over the Falkland Islands in return for basing rights. Nothing came of it. Similar discussions were also held over surrendering Gibraltar to Spain in return for Spanish neutrality.

58 Spears, *Assignment to Catastrophe*, p.38

59 Ibid.

60 Coote, *A Churchill Reader*, p.48

61 Churchill, *The Second World War, Volume I, The Gathering Storm*, p.345

62 Ibid.

63 Ibid.

CHAPTER 12: MASTER AND COMMANDER

1 Captain Donald Macintyre, *Narvik*, London: Pan, 1962, p.14

2 Lamb, *The Wisdom of Winston Churchill*, p.343

3 Craster, *Speeches on Foreign Policy by Viscount Halifax*, p.354

4 Anthony Dix, *The Norway Campaign and the Rise of Churchill 1940*, Barnsley: Pen & Sword, 2014, p.34

5 Ibid.

6 Ibid., p.83

7 Owen, *Tempestuous Journey*, p.746

8 Ibid, p.747

9   Ibid.

10 Paterson, *Winston Churchill*, p.251

11 *New York World Telegram*, 10 May 1940

12 Avon, *The Eden Memoirs: The Reckoning*, p.97

13 Owen, *Tempestuous Journey*, p.750

14 Ibid., p.751

15 Craster, *Speeches on Foreign Policy by Viscount Halifax*, p.353

16 Ibid., p.354

17 Len Deighton, *Blitzkrieg: From the Rise of Hitler to the Fall of Dunkirk*, London: Jonathan Cape, 1979, p.261

18 Ponting, *Churchill*, p.442

19 Moran, *Winston Churchill*, p.292

20 Avon, *The Eden Memoirs: The Reckoning*, p.109

21 Deighton, *Blitzkrieg*, p.285. There seems to be some confusion over when this message was sent. Major General Julian Thompson records that it was delivered by boat on the night of 25 May; see *Dunkirk: Retreat to Victory*, London: Sidgwick & Jackson, 2008, pp.169–70. In contrast Robert Jackson says it was sent at 2100 hours on 26 May after the garrison were overwhelmed; see *Dunkirk*, London: Granada, 1978, pp.74–5

22 Moran, *Winston Churchill*, p.292

23 Patrick Wilson, *Dunkirk: From Disaster to Deliverance*, Barnsley: Leo Cooper, 1999, p.32

24 Ibid., p.34

25 Ponting, *Churchill*, p.447

26 Spears, *Assignment to Catastrophe*, p.292

27 Ibid., p.294

28 Wilson, *Dunkirk*, p.152

29 Spears, *Assignment to Catastrophe*, p.337

30 This is the figure issued by the Admiralty's Historical Section/Tactical and Staff Duties Department and does not tally with the 315,567 reported by Ramsey's Dover Report; see Hugh Sebag-Montefiore, *Dunkirk: Fight to the Last Man*, London: Penguin, 2007, p.541. As with all historical statistics no two historians can agree on any of the numbers relating to Dunkirk.

31 Nicholas Atkin, *The Forgotten French: Exiles in the British Isles 1940–44*, Manchester: Manchester University Press, 2003, p.94

32 Nicholas Harman, *Dunkirk: The Necessary Myth*, London: Coronet, 1990, p.261

33 Ibid., p.277

34 Spears, *Assignment to Catastrophe*, 1956, p.361

35 Robert Wernick, *Blitzkrieg*, New York: Time-Life Books, 1976, p.190

CHAPTER 13: HIS FINEST HOUR

1   Len Deighton, *Battle of Britain*, London: Jonathan Cape, 1980, p.68

2   Norman Franks, *RAF Fighter Command 1936–1968*, Sparkford: Patrick Stevens, 1992, p.61

3   Len Deighton, *Fighter: The True Story of the Battle of Britain*, London: Jonathan Cape, 1977, p.72

4   Leonard Mosley, *The Battle of Britain*, Alexandria, Virginia: Time-Life, 1984, p.50 and Jon Lake, *Battle of Britain*, London: Amber, 2019, p.92

5 Richard Collier, *Eagle Day: The Battle of Britain*, London: J.M. Dent & Sons, 1980, p.13

6 H. Tatlock Miller and Loudon Sainthill, *Churchill: The Walk with Destiny*, London: Hutchinson, 1959, p.156

7 Deighton, *Battle of Britain*, p.77

8 John Ray, *The Battle of Britain: Dowding and the First Victory, 1940*, London: Cassell, 2000, p.31

9 Ibid., p.171

10 Dowding's retirement dates were June 1939, March 1940, 14 July 1940 and 31 October 1940.

11 Deighton, *Fighter*, p.150

12 This was achieved on 22 May 1940; the German naval code was cracked in June 1941 and the army code three months later. The resulting decrypts were highly restricted and were given the security classification Ultra. Apart from the decoders only 31 people knew about this source of intelligence. See Roberts, *Churchill: Walking with Destiny*, pp.538–9

13 Ray, *The Battle of Britain*, p.50 & p.143; Michael Kerrigan, *How Bletchley Park Won World War II*, London: Amber, 2018, p.84. Many sources also claim Churchill gave Keith Park access as well.

14 Joshua Levine, *Forgotten Voices of the Blitz and the Battle of Britain*, London: Ebury, 2007, p.148

15 Ibid., p.149

16 Ibid., p.148

17 Roger Parkinson, *Dawn on our Darkness: The Summer of 1940*, St Albans: Granada, 1977, p.153

18 Ibid.

19 Dennis Knight, *Harvest of Messerschmitts: The Chronicle of a Village at War 1940*, London: Frederick Warne, 1981, p.110

20 Dilip Sarkar, *The Few: The Story of the Battle of Britain in the Words of the Pilots*, Stroud: Amberley, 2012, p.157

21 Frank and Joan Shaw, *We Remember the Home Guard*, London: Ebury, 2012, p.177

22 Ronald Wheatley, *Operation Sea Lion*, London: Oxford University Press, 1962, p.77

23 Peter Fleming, *Invasion 1940*, London: Rupert Hart-Davis, 1957, p.281

24 Collier, *Eagle Day*, p.182 and Richard Overy, *The Battle of Britain*, London: Penguin, 2004, p.93

25 Shaw, *We Remember the Home Guard*, p.150

26 Mosley, *The Battle of Britain*, p.126

27 Deighton, *Fighter*, p.22

28 Collier, *Eagle Day*, p.190

29 Ibid., p.194

30 Many early accounts state Churchill turned up at Uxbridge on a whim, but this is not true. Group Captain Frederick Winterbotham, Deputy Chief of the Secret Intelligence Service, subsequently confirmed Ultra had advance warning and that Churchill was briefed. See Levine, *Forgotten Voices of the Blitz and the Battle of Britain*, p.289

31 Collier, *Eagle Day*, p.196

32 Ibid., p.198

33 Ibid.
34 Patrick Bishop, *Battle of Britain*, London: Quercus, 2010, p.302
35 Collier, *Eagle Day*, p.196
36 Levine, *Forgotten Voices of the Blitz and the Battle of Britain*, p.289
37 Ibid.
38 Collier, *Eagle Day*, p.213
39 Once the dust had settled German losses were reassessed to 61 aircraft, while the RAF lost 27 aircraft and 16 pilots.
40 Collier, *Eagle Day*, p.218
41 '175 Shot Down', *Daily Express*, Monday 16 September 1940
42 Bishop, *Battle of Britain*, p.312
43 AIR 22/72, 'Air Ministry Weekly Intelligence Summary', London: Public Records Office, dated 19 September 1940, pp.4–5
44 Franks, *RAF Fighter Command*, p.103
45 Air Vice-Marshal Sandy Johnstone, *Spitfire into War*, London: Grafton, 1988, p.214
46 Mosley, *The Battle of Britain*, p.146

CHAPTER 14: STRATEGIC DILEMMA

1 Bernard Edwards, *Churchill's Thin Grey Line: British Merchant Ships at War 1939– 1945*, Barnsley: Pen & Sword, 2017, p.222
2 Ibid.
3 Roskill, *Churchill and the Admirals*, p.119
4 Ibid.
5 Ibid., p.121
6 Ibid.
7 Lamb, *The Wisdom of Winston Churchill*, p.342
8 Coote, *A Churchill Reader*, p.238
9 For a detailed account of Churchill's relationship with Stalin see Martin Folly, Geoffrey Roberts and Oleg Rzheshevsky, *Churchill and Stalin: Comrades-in-Arms during the Second World War*, Barnsley: Pen & Sword, 2019
10 Lamb, *The Wisdom of Winston Churchill*, p.68
11 Dr David J. Coles and David Gregory, 'German Submarine Offensive along Florida's Coast', *Florida World War II Heritage Trail*, Tallahassee: Florida Department of State, Division of Historical Resources, 2015, p.21
12 *Daily Mirror*, 6 March 1942
13 Bernard Edwards, *The Road to Russia: Arctic Convoys*, Barnsley: Leo Cooper, 2002, p.106
14 Roskill, *Churchill and the Admirals*, p.130
15 Edwards, *The Road to Russia*, p.197
16 Ibid., p.184
17 Ibid., p.78
18 Edwards, *Churchill's Thin Grey Line*, p.221
19 Sea convoy losses equated to 0.7 per cent, while coastal convoy losses were double this, which shows just how successful the convoy system was. David Wragg, *Second World War Carrier Campaigns*, Barnsley: Pen & Sword Maritime, 2004, p.54

20 Churchill, *The Second World War, Volume V, Closing the Ring*, p.8
21 Ibid.
22 Ibid.

CHAPTER 15: OLD FOES

1   Lieutenant-Colonel Michael Dewar, *The British Army in Northern Ireland*, London: Arms and Armour Press, 1985, p.16
2   John W. Wheeler-Bennett, *King George VI: His Life and Reign*, London: The Reprint Society, 1959, p.381
3   Avon, *The Eden Memoirs: The Reckoning*, p.69
4   Ponting, *Churchill*, p.473
5   Lamb, *The Wisdom of Winston Churchill*, p.212
6   Churchill, *The Second World War, Volume I, The Gathering Storm*, p.232
7   Ibid.
8   Avon, *The Eden Memoirs: The Reckoning*, p.70
9   Moran, *Winston Churchill*, p.261
10 Richard J. Aldrich and Rory Cormac, *The Black Door: Spies, Secret Intelligence and British Prime Ministers*, London: William Collins, 2017, p.94
11 Field Marshal the Viscount Montgomery, *The Memoirs*, London: Collins, 1958, p.70
12 Ponting, *Churchill*, p.475
13 Avon, *The Eden Memoirs: The Reckoning*, p.69
14 Alex Danchev and Daniel Todman (ed.), *War Diaries 1939–1945: Field Marshal Lord Alanbrooke*, London: Phoenix Press, 2002, p.94
15 Ibid., p.95
16 Churchill, *The Second World War, Volume III, The Grand Alliance*, p.648
17 Moran, *Winston Churchill*, p.261
18 Ibid.
19 Lamb, *The Wisdom of Winston Churchill*, p.211
20 E. Royston Pike, 'The Strange Case of Mr. De Valera's Ireland', *The War Illustrated*, 28 February 1942
21 Ibid.
22 Avon, *The Eden Memoirs: The Reckoning*, p.70
23 Gordon Corrigan, *Blood, Sweat and Arrogance and the Myths of Churchill's War*, London: Weidenfeld & Nicolson, 2006, p.162
24 Ibid. Northern Ireland provided 37,000 recruits.

CHAPTER 16: HITTING BACK

1   Anthony Verrier, *The Bomber Offensive*, London: Pan, 1974, p.81
2   Robert Jackson, *Before the Storm: The Story of Bomber Command 1939–42*, London: Cassell, 2001, p.129
3   Max Hastings, *Bomber Command*, London: Pan, 1999, p.97
4   Ibid., p.117
5   Ibid., p.76
6   John Sweetman, *Bomber Crew: Taking on the Reich*, London: Abacus, 2005, p.62

7 Ibid., p.66

8 Lamb, *The Wisdom of Winston Churchill*, p.57

9 Jackson, *Before the Storm*, pp.171–2

10 Ibid., p.172

11 Hastings, *Bomber Command*, p.121

12 Jackson, *Before the Storm*, p.129

13 Harris, *Bomber Offensive*, p.109

14 Ibid., p.110

15 Ministry of Information, *Bomber Command Continues: The Air Ministry Account of the Rising Offensive Against Germany July 1941–June 1942*. London: HMSO, 1942, p.45

16 Ibid., p.51

17 Harris, *Bomber Offensive*, p.112

18 Hastings, *Bomber Command*, p.255. This remark was made to Hastings on 25 April 1978, so well after the war. However, Harris said almost the same thing in 1947: 'He is a bad listener, and frequently interrupts anyone …' Arthur Harris, *Bomber Offensive*, p.152

19 Robert Jackson, *Bomber! Famous Bomber Missions of World War II*, London: Arthur Barker, 1980, p.109 records 30,482 dead.

20 Hastings, *Bomber Command*, p.257

21 Frederick Taylor, *Dresden: Tuesday 13 February 1945*, London: Bloomsbury, 2005, p.170

22 Victor Klemperer, *To the Bitter End: The Diaries of Victor Klemperer 1942–1945*, London: Weidenfeld & Nicolson, 1999, p.404. Klemperer survived the bombing of Dresden and noted this figure twice, on 21 and 22 February 1945. Sinclair McKay, *Dresden: The Fire and the Darkness*, London: Viking, 2020, p.296, citing David Irving, *The Destruction of Dresden*, London: Kimber, 1963, says the death toll may have been anything between 135,000 and 200,000.

23 *Manchester Guardian*, 7 March 1945

24 Taylor, *Dresden*, p.430

25 Ibid.

26 Patrick Bishop, *Bomber Boys: Fighting Back 1940–1945*, London: Harper Perennial, 2008, p.353

27 Harris, *Bomber Offensive*, p.58

28 Lamb, *The Wisdom of Winston Churchill*, p.185

29 Harris, *Bomber Offensive*, p.152

CHAPTER 17: 'BANDS OF BROTHERS'

1 Stephen Bull, *Churchill's Army 1939–1945*, London: Conway, 2016, p.293

2 John Laffin, *Raiders: Elite Forces Attacks*, London: Chancellor Press, 2000, p.4

3 Robin Neillands, *The Raiders: The Army Commandos 1940–1946*, London: Fontana, 1990, p.9

4 Laffin, *Raiders*, p.10

5 Ibid., p.4

6 Lord Lovat, *March Past*, London: Weidenfeld & Nicolson, 1978, p.186

7 Neillands, *The Raiders*, p.37

8 Lovat, *March Past*, p.187
9 David Niven, *The Moon's a Balloon*, London: Coronet, 1972, p.222
10 Ibid.
11 Roskill, *Churchill and the Admirals*, p.111
12 Lovat, *March Past*, p.189
13 Ibid., p.222
14 Roskill, *Churchill and the Admirals*, p.176
15 Lovat, *March Past*, p.222
16 Brigadier Peter Young, *Commando*, London: Macdonald & Co, 1970, p.16
17 Ibid.
18 Roskill, *Churchill and the Admirals*, p.177
19 Ibid., p.176
20 Philip Ziegler, *Mountbatten: The Official Biography*, London: Collins, 1985, p.1444
21 Mountbatten foreword to Warren Tute, John Costello and Terry Hughes, *D-Day*, London, Pan, 1975, p.4
22 Ibid.
23 Ibid.
24 Canadian historian David O'Keefe, in *One Day in August: Ian Fleming, Enigma and the Deadly Raid on Dieppe*, London: Icon Books, 2020, explains the raid was also intended to capture vital Enigma intelligence to assist the Battle of the Atlantic. This aspect was a closely guarded secret at the time.
25 Laffin, *Raiders*, 2000, p.140
26 Ibid.
27 Tute, Costello and Hughes, *D-Day*, p.4

CHAPTER 18: MEDITERRANEAN SHOWDOWN

1 Lamb, *The Wisdom of Winston Churchill*, p.214
2 Roskill, *Churchill and the Admirals*, p.169
3 Ibid.
4 For more on this operation see Angus Konstam, *Taranto 1940: The Fleet Air Arm's precursor to Pearl Harbor*, Oxford: Osprey, 2015
5 Lamb, *The Wisdom of Winston Churchill*, p.255
6 Kenneth Macksey, *Beda Fomm*, London: Pan/Ballatine, 1972, p.155
7 Ibid., p.151
8 Ibid.
9 Ibid.
10 Graham Stewart, *His Finest Hours: The War Speeches of Winston Churchill*, London: Quercus, 2007, p.98
11 Ibid.
12 Churchill, *The Second World War, Volume III, The Grand Alliance*, pp.56–8
13 Barrie Pitt, *Churchill and the Generals*, Barnsley: Pen & Sword Military Classics, 2004, p.62
14 Avon, *The Eden Memoirs: The Reckoning*, p.192
15 Ibid.
16 Churchill, *The Second World War, Volume III, The Grand Alliance*, p.84

17 Ibid.

18 Ibid., p.194

19 Alan Clark, *The Fall of Crete*, London: Cassell, 2001, p.17

20 Ibid.

21 Ibid.

22 Antony Beevor, *Crete: The Battle and the Resistance*, London: Penguin, 1992, p.54

23 Ibid.

24 Coote, *A Churchill Reader*, p.77

25 Churchill, *The Second World War, Volume III, The Grand Alliance*, p.192

26 Ibid., p.268

27 Ibid., p.291

28 Ibid., 307

29 Ibid., 309

30 Ibid., p.354

31 Eisenhower, *Churchill The Life Triumphant*, p.93

32 Danchev and Todman, *War Diaries*, p.269

33 Moran, *Winston Churchill*, p.38

34 Ibid.

35 Coote, *A Churchill Reader*, p.246

36 Stewart, *His Finest Hours*, p.133

37 Ibid, p.134

38 Ibid.

39 Moran, *Winston Churchill*, p.48

40 Soames, *Speaking for Themselves*, p.466

41 Danchev and Todman, *War Diaries*, p.297

42 Moran, *Winston Churchill*, p.53

43 Field Marshall Alexander, *The Alexander Memoirs*, 1940–1945, London: Cassell, 1962, p.13

44 Ibid., p.10

45 Montgomery, *The Memoirs*, p.106

46 Soames, *Speaking for Themselves*, p.466

47 Brian Montgomery, *A Field Marshal in the Family*, London: Constable, 1973, p.272

48 Alexander, *The Alexander Memoirs*, p.28

49 Stewart, *His Finest Hours*, p.138

CHAPTER 19: AN AMERICAN FRIEND

1 Stewart, *His Finest Hours*, p.128

2 Charles Chaplin, *My Auto-Biography*, London: The Bodley Head, 1964, p.364

3 Soames, *Speaking for Themselves*, p.347. In this context Churchill meant he thought Chaplin was a Bolshevik or Socialist, which would have been considered a political slur.

4 Ibid.

5 Coote, *A Churchill Reader*, p.361

6 Brendon, *The Dark Valley*, p.239

7   Churchill, *The Second World War, Volume I, The Gathering Storm*, p.199
8   Avon, *The Eden Memoirs: The Reckoning*, p.41
9   Ibid.
10 Robert Wernick, *Blitzkrieg*, New York: Time-Life Books, 1976, p.138
11 Avon, *The Eden Memoirs: The Reckoning*, p.134
12 Churchill, *The Second World War, Volume I, The Gathering Storm*, p.435
13 Wheeler-Bennett, *King George VI*, p.511
14 Stewart, *His Finest Hours*, p.91
15 Ibid.
16 Wheeler-Bennett, *King George VI*, p.513
17 Avon, *The Eden Memoirs: The Reckoning*, p.135
18 Ibid.
19 Parkinson, *Dawn on our Darkness*, p.5
20 Wheeler-Bennett, *King George VI*, p.511 citing Churchill, *The Second World War, Volume II*, pp.125–6
21 Franklin D. Roosevelt, *Radio Address to the Democratic National Convention Accepting the Nomination*, 19 July 1940
22 Coote, *A Churchill Reader*, p.303
23 Roskill, *Churchill and the Admirals*, p.126
24 Ibid.
25 Lamb, *The Wisdom of Winston Churchill*, p.232
26 Wheeler-Bennett, *King George VI*, p.521
27 WSC to President Franklin Roosevelt, 7 December 1940, FDR Library
28 Lamb, *The Wisdom of Winston Churchill*, p.232
29 Stewart, *His Finest Hours*, p.102
30 Dr Daniel L. Schafer and Frederick P. Gaske, 'British Wings over Florida in World War II', *Florida British Heritage Trail*, Tallahassee: Florida Department of State, Division of Historical Resources, 2014, p.58
31 Since diagnosed as Guillain-Barré syndrome, an autoimmune illness.
32 Michael Kluger and Richard Evans, *Roosevelt and Churchill: The Atlantic Charter – A Risky Meeting at Sea that Saved Democracy*, Barnsley: Frontline, 2020, p.24
33 Ibid., pp.24–5
34 Ibid., p.25
35 Arthur, *Churchill: The Life*, p.180
36 Hilton, *Hitler's Secret War in South America*, p.315
37 Aldrich and Cormac, *The Black Door*, p.111
38 Franklin Roosevelt, 'Navy Day Address' on the Attack on the Destroyer *Kearny*, 27 October 1941
39 Coote, *A Churchill Reader*, p.371
40 Bercuson and Herwig, *One Christmas in Washington*, p.94
41 Moran, *Winston Churchill*, p.10
42 Bercuson and Herwig, *One Christmas in Washington*, p.140
43 Stewart, *His Finest Hours*, p.121
44 Ibid., p.125
45 Moran, *Winston Churchill*, p.15
46 Ibid., pp.16–7

47 Ibid., p.17
48 Ibid., p.21

CHAPTER 20: JOAN OF ARC

1 Brigadier Stanley Clark, *The Man Who is France: The Story of Charles de Gaulle*, London: George G. Harrap, 1960, p.100
2 Spears, *Assignment to Catastrophe*, p.381
3 Ibid., p.102
4 Ibid., p.103
5 Ibid., p.104
6 Ibid.
7 Ibid., p.516
8 Ibid., p.620
9 Clark, *The Man Who is France*, p.113
10 Coote, *A Churchill Reader*, p.117
11 Aidan Crawley, *de Gaulle*, London: Collins, 1969, p.23
12 Andrew, *The Defence of the Realm*, p.239
13 Max Hastings, *The Secret War: Spies, Codes and Guerrillas 1939–45*, London: William Collins, 2017, p.207
14 Aldrich and Cormac, *The Black Door*, p.91
15 Crawley, *de Gaulle*, p.138
16 Ibid., pp.164–5
17 Clark, *The Man Who is France*, p.158
18 David Irving, *The War Between the Generals*, London: Allen Lane, 1981, p.130
19 Coote, *A Churchill Reader*, p.345
20 Jean Lacouture, *De Gaulle: The Rebel 1890–1944*, London: Harvill, 1993, p.411
21 Jeffrey, *MI6*, pp.743–5
22 Coote, *A Churchill Reader*, p.345
23 Lacouture, *De Gaulle*, p.430
24 Avon, *The Eden Memoirs: The Reckoning*, p.386
25 Ibid., p.387
26 Lacouture, *De Gaulle*, p.433
27 Robert Aron, *De Gaulle Before Paris: The Liberation of France June 1944–August 1944*, London: Putnam, 1962, p.55
28 Ibid., p.58
29 Ibid., p.57
30 Julian Jackson, *Charles de Gaulle*, London: Cardinal, 1990, p.13
31 Coote, *A Churchill Reader*, p.117

CHAPTER 21: COURTING THE RED CZAR

1 Lamb, *The Wisdom of Winston Churchill*, p.56
2 Simon Sebag Montefiore, *Stalin: The Court of the Red Tsar*, London: Weidenfeld & Nicolson, 2003, p.309
3 Hough, *Winston and Clementine*, p.547

4 Gilbert, *Churchill: A Life*, p.701

5 Ibid.

6 Stewart, *His Finest Hours*, p.103

7 Thomas B. Allen and Norman Polmar, *Code-Name Downfall: The Secret Plan to Invade Japan – and Why Truman Dropped the Bomb*, New York: Simon & Schuster, 1995, p.177

8 Carter, *Porton Down*, p.39

9 Ibid., p.44

10 Churchill and Roosevelt also threatened similar retaliation if biological weapons were employed against Allied troops. Churchill authorised biological warfare experiments, which culminated in Gruinard Island being contaminated with anthrax. This research was shared with America and Canada, but not the Soviet Union. Under Operation *Vegetarian* the Allies planned to drop five million anthrax-infected cattle-cakes onto Germany's pastures. Again like the mustard gas, although the cakes were manufactured and stockpiled Churchill never authorised their use.

11 Sebag Montefiore, *Stalin*, p.362

12 Avon, *The Eden Memoirs: The Reckoning*, p.329

13 Wheeler-Bennett, *King George VI*, pp.539–40

14 Ibid., p.540

15 Arthur Bryant, *The Turn of the Tide 1939–1943*, London: The Reprint Society, 1958, p.326

16 Ibid., p.327

17 Avon, *The Eden Memoirs: The Reckoning*, p.330

18 Sebag Montefiore, *Stalin*, p.362

19 Avon, *The Eden Memoirs: The Reckoning*, p.330

20 Coote, *A Churchill Reader*, p.116

21 Churchill, *The Second World War, Vol. V, Closing the Ring*, p.229

22 Sinclair McKay, *The Secret Life of Bletchley Park*, London: Aurum, 2011, p.233

23 Captain Jerry Roberts, *Lorenz: Breaking Hitler's Top Secret Code at Bletchley Park*, Stroud: The History Press, 2017, p.135

CHAPTER 22: LOSS OF FAITH

1 Stewart, *The Savage Border*, pp.193–4. Other sources state that over 60,000 British and Indian troops were involved.

2 Also known as the Indian National Congress.

3 In 1939 the Indian Army totalled 205,000 regulars; 90 per cent of the officers were British, plus 84,000 auxiliaries. There were also 61,000 British troops in India. By 1945 India had 2.5 million men under arms. Boris Mollo, *The Indian Army*, Poole: Blandford, 1981, pp.164–5

4 Fischer, *The Life of Mahatma Gandhi*, p.439

5 Geoffrey Regan, *Someone Had Blundered... A Historical Survey of Military Incompetence*, London: B.T. Batsford, 1987, p.267

6 Ibid., p.269

7 Churchill, *The Second World War, Volume III, The Grand Alliance*, p.376

8 Ibid., p.379

9   Victoria Schofield, *Wavell: Soldier & Statesman*, London: John Murray, 2006, p.92

10   Christopher Bayly and Tim Harper, *Forgotten Armies: Britain's Asian Empire & The War with Japan*, London: Penguin, 2005, p.107

11   Niven, *The Moon's a Balloon*, p.228

12   John Toland, *Infamy: Pearl Harbor and its Aftermath*, London: Penguin, 2001, p.16

13   Niven, *The Moon's a Balloon*, p.228

14   Jeffrey, *MI6*, p.574

15   Ibid.

16   Andrew, *The Defence of the Realm*, p.220

17   Brian P. Farrell, *The Defence and Fall of Singapore 1940–1942*, Stroud: Tempus, 2005, p.126 and McKay, *The Secret Life of Bletchley Park*, p.176

18   Danchev and Todman, *War Diaries*, p.210 and Bryant, *The Turn of the Tide*, p.232.

19   Churchill, *The Second World War, Volume III, The Grand Alliance*, p.564

20   Schofield, *Wavell*, p.235

21   Bayly and Harper, *Forgotten Armies*, p.107

22   Schofield, *Wavell*, p.235

23   Moran, *Winston Churchill*, p.27

24   Ibid.

25   Farrell, *The Defence and Fall of Singapore*, p.355

26   Ibid., p.356

27   Reg Twigg, *Survivor on the River Kwai: The Incredible Story of Life on the Burma Railway*, London: Penguin, 2014, pp.117-8

28   Alistair Urquhart, *The Forgotten Highlander: My Incredible Story of Survival during the War in the Far East*, London: Little Brown, 2010, p.100

29   Lamb, *The Wisdom of Winston Churchill*, p.318

30   Ibid.

31   Avon, *The Eden Memoirs: The Reckoning*, p.321

32   Ibid.

33   Mark Logue and Peter Conradi, *The King's War*, London: Quercus, 2019, p.144

34   Gilbert, *Churchill: A Life*, p.718

35   Ibid.

36   This enquiry never happened, and recriminations have abounded ever since.

37   Moran, *Winston Churchill*, p.27

CHAPTER 23: INDIA IN REVOLT

1   Wilson, *When Tigers Fight*, p.194

2   Moran, *Winston Churchill*, p.31.

3   E. Royston Pike, 'India: Sir Stafford Opens the Door', *The War Illustrated*, 1 May 1942

4   Enright, *The Wicked Wit of Winston Churchill*, p.112

5   Nirad C. Chaudhuri, *Thy Hand, Great Anarch! India: 1921–1952*, London: Chatto & Windus, 1987, p.691. It should be noted that Chaudhuri since his student days was a Churchill supporter.

6   Owen, *Tempestuous Journey*, p.722

7   Chaudhuri, *Thy Hand, Great Anarch!* p.691

8   Ibid.

9   Patrick French, *Liberty or Death: India's Journey to Independence and Division*, London: HarperCollins, 1997, pp.145–6

10 Fischer, *The Life of Mahatma Gandhi*, p.451

11 John Clancy, *'The Most Dangerous Moment of the War': Japan's Attack on the Indian Ocean, 1942*, Oxford: Casemate, 2017, p.152

12 Roskill, *Churchill and the Admirals*, p.206

13 Clancy, *'The Most Dangerous Moment of the War'*, p.170

14 James Holland, *Burma '44: The Battle that Turned Britain's War in the East*, London: Corgi, 2016, p.118

15 Ronald H. Spector, *Eagle Against the Sun: The American War with Japan*, London: Cassell, 2000, p.337

16 'Congress members arrested in India', *The War in Pictures*, 9 August 1942. A total of 148 Congress leaders were rounded up that day.

17 Srinath Raghavan, *India's War: The Making of Modern South Asia, 1939–1945*, London: Penguin, 2017, p.273

18 Stewart, *The Savage Border*, p.182

19 Fischer, *The Life of Mahatma Gandhi*, p.413

20 Philip Mason, *A Matter of Honour. An Account of the Indian Army its Officers and Men*, London: Jonathan Cape, 1974, p.478

21 French, *Liberty or Death*, p.161

22 Christopher Somerville, *Our War: How the British Commonwealth Fought the Second World War*, London: Weidenfeld & Nicolson, 1998, p.118

23 Bayly and Harper, *Forgotten Armies*, p.304, citing a letter from GHQ India, dated 26 February 1943.

24 Robert Palmer, *A Concise History of 50th Indian Tank Brigade*, Barnstaple: British Military History, 2014, p.7

25 These were the 20th, 25th and 26th Infantry plus the 14th, 19th and 23rd respectively. The Indian Army also had five divisions in the Middle East, plus one retreating from Burma. Two others were lost in Singapore. Robert Palmer, *A Concise History of the 25th Indian Infantry Division*, Barnstaple: British Military History, 2012, p.3

26 Schofield, *Wavell*, p.271

27 Raghavan, *India's War*, p.275

28 Field Marshal Sir William Slim, *Defeat into Victory*, London: Cassell, 1956, p.138

29 Ibid., p.136

30 French, *Liberty or Death*, p.161

31 Bayly and Harper, *Forgotten Armies*, p.248 & 277. These figures vary; some sources record 1,000 deaths and up to 100,000 arrests.

32 Mike Calvert, *Slim*, London: Pan, 1973, p.48. Lawrence James in *Churchill and Empire: Portrait of an Imperialist*, London: Weidenfeld & Nicolson, 2014, p.297 records 35,000 troops supported the police, but this number may only represent those actually deployed on the streets.

33 Coote, *A Churchill Reader*, p.328

34 Stewart, *His Finest Hours*, p.149

35 Somerville, *Our War*, p.118

36 Chaudhuri, *Thy Hand, Great Anarch!* pp. 703–4

37 Ibid.
38 Philip Jowett, *Japan's Asian Allies 1941–45*, Oxford: Osprey, 2020, p.13 & p.18
39 Slim, *Defeat into Victory*, p.232
40 Ibid., p.539
41 Schofield, *Wavell*, p.341
42 Slim, *Defeat into Victory*, p.539

CHAPTER 24: STRAINED RELATIONS

1   French, *Liberty or Death*, p.162
2   Aldrich and Cormac, *The Black Door*, p.110
3   Schofield, *Wavell*, p.272
4   Robert Palmer, *A Concise Biography of Captain J.N. Randle, VC*, Barnstaple: British Military History, 2014, p.7
5   Jon Latimer, *Burma: The Forgotten War*, London: John Murray, 2004, pp.148–9
6   Ibid., p.149
7   French, *Liberty or Death*, p.163
8   Aldrich and Cormac, *The Black Door*, p.127
9   John Masters, *The Road Past Mandalay*, London: Cassell, 2002, p.139
10 Ibid., p.140
11 Ibid., p.141
12 Sir Charles Wilson was awarded a peerage in March 1943, becoming Lord Moran.
13 Moran, *Winston Churchill*, p.107
14 Ibid., p.108
15 Masters, *The Road Past Mandalay*, p.157
16 Somerville, *Our War*, p.204
17 Schofield, *Wavell*, p.300
18 Ibid., p.299
19 It has been estimated that between one and three million people died over the three years of the famine.
20 Robert Palmer, *A Concise Biography of Major General D. Stuart*, Barnstaple: British Military History, 2020, p.17
21 Andrew Roberts presents a convincing case that Churchill did all he could under the circumstances and had instructed Wavell to act; see *Churchill: Walking with Destiny*, pp.785–9
22 French, *Liberty or Death*, p.132
23 Slim, *Defeat into Victory*, p.128
24 Ibid., pp.218–9
25 Ibid., p.204
26 Danchev and Todman, *War Diaries*, p.445 and Bryant, *The Turn of the Tide*, p.583
27 Ibid.
28 This was Mountbatten's proposed Operation *Culverin*. It was scaled down to Operation *Buccaneer*, the recapture of the Indian Andaman Islands, but this was also abandoned due the ongoing lack of landing craft.
29 Andrew Roberts, *Masters and Commanders: How Roosevelt, Churchill, Marshall and Alanbrooke Won the War in the West*, London: Allan Lane, 2008, p.470

30 Churchill appointed Smuts an Honorary Field Marshal in 1941 as a way of thanking him for South Africa's military support in Egypt.

31 Jeffrey, *MI6*, p.595

32 Ibid., 593

33 Danchev and Todman, *War Diaries*, p.581 and Arthur Bryant, *Triumph in the West 1943–1946*, London: The Reprint Society, 1960, p.200

CHAPTER 25: SECOND FRONT NOW

1 For more on this campaign see Anthony Rogers, *Kos and Leros 1943: The German Conquest of the Dodecanese*, Oxford: Osprey, 2019

2 Churchill, *The Second World War, Vol. V, Closing the Ring*, p.292

3 Wheeler-Bennett, *King George VI*, p.602

4 Ibid., p.605

5 Ibid.

6 Ibid., p.606

7 Logue and Conradi, *The King's War*, p.199

8 Wheeler-Bennett, *King George VI*, p.606

9 Stewart, *His Finest Hours*, p.169

10 Ibid.

11 Bryant, *Triumph in the West*, p.170

12 Montgomery, *The Memoirs*, p.253

13 Alistair Horne and David Montgomery, *The Lonely Leader: Monty 1944–1945*, London: Pan, 1995, p.130

14 Danchev and Todman, *War Diaries*, p.557 and Bryant, *Triumph in the West*, p.172

15 Horne and Montgomery, *The Lonely Leader*, p.130

16 Montgomery, *The Memoirs*, p.253

17 Bryant, *Triumph in the West*, p.173

18 Irving, *The War Between the Generals*, p.166

19 Ibid.

20 Wheeler-Bennett, *King George VI*, p.609

21 Holmes, *In the Footsteps of Churchill*, 'Mustard Gas Minute of 6 July 1944', pp.311–2

22 Carlo D'Este, *Eisenhower*, London: Weidenfeld & Nicolson, 2003, p.551

23 Ibid., p.566

24 Dwight D. Eisenhower, *Crusade in Europe*, London: William Heinemann, 1948, p.309

25 Gilbert, *Churchill: A Life*, p.787

26 Ibid., p.788

27 Max Hastings, *Finest Years: Churchill as Warlord 1940–45*, London: HarperPress, 2009, p.491

28 Coote, *A Churchill Reader*, p.254

29 Churchill helped facilitate this by deliberately abandoning the Yugoslav royalists; see Christopher Catherwood, *Churchill and Tito: SOE, Bletchley Park and Supporting the Yugoslav Communists in World War II*, Barnsley: Frontline, 2017

30 Alexander, *The Alexander Memoirs*, p.141

31 Ibid., p.142 Initially the weak British and Greek Royalist forces were facing at least 40,000 Communists organized into ten divisions, about half of whom were in Athens. Ironically they were armed with British, German and Italian weapons. British units deployed to Greece included the 23rd Armoured and 2nd Parachute Brigades plus the 4th Indian, 4th Infantry and 46th Infantry Divisions. By 1945 they numbered 75,000 men at a time when Britain could hardly spare the manpower.

32 Elizabeth Nel, *Mr Churchill's Secretary*, London: Hoffer and Stoughton, 1961, p.158 – Layton was her maiden name.

33 Moran, *Winston Churchill*, p.214

34 Ibid.

CHAPTER 26: 'DEATH WISH'

 1 Major-General Sir Francis de Guingand, *Operation Victory*, London: Hodder and Stoughton, 1947, p.440

 2 Charles Whiting, *West Wall: The Battle for Hitler's Siegfried Line September 1944–March 1945*, London: Pan, 2002, p.170

 3 Charles Whiting, *Siegfried: The Nazis' Last Stand*, London: Pan, 2003, p.211

 4 Danchev and Todman, *War Diaries*, p.668 and Bryant, *Triumph in the West*, p.333

 5 Bryant, *Triumph in the West*, p.334

 6 de Guingand, *Operation Victory*, p.441

 7 Charles Whiting, *Bounce the Rhine*, London: Leo Cooper, 1985, p.95

 8 Ibid.

 9 Nigel Hamilton, *Monty the Field Marshal 1944–1976*, London: Hamish Hamilton, 1986, p.421

10 de Guingand, *Operation Victory*, 1947, p.441

11 Bryant, *Triumph in the West*, p.339

12 Hamilton, *Monty the Field Marshal*, p.421

13 Danchev and Todman, *War Diaries*, p.673 and Bryant, *Triumph in the West*, p.339

14 Danchev and Todman, *War Diaries*, p.674 and Bryant, *Triumph in the West*, p.340

15 Richard Collier, *The Warcos: The War Correspondents of World War Two*, London: Weidenfeld & Nicolson, 1989, p.185

16 Eisenhower, *Crusade in Europe*, p.426

17 Danchev and Todman, *War Diaries*, p.675 and Bryant, *Triumph in the West*, p.341

18 Whiting, *Bounce the Rhine*, p.128

19 Eisenhower, *Crusade in Europe*, p.427.

20 Whiting, *Bounce the Rhine*, p.128

21 Ibid.

22 Danchev and Todman, *War Diaries*, p.676 and Bryant, *Triumph in the West*, p.341

23 D'Este, *Warlord*, p.790

24 Danchev and Todman, *War Diaries*, p.677 and Bryant, *Triumph in the West*, p.344

25 Danchev and Todman, *War Diaries*, p.676 and Bryant, *Triumph in the West*, p.343

26 Churchill received some sad news when he was informed that Lloyd George had died at the age of 82 on 26 March 1945. He had only just recommended him for a peerage in the New Year Honours List, making him the Earl Lloyd-George of

Dwyfor and Viscount Gwynedd. Lloyd George had been grateful for Churchill's support in gaining entry to the House of Lords, as he knew his failing health would have prevented him fighting the next general election.

27 Alan Moorehead, *Montgomery: A Biography*, London: Hamish Hamilton, 1946, p.221

28 Danchev and Todman, *War Diaries*, p.678 and Bryant, *Triumph in the West*, p.345

29 Lamb, *The Wisdom of Winston Churchill*, p.308

30 Coote, *A Churchill Reader*, p.371

31 Moorehead, *Montgomery*, p.223

32 Stewart, *His Finest Hours*, p.195

33 Nel, *Mr Churchill's Secretary*, p.177

34 Ibid.

35 Stewart, *His Finest Hours*, p.195

36 Hastings, *Finest Years*, p.569

37 Ibid., p.568

38 Danchev and Todman, *War Diaries*, p.689

CHAPTER 27: MIRACLE OF DELIVERANCE

1 French, *Liberty or Death*, p.188

2 These consisted of 5th, 7th, 25th and 26th Divisions, which were grouped into the 34th Indian Corps for the liberation of Malaya. Holland, *Burma '44*, pp.369–70

3 French, *Liberty or Death*, p.189

4 Ibid., p.200

5 David Rooney, *Burma Victory: Imphal, Kohima and the Chindit Issue, March 1944 to May 1945*, London: Arms and Armour Press, 1995, p.92

6 A few troopers of the Gwalior Lancers went over to the INA near Taung Bazaar in early February 1944. However, they were members of the Indian State Forces and not part of the regular Indian Army.

7 Mason, *A Matter of Honour*, p.519

8 Slim, *Defeat into Victory*, p.327

9 Chaudhuri, *Thy Hand, Great Anarch!*, p.794

10 Mollo, *The Indian Army*, p.162. Mason, *A Matter of Honour*, p.511 cites an even higher figure of 15,740.

11 Stephen Harper, *Miracle of Deliverance: The Case for the Bombing of Hiroshima and Nagasaki*, London: Sidgwick & Jackson, 1985, p.10

12 Harris, *Bomber Offensive*, p.155

13 Avon, *The Eden Memoirs: The Reckoning*, p.549

14 Ibid.

15 Niven, *The Moon's a Balloon*, p.231

16 Allen and Polmar, *Code-Name Downfall*, p.267

17 Harper, *Miracle of Deliverance*, p.87

18 Gilbert, *Churchill: A Life*, p.852

19 Somerville, *Our War*, p.287

20 Avon, *The Eden Memoirs: The Reckoning*, p.550

21 Moran, *Winston Churchill*, p.286

22 Ibid., p.287

23 Montgomery, *The Memoirs*, p.392

24 Alexander, *The Alexander Memoirs*, p.160

25 Dirk Bogarde, *Backcloth*, London: Penguin, 1987, pp.173–4

26 Ballard, *Miracles of Life*, p.123

27 Harper, *Miracle of Deliverance*, p.102

28 Capturing Iwo Jima cost the US armed forces 6,766 dead and 19,189 wounded. Okinawa, the last island before the Japanese mainland, cost 11,900 dead and 36,000 wounded. Derrick Wright, *Pacific Victory: Tarawa to Okinawa 1943–1945*, Stroud: Sutton, 2005, p.195 & p.233

29 Ted Gup, 'When the Bomb Fell', *National Geographic*, June 2020, p.88

30 Nel, *Mr Churchill's Secretary*, p.185

CHAPTER 28: THE WHOLE SCENE

1 Dwight D. Eisenhower, *At Ease: Stories I Tell to Friends*, London: Robert Hale, p.272

2 Churchill, *The Second World War, Volume I, The Gathering Storm*, pp.526–7

3 Eisenhower, *Churchill The Life Triumphant*, p.134

4 Catherwood, *Churchill*, p.15

5 Randolph Churchill, *Winston S. Churchill*,Vol. I, p.115 and Arthur, *Churchill: The Life*, p.30

6 Ponting, *Churchill*, p.14

7 Randolph Churchill, *Winston S. Churchill*,Vol. I, p.243

8 Ibid., p.526

9 Montgomery, *The Memoirs*, p.536

10 Eisenhower, *Crusade in Europe*, p.401

11 Spears, *Assignment to Catastrophe*, p.141

12 Harris, *Bomber Offensive*, p.152

13 Tatlock Miller and Sainthill, *Churchill: The Walk with Destiny*, p.153

14 Ibid.

15 Churchill, *The Second World War, Volume I, The Gathering Storm*, p.527

16 Avon, *The Eden Memoirs: The Reckoning*, p.552

17 Ibid.

18 Alexander, *The Alexander Memoirs*, p.32

19 Moorehead, *Montgomery*, p.239

20 Harris, *Bomber Offensive*, p.151

21 Danchev and Todman, *War Diaries*, p.194

22 Eisenhower, *Churchill The Life Triumphant*, p.4

23 Eisenhower, *Crusade in Europe*, p.265

24 Harris, *Bomber Offensive*, p.151

25 Eisenhower, *Churchill The Life Triumphant*, p.133

26 Spears, *Assignment to Catastrophe*, p.18

27 Eisenhower, *Crusade in Europe*, p.69

28 Moran, *Winston Churchill*, p.292

29 Danchev and Todman, *War Diaries*, p.141
30 Eisenhower, *Churchill The Life Triumphant*, p.133
31 Chaudhuri, *Thy Hand, Great Anarch!* p.704
32 Moorehead, *Montgomery*, p.239
33 Montgomery, *The Memoirs*, p.535
34 Montgomery, *A Field Marshal in the Family*, p.272
35 Lamb, *The Wisdom of Winston Churchill*, p.252
36 Wheeler-Bennett, *King George VI*, p.447
37 Ibid.
38 Soames, *Speaking for Themselves*, p.467
39 Churchill, *The Second World War, Volume III, The Grand Alliance*, p.679
40 Moran, *Winston Churchill*, p.146
41 Avon, *The Eden Memoirs: The Reckoning*, p.350
42 Moran, *Winston Churchill*, p.146
43 Harris, *Bomber Offensive*, p.152
44 Enright, *The Wicked Wit of Winston Churchill*, p.64
45 Owen, *Tempestuous Journey*, p.753
46 Danchev and Todman, *War Diaries*, p.226
47 Ibid., p.713
48 Slim, *Defeat into Victory*, p.523
49 While this neglect was seen as a slight to 14th Army's achievements, it did Slim's career no harm as he subsequently served as Allied Land Forces Commander, South East Asia, Chief of the Imperial General Staff and was appointed Field Marshal in 1949.
50 Coote, *A Churchill Reader*, p.224
51 Holmes, *In the Footsteps of Churchill*, p.254
52 Ibid.
53 Eisenhower, *Churchill The Life Triumphant*, p.4
54 Ibid.
55 Nikita Khrushchev, *Khrushchev Remembers*, London: Andre Deutsch, 1971, p.222
56 Ibid.
57 Chaudhuri, *Thy Hand, Great Anarch!*, p.757
58 Ibid.

EPILOGUE: GONE PAINTING

1 *A View of Marrakech, with the tower of the Katoubia mosque, January 1943.* See Soames, *Winston Churchill: His Life as a Painter*, p.133
2 During his premiership Churchill spent over a year abroad, making 25 trips to see allies. These included six journeys to lobby Roosevelt. See 'Winston Churchill: Wartime Traveller', by Ged Martin in Folly, Roberts and Rzheshevsky, *Churchill and Stalin*, p.285
3 Soames, *Speaking for Themselves*, p.537
4 Sarah Churchill, *A Thread in the Tapestry*, London: Deutsch, 1967, p.95
5 Alexander, *The Alexander Memoirs*, p.160
6 Ibid.

7 *Scene on Lake Como*, September 1945, The National Trust, Chartwell. See Soames, *Winston Churchill: His Life as a Painter*, p.141

8 Ibid., p.147

9 Moran, *Winston Churchill*, p.301

10 Sarah Churchill, *A Thread in the Tapestry*, p.91. The 'boys' in question included Major John Ogier and Lieutenant Tim Rogers, both from the 4th Hussars. The two officers and 24 men were deployed specially from Austria to guard Churchill.

11 During Churchill's second premiership of 1951–55 he had to contend with two more conflicts, the Malayan Emergency which lasted from 1948 to 1960 and the Mau Mau Uprising of 1952, which also continued until 1960. In case of the former, it was held up as a textbook counter-insurgency war; however, the latter, fought in Kenya, witnessed war crimes committed by both sides.

WINSTON CHURCHILL'S MILITARY CAREER AT A GLANCE: 1895–1945

1 General Hamilton's account of seeking recognition for Churchill during the Boer War does not make clear whether he actually recommended him for a VC, as some historians interpret. Hamilton referenced the VC in terms of 'conspicuous gallantry' shown by Winston, but only added, 'Persistent efforts were made by me to get some mention made or notice taken of Winston's initiative and daring...'. Hamilton claimed his efforts were thwarted by Field Marshal Roberts and General Kitchener, who were not receptive. Randolph Churchill, *Winston S. Churchill*, Vol. I, pp.530–1

Bibliography

As any self-respecting Churchill historian will warn, the works by Winston Churchill are quite simply legion and those books about him and World War II seemingly inexhaustible. According to that doyen of all things Churchillian, Professor Andrew Roberts, there have been over a thousand books written on Churchill. The vast majority of them, though, tend to be largely framed by his long political career or certain narrow aspects of his life. To give this figure some context biographer Volker Ullrich noted there are about 128,000 books on Hitler, so Winston has some considerable way to go to catch up.

Despite the absolutely vast wealth of archive and published material, anyone studying Churchill must inevitably pay tribute to the works of Christopher Catherwood, Carlo D'Este, Martin Gilbert, Barry Gough, Max Hastings, Roy Jenkins, Lord Moran, Allen Packwood, Clive Ponting and last but not least Andrew Roberts, to name but a few. Whilst countless Churchill and related military history titles have been of background interest, the following bibliography lists those works that directly helped shape this book or are quoted from in the text. Date of publication is the edition consulted.

BOOKS

Aldrich, Richard J. & Cormac, Rory, *The Black Door: Spies, Secret Intelligence and British Prime Ministers*, London: William Collins, 2017

Alexander, Field Marshal, *The Alexander Memoirs 1940–1945*, London: Cassell, 1962

Allen, Thomas B. & Polmar, Norman, *Code-Name Downfall: The Secret Plan to Invade Japan – and Why Truman Dropped the Bomb*, New York: Simon & Schuster, 1995

Andrew, Christopher, *The Defence of the Realm: The Authorized History of MI5*, London: Allen Lane, 2009

Arnn, Larry P., *Churchill's Trial: Winston Churchill and the Salvation of Free Government*, Nashville, Tennessee: Nelson, 2015

Aron, Robert, *De Gaulle Before Paris: The Liberation of France June 1944–August 1944*, London: Putnam, 1962

Arthur, Max, *Churchill: The Life: An Authorized Pictorial Biography*, London: Cassell, 2017

Arthur, Max, *Last Post: The Final Word from our First World War Soldiers*, London: Weidenfeld & Nicolson, 2005

Arthur, Max, *Symbol of Courage: The Men Behind the Medal*, London: Pan, 2005

Atkin, Nicholas, *The Forgotten French: Exiles in the British Isles 1940–44*, Manchester: Manchester University Press, 2003

Atkin, Ronald, *Dieppe 1942: The Jubilee Disaster*, London: Macmillan, 1980

Attlee, Clement, *As It Happened*, London: Heinemann, 1954

Atwood, Rodney, *Roberts & Kitchener in South Africa 1900–1902*, Barnsley: Pen & Sword, 2011

Avon, The Rt. Hon. The Earl of, *The Eden Memoirs: The Reckoning*, London: Cassell, 1965

Ballard, J.G., *Miracles of Life: Shanghai to Shepperton: An Autobiography*, London: Harper Perennial, 2008

Barnett, Correli, *The Desert Generals*, London: Pan, 1983

Bayly, Christopher & Harper, Tim, *Forgotten Armies: Britain's Asian Empire & The War with Japan*, London: Penguin, 2005

Belfield, Eversley, *The Boer War*, London: Leo Cooper, 1975

Bennett, Richard, *The Black and Tans*, Barnsley: Pen & Sword, 2020

Bercuson, David J. & Herwig, Hologer H., *One Christmas in Washington: Churchill and Roosevelt Forge the Grand Alliance*, London: Phoenix, 2006

Best, Geoffrey, *Churchill: A Study in Greatness*, New York: Oxford University Press, 2003

Bishop, Patrick, *Air Force Blue: The RAF in World War Two – Spearhead of Victory*, London: William Collins, 2017

Bishop, Patrick, *Battle of Britain*, London: Quercus, 2010

Bishop, Patrick, *Bomber Boys: Fighting Back 1940–1945*, London: Harper Perennial, 2008

Bishop, Patrick, *Fighter Boys: Saving Britain 1940*, London: Harper Perennial, 2004

Blundell, Nigel, *Winston Churchill: The Pictorial History of a British Legend*, Barnsley: Pen & Sword, 2011

Bogarde, Dirk, *Backcloth*, London: Penguin, 1987

Brendon, Piers, *The Dark Valley: A Panorama of the 1930s*, London: Jonathan Cape, 2000

Bryant, Arthur, *The Turn of the Tide 1939–1943*, London: The Reprint Society, 1958

Bryant, Arthur, *Triumph in the West 1943–1946*, London: The Reprint Society, 1960

Bull, Stephen, *Churchill's Army 1939–1945*, London: Conway, 2016

Burridge, Trevor, *Clement Attlee*, London: Jonathan Cape, 1985

Calvert, Mike, *Slim*, London: Pan, 1973

Carter, G.B., *Porton Down: 75 Years of Chemical and Biological Research*, London: HMSO, 1992

Catherwood, Christopher, *Churchill and Tito: SOE, Bletchley Park and Supporting the Yugoslav Communists in World War II*, Barnsley: Frontline, 2017

Catherwood, Christopher, *Churchill: The Story of the Greatest Briton in Words, Photographs and Documents*, London: SevenOaks, 2018

Chandler, David, *Marlborough as Military Commander*, London: Batsford, 1979

Chandler, David, *The Art of Warfare in the Age of Marlborough*, London: Batsford, 1976

Chang, Iris, *The Rape of Nanking: The Forgotten Holocaust of World War II*, London: Penguin, 1998

Charlwood, David, *Churchill and Eden: Partners Through War and Peace*, Barnsley: Pen & Sword, 2020

Chaudhuri, Nirad C., *Thy Hand, Great Anarch! India: 1921–1952*, London: Chatto & Windus, 1987

Churchill, Randolph S., *Winston S. Churchill*, Volume I, Youth 1874–1900, London: Heinemann, 1966

Churchill, Randolph S., *Winston S. Churchill*, Volume II, Young Statesman 1901–1914, London: Heinemann, 1967

Churchill, Sarah, *A Thread in the Tapestry*, London: Deutsch, 1967

Churchill, Winston S., *A History of the English-Speaking Peoples*, Volume IV, London: The Folio Society, 2003

Churchill, Winston S., *The Second World War*, Volumes I–VI, London: Cassell, 1948-54

Clancy, John, '*The Most Dangerous Moment of the War': Japan's Attack on the Indian Ocean, 1942*, Oxford: Casemate, 2017

Clark, Brigadier Stanley, *The Man Who is France: The Story of Charles De Gaulle*, London: Harrap, 1960

Clarke, Peter, *Mr Churchill's Profession: Statesman, Orator, Writer*, London: Bloomsbury, 2013

Coles, Dr David J. & Gregory, David, *Florida World War II Heritage Trail*, Florida Department of State, Division of Historical Resources, 2015

Collier, Richard, *Eagle Day: The Battle of Britain*, London: J.M. Dent & Sons, 1980

Collier, Richard, *The Warcos: The War Correspondents of World War Two*, London: Weidenfeld & Nicolson, 1989

Collier, Richard, *The War that Stalin Won*, London: Hamish Hamilton, 1983

Coote, Colin R., *A Churchill Reader: The Wit and Wisdom of Sir Winston Churchill*, Boston: Houghton Mifflin, 1954

Corrigan, Gordon, *Blood, Sweat and Arrogance and the Myths of Churchill's War*, London: Weidenfeld & Nicolson, 2006

Craddock, Percy, *Know Your Enemy: How the Joint Intelligence Committee Saw the World*, London: John Murray, 2002

Craster, H.H.E (ed.), *Speeches on Foreign Policy by Viscount Halifax*, London: Oxford University Press, 1940

Crawley, Aidan, *de Gaulle*, London: Collins, 1969

Danchev, Alex & Todman, Daniel (ed.), *War Diaries 1939–1945: Field Marshal Lord Alanbrooke*, London: Phoenix Press, 2002

de Guingand, Major-General Sir Francis, *Operation Victory*, London: Hodder and Stoughton, 1947

Deighton, Len, *Battle of Britain*, London: Jonathan Cape, 1980

Deighton, Len, *Blitzkrieg: From the Rise of Hitler to the Fall of Dunkirk*, London: Jonathan Cape, 1979

Deighton, Len, *Fighter: The True Story of the Battle of Britain*, London: Jonathan Cape, 1977

Delmas, Vincent, Cammardella, Alessio, Kersaudy, François & Regnault, Christophe, *Churchill: A Graphic Biography*, Barnsley: Greenhill Books, 2020

D'Este, Carlo, *Eisenhower*, London: Weidenfeld & Nicolson, 2003

D'Este, Carlo, *Warlord: A Life of Churchill at War, 1874–1945*, London: Allen Lane, 2009

Dewar Gibb, Major Andrew, *With Winston Churchill at the Front: Winston in the Trenches 1916*, Barnsley: Frontline, 2016

Dewar, Lieutenant-Colonel Michael, *The British Army in Northern Ireland*, London: Arms and Armour Press, 1985

Dilks, David, *Churchill and Company: Allies and Rivals in Peace and War*, London: I.B. Tauris, 2012

Dix, Anthony, *The Norway Campaign and the Rise of Churchill 1940*, Barnsley: Pen & Sword, 2014

Durnford-Slater, John, *Commando: Memoirs of a Fighting Commando in World War Two*, Barnsley: Greenhill Books, 2020

Edwards, Bernard, *Churchill's Thin Grey Line: British Merchant Ships at War 1939–1945*, Barnsley: Pen & Sword, 2017

Edwards, Bernard, *The Road to Russia: Arctic Convoys*, Barnsley: Leo Cooper, 2002

Enright, Dominique, *The Wicked Wit of Winston Churchill*, London: Michael O'Mara, 2001

Eisenhower, Dwight D., *Crusade in Europe*, London: William Heinemann, 1948

Eisenhower, Dwight D., 'Introduction', in *Churchill The Life Triumphant: The Historical Record of Ninety Years*, New York: American Heritage Publishing, 1965

Elson, Robert T., *Prelude to War*, New York: Time-Life Books, 1976

Eshel, David, *Bravery in Battle: Valour on the Front Line*, London: Cassell, 1999

Fabb, John & Carman, W.Y., *The Victorian and Edwardian Army from Old Photographs*, London: B.T. Batsford, 1975

Farrell, Brian P., *The Defence and Fall of Singapore 1940–1942*, Stroud: Tempus, 2005

Featherstone, Donald, *At Them with the Bayonet: The First Sikh War*, London: Jarrolds, 1968

Featherstone, Donald, *Omdurman 1898: Kitchener's Victory in the Sudan*, Oxford: Osprey, 1994

Featherstone, Donald, *Weapons & Equipment of the Victorian Soldier*, Poole: Blandford Press, 1978

Fischer, Louis, *The Life of Mahatma Gandhi*, London: HarperCollins, 1997

Fitzgerald, Michael, *Hitler's War Beneath the Waves*, London: Arcturus, 2020

Fleming, Peter, *Invasion 1940*, London: Rupert Hart-Davis, 1957

Folly, Martin, Roberts, Geoffrey & Rzheshevsky, Oleg, *Churchill and Stalin: Comrades-in-Arms during the Second World War*, Barnsley: Pen & Sword, 2019

Ford, Ken, *El Alamein 1942: The Turning of the Tide*, Oxford: Osprey, 2001

Ford, Ken, *Operation Crusader 1941: Rommel in Retreat*, Oxford: Osprey, 2010

Forty, George & Anne, *They Also Served*, Speldhurst: Midas, 1979

Franks, Norman, *Battle of Britain*, London: Bison, 1981

Franks, Norman, *RAF Fighter Command 1936–1968*, Sparkford: Patrick Stevens, 1992

Fraser, David, *Alanbrooke*, London: Hamlyn, 1983

French, Patrick, *Liberty or Death: India's Journey to Independence and Division*, London: HarperCollins, 1997

Gardiner, Juliet, *Wartime Britain 1939–1945*, London: Review, 2005

Gibney, John (ed.), *The Irish War of Independence and Civil War*, Barnsley: Pen & Sword, 2020

Gilbert, Martin, *Churchill: A Life*, London: Pimlico, 2000

Gough, Barry, *Churchill and Fisher: Titans at the Admiralty*, Barnsley: Seaforth, 2017

Graves, Robert, *Goodbye to All That*, Harmondsworth: Penguin, 1977

Green, David, *Blenheim*, London: Purnell, 1974

Hamilton, Nigel, *Monty: The Field-Marshal 1944–1976*, London: Hamish Hamilton, 1986

Hamilton, Nigel, *Monty: The Making of a General 1887–1942*, London: Hamish Hamilton, 1981

Harman, Nicholas, *Dunkirk: The Necessary Myth*, London: Coronet, 1990

Harper, Stephen, *Miracle of Deliverance: The Case for the Bombing of Hiroshima and Nagasaki*, London: Sidgwick & Jackson, 1985

Harris, Marshal of the RAF Sir Arthur, *Bomber Offensive*, London: Collins, 1947

Harris, John, *The Indian Mutiny*, London: Granada, 1973

Hastings, Max, *Bomber Command*, London: Pan, 1999

Hastings, Max, *Finest Years: Churchill as Warlord 1940–45*, London: HarperPress, 2009

Hastings, Max, *The Secret War: Spies, Codes and Guerrillas 1939–45*, London: William Collins, 2017

Haythornthwaite, Philip J., *Gallipoli 1915: Frontal Assault on Turkey*, Oxford: Osprey, 1991

Haythornthwaite, Philip J., *The Colonial Wars Source Book*, London: Caxton, 2000

Heiden, Konrad, *Der Fuehrer: Hitler's Rise to Power*, London: Victor Gollancz, 1944

Hemingway, Ernest (ed & intro.), *Men at War*, London: Fontana, 1972

Herder, Brian Lane, *Operation Torch 1942: The Invasion of French North Africa*, Oxford: Osprey, 2017

Hilton, Stanley E., *Hitler's Secret War in South America 1939–1945*, Baton Rouge: Louisiana State University Press, 1981

Holland, James, *Burma '44: The Battle that Turned Britain's War in the East*, London: Corgi, 2016

Holmes, Richard, *Complete War Walks: From Hastings to Normandy*, London: BBC Worldwide, 2003

Holmes, Richard, *In the Footsteps of Churchill*, London: BBC Books, 2005

Holmes, Richard, *The Western Front*, London: BBC Worldwide, 1999

Horne, Alistair & Montgomery, David, *The Lonely Leader: Monty 1944–1945*, London: Pan, 1995

Hough, Richard, *Winston and Clementine: The Triumphs and Tragedies of the Churchills*, London: Bantam, 1991

Irons, Roy, *Churchill and the Mad Mullah of Somaliland: Betrayal and Redemption 1899–1921*, Barnsley: Pen & Sword, 2013

Irving, David, *The War Between the Generals*, London: Allen Lane, 1981

Jackson, Julian, *Charles de Gaulle*, London: Cardinal, 1990

Jackson, Robert, *Before the Storm: The Story of Bomber Command 1939–42*, London: Cassell, 2001

Jackson, Robert, *Bomber! Famous Bomber Missions of World War II*, London: Arthur Barker, 1980

Jackson, Robert, *Dunkirk*, London: Granada, 1978

James, Lawrence, *Churchill and Empire: Portrait of an Imperialist*, London: Weidenfeld & Nicolson, 2014

Jeffrey, Keith, *MI6: The History of the Secret Intelligence Service, 1909–1949*, London: Bloomsbury, 2011

Jenkins, Roy, *Churchill: A Biography*, New York: Farrar, Straus and Giroux, 2001

Johnson, Boris, *The Churchill Factor: How One Man Made History*, London: Hodder & Stoughton, 2015

Johnstone, Air Vice-Marshal Sandy, *Spitfire into War*, London: Grafton, 1988

Jowett, Philip, *Japan's Asian Allies 1941–45*, Oxford: Osprey, 2020

Judd, Denis, *The Boer War*, London: Granada, 1977

Kennedy, Michael & Laing, Victor (ed.), *The Irish Defence Forces 1940–1949: The Chiefs of Staff's Report*, Dublin: Irish Manuscripts Commission, 2011

Khrushchev, Nikita, *Khrushchev Remembers*, London: Andre Deutsch, 1971

Kingston, William H.G., *Our Soldiers: Gallant deeds of the British Army during the reign of Queen Victoria*, London: Griffith Farran Browne, 1899

Kinvig, Clifford, *Churchill's Crusade: The British Invasion of Russia 1918–1920*, New York: Hambledon Continuum, 2006

Klemperer, Victor, *To the Bitter End: The Diaries of Victor Klemperer 1942–1945*, London: Weidenfeld & Nicolson, 1999

Kluger, Michael & Evans, Richard, *Roosevelt and Churchill: The Atlantic Charter – A Risky Meeting at Sea that Saved Democracy*, Barnsley: Frontline, 2020

Knight, Dennis, *Harvest of Messerschmitts: The Chronicle of a Village at War 1940*, London: Frederick Warne, 1981

Kochan, Lionel, *Russia in Revolution*, London: Paladin, 1978

Kruger, Rayne, *Good-bye Dolly Gray: The Story of the Boer War*, London: Pan, 1974

Konstam, Angus, *Taranto 1940: The Fleet Air Arm's precursor to Pearl Harbor*, Oxford: Osprey, 2015

Lacoute, Jean, *De Gaulle: The Rebel 1890–1944*, London: Harvill, 1993

Laffin, John, *Raiders: Elite Forces Attacks*, London: Chancellor Press, 2000

Lake, Jon, *Battle of Britain*, London: Amber, 2019

Lamb, Sean (ed.), *The Wisdom of Winston Churchill: Words of War and Peace*, London: Arcturus, 2019

Latimer, Jon, *Burma: The Forgotten War*, London: John Murray, 2004

Lawrence, T.E., *Revolt in the Desert*, London: Jonathan Cape, 1927

Lawrence, T.E., *Seven Pillars of Wisdom*, Vol. 1, London: Reprint Society, 1939

Lavery, Brian, *Churchill's Navy: The Ships, People and Organization 1939–1945*, London: Conway, 2016

Lavery, Brian, *Churchill Warrior: How a Military Life Guided Winston's Finest Hours*, Oxford: Casemate, 2017

Levine, Joshua, *Dunkirk: The History Behind the Major Motion Picture*, London: William Collins, 2017

Levine, Joshua, *Forgotten Voices of the Blitz and the Battle of Britain*, London: Ebury, 2007

Levine, Joshua, *The Secret History of the Blitz*, London: Simon & Schuster, 2015

Liddell Hart, B.H., *History of the First World War*, London: Cassell, 1971

Lloyd George, David, *War Memoirs of David Lloyd George*, Volume II, London: Odhams, 1937

Logue, Mark & Conradi, Peter, *The King's War*, London: Quercus, 2019

Lovat, Lord, *March Past*, London: Weidenfeld & Nicolson, 1978

Lukacs, John, *Five Days in London, May 1940*, London: The Folio Society, 2011

Lyman, Robert, *Japan's Last Bid for Victory: The Invasion of India 1944*, Barnsley: Pen & Sword, 2020

Macintyre, Captain Donald, *Narvik*, London: Pan, 1962

Macrae, Stuart, *Winston Churchill's Toyshop: The Inside Story of Military Intelligence (Research)*, Stroud: Amberley, 2012

Marix Evans, Martin, *1918 The Year of Victories*, London: Arcturus, 2002

Mason, Philip, *A Matter of Honour: An Account of the Indian Army its Officers and Men*, London: Jonathan Cape, 1974

Masters, John, *The Road Past Mandalay*, London: Cassell, 2002

Mayer, S.L. (ed.), *The Japanese War Machine*, Feltham: Bison, 1976

McCarten, Anthony, *Darkest Hour: How Churchill Brought Us Back from the Brink*, London: Penguin, 2017

McKay, Sinclair, *Dresden: The Fire and the Darkness*, London: Viking, 2020

McKay, Sinclair, *The Secret Life of Bletchley Park*, London: Aurum, 2011

Messenger, Charles, *Broken Sword: The Tumultuous Life of General Frank Crozier 1879–1937*, Barnsley: Praetorian Press, 2013

Mollo, Boris, *The Indian Army*, Poole: Blandford, 1981

Montgomery, Field-Marshal the Viscount, *A Concise History of Warfare*, London: Collins, 1972

Montgomery, Field-Marshal the Viscount, *The Memoirs*, London: Collins, 1958

Moore, Kate, *The Battle of Britain*, Oxford: Osprey, 2015

Moorehead, Alan, *Montgomery: A Biography*, London: Hamish Hamilton, 1946

Moran, Lord, *Winston Churchill: The Struggle for Survival 1940–1965*, London: Constable, 1966

Mosley, Leonard, *The Battle of Britain*, Alexandria, Virginia: Time-Life, 1984

Moynaham, Brian, *The Claws of the Bear: A History of the Soviet Armed Forces from 1917 to the Present*, London: Hutchinson, 1989

Nel, Elizabeth, *Mr Churchill's Secretary*, London: Hodder and Stoughton, 1961

Neillands, Robin, *The Raiders: The Army Commandos 1940–1946*, London: Fontana, 1990

Nester, William, *Winston Churchill and the Art of Leadership*, Barnsley: Frontline Books, 2020

Niven, David, *The Moon's a Balloon*, London: Coronet, 1972

Norman, Dr Andrew, *Winston Churchill: Portrait of an Unquiet Mind*, Barnsley: Pen & Sword, 2012

O'Ballance, Edgar, *The Red Army*, London: Faber and Faber, 1964

Overy, Richard, *Russia's War*, London: Penguin, 1998

Overy, Richard, *The Battle of Britain*, London: Penguin, 2004

Overy, Richard, *The Dictators: Hitler's Germany Stalin's Russia*, London: Penguin, 2004

Overy, Richard & Wheatcroft, Andrew, *The Road to War*, London: Macmillan, 1989

Owen, Frank, *Tempestuous Journey: Lloyd George His Life and Times*, London: Hutchinson, 1954

Packwood, Allen, *How Churchill Waged War: The Most Challenging Decisions of the Second World War*, Barnsley: Frontline, 2019

Pakenham, Thomas, *The Boer War*, London: Abacus, 2009

Palmer, Robert, *A Concise Biography of Captain J.N. Randle, VC*, Barnstaple: British Military History, 2014

Palmer, Robert, *A Concise Biography of Major General D. Stuart*, Barnstaple: British Military History, 2020

Palmer, Robert, *A Concise History of Northern Ireland District*, Barnstaple: British Military History, 2019

Palmer, Robert, *A Concise History of the 25th Indian Infantry Division*, Barnstaple: British Military History, 2012

Palmer, Robert, *A Concise History of 50th Indian Tank Brigade*, Barnstaple: British Military History, 2014

Parkinson, Roger, *Dawn on our Darkness: The Summer of 1940*, St Albans: Granada, 1977

Paterson, Michael, *Winston Churchill: His Military Life 1895–1945*, Newton Abbot, 2005

Pendle, George, *A History of Latin America*, London: Penguin, 1990

Pitt, Barrie, *Churchill and the Generals*, Barnsley: Pen & Sword Military Classics, 2004

Ponting, Clive, *Churchill*, London: Sinclair-Stevenson, 1994

Raghavan, Srinath, *India's War: The Making of Modern South Asia 1939–1945*, London: Penguin, 2017

Rankin, Nicholas, *Churchill's Wizards: The British Genius for Deception 1914–1945*, London: Faber and Faber, 2009

Ray, John, *The Battle of Britain: Dowding and the First Victory, 1940*, London: Cassell, 2000

Regan, Geoffrey, *Someone Had Blundered... A Historical Survey of Military Incompetence*, London: B.T. Batsford, 1987

Remarque, Erich Maria, *All Quiet on the Western Front*, London: Mayflower, 1972

Riasanovsky, Nicholas V., *A History of Russia*, New York: Oxford University Press, 1993

Roberts, Andrew, *Churchill: Walking with Destiny*, London: Penguin, 2019

Roberts, Andrew, *Masters and Commanders: How Roosevelt, Churchill, Marshall and Alanbrooke Won the War in the West*, London: Allen Lane, 2008

Roberts, Captain Jerry, *Lorenz: Breaking Hitler's Top Secret Code at Bletchley Park*, Stroud: The History Press, 2017

Rogers, Anthony, *Kos and Leros: The German Conquest of the Dodecanese*, Oxford: Osprey, 2019

Rooney, David, *Burma Victory: Imphal, Kohima and the Chindit Issue, March 1944 to May 1945*, London: Arms and Armour Press, 1995

Roskill, Stephen, *Churchill and the Admirals*, Barnsley: Pen & Sword, 2013

Ruane, Kevin, *Churchill and the Bomb: In the War and the Cold War*, London: Bloomsbury Academic, 2018

Ryder, Chris, *The Fateful Split: Catholics and the Royal Ulster Constabulary*, London: Methuen, 2004

Sangster, Andrew, *Alan Brooke: Churchill's Right-Hand Critic*, Oxford: Casemate, 2021

Sarkar, Dilip, *The Few: The Story of the Battle of Britain in the Words of the Pilots*, Stroud: Amberley, 2012

Schafer, Dr L. & Gaske, Frederick P., *Florida British Heritage Trail*, Tallahassee: Florida Department of State, Division of Historical Resources, 2014

Schofield, Victoria, *Wavell: Soldier & Statesman*, London: John Murray, 2006

Sebag Montefiore, Hugh, *Dunkirk: Fight to the Last Man*, London: Penguin, 2007

Sebag Montefiore, Simon, *Stalin: The Court of the Red Tsar*, London: Weidenfeld & Nicolson, 2003

Shakespeare, Nicholas, *Six Minutes in May: How Churchill Unexpectedly Became Prime Minister*, London: Vintage, 2018

Shaw, Frank & Joan, *We Remember the Home Guard*, London: Ebury, 2012

Sibley, Major J.R., *Tanganyikan Guerrilla: East African Campaign 1914–18*, London: Pan/Ballatine, 1973

Slim, Field Marshal Sir William, *Defeat into Victory*, London: Cassell, 1956

Soames, Mary (ed.), *Speaking for Themselves: The Personal Letters of Winston and Clementine Churchill*, London: Black Swan, 1999

Soames, Mary, *Winston Churchill: His Life as a Painter*, London: Collins, 1990

Somerville, Christopher, *Our War: How the British Commonwealth Fought the Second World War*, London: Weidenfeld & Nicolson, 1998

Spears, Major-General Sir Edward, *Assignment to Catastrophe*, London: The Reprint Society, 1956

Spector, Ronald H., *Eagle Against the Sun: The American War with Japan*, London: Cassell, 2000

Stephenson, Charles, *The Eastern Fleet and the Indian Ocean 1942–1944: The Fleet that Had to Hide*, Barnsley: Pen & Sword, 2020

Stevens, Philip, *The Great War Explained*, Barnsley: Pen & Sword, 2014

Stewart, Graham, *His Finest Hours: The War Speeches of Winston Churchill*, London: Quercus, 2007

Stewart, Jules, *The Savage Border: The Story of the North-West Frontier*, Stroud: Sutton, 2007

Stille, Mark, *Malaya and Singapore 1941–42*, Oxford: Osprey, 2016

Stone, Norman, *Europe Transformed 1878–1919*, Glasgow: Fontana, 1983

Strachan, Hew, *The First World War*, London: Simon & Schuster, 2003

Strawson, John, *Churchill and Hitler: In Victory and Defeat*, London: Constable, 1997

Sweetman, John, *Bomber Crew: Taking on the Reich*, London: Abacus, 2005

Tatlock Miller, Harry & Sainthill, Loudon, *Churchill: The Walk with Destiny*, London: Hutchinson, 1959

Taylor, Frederick, *Dresden: Tuesday 13 February 1945*, London: Bloomsbury, 2005

Thesiger, Wilfred, *The Marsh Arabs*, Harmondsworth: Penguin, 1967

Thompson, Major-General Julian, *Dunkirk: Retreat to Victory*, London: Sidgwick & Jackson, 2008

Thompson, Robert Smith, *Pledge to Destiny: Charles de Gaulle and the Rise of the Free French*, New York: McGraw-Hill, 1974

Toland, John, *Infamy: Pearl Harbor and its Aftermath*, London: Penguin, 2001

Toye, Richard (ed.), *Winston Churchill: Politics, Strategy and Statecraft*, London: Bloomsbury Academic, 2017

Tucker-Jones, Anthony, *D-Day 1944: The Making of Victory*, Stroud: The History Press, 2019

Tucker-Jones, Anthony, *Kursk 1943: Hitler's Bitter Harvest*, Stroud: The History Press, 2018

Tucker-Jones, Anthony, *Operation Dragoon: The Liberation of Southern France 1944*, Barnsley: Pen & Sword, 2009

Tucker-Jones, Anthony, *Slaughter on the Eastern Front: Hitler and Stalin's War 1941–1945*, Stroud: The History Press, 2017

Tucker-Jones, Anthony, *Spitfire to Reaper: The Changing Face of Aerial Warfare – 1940–Present Day*, Stroud: The History Press, 2018

Tucker-Jones, Anthony, *Sun Tzu's The Art of War: Illustrated Edition*, London: Bloomsbury, 2019

Tucker-Jones, Anthony, *The Battle for the Mediterranean: Allied and Axis Campaigns from North Africa to the Italian Peninsula, 1940–45*, London: Arcturus, 2021

Tucker-Jones, Anthony, *The Devil's Bridge: The German Victory at Arnhem, 1944*, Oxford: Osprey, 2020

Tucker-Jones, Anthony, *The Killing Game: A Thousand Years of Warfare in Twenty Battles*, Stroud: The History Press, 2018

Tute, Warren, *The Reluctant Enemies: The Story of the Last War between Britain and France 1940–1942*, London: Collins, 1990

Tute, Warren, Costello, John & Hughes, Terry, *D-Day*, London: Pan, 1975

Twigg, Reg, *Survivor on the River Kwai: The Incredible Story of Life on the Burma Railway*, London: Penguin, 2014

Urquhart, Alistair, *The Forgotten Highlander: My Incredible Story of Survival during the War in the Far East*, London: Little Brown, 2010

Vale, Allister & Scadding, John, *Winston Churchill's Illnesses 1886–1965: Courage, Resilience and Determination*, Barnsley: Frontline Books, 2020

Verrier, Anthony, *The Bomber Offensive*, London: Pan, 1974

Warner, Denis & Peggy, *The Tide at Sunrise: A History of the Russo-Japanese War 1904–1905*, London: Angus & Robertson, 1975

Wells, H.G., *The War of the Worlds*, Harmondsworth: Penguin, 1971

Wernick, Robert, *Blitzkrieg*, New York: Time-Life Books, 1976

West, Anthony, *H.G. Wells: Aspects of a Life*, London: Hutchinson, 1984

Wheatley, Ronald, *Operation Sea Lion*, London: Oxford University Press, 1962

Wheeler-Bennett, John W., *King George VI: His Life and Reign*, London: The Reprint Society, 1959

White, Dorothy Shipley, *Seeds of Discord: De Gaulle, Free France and the Allies*, New York: Syracuse University Press, 1964

Whiting, Charles, *Bounce the Rhine*, London: Leo Cooper, 1985

Whiting, Charles, *Siegfried: The Nazis' Last Stand*, London: Pan, 2003

Whiting, Charles, *West Wall: The Battle for Hitler's Siegfried Line September 1944–March 1945*, London: Pan, 2002

Wilkinson-Latham, Christopher, *The Boer War*, London: Osprey, 1977

Wilkinson-Latham, Christopher, *The Indian Mutiny*, London: Osprey, 1977

Wilkinson-Latham, Robert, *The Sudan Campaigns 1881–1898*, London: Osprey, 1976

Wilmot, Chester, *The Struggle for Europe*, London: Collins, 1952

Wilson, Dick, *When Tigers Fight: The Story of the Sino-Japanese War 1937–45*, London: Hutchinson, 1982

Wilson, Patrick, *Dunkirk: From Disaster to Deliverance*, Barnsley: Leo Cooper, 1999

Wolf, Klaus, *Victory at Gallipoli 1915: The German-Ottoman Alliance in the First World War*, Barnsley: Pen & Sword, 2020

Wright, Derrick, *Pacific Victory: Tarawa to Okinawa 1943–1945*, Stroud: Sutton, 2005

Wynn, Stephen, *Churchill's Flawed Decisions: Errors in Office of the Greatest Briton*, Barnsley: Pen & Sword, 2020

Young, Brigadier Peter, *Commando*, London: Macdonald & Co, 1970

Ziegler, Philip, *Mountbatten: The Official Biography*, London: Collins, 1985

Zulfo, 'Ismat Hasan, *Karari: The Sudanese Account of the Battle of Omdurman*, London: Frederick Warne, 1980

JOURNALS

Daily Express
Daily Graphic
Daily Mail
Daily Mirror
Financial Express

Harijan
Illustrated London News
Irish Independent
Irish Times
Manchester Evening News
Morning Post
National Geographic
New York World Telegram
Pearson's Illustrated War News
People's War
Times
Times of India
The War Illustrated
The War in Pictures

ONLINE RESOURCES

Blenheim Palace
www.blenheimpalace.com
Churchill Central
www.churchillcentral.com
International Churchill Society
www.winstonchurchill.org

ICS Partners
America's National Churchill Museum, Fulton, Missouri
www.nationalchurchillmuseum.org
Chartwell, The National Trust, England, UK
www.nationaltrust.org.uk/chartwell
Churchill Archives Centre, Churchill College, Cambridge, UK
www.churchillarchive.com
Churchill War Rooms
www.iwm.org.uk/visits/churchill-war-rooms
Imperial War Museum, London UK
www.iwm.org.uk
National Churchill Leadership Center, Washington, DC
www.winstonchurchill.org/visit/national-churchill-leadership-center
The Queen Mary, Long Beach California
www.queenmary.com
Winston Churchill Memorial Trust, London, UK
www.wcmt.org.uk

Index

References to maps are in **bold**.

Abdulla, Khalifa   16, 19, 20, 25
Abdullah I of Jordan, Emir   118
Abyssinia   16, 42, 136, 208, 215
Aden   41, 119, 188, 207
Admiralty   72–74, 83
Afghanistan   11, 41, 42, 100, 251
Afridis   45
Ahmad, Sharif Mahmud   16
aircraft, British   156–57, 188, 191, 192, 194
Albania   136, 300
Alexander, Albert   175
Alexander, FM Harold   151, 152, 292, 316, 328
    and Egypt   219, 220
    and Greece   301, 302
Alexandria   12
Allenby, Col E.H.H.   63
America *see* United States of America
Amery, Leo   144, 272, 283, 311
amphibious operations   12, 197, 284, 296
Amritsar massacre (1919)   117
Anderson, William   85
Andrews, John M.   184
Arab Revolt (1916–18)   116–17, 119
Arctic convoys   171, 173–76, 248–49
Argentina   136
Ark Royal, HMS   101, 211
Arras, battle of (1940)   148
Asquith, Herbert Henry   69, 72, 73, 78, 81, 104
Atkins, John   50, 51, 54
Atlantic Ocean   170, 171–72, 175–76, 200
atomic bomb   11, 314–15, 316–17, 327

Attlee, Clement   122, 132, 133, 246, 262, 317
    and De Gaulle   240
    and general election   314, 315–16
Auchinleck, Gen Claude   216–17, 219, 280, 281, 282, 311–12
Augusta, USS   228
Australia   79, 199, 214, 215, 259
Australian Army   264
Austria   127

Bader, Douglas   166
Baldwin, Stanley   121, 127
Balfour, Arthur   70, 78
Ballard, J.G.   129, 130, 316
Baltic States   246
"bands of brothers" *see* Commandos
Baring, Hugo   41, 46
Barnes, Peter   178
Barnes, Lt Reginald 'Reggie'   36, 37–38, 41, 50
Barry, Tom   178
Beatty, Lt David   19, 22, 26
Beaverbrook, Max Aitken, Lord   84–85, 93, 94, 155, 156–57, 202–3
BEF *see* British Army
Belgian Army   149
Belgium   73, 82–83, 147
Bell, Gertrude   115, 118
Bellairs, Rear Adm Roger Mowbray   226–27
Bengal famine   269, 282–83, 286–87
Bensusan-Butt, David   190
Bentick, Bill   244
Beresford, Charles, Lord   105
Berlin   161, 162, 190–91, 194, 303
    and Blockade   328
    and British Victory Parade   315

Blenheim Palace 34
Bletchley Park 146, 158–59, 167, 243, 244, 249
Blitz 161–67, 184
Blood, Brig-Gen Sir Bindon 43, 44
Blunt, Anthony 249
Boer War (1899–1902) 48–56, 57–58, 60–63, 196, 198, 319
    map 59
Bogarde, Dirk 316
Bolshevism 11, 87–91, 93–96, 319
Bomber Command 12, 175, 187–95, 294
Botha, Louis 51, 61, 63, 68
Bourne, Lt-Gen Sir Alan 198
Brabazon, Col John 36, 44, 58, 62
Brazil 135–36, 176, 229
Brimah, Aziz 281
Britain, Battle of (1940) 12, 13, 159, 161–67
British Army 114–15, 315, 316
    and India 269–71, 272
    and Ireland 104–5, 106, 107–8, 109–11
    see also Commandos
British Army (units):
    8th Army 217–18, 219–20
    2nd Grenadier Guards Rgt 10
    4th Hussars Rgt 9, 10, 14, 35–36, 40–41
    5th Dragoon Guards Rgt 51
    5th Lancers Rgt 51
    9th Lancers Rgt 40
    20th Hussars Rgt 18
    21st Lancers Rgt 10, 22
    Royal Scots Fusiliers Rgt 10, 81–83
British Empire 27, 42, 68, 100–1, 291, 319
Broadwood, Col R.G. 18, 26
Brooke, Lt-Gen Alan 151, 153, 171, 183, 289
    and Churchill 310, 321, 324, 325
    and D-Day 294, 296, 297
    and Dragoon 299–300
    and Egypt 219
    and India 286
    and Rhine 304, 305, 306, 307, 308, 309
    and Royal Navy 173–74
Brooke-Popham, ACM Sir Robert 255, 256, 259, 262, 263
Browne-Clayton, Lt William 44
Bulgaria 213, 300
Buller, Gen Redvers 50, 51, 57, 58, 60
Burleigh, Bennet 24
Burma 11, 12, 14, 250–51, 255, 256, 258
    and Chiang Kai-shek 277–78, 311–12
    and independence 273
    and India 269–70

and Indian Army 312–13
and Japan 264–65
and Wingate 279–81
Byng, Lt-Col Julian 'Bungo' 58
Byrne, Joseph 108
Byrne, Pvt Thomas 23–24

Cairncross, Capt John 249
Cairo Conferences (1921/43) 115, 117, 290
Calcutta, HMS 209
Campbell-Bannerman, Sir Henry 68, 69
Campbeltown, HMS 202
Campos, Marshal Martínez 37
Canada 171, 182, 199, 202–3, 221, 238; see also King, Mackenzie
Carden, Vice-Adm Sir Sackville 73–74, 76–77
Carrington, Lt-Gen Sir Robert 183
Carson, Edward 104
Casablanca Conference (1943) 289
Casement, Roger 178
Catroux, Gen Georges 236
Cavendish-Bentick, William 146
Ceylon 267
Chaco War (1932–35) 135
Chamberlain, Joseph 49, 63
Chamberlain, Neville 127, 132, 133, 136–37, 144–46
    and Ireland 180
    and Norway 142, 143
Channel ports 187–88
Chaplin, Charlie 221
Chapman, Gen E.F. 36
Chapman, Lt P. 16
Chaudhuri, Nirad 265–66, 273, 313, 323, 326
chemical weapons see mustard gas
Cherwell, Lord 175, 193
Chiang Kai-shek 126, 129–30, 131, 251, 259
    and Burma 264–65, 277–78, 311–12
    and India 266, 273
    and USA 286, 291
China 11, 125–26, 129–31, 134, 250
    and USA 222–23, 265
Chisholme, Lt-Col Scott 51
Churchill, Clementine (wife) 69, 114, 327
Churchill, Jack (brother) 58, 62, 221
Churchill, Jennie, Lady Randolph (mother) 35, 47, 57–58
Churchill, Johnnie (nephew) 221
Churchill, Lord Randolph (father) 17, 33, 34, 35
Churchill, Randolph (son) 104, 123, 221

Churchill, Winston 9–14, 33–34, 309–10, 318–26, 327–28
  and 4th Hussars 35–36
  and 1945 election 315–16
  and Battle of Britain 159, 161–67
  and Bengal famine 282–83, 286–87
  and Boer War 50–56, 57–58, 60–63
  and Bomber Command 187–95
  and books 26, 63
  and Burma 264–65, 279–81, 312
  and China 125–26, 130–31
  and Commandos 196–203
  and Cuba 36–38
  and D-Day 294–98
  and Dardanelles 73–74, 76–79
  and De Gaulle 232–41
  and *Dragoon* 298–300
  and Dunkirk 149–54
  and Egypt 114–15, 219–20
  and First Lord of the Admiralty 72–73, 136–37
  and Greece 212–13, 214–15, 301–2
  and Home Secretary 69–72
  and India 40–47, 121–22, 251–52, 265–66, 268–74
  and Ireland 104, 105, 106–8, 109–13, 177–80, 181–86
  and Japan 313–14
  and Libya 216–17, 218
  and Middle East 117–20
  and Minister of Munitions 85–86
  and Mussolini 208, 209–11
  and Nazism 123–25, 126–28
  and Norway 148–49
  and Omdurman 16–20, 22–27
  and politics 67, 68
  and Potsdam 314–15
  and Rhine River 304–6, 307–9
  and Royal Air Force 99–100, 101, 102–3, 155–56
  and Royal Navy 141–42, 143–44, 168–76
  and Russian Civil War 87–90, 91, 93, 94, 95–96
  and Second Front 288, 289–90, 291–92
  and Singapore 253, 255, 255–56, 257–63
  and South America 135–36
  and Spanish Civil War 128–29, 131, 132–33, 134
  and Stalin 242–49
  and Sumatra 284, 285, 286
  and tanks 83–84
  and USA 157–58, 221–22, 224–31, 278–79
  and War Cabinet 145–47
  and Western Front 80–83
  and Yalta 302–3
City of Flint, USS 223–24
Clarke, Lt-Col Dudley 197, 198, 199
Clayton Mission (1925) 119
Cochrane, Sir Archibald 251
Cockran, Bourke 37
Cold War 319, 328
Collins, Michael 112, 113
Cologne 192
Colville, Jock 245, 306
Commandos 12, 197–203
Communism 125, 126, 128, 129–30, 131, 133
  and Greece 300–2
  and India 269
  and Stalin 242, 244
  and USA 223
Cotton, Sidney 184
Courageous, HMS 141
Coventry, HMS 209
Cranborne, Lord 184
Craster, H.H.E. 131
Crete 12, 185, 215–16, 200, 322
Crimean War (1853–56) 33
Cripps, Sir Stafford 175, 245, 265, 266
Cronje, Gen Piet 49
Crozier, Brig-Gen Frank 108–9
Cuba 9, 36–38, 39, 135, 172
Cunningham, Adm Andrew 169, 209, 210, 213
Curtin, John 264, 324
Curzon, Lord 64
Czech Legion 90–91, 93–94, 95–96
Czechoslovakia 127–28, 223

D-Day 12, 202, 203, 240–41, 291–92, 294–98
Dakar (Senegal) 236
Dalrymple-Hamilton, Adm Sir Frederick 295, 296
Dardanelles campaign (1915–16) 73–74, 76–79
  map **75**
Darlan, Adm Jean François 169, 233, 234, 235, 239
De Gaulle, Gen Charles 169, 232–41
De Guingand, Maj-Gen Francis 304, 305, 306, 308
De Valera, Éamon 111, 113, 177–78, 179–80, 181–82, 184–86

Dempsey, Lt-Gen Sir Miles 297, 308
Denmark 143
Dervishes 18, 19–20, 22–23, 25, 26, 42
Deutschland (ship) 223–24
Dewar Gibb, Capt Andrew 81, 82, 83
Dewsnap, Dan 56
Dhingra, Madan Lal 79
Dieppe raid (1942) 153, 202–3, 247, 292
Dill, Gen Sir John 197, 201, 210, 212–13, 245, 255
    and Malaya 264
    and Singapore 256
Disraeli, Benjamin 34
Dobbie, Lt-Gen Sir William 253
Dorman-Smith, Sir Reginald 256
Douglas, AVM Sholto 166
Douglas-Jones, WC Eric 163–64, 165
Dowding, ACM Sir Hugh 152, 155–56, 158, 159, 162, 166–67
Dresden 194–95
Dundonald, Lord 60
Dunkirk 13, 149–54
Dutch East Indies 251, 256, 317

East Africa 80
Easter Rising (1916) 105–6, 178
Eastern Europe 291, 300
Eden, Anthony 129, 132, 133, 134, 145, 324
    and Churchill 314, 315–16, 320
    and De Gaulle 234, 235, 236, 240
    and Dunkirk 149, 152
    and Greece 212–13, 214, 301
    and Ireland 179, 180, 182, 183, 185
    and Mussolini 136
    and North Africa 289, 322
    and Singapore 262
    and Stalin 245, 246, 247
    and USA 223, 224, 225
Edward VII, King 48
Edward VIII, King 127, 177
Egypt 14, 16, 42, 47, 114–15, 165
    and Commandos 199
    and defence 207, 209–10, 218–20
Egyptian Army 17, 18, 19
Eire *see* Ireland
Eisenhower, Gen Dwight 13, 241, 299, 303
    and Churchill 318, 320, 321, 326
    and D-Day 292, 294, 296, 298
    and Rhine 304, 305, 307
El Alamein 13, 323

Elandslaagte, battle of (1899) 51
Elgin, Lord 46, 68
Empire Heritage, SS 186
Enigma codes 244, 249
Eritrea 208
espionage 72, 176, 180–81, 186, 249

Faisal I of Iraq, King 116, 117, 118, 120
Fascism 128, 133, 178
Fergusson, Gen Sir Charles 82
Finland 88, 142–43
First Sikh War (1845–46) 41
Fisher, Adm Sir John 72, 73, 76, 78
Forbes, Adm Sir Charles 169–70
Ford, Henry 157
France 12, 80–82, 95, 115, 117, 169
    and Commando raids 198–99, 202
    and *Dragoon* 298–99
    and Mussolini 207, 208
    see also D-Day; De Gaulle, Gen Charles;
        Dieppe raid; Dunkirk; Free France;
        Indochina; Vichy France
Franco, Gen Francisco 128, 131, 132, 133–34, 243
Frankland, 2Lt Thomas 52, 55, 63
Free France 169, 235, 236, 238–39
French, FM Sir John 81, 106, 107
French Army 141, 147–48, 149
French Navy 169
French resistance 236, 239
French West Africa 236

Gajda, Gen Radola 91, 95
Gallacher, William 133
Gallipoli campaign (1915–16) 76–79, 319
    map 75
Gandhi, Mahatma 57, 61, 79, 122, 252
    and Burma 281
    and Chiang Kai-shek 264
    and Quit India 266, 268, 269
Gatacre, Gen 51
George II of Greece, King 301
George V of Great Britain, King 71
George VI of Great Britain, King 145, 246, 262, 310, 323
    and D-Day 294–96, 298
    and Roosevelt 224, 225
Gerard, William, Lord 50
German Air Force *see* Luftwaffe
German-American Bund 223

German Condor Legion   134
German East Africa   74, 80
German South West Africa   80
Germany   11, 69, 72, 142, 309–10
    and Bomber Command   193–95
    and Brazil   135
    and Ireland   178, 180–81, 182
    and southern attack plans   **293**
    and Turkey   115–16
    and World War I   73–74
    see also Berlin; Hitler, Adolf; Luftwaffe;
        Nazism; Rhine River; U-boats
Giraud, Gen Henri   240
Gómez, Máximo   36, 37
Gordon, Gen Charles   16
Gort, Lord   141, 147, 148, 149, 151
Görtz, Hermann   180–81
Gough, Gen Sir Hubert   45, 62, 104
Graf Spee (ship)   141
Graves, Lt Robert   86, 115
Graziani, Marshal Rodolfo   208
Greece   12, 73, 115, 290, 300–2, 322
    and defence   209–10, 212–13, 214–15
Greenwood, Sir Hamar   107, 110
Grenfell, Lt Robert   16, 17, 23, 24, 25
Grey, Sir Edward   72, 73, 118–19
Grigg, Sir James   298, 306
Gubbins, Lt-Col Colin   197
Guernica bombing (1937)   134
guerrilla warfare   197

Haig, FM Douglas   17, 25, 63, 81, 84
Hakewill Smith, Lt Edmund   82
Haldane, Gen Aylmer   46–47, 51, 52, 53, 55
    and Cairo   114
    and Iraq Revolt   103
    and Russia   67
Halifax, Lord   119, 130, 131–32, 141–42, 147
    and Chamberlain   144, 145
    and De Gaulle   234, 235
Hamburg   193–94
Hamilton, Lt-Gen Ian   46, 63, 77, 78
Harris, ACM Arthur   100, 120, 175
    and Bomber Command   189, 191–92, 193,
        194, 195
    and Churchill   314, 320, 321, 324
Harrow School   33, 35, 318
Hasheen, battle of (1885)   18
Hassan, Muhammed Abdullah   42–43, 101
Hess, Rudolf   244

Higginson, Brig-Gen H.W.   110
Hillman, Sidney   228
Hindenburg, Paul von   124
Hitler, Adolf   11, 12, 13–14, 122, 123–25, 150
    and air bases   157
    and Battle of Britain   161
    and expansionism   126–28
    and France   147–48, 169
    and Greece   213, 214
    and Ireland   182–83, 185
    and Italy   289
    and Norway   143
    and Poland   136–37
    and Soviet Union   171, 173, 243, 244,
        245–46, 249, 255
    and Spanish Civil War   134
    and suicide   309
    and USA   230
Holland, Gen Sir Arthur   93
Home Guard   162
Hong Kong   130–31, 257, 259
Horrocks, Gen Brian   90, 91
Howard, Hubert   16, 25
Howard, John   56
Huddleston, Maj-Gen Sir Hubert   182, 183, 185
Hull, Cordell   222, 225
Huntziger, Gen Charles   233
Hussein bin Ali, Sharif of Mecca   116, 119

Ibn Saud, Abdullaziz   119
Illustrious, HMS   209, 210
Imperial Yeomanry   62
Independent Companies   197, 198, 199
India   9, 12, 40–47, 64, 68, 277, 311
    and Afghanistan   100
    and Amritsar   117
    and Churchill   319, 323
    and famine   282–83, 286–87
    and independence movement   11, 79, 313,
        328
    and Japan   267–68
    and nationalism   121–22, 251–52, 265–66,
        268–72
    and Punjab mutiny   109, 113
    and RAF   120–21
    and USA   222, 229, 278–79
    and Wavell   281–82
Indian Army   41–42, 64, 116, 272–74, 312–13,
    317
    9th Bengal Lancers Rgt   18

31st Punjab Rgt 10
35th Sikh Infantry Rgt 10
45th Sikh Infantry Rgt 42–43
Indian Mutiny 41
Indian National Army (INA) 273, 312–13
Indian National Congress 79, 121–22, 252, 268–69
Indochina 131, 251, 256, 317
intelligence 239, 252, 278–79, 277; *see also* Bletchley Park; MI5; MI6
Iraq 11, 102–3, 114, 118, 119–20, 207
Ireland 104–13, 177–86, 319, 328
Irish Army 185
Irish Republican Army (IRA) 106–7, 109–11, 112–13, 177–79, 180–81, 185
iron ore 142, 143
Ironside, Gen Edmund 89, 93, 114, 149
Ismay, Gen Sir Hastings 196, 295, 304, 310
Italian Army 208–9, 210–11
Italy 115, 134, 135, 187, 211, 290; *see also* Mussolini, Benito

Jackson, Capt Thomas 67
Jam Sahib of Nawanagar, Maharajah 277
Jamaica 68
James, Lionel 17
Jameson, Dr Leander Starr 49
Janin, Gen Maurice 95
Japan 11, 12, 250–51, 258–60, 322
  and atomic bombings 314–15, 316–17
  and Burma 264–65, 312, 313
  and China 125–26, 129–31, 134
  and India 267–68, 273–74
  and Russia 67, 90, 95
  and Singapore 252–53, 256–57, 261–63
  and Stalin 291
  and Tehran Conference 284–85
  and Tokyo 313–14
  and USA 222–23, 229, 230, 255–56
Jeffreys, Gen 43, 44
Jerusalem 116, 117–18
Jews 116, 118, 124, 223
Jinnah, Muhammed Ali 252, 266
Johnstone, Sqn Ldr Sandy 167
Joint Intelligence Committee 146, 181, 244
Joubert, Gen Piet 49, 51, 52, 54, 55
Jutland, battle of (1916) 83

Kearny, USS 229
Kelvin, HMS 296, 298

Kemal, Gen Mustafa 102, 121
Kenna, Capt Paul 23, 24
Kennedy, Joe 142, 157–58
Kennedy, Maj-Gen Sir John 259–60
Kenya 209, 215
Kerr, Philip 88
Keyes, Adm Sir Roger 198, 199–201, 202
Khan, Abdul Gaffar 269
Khrushchev, Nikita 325–26
Khyber Pass 45–46
King, Mackenzie 171, 229, 231, 289, 324
Kitchener, Maj-Gen Sir Herbert 40, 42, 47, 80, 119
  and Omdurman 15, 17, 18, 19, 20, 25, 48
  and South Africa 63–64
  and World War I 73, 74, 76, 79, 84
Knox, Gen Alfred 89, 91
Knudsen, William 228
Koenig, Gen Pierre 238
Kolchak, Adm Alexander 89–90, 91, 93, 95
Königsberg (ship) 80
Korean War (1950–53) 328
Kruger, Paul 49
Kut, siege of (1916) 116

Ladysmith 60–61, 62
Lansdowne, Lord 40
Lascelles, Sir Alan 295
Lawrence, Col T.E. 115, 116, 117, 118, 119, 196
Layton, Elizabeth 310, 317
Layton, Vice-Adm Sir Geoffrey 255, 267
League of Nations 125–26
Lebanon 117
Lee, Arthur 68
Lee, Col Raymond E. 161
Leigh-Mallory, ACM Trafford 156, 166
Lenin, Vladimir 87, 125
Lentaigne, Brig Joe 280
Libya 12, 169, 200, 238, 322
  and defence 207–8, 210–11, 212, 214, 216–18
Liddell Hart, Capt B.H. 86
Lindsay, Capt Lionel 71
Linlithgow, Lord 252, 268, 270, 271, 272, 282–83
Lloyd, Maj-Gen Wilfred 278
Lloyd George, David 67, 77, 78, 85, 144, 324
  and Ireland 106, 107, 108, 110–11, 112, 113
  and resignation 121

and Russia　87, 88–89, 90, 91, 95–96
and tanks　84, 85
and War Cabinet　145–46
Lockhart, Lt-Gen Sir William　45, 46, 47
Long, Col Charles　51–52
Long, Leo　249
Long, Walter　108
Lovat, Simon Fraser, 15th Lord　198, 199, 200, 203
Lucas, Brig-Gen Cuthbert　109, 110
Luftwaffe　124, 143–44, 156, 165, 184, 296–97
Lyttleton, Maj-Gen　60, 61

MacArthur, Gen Douglas　259, 279
McBride, Sean　178
McCormick, Patrick　178
MacCurtain, Thomas　107
McDavid, Lt Jock　81, 82
MacDonald, Malcolm　182
MacDonald, Flt Lt Peter　166
MacDonald, Ramsay　121, 127
Mckenna, Reginald　72
McLeod, Maj-Gen D.K.　251, 256
MacNeill, Gen Hugo　182
Macpherson, Ian　106, 107
Macready, Gen Sir Nevil　70–71, 113, 106, 108, 110, 111
'Mad Mullah' see Hassan, Muhammed Abdullah
Madagascar　238
Maffey, Sir John　179, 181
Mahdi (Mohammed Ahmed)　16, 22
Maisky, Ivan　244, 246
Majendie, Maj-Gen Vivian　185
Malaya　12, 230, 251
and Japan　253, 255, 256, 259, 260
Malaya, HMS　211
Malta　207, 209, 321–22
Manchuria　125, 126, 317
Mao Zedong　125, 126, 130, 131, 286
maps:
Boer War　59
Britain's air defences　160
Dardanelles and Gallipoli　75
Dunkirk evacuation　150
Far East　254
Omdurman, battle of　21
Russian Civil War　92
southern Germany attack plans　293
Marlborough, Charles Spencer-Churchill ('Sunny'), 9th Duke of (cousin)　34, 62

Marlborough, George Churchill, 8th Duke of (uncle)　34
Marlborough, John Churchill, 1st Duke of　33–34, 122
Martí, José　36
Martin, Col R.M.　15, 16, 18, 20, 22, 23, 24–25
Masaryk, Tomáš　91, 94, 95
Mashona　40
Masters, Maj John　280
Matabele　40
Maynard, Gen Charles　89
Mayne, Lt-Gen Mosley　282
Mediterranean Sea　168–69, 207
Meiklejohn, Lt Ronald　18, 19, 25
Meltzer, Pvt Sam　315
Menzies, Sir Robert　184
Menzies, Sir Stewart　235–36, 239
merchant shipping　168
Mers-el-Kebir (Algeria)　235, 237, 322
Mesopotamia　101–3, 115, 118
Methuen, Lord　51
Mexico　135, 136
MI5:　11, 71–72, 79, 172, 235–36
and Ireland　177, 186
MI6:　11, 71, 127, 136, 235–36
and Ireland　177, 181, 184
and Japan　258, 262–63
Miaja, Gen José　132
Milner, Sir Alfred　49
Miquelon Island　237–38
Moleyns, Capt Frederick de　42
Molotov, Vyacheslav　174, 246–47, 288
Molyneux, Lt Richard　17, 23–24, 26
Mongolia　250
Montgomery, FM Bernard　110–11, 129, 151, 182, 219–20
and Churchill　316, 318, 320–21, 323
and D-Day　292, 294, 296–97, 298
and Rhine　305, 306–9
Montmorency, Lt Raymond de　24
Moran, Lord　217, 219, 280, 281, 315, 316
Morgan, Lt-Gen Sir Frederick　292
Morton, Maj Desmond　85, 127, 146–47, 235–36
Mountbatten, Louis, Lord　201–3, 283–84, 312, 315, 317
Mudaliar, Sir Ramaswami　277
Müller, Filinto　135
Munro, Lt-Gen Sir Charles　78
Muselier, Adm Émile　235, 236, 238

Muslim League   252, 266, 268
Mussolini, Benito   12, 13, 14, 136, 289, 322
    and Egypt   165
    and Spanish Civil War   132–33
    and strategy   168–69, 207–10
    and USA   230
Mussolini, Bruno   135
mustard gas   11, 85–86, 93, 183, 245–46
    and RAF   100, 103

Nanking massacre (1937)   131
Napoleon Bonaparte   34, 69
Narayan, Jai Prakash   269
nationalism   79, 114–15
    and India   121–22, 222, 251–52, 265–66,
        268–72
    and Ireland   104, 105–7, 181
Nazism   123–25, 126–28, 129–30, 133, 320
    and USA   223, 229
Nesbit, Randolph   40
Netherlands   147, 256; see also Dutch East Indies
New Zealand   79, 214, 215, 216
Newall, Sir Cyril   155, 156, 167, 188
Nicolson, Brig Claude   149
Niven, Capt David   199, 257, 258, 314
Noel-Baker, Philip   132
Nolan, Capt Louis   22
North Africa   13, 238–39, 288–89; see also
    Egypt; Libya; Tunisia
North-West Frontier   10, 41, 42–43, 45–46, 100,
    251, 318
    and INC   269
Norway   142–44, 148–49, 197, 199–200
Nuffield, Lord   156–57
Nye, Capt Charles   93

O'Connor, Gen Richard   210, 211, 214, 297
O'Donovan, Jim   178
O'Duffy, Gen Eoin   178, 181
oil   118, 119, 172–73, 256
Oldham   48, 56, 63
Omdurman, Battle of (1898)   15–20, 22–27, 47,
    48, 318
    map   21
operations:
    Barbarossa (1941)   244
    Battleaxe (1941)   216
    Brevity (1941)   215
    Chariot (1942)   202
    Compass (1940–41)   210–11

    Crusader (1941)   217, 322
    Dervish (1941)   245
    Dragoon (1944)   298–300
    Dynamo (1940)   150–53
    Gomorrah (1943)   193–94
    Jubilee (1942)   202
    Kathleen (1940)   181
    Lustre (1941)   212–13
    Matador (1941)   256
    Overlord (1944)   240–41, 289–90, 291–92,
        294–98
    Pilgrim (1941)   200
    Plunder (1945)   304–9
    Wilfred (1939)   142, 143–44
    Zipper (1945)   317
Orakzais   45
Orwell, George   129, 133–34
Ottoman Empire   72, 101, 114, 115, 116–17

Page Croft, Sir Henry   133
Paget, Gen Sir Arthur   105
painting   82–83, 117–18, 327, 328
Pakenham, Capt William Christopher   67
Palestine   115, 116, 117–18, 207
Panama Canal   68, 135
Papandreou, Georgios   301
Paris Peace Conference (1919)   88–89
Park, Keith   155, 163, 166
Pathans   42–44, 45, 47, 251
Pearl Harbor (1941)   184, 230, 257
Peck, John   315
Peirse, AM Sir Richard   188, 189, 191
Percival, Maj-Gen Arthur   253, 255, 259, 260,
    261, 263
Pétain, Philippe   169, 232, 233–35, 236–37
Petrie, Sir David   235
Pfaus, Oscar   178
Philippines   131, 230, 251
Phillips, Adm T.S.V.   166–67
Phillips, William   278–79
'Phoney War'   141
Pim, Capt Richard   262
Pink, WC Richard   120–21
Plumer, Lt-Col H.   63
poison gas see mustard gas
Poland   88, 93–94, 136–37, 246, 300
Portal, AM Sir Charles   167, 173–74, 188, 294
    and Bomber Command   189, 190–91, 193,
        194, 195
Portugal   11, 200, 285–86

Potsdam Conference (1945)   314–15, 327
Pound, Adm Sir Dudley   137, 142, 173, 201
Pownall, Lt-Gen Sir Henry   283
Prescott-Decie, Brig-Gen Cecil   109, 110
Prince of Wales, HMS   173, 228, 257, 258, 262, 322
prisoners of war (POWs)   153–54, 178, 261
Puerto Rico   37, 39

Queen's Own Oxfordshire Hussars   80–81

Radio Direction Finding (RDF)   156
Raeder, Adm Erich   143
Ramsay, Adm Sir Bertram   148, 150–51, 295
Ramsay, Col William   40
Red Army   131, 243–44, 249
    and Russian Civil War   88, 89, 91, 93–94
refugees   133, 134
Remarque, Erich Maria: All Quiet on the Western Front   86
Renown, HMS   211
Repulse, HMS   173, 257, 258, 262, 322
Reynaud, Paul   143, 148, 153, 232, 233
    and Dunkirk   149–50, 152
Rhine River   10, 300, 304–9
Rhodes, Cecil   49
Rhodesia   40
Ritchie, Gen Neil   217
Rix, Pvt Wade   23, 24
Robeck, Adm de   77
Roberts, Capt Jerry   249
Roberts, FM Lord   57, 62, 63
Rommel, Gen Erwin   13, 200, 214, 216, 219, 220
    and Libya   217, 218, 322
Roosevelt, Franklin D.   13, 137, 185, 193, 302–3, 309
    and Churchill   228–31, 325–26
    and De Gaulle   237, 238, 239, 240, 241
    and India   266, 268, 272–73, 278–79
    and Japan   256, 257–58, 259
    and Lend-Lease   227–28
    and Libya   217
    and Neutrality Act   222–23
    and re-election   153, 158, 226
    and Second Front   288, 289, 291–92
    and Soviet Union   171, 246–47
    and warships   224–25
Roosevelt, Theodore   68
Rorke's Drift, battle of (1879)   35

Rougier, Louis   237
Royal Air Force (RAF)   11, 99–101, 102–3, 175, 319
    and Battle of Britain   161–63
    and Dowding   155–56, 158, 159
    and Dunkirk   152–53
    and India   120–21, 269–70, 272
    and Iraq   119–20
    and Ireland   107, 183
    and Singapore   253
    and USA   228
    see also Bomber Command
Royal Irish Constabulary   108–9
Royal Marines   196–97, 198
Royal Military College, Sandhurst   35, 318
Royal Navy   12, 68, 141–42, 143–44, 169–76
    and Greece   290
    and Ireland   105, 179–80, 185–86
    and Japan   267
    and Mediterranean Fleet   209, 210
    and RAF   166–67
    and Singapore   253
    and USA   225
    and World War I   72–74, 76–77
Royal Oak, HMS   141, 169
Ruhr   187, 309
Rushdi Pasha   114
Russia   73, 74
Russia in the Shadows (Wells)   94
Russian Civil War (1917–22)   11, 87–91, 92, 93–96, 242, 319
Russo-Japanese War (1904–5)   67–68
Ryan, Frank   181

Saint-Pierre Island   237–38
Sakabulas   58
Salmond, AM Sir John   120
Sandhurst see Royal Military College, Sandhurst
Saudi Arabia   119
Schall, Thomas D.   222
Schlosberg, Freda   54–55
Scissorforce   197
Scobie, Lt-Gen Ronald   301, 302
Scotland   183, 199
Second Front   288–89, 291–92; see also D-Day
sectarianism   11, 105, 107, 111, 112–13, 177
Sedan, battle of (1940)   147–48
Seven Pillars of Wisdom, The (Lawrence)   119
Sèvres, Treaty of (1920)   101, 115, 117, 121
Shaw, George Bernard   242–43

Sheffield, HMS 211
Sicily 13, 289
Sidney Street, siege of (1911) 69–70
Sikhs 42, 43–44
Silver Shirt Legion 223
Simpson, Wallis 127
Simpson, Gen William 304, 305, 306, 307–8
Sinclair, Maj Sir Archibald 81, 82, 83, 143, 145, 155, 162
Singapore 12, 199, 251, 261–63, 317
    and Japan 252–53, 255, 256–57, 259–61
    and Sumatra 284, 285, 286
Slim, Gen William 271–72, 273–74, 278, 281, 312–13, 325
Smith, Lt Robert 20, 22
Smuts, FM Jan Christiaan 54, 68, 80, 111, 285
    and Churchill 321, 323–24
    and D-Day 296, 297
Smyth, Lt-Col Gerald 109
Smyth, Capt Nevill 24
Somaliland 101, 207, 209
Somervell, Robert 33
Somerville, Adm James 169, 175, 211, 267
Somme, battle of the (1916) 83–84
South Africa 9, 10, 38, 40, 68, 80; *see also* Boer War
Soviet Union 125, 131, 171, 173; *see also* Stalin, Joseph
Spaatz, Gen Carl 294
Spain 11, 170, 200; *see also* Cuba; Spanish Civil War
Spanish Civil War (1936–39) 128–29, 131–34, 181
Spears, Maj-Gen Sir Edward 81, 137, 153, 320, 321
    and De Gaulle 232, 233, 234, 236
Spion Kop 60–61
Stalin, Joseph 13, 95, 125, 126, 242–49, 288
    and Arctic convoys 173, 174–76
    and Churchill 325–26
    and Finland 142, 143
    and Japan 284, 316, 317
    and Potsdam 314–15
    and Second Front 291, 292
    and territory 290
    and Yalta 302–3
Stalingrad, battle of (1942–43) 13, 248
Stark, Adm Harold 225
Steevens, G.W. 19, 20, 22
Stent, Vere 61

Stephenson, Sir William 277
Stevenson, AVM Donald 189, 190
Stilwell, Maj-Gen Joseph W. 259, 264, 283, 286
Stokes, Richard 195
Story of the Malakand Field Force, The (Churchill) 45
Strickland, Maj-Gen Sir Peter 111
Stuart, Maj-Gen Douglas 282
Sudan 9, 10, 40, 42, 115
    and defence 207, 209, 215
    see also Omdurman, Battle of
Suez Canal 12, 115, 116, 207, 288
Sumatra 284, 285, 286, 313
Sweden 142, 143
Sweetenham, Sir Alexander 68
Swinton, Lt-Col Ernest 68, 84
Syria 115, 116, 117, 216, 237

Taiwan 130
Tanga, battle of (1914) 74
tanks 83–84, 85, 87
Tannenbaum, Frank 136, 229
Tedder, ACM Sir Arthur 294, 322
Tegart, Charles 181
Tehran Conference (1943) 284–85, 290, 291
Telfer-Smollett, Gen Alexander 130
Tennant, Capt William 151
Territorial Army 80, 197
Tewari, Krishen 270, 273
Thailand 251, 253, 256
Thesiger, Wilfred 118
Third Anglo-Afghan War (1919) 100
Thoma, Gen Wilhelm von 324
Thompson, Cmdr Charles Ralfe 'Tommy' 306, 308
Thompson, Walter 145, 163
Thorneycroft, Lt-Col Alex 60
Tirpitz (ship) 173
Tizard, Henry 225
Tod, Maj R.J.F. 'Ronnie' 198
Tonypandy riots (1910–11) 70–71
Tovey, Adm Sir John 170, 171, 173, 175
Transjordan 114, 118, 119, 207
trench warfare 67–68
Trenchard, Hugh 99–100, 101, 102, 114
Trident Conference (1943) 279
Truman, Harry S. 11, 314–15, 316, 327
Tudor, Gen Sir Hugh 83, 107–8, 109, 110
Tunisia 13, 186, 208, 289
Turkey 72, 73, 77, 101–2, 115–16, 121

U-boats   72, 78, 124, 141, 200, 229
  and Atlantic Ocean   170, 171, 176
  and Ireland   180, 181, 184, 186
Ukraine   93–94
uniforms   12, 81, 306
United States of America (USA)   12, 38–39, 68,
    126, 142
  and China   265, 286
  and Churchill   221–22
  and IRA   178
  and Ireland   184
  and Japan   255–56
  and Neutrality Act (1939)   222–24
  and Russian Civil War   90, 95
  and Tokyo   313–14
  see also Roosevelt, Franklin D.
US Army Air Force (USAAF)   189, 192, 194
US Marine Corps   68
US Navy   37, 68, 222, 226–27
  and Atlantic Ocean   173, 174, 175

Valdez, Gen   37, 38
Valiant, HMS   209
Vargas, Getúlio   135–36, 176
VE Day   310
Versailles, Treaty of (1919)   88, 115, 124–25
Vichy France   14, 169, 235, 236–37
Victoria, Queen   42
Victorious, HMS   173

Wagner, Charles   52, 53, 54
Wakely, Maj-Gen Arthur   282
Wales   70–71
Ward, Col John   89
Wardlaw-Milne, Sir John   218
Warren, Gen Sir Charles   58, 60, 61
Wavell, FM Archibald   207–9, 210–11, 212,
    216, 237, 267
  and Burma   255, 258–59, 278
  and Greece   212–13, 214, 215
  and India   271, 272, 281–82, 286–87, 311,
    313
  and Singapore   256–57, 259, 260–61
weaponry   225–26, 227–28

Weber-Drohl, Ernst   180
Wedemeyer, Gen Albert   279, 283, 286
Weir, Sir William   99
Wellington, Arthur Wellesley, Duke of   33–34
Wells, H.G.   84, 93–94, 242
Weygand, Gen Maxime   233, 234
Wheeler, Burton K.   223
White, Gen Sir George   46
White Russians   87–91, 93, 93–96
Wiart, Carton de   286
Wilhelm II, Kaiser   69
Wilkie, Wendell   158, 226
Wilkinson, Ellen   132, 133
Wilkinson, Gerald   279
Wilson, Sir Charles   180, 184, 230, 231
Wilson, FM Sir Henry   88, 106, 109, 110, 111,
    113
Wilson, Hugh   223
Wilson, Gen Maitland   290, 292
Wilson, Woodrow   88
Winant, John Gilbert   245, 246
Wingate, Maj-Gen Orde   279–81, 283
Winterbotham, Petrea   159
Wodehouse, Brig Edmund   179
Wodehouse, Maj Frederick   69
Wolseley, Lord   36
Women's Auxiliary Air Force (WAAF)   159, 163
Woodgate, Maj-Gen Sir Edward   60
World War I (1914–18)   10, 12, 67, 72–74,
    76–79, 87, 196
  and Churchill   319
  and Western Front   80–86
Wylie, Capt James   52, 53, 54
Wyllie, Sir William Curzon   79
Wyndham, Maj Crole   23

Yalta Conference (1945)   12, 302–3
Ypres, battle of (1915)   74
Yugoslavia   214, 300

Zaghloul, Saad   114–15
Zec, Philip   172–73
Zhukov, Gen Georgi   250
Zulus   42, 49